NOVEL CLEOPATRAS

Romance Historiography and the Dido Tradition in English Fiction, 1688–1785

Novel Cleopatras

Romance Historiography and the Dido Tradition in English Fiction, 1688–1785

NICOLE HOREJSI

UNIVERSITY OF TORONTO PRESS
Toronto Buffalo London

Toronto Buffalo London
utorontopress.com

ISBN 978-1-4426-4714-5

Library and Archives Canada Cataloguing in Publication

Horejsi, Nicole, 1978–, author
Novel Cleopatras : romance historiography and the Dido tradition in English fiction, 1688–1785 / Nicole Horejsi.

Includes bibliographical references and index.
ISBN 978-1-4426-4714-5 (hardcover)

1. English fiction – 18th century – History and criticism. 2. English fiction – Women authors – History and criticism. 3. Cleopatra, Queen of Egypt, –30 B.C. – In literature. 4. Dido (Legendary character) in literature. 5. History in literature. 6. Mythology in literature. I. Title.

PR851.H67 2019 823′.509 C2018-905356-9

This book has been published with the assistance of the Warner Fund at the University Seminars at Columbia University.

University of Toronto Press acknowledges the financial assistance to its publishing program of the Canada Council for the Arts and the Ontario Arts Council, an agency of the Government of Ontario.

Canada Council for the Arts Conseil des Arts du Canada

Funded by the Government of Canada Financé par le gouvernement du Canada

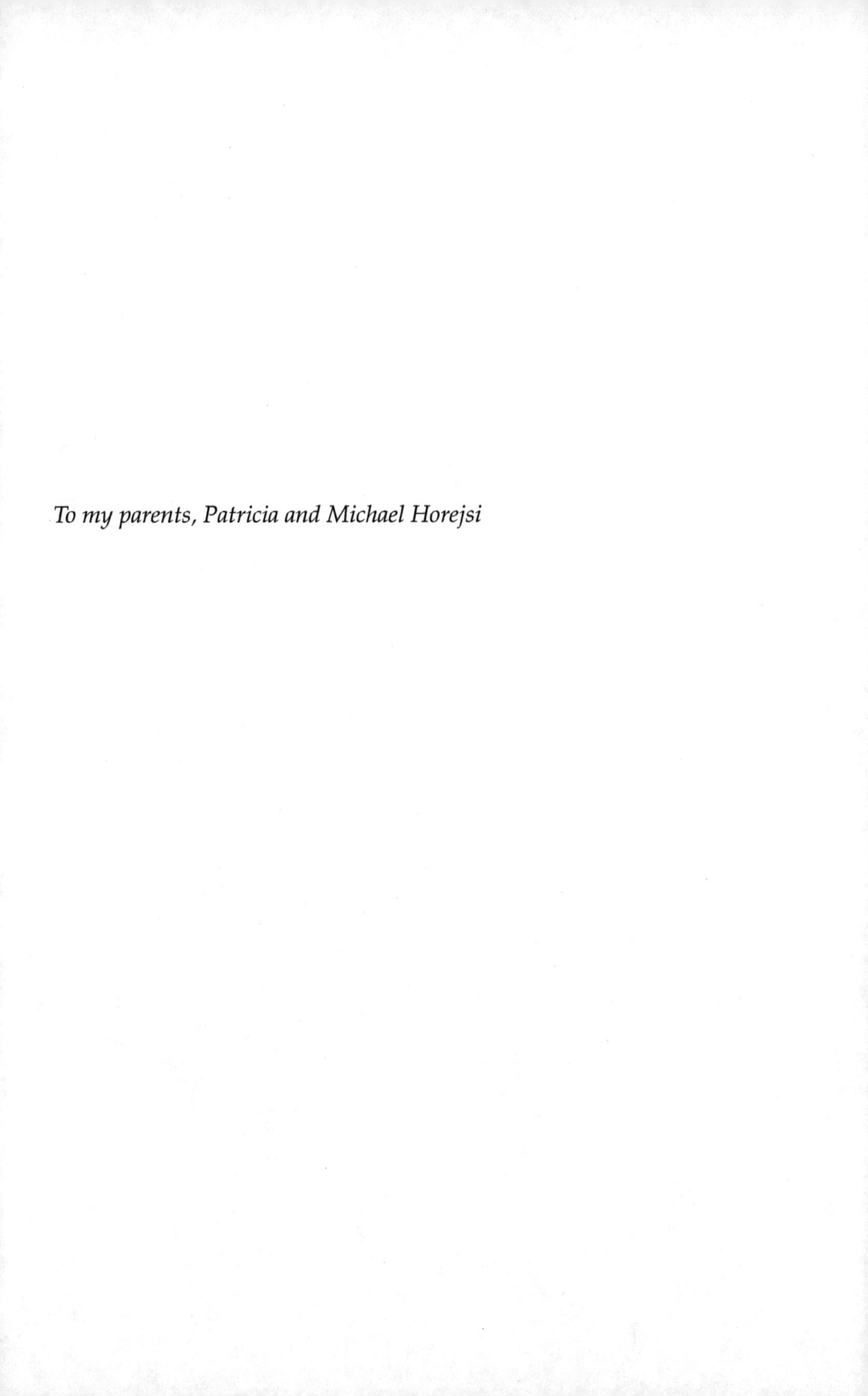

To my parents, Patricia and Michael Horejsi

Contents

List of Illustrations ix

Acknowledgments xi

Introduction 3

PART 1: Demythologizing Dido: Epic and Romance

1 "Pulcherrima Dido": Jane Barker and the Epic of Exile 25

2 "What Is There of a Woman Worth Relating?" Revising the *Aeneid* in Henry Fielding's *Amelia* 54

PART 2: Mythologizing Cleopatra: Romance Historiography and the Queens of Egypt

3 "A Pattern to Ensuing Ages": Reinventing Historical Practice in Charlotte Lennox's *Female Quixote* 89

4 Performing Augustan History in Sarah Fielding's *Lives of Cleopatra and Octavia* 125

5 Whose "Wild and Extravagant Stories"? Clara Reeve's *The Progress of Romance* and *The History of Charoba, Queen of Ægypt* 166

Epilogue 199

Notes 209

Bibliography 249

Index 269

Illustrations

1.1 Jacopo Amigoni (c. 1675–1752), *Hannibal swearing eternal enmity to Rome* 41

2.1 Thomas Gainsborough, *Cottage Door* (c. 1780) 66

3.1 Richard Samuel, *Portraits in the Characters of the Muses in the Temple of Apollo* (1778) 91

3.2 From Pierre Le Moyne's *Galerie des femmes fortes* (1647) 103

3.3 From Pierre Le Moyne's *Galerie des femmes fortes* (1647) 104

3.4 From Madeleine de Scudéry's *Femmes illustres*, inscribed "To the Glory of the [Female] Sex" (1642) 105

3.5 The *Carte de Tendre*, from Madeleine de Scudéry's *Clelia, ou histoire romaine* (1654–60) 115

3.6 Engraving of Clelia, from Pierre Le Moyne's *Galerie des femmes fortes* (1647) 117

3.7 Engraving of Lucretia, from Pierre Le Moyne's *Galerie des femmes fortes* (1647) 118

4.1 Angelica Kauffman, *Virgil Reading the Aeneid to Augustus* (1788) 155

Acknowledgments

This project began in Fall 2000 when I took my first graduate seminar at the University of California, Los Angeles, a course on the Bluestockings with Felicity Nussbaum. That course seized my imagination, forever changing my academic career. I am grateful to Felicity for recruiting me to the eighteenth century, and for being a truly superlative mentor from that first Bluestockings seminar to this day. I would also like to thank the wonderful cohort of students I met during that period, including Nush Powell, Chris Loar, Noelle Chao, Melissa Sodeman, and Derek Pacheco, who provided feedback on various aspects of early drafts. Later, Jayne Lewis, Robert Gurval, and especially Helen Deutsch offered invaluable insights for future publication.

I have been fortunate to receive support for this project at every step of the way. As a graduate student at UCLA, I earned a Summer Research Mentorship Award under Felicity Nussbaum, during which I refined an article on Steele's *Spectator* 11 that would later become part of the framework of my argument. This article subsequently appeared in *Eighteenth-Century Studies* 39.2 (2006): 201–26, and elaborates the current discussion of Inkle and Yarico in the Introduction. I also earned a Thayer Fellowship to use the UCLA Young Research Library Department of Special Collections to study oriental tales; travel grants from the UCLA Department of English and the UCLA Center for the Study of Women to read seventeenth-century French romances at the British Library; and two dissertation fellowships, the William Andrews Clark Memorial Library Dissertation Fellowship from the UCLA Center for Seventeenth- and Eighteenth-Century Studies and the Alfred E. Longueuil Dissertation Fellowship from the UCLA Department of

English. I also benefited from the feedback and camaraderie of my fellow colleagues at the Annual Seminar for Young Scholars (as it was then called) sponsored by the International Society for Eighteenth-Century Studies.

As an assistant professor in the Department of English and Comparative Literature at Columbia University in the City of New York, I received summer support as well as a year-long Chamberlain Fellowship to conduct research. I am thankful for the feedback of my colleagues during this period, especially Jenny Davidson and the members of the Columbia University Seminar on Eighteenth-Century European Culture. In addition to the lively discussion I enjoyed while presenting a portion of chapter 1 to my fellow seminarians, the Seminar has generously provided financial support for the publication of this project through the Warner Fund at the University Seminars at Columbia University.

My colleagues in the English Department at California State University, Los Angeles have also provided helpful suggestions and advice, especially Michael Calabrese and Linda Greenberg, a dear friend who has followed this project in its many stages since we met nearly two decades ago at UCLA. Now that I've returned to Southern California, the Huntington Library and its staff also deserve special thanks. In addition to having received a short-term fellowship to pursue my interest in French romances, I'm fortunate to live only a short distance from the library and have spent many days among its collections since the summer of 2014.

Although it is impossible to name every person who has generously offered feedback and support over the years, I would like to thank several people in particular who, aside from Felicity, have gone above and beyond in reading and commenting on various drafts. I am eternally grateful to Nush Powell for her thoughts on whole iterations of this project at various stages, and to Rivka Swenson for guidance and moral support. My writing group of California State University faculty, including Regulus Allen and Susan Carlile, read and commented on several chapters, and cheered me along the way. Ros Ballaster's comments, especially on my Lennox chapter, have changed the entire project for the better.

I am also grateful to the team at University of Toronto Press, including Mark Thompson, Richard Ratzlaff, and Barb Porter, and to my copy-editor, Judith Williams. This book would not exist without them, nor without the mentorship of John Richetti, who introduced me to

Richard at a meeting of the American Society for Eighteenth-Century Studies.

I would like to conclude by expressing gratitude to my parents, Patricia and Michael Horejsi, for their love and support. I couldn't be more pleased to dedicate this project to both of them.

NOVEL CLEOPATRAS

Introduction

In 1711, the *Spectator* published the story of Inkle and Yarico, transforming a minor episode from Richard Ligon's 1657 history of Barbados into a legend that would reverberate throughout the eighteenth century. Immediately following Joseph Addison's call, in *Spectator* 10, to create a periodical capable of gracing "Tea Tables" as well as "Coffee-Houses," Richard Steele devotes one of the earliest issues of the *Spectator* to the frequent hostility of classical literature towards female characters and readers, both in the past and in the British present.[1] Mr Spectator relates how Arietta, a woman whose "Conversation is so mixed with Gaiety and Prudence, that she is agreeable both to the Young and the Old" (1:47–8), rebukes a "common-place talker" who rudely employs the classical story of the Ephesian Matron to chastise his hostess. Turning to "the old Topic, of Constancy in Love," the Commonplace Talker desires to illustrate "the Perjuries of the Fair, and the general Levity of Women." He concludes by relating the well-known account of the Widow of Ephesus, a story remembered from Petronius's Latin novel, the *Satyricon* (dating to the mid-first century CE), which enjoyed, even before Petronius, a wide folkloric currency.[2] The tale of the Ephesian Matron, a famous misogynist *sententia*, depicts the Widow's seduction by a Roman soldier at the very tomb of her dead husband; in order to prevent the soldier's death, she subsequently offers her husband's body as a substitute for one of the corpses that has gone missing on her lover's watch. In response to her interlocutor's "murdering" of Petronius's anecdote (1:48), Arietta relates a story that would ignite the eighteenth-century imagination. *Spectator* 11 features the tale of the English merchant Inkle, shipwrecked on the island of Barbados, and the Amerindian Yarico, the indigenous woman who saves him from her countrymen. Although the pair fall in love, and Yarico even becomes pregnant with their child, Inkle reneges on his promises to convey Yarico to England, and instead sells her into slavery. She attempts to dissuade him with news of her pregnancy, but "he only made Use of that Information, to rise in his Demands upon the Purchaser" (1:51). The moving scene leads Mr Spectator to declare that Inkle and Yarico should always be a "counterpart to the *Ephesian Matron*" (1:51) as he, unlike the Commonplace Talker, appropriately weeps for Yarico's loss.

The first to present a literary account of Yarico's story, Steele's version soon transcended history, much like its most famous, yet unnamed intertext: the story of Aeneas and Dido.[3] In telling the tale of Inkle and Yarico to combat the anecdote of the Ephesian Matron – itself based, in Petronius, on Dido's betrayal of her dead husband, Sychaeus – Steele thus returns to Virgilian epic in an attempt to enact a new originary narrative for an early eighteenth-century audience that self-consciously modelled itself after Augustan Rome. By irresponsibly invoking Petronius, Arietta's interlocutor demonstrates the problematic reading practices – associated first with the Commonplace Talker, then with Petronius and his narrator – that Steele seeks, in *Spectator* 11, to correct: even as Arietta's guest inappropriately turns to Petronius to use the weight of the classical tradition against her, he also "murders" his so-called evidence for women's inconstancy. In this way, he reveals himself, twice over, to be a selective reader of the classics, his partial knowledge of Petronius deployed to misogynist ends. By contrast, Arietta models the right use of classical learning: readers properly motivated by fellow feeling should follow Virgilian epic in sympathizing with Dido's plight. The problem, then, as Steele articulates it, is not only the *Aeneid* itself, but the improper understanding of Book 4 inherited from the Matron's story. Where Petronius relies on the Dido episode to mock Dido's misfortune, Yarico's sad conclusion foregrounds the unjustness of each heroine's fate.

As a result, Arietta's appropriation of the *Aeneid* is both apt and wanting. On the one hand, the story of Inkle and Yarico, as a parallel to Aeneas and Dido, allows Arietta, because of the *Aeneid*'s sympathy for Dido, to refute the Commonplace Talker's common misogyny. Yet it also suggests the difficulty of recuperating a narrative that requires Dido's demise. "Inkle and Yarico," in transposing Virgilian epic to the New World, does nothing to prevent Yarico's abandonment or servitude. Relying on Yarico's story to invert the critique offered by the Ephesian

Matron – to argue that men, rather than women, are inconstant – paradoxically affirms the battle-of-the-sexes model that underpins the Widow's story. Arietta's response, no matter how sobering, not only fails to provide an alternative paradigm but also reinforces an existing template that will continue to enable both Dido's and Yarico's betrayals; it suggests a pattern so entrenched that it can only be turned against its "heroic" perpetrators, not escaped entirely. Indeed, the subsequent translation of Yarico's story into an epistolary tradition reminiscent of Ovid's *Heroides* indicates the ease with which eighteenth-century writers assimilated her to the Dido model and, I should add, to the numerous mythological examples of similarly abandoned heroines.[4]

In this way, the story of Inkle and Yarico vividly epitomizes how the narrative example of the *Aeneid* continued to shape understandings of the British present, echoing not only Dido in Yarico, but Rome in England, and Carthage in Barbados. In Steele's rendition, Ligon's history, Petronius's novel, Aeneas's epic, and Dido's romance meet in a New World fable that, in many ways, parallels the *Aeneid*'s narrative of conquest and imperial domination. In other words, it takes on the status (to use Laura Brown's term) of a "cultural fable" that "transcends particular writers and texts: it is generated collectively in many texts over a period of time" and "has a narrative trajectory that moves beyond the local or static effect of a trope or a figure," telling "a story whose protagonist is an emanation of contemporary experience and whose action reflects an imaginative negotiation with that experience."[5] However, although *Spectator* 11 achieves the cultural fable's goal of demystifying the heroic demands of Virgilian epic and illuminating the continued relevance of that model in the present,[6] it never succeeds in becoming an originary narrative in its own right for the reasons I suggest: Arietta's strategy of simple inversion reinforces, even as it critiques, Dido's story. Signalling the success of Virgil's epic, it never seems to occur to Arietta that some other outcome might be possible; though Steele turns away from Old World geographies to New, he also naturalizes Yarico's defeat through the force of classical precedent. At the same time, the history of the eighteenth-century novel shows that Steele's response in *Spectator* 11 is not the only possible engagement with the Dido story. In its dissatisfaction with existing myths, the story of Inkle and Yarico in fact anticipates the revisionist strand of neoclassical culture represented by reimaginings of the Dido story in the novels of the long eighteenth century.

In *Novel Cleopatras,* I argue that eighteenth-century writers eager to complicate their classical heritage find in Virgilian epic – with its sympathy, however limited, for Dido's plight – the groundwork for inventing new histories and mythologies for contemporary readers traditionally marginalized by classical authority. Turning away from the formal and ideological exclusivity of epic, which requires Dido's demise, these writers take advantage of the emerging genre of the novel to create a parallel, supplementary, and even competing tradition for eighteenth-century readers. For writers such as Jane Barker, Henry Fielding, Charlotte Lennox, Sarah Fielding, and Clara Reeve, the capacious nature of the novel and its easy accessibility position the emerging form as an ideal challenger both to the authority of the *Aeneid* and to contemporary uses of Virgilian epic and Augustan history. Because Dido and the historical figure she represents – Cleopatra – take centre stage in the twin projects of reimagining epic and history, I contend that turning to the doomed queens who haunted the Roman imagination enables eighteenth-century novelists to seize the productive overlap among genres – history, romance, novel, even epic – and therefore to disrupt one of the founding narratives of Western civilization and rewrite it for their own ends. I refer to these stories as "originary narratives" because they at once engage and revise the *Aeneid* and Augustan history. These new myths privilege heroines as a way of expanding heroic models, but they also avoid simplistically inverting the Virgilian paradigm – which would reinforce the perceived defects of the *Aeneid* – and instead break from it altogether by rejecting traditional categories of victory and defeat.

As early as antiquity, readers would have known that the *Aeneid* forever altered the mythology traditionally associated with Dido; Virgil is the first to subordinate Dido's narrative to his hero's, despite an earlier tradition celebrating Carthage's founding. Thanks to Cupid's orders from Venus, Dido falls victim to a mad desire for her foreign guest, and eventually commits suicide when Aeneas rejects his vows to her. Although he tarries in Carthage, even helping Dido to build her city, he ultimately repudiates their marriage and leaves at Mercury's behest. Yet the founding of Carthage famously postdates the Trojan exile by over three hundred years, so that, until Virgil, Dido had existed as a legendary figure of her own. In Punic legend, Dido, a Phoenician princess, finds herself exiled in Libya after her bloodthirsty brother, Pygmalion, murders her husband, Sychaeus, in order to obtain his fortune. The local king, Iarbas, then grants Dido only as much land as she can cover with an ox-hide; she unexpectedly satisfies his injunction by cutting the hide into strips and stretching it as far as she can, thus marking the boundaries of one of the greatest civilizations of the ancient world.[7] When Iarbas attempts to force Dido to marry him, she then immolates herself in order to escape his demands and remain loyal to Sychaeus. The figure of Dido therefore initiates two competing mythologies: the chaste, clever Dido of legend and history vs the Virgilian Dido who – like the Ephesian Matron – betrays the memory of her dead husband. At the same time, because of the positioning of the *Aeneid*, Dido's subsequent subordination to Aeneas's narrative, though unknown before Virgil, assumes the weight of inevitability despite the violence it does to the original Dido myth. Just as Virgil translates the chaste Dido of Carthaginian legend into the lovelorn queen of Augustan historiography, the Virgilian Dido becomes the literary version of the historical Cleopatra, driven from history into romance – transformed from the politically savvy queen of Egypt to Antony's foredoomed seductress.

In this way, I would like to stress that *Novel Cleopatras* is not an argument about Virgil or even about Dido or Cleopatra per se, despite their prominence in this project. Rather, my claim is about the politics of gender and genre in the long eighteenth century, and the originary role of Dido's story. There are, of course, other similar tales of betrayal, with more ancient pedigrees than Aeneas's abandonment of Dido. But the Dido story takes on particular significance because of its literary-historical positioning after the defeat of Cleopatra at the Battle of Actium. The Augustan propaganda that aggressively rewrites Cleopatra as an Egyptian "whore" and Antony as her effeminate love-slave has significant consequences for subsequent narratives: in naturalizing the hierarchic relationships between victors and losers, epic and romance, the *Aeneid* reinforces available discourses in ways that would continue to produce future Didos. Cleopatra thus enters the project as the historical model for Dido, and together the two women become figures for thinking about myth (represented by Dido) and history (represented by Cleopatra), but also for exploring the fluid boundaries between history and fiction. *Novel Cleopatras* is therefore an argument about the uses of narrative to circumscribe or expand available storytelling possibilities, the effects of these originary stories on characters marginalized by conventional epic and history, and the prospect of innovating new mythologies from the same tradition that had served as the basis of Western education since antiquity. The plurality of Cleopatras, like the plurality of Didos, makes visible the fictions that engender history, literature, and literary history.

The goals of this project are twofold. I advocate a revised history of the eighteenth-century novel that foregrounds its ancient origins, its dynamic relationship to epic, and its centrality to neoclassical print culture. At the same time, I reinscribe the essential role of women writers in this history. Critics have tended to underestimate women as agents of neoclassical culture because they were formally excluded from the system of education that taught their brothers Greek and Latin. In reality, a number of exceptional middle- and upper-class women were serious students of the classics, and some – including Barker, Fielding, and Reeve – even received training in the ancient languages with the help of male relatives and family friends. Because the novel was one of the genres most accessible to women in this period, critics' exclusion of the novel as a (neo)classical form works hand in hand with the marginalization of women as neoclassical writers.

In emphasizing the novel's indebtedness to the historical and romance legacies of the *Aeneid*, I have chosen these writers for the breadth of coverage they offer – spanning the period between 1688 and 1785 – and for their representativeness for twenty-first- as well as eighteenth-century readers. To this end, I have also included chapters on Charlotte Lennox and Henry Fielding. I include Henry in this project for the same reason that I began this Introduction with Richard Steele: in order to suggest that women writers weren't alone in reimagining their classical heritage. So too did their male allies, such as Steele and Fielding, who went so far as to rewrite the *Aeneid* in his 1751 novel, *Amelia*. Although Barker, Sarah Fielding, and Reeve may appear less self-evidently canonical than Lennox and Henry Fielding, Barker was both a popular originator of the English novel and the foremost Jacobite writer of her day. Her *Exilius* (finished by 1688 but published in 1715) demonstrates that the novel – with its origins, for Barker, at the nexus of romance, epic, and history – had, since the beginning, taken inspiration from Virgil's epic, and from Dido's story in particular. At the same time, recent scholarship continues to stress Sarah Fielding's position at the very heart of mid-eighteenth-century fiction: Betty Schellenberg, for example, has described Fielding as one of the top ten producers of fiction around mid-century, and Clara Reeve ranked her, in *The Progress of Romance* (1785), just behind Henry Fielding and Samuel Richardson in her importance as an English novelist. Reeve, for her part, remains one of the most prolific and significant innovators of British fiction at the end of the eighteenth century, the first to write a gothic novel following Horace Walpole's *Castle of Otranto* – the wildly successful *Old English Baron, or Champion of Virtue* (1777) – and the first woman to publish a literary-critical history of the novel in 1785.

That three of these novelists – Lennox and the Fieldings – were writing in the 1750s further underscores the fundamental relationship between Augustan mythology and the emerging form. At a historical moment when novels comprised only a small fraction of the literary marketplace, and publishing new novels proved extraordinarily difficult, Charlotte Lennox and Henry and Sarah Fielding all turned, in various ways, to Virgilian epic and Augustan history for their subject matter. Thus, when Lennox wished to satirize the vogue for (but also contemporary mockery of) romances, she created a heroine deluded by stories of ancient princesses, such as Cleopatra; when Henry decided, in *Amelia*, to experiment with sentimental fiction, he chose to rewrite Virgil's *Aeneid*; and when Sarah Fielding took up fictional biography because translation and history were more lucrative than novels, she turned to Cleopatra and Octavia. That these influential writers embraced the fictions of Augustan propaganda at such a vexed period in the publication of new fiction attests to the centrality of Virgilian epic, and the immediate culture that produced it, in the development of the novel in eighteenth-century Britain. The stories of Dido and Cleopatra – at once traditional and familiar, yet generative of new narrative possibilities – fundamentally shaped the course of British fiction; Dido's legacy haunts the novel because "Dido" represents narrative itself.

My argument unfolds in two parts. The first, "Demythologizing Dido: Epic and Romance," focuses on the figure of Dido as the literary emblem of a Cleopatra tamed by epic and at once relegated to, and recuperated by, romance. In chapters 1 and 2, Jane Barker and Henry Fielding attempt to recover Dido as a powerful symbol of resistance for the dissenting readers who see, in her narrative, the origins of conflicts that would structure literary history. In turn, Part 2, "Mythologizing Cleopatra: Romance Historiography and the Queens of Egypt," takes up the legacy of Dido's counterpart, whose vilification at the hands of ancient and modern historians highlights the uneasy affinities between fact and fiction. In chapters 3 through 5, I emphasize the stakes of the first two chapters by exploring the afterlife of the Dido fable in Charlotte Lennox, Sarah Fielding, and Clara Reeve, and the violence it does to fiction and history. The repercussions of Dido's taming are not only mythic, but historical: the ready translation of the real Cleopatra into the fictional Dido, and the creation of a Cleopatra, like Dido, undone by love, have far-reaching consequences, both political and literary. From contemporary fears that the Dido and Aeneas episode, in the hands of unsympathetic readers, would justify a ruthless imperial impulse to suspicions that Dido's fate limits narrative possibilities for other heroines, the Dido story inhabits subsequent literature and history.

Rites of Initiation: Reading Epic in Eighteenth-Century Britain

In the project of rewriting epic, Virgil offered a particularly fitting point of departure. In 1785, the critic and novelist Clara Reeve would polemically argue, in her literary-critical dialogue *The Progress of Romance*, that Homer was the very "parent of Romance" and Virgil "the most successful of his Imitators," despite eighteenth-century critics' frequent construction of "romance" and "epic" as opposing forms.[8] Although it is by now well known that authors of the period expressed scepticism towards classical culture, ancient writers continued to set authoritative literary standards, so that novelists, no less than poets, turned to Virgil, and especially to the *Aeneid*, in rethinking the role of classical culture for an eighteenth-century audience whose diversity meant varying degrees of familiarity with the ancients.

Despite its indebtedness to ancient Rome, the eighteenth century expressed ambivalence not only towards Augustan culture and its most famous epic but, for the first time, towards the educational system that privileged Latin over other subjects.[9] Yet challenges to traditional schooling did little to dethrone Virgil from his prominence in the formal curriculum. Taking precedence even over Homer, Virgil towered over the ancients for eighteenth-century readers. Culturally and linguistically, the *Aeneid* was more readily accessible than its Greek counterparts. Formal instruction centred on the transmission of Roman culture and Latin texts, and reading Latin meant reading Virgil: "for several hundred years, Virgil's poetry formed an integral part of the common educational experience of almost every educated person wherever the Latin secondary education of Europe took hold."[10] Although, as the century progressed, the *Aeneid* came to represent an entrenched but impractical paradigm increasingly undermined by the democratization of print culture and the rise of a middle-class readership, Virgil's poem remained a powerful literary standard. Most eighteenth-century students would have read the *Aeneid* at least twice during their primary education.[11]

Unlike the *Iliad*, which staged the conflict between Greeks (themselves barbarous by Roman standards) and the Trojans of Asia Minor, the *Aeneid*'s foundation myth, detailing the origins of Rome and its eponymous hero, played a significant role in legitimating England's mythic history. By the eighteenth century, there was already a long tradition of locating English origins in the Fall of Troy, marking a steady rise to greatness that mirrored the Roman Empire's. From the legendary founding of Rome, medieval historians such as Geoffrey of Monmouth had constructed a similar myth for Britain: the Trojan Brutus founded Nova Troia on the site of modern London, making the Romans ancestors of the English, and the English natural inheritors of Rome's cultural legacy. Along with the prominence of Virgil thus came the dream of empire that the *Aeneid* had engendered: to be an elite eighteenth-century schoolboy was to strive to emulate the noble virtues that Aeneas embodied, and to identify with Aeneas meant identifying, in some measure, against Dido and his Latin rival, Turnus, even as England consciously constructed its own imperial destiny. Craig Kallendorf has argued that, "As a school text, the *Aeneid* proved crucial in the formation of the early modern Self, for generations of schoolchildren learnt to see themselves through the eyes of Aeneas as they absorbed the values according to which they would live their lives."[12] These values involved, moreover, a "class-specific performance of masculinity" and cultural identity: "As a school text used to instruct male students in the Latin language, Virgil's *Aeneid* was, until the [nineteenth] century, an important part of the initiation rite schoolboys underwent in their acquisition of a public language basic to their acquisition of a mature masculine identity."[13] The Virgilian model constructed that "mature masculine identity" in opposition to a feminine (or feminized) foreign Other – the Latin chieftain who incites Aeneas's Achillean rage, the queen of Carthage who outrageously immolates herself on his departure. Though the system of Latin learning received its first real challenges in the eighteenth century, it would continue to dominate elite British education for at least another two hundred years.

At the other end of the spectrum, informal networks – and, in rare cases, even formal schooling – allowed women of a certain class to participate in the transmission of classical culture. Though women's education typically excluded instruction in ancient languages – limited instead to subjects such as sewing, dancing, music, French, and Italian – a small number of schools included Latin in the girls' curriculum.[14] Outside of the very limited opportunities available through formal schooling, it was more common still for bright and motivated women to receive informal instruction under the auspices of male relatives and family friends. Jane Stevenson, in her impressive survey, *Women Latin Poets*, reminds us that "[m]embers of the upper gentry and relatively minor aristocracy and educated citizens continued to behave [in the seventeenth and eighteenth centuries] much as their grandfathers had done, and educate, or fail to educate, their daughters according to the traditional practice of their own specific family."[15] Of the women I discuss in this project, Jane Barker learned Latin from her brother, a medical student at Cambridge; Sarah Fielding from a family friend, the Reverend Arthur Collier; and Clara Reeve from her father, William, a rector and curate. Fielding even mastered Greek, reputedly surpassing her brother's skills in that language,[16] and both Fielding and Reeve became accomplished translators of Greek and Latin. In addition to the research required for *The Lives of Cleopatra and Octavia* (1757), Fielding produced an edition of Xenophon's *Memoirs of Socrates* (1762), parts of which remained in print through the twentieth century. Reeve likewise completed a translation of John Barclay's Latin romance, the *Argenis* (1621), in 1772. Though Barker, Fielding, and Reeve remain atypical, even for their class, they are joined by other familiar figures such as Anne Finch, Hester Thrale, Hannah More, Anna Seward, and Elizabeth Carter.[17] Although Joseph Levine argues that it was "natural for the few women writers in the period largely to disregard [the] quarrel [between Ancients and Moderns]," insisting that "they must inevitably have inclined to the modern side,"[18] classically educated female authors actively shaped the reception of Augustan literature and culture in eighteenth-century Britain.

Returning to Narrative Origins: Finding Alternatives in Virgil's *Aeneid*

On 2 September 31 BCE, Octavian defeated Antony and Cleopatra at Actium. That victory gave birth to the Roman Empire – to the so-called Golden Age of Augustus and the *pax Romana* – and to a Western civilization that would, in many ways, continue to fashion itself after Rome's exemplar for the next two thousand years.[19] More than the defeat of the ambitious Triumvir Mark Antony and his Egyptian queen, Octavian's conquest of Egypt became an emblem of the triumph of Roman over barbarian, stolid *romanitas* over Egyptian effeminacy, West over East. As I have argued, Cleopatra's loss became an originary myth in

Western culture, and Virgil's *Aeneid*, the mythic retelling of her defeat, further enshrined the generic victory of epic over romance.[20] The famed Dido and Aeneas episode, in its seamless fusion of myth and fact – celebrating the fall of Antony and Cleopatra and Octavian's prophetic rise to power – had changed the course of literary history, and historiography itself, as a result of Cleopatra's challenge to Roman rule.

Demonstrating the power of the *Aeneid*'s version of history, by 1377 the term "Dido" had emerged, in English, as a byword for storytelling itself. Signifying an "old story, a thrice-told tale," it attests to the extent to which the fate of Virgil's heroine had become synonymous with the very act of generating narrative meaning.[21] From the moment of its first appearance, the story of Dido became the most popular episode of Virgil's epic. "No part of the whole work," Ovid writes in the *Tristia*, "is more read than that illicit union of love."[22] From Augustine to Chaucer to Nahum Tate's libretto for Purcell's *Dido and Aeneas*, the Dido narrative found a number of post-Virgilian champions, and scholars such as Marilynn Desmond and Margaret Ferguson have superbly documented Dido's role as a figure of resistance in the larger literary culture of medieval and early modern France and England.[23] *Novel Cleopatras* extends the tradition of rereading Dido into the eighteenth century, taking up a single national literature and a specific genre – the novel – at a time when women were entering the literary marketplace on an unprecedented scale, making Dido a potent emblem for male and female writers alike.

For Virgil's Augustan audience, Dido was a convenient figure for certain defeat because she represented the fates of Carthage and Egypt. The legendary founder of Carthage, she at once embodied the origins of that empire – destined, thanks to her dying curse, to wage war against Rome – and its well-known and seemingly compulsory demise. In yoking together the twin deaths of Dido and her empire, Virgil's subordination of Dido's story to Aeneas's thus participates in a larger narrative pattern: it anticipates and justifies Dido's demise, and hence Carthage's subsequent downfall, while it casts Cleopatra's failure as a *fait accompli* by mythologizing her as Dido. Depending, as it did, on Dido's unrequited love for Aeneas, Virgil's novel explanation for the hostility between Carthage and Rome suggests that any such challenge to Roman supremacy, let alone on the part of a foreign woman, could never succeed; Dido and Cleopatra exist, in Augustan mythology, as always already conquered. Augustus apparently imagined the conflict in global terms. According to the historian Cassius Dio, he proclaimed that he fought on behalf of Rome – indeed, on behalf of all men – "to conquer and rule all mankind, [and] to allow no woman to make herself equal to a man."[24] Dio's characterization perfectly illustrates the stakes of the Dido-Cleopatra story: Dido comes to stand for the very category "woman" and, as I will argue, for the potent intersections between "woman" and "defeat."

I call this freighted conjunction the "Dido position" because it suggests the ways in which the character "Dido" comes to embody the fact of loss more generally. Dido, then, is not merely the queen of Carthage, but an emblem of necessary defeat. She represents, in the context of my argument, categories of identity marginalized by epic convention – not only, in this case, "woman" and "foreigner," but also, for Barker, the Jacobite supporters of James II, and even, for Reeve, the Islamic tradition represented by *The History of Charoba*. Instead of rejecting romance, as the *Aeneid* had done in Dido's suicide, eighteenth-century novelists seek to embrace the Dido figure, the foreign, feminine subject, as the very embodiment of modern heroism. Where ancient authors tamed Dido, and similar heroines, through dilatory and often tragic romance narratives, eighteenth-century writers profit from romance elements to reappropriate Dido's story and the subject position she typifies for epic's outcasts.[25]

This is especially true of one of the novel's immediate forebears, the seventeenth-century French romance (sometimes called the Baroque or heroic novel), best exemplified in the works of Madeleine de Scudéry and Gauthier de Costes, Seigneur de la Calprenède. Between them, Scudéry and La Calprenède produced some of the most famous romances of the period, including Scudéry's *Artamène, ou le Grand Cyrus* (1649–53) and *Clélie, histoire romaine* (1654–60) and La Calprenède's *Cassandre* (1642–5) and *Cléopâtre* (1648–58) – stories so well known that, even by the time of publication of Lennox's *Female Quixote* in 1752, passing allusions sufficed to convey her satire to contemporary readers. The tremendous success of Scudéry and La Calprenède followed on the revival of Heliodorus's *Aithiopika*.[26] A fourth-century Greek writer from Emesa (modern-day Syria), Heliodorus gained newfound popularity in sixteenth-century Europe when his *Ethiopian Story* was rediscovered and promptly enshrined in the literary landscape.[27] Though discussions of the British novel have tended to overstate its newness, emphasizing its modernity over its antiquity, classicists widely regard Heliodorus as one of the ancient progenitors of the form; the *Aithiopika* influenced the English novel both in its own right and through its relationship to the French romances of the seventeenth century. In addition to Lennox, all of the writers in my project draw, to varying extents, on the legacy of Heliodorus, from Barker's 1688 tale of North African intrigue to Reeve's 1785 explication of the novel's ancient origins.[28]

Romance's capacity to facilitate generic blending encourages writers to exploit the blurred lines between romance and other genres, not only epic but its longtime conspirator, history. Indeed, "romance," "history," and even "novel" were highly vexed terms at the beginning of the eighteenth century, often used interchangeably until critics such as Samuel Johnson attempted to redefine "romance" and "novel" as opposing forms, and history began to emerge as an independent discipline.[29] Certainly, for seventeenth- and eighteenth-century writers and readers, romance could be, and frequently was, historical, taking up ancient histories, such as Herodotus and Livy, and elaborating them with the deeds of heroines and heroes, often real-life figures of varying note.[30] A more inclusive mode, one with its own claims to legitimate historicity, romance offered an ideal genre to supplant epic, and to revalue the position of subjection associated with Dido, whose carefully plotted submission to romance convention had thoroughly symbolized, in epic and history, her defeat.

In this way, writers like Scudéry and La Calprenède profit from what I call "romance historiography" in theorizing the relationship between history and fiction. This might seem, at first, a paradoxical term, but, by yoking together the superficially disparate concepts of romance and history, I hope to suggest the complex understanding of history exhibited by seventeenth-century romance and reproduced by many eighteenth-century novelists. That is, "romance historiography" establishes an authoritative framework for thinking about its constitutive parts, romance and history, and their relationship to one another – the self-conscious intersection of canonical history, fiction, and alternative modes of historiography. Here, again, the story of Cleopatra is instructive. In focusing on the aftermath of the Battle of Actium, La Calprenède's romance examines the history following Cleopatra's demise: centred on the stories of her children with Antony and Julius Caesar, it at once illuminates a history largely obscured by Greek and Roman historians and refutes the Augustan (and Virgilian) narrative of the *pax Romana*, depicting the emperor as a tyrant while cultivating sympathy for its foreign heroines and heroes.[31] Indeed, the French romances of the seventeenth century focus almost exclusively on characters and geographical regions unchampioned by conventional histories.

In particular, the turn to Eastern climes by seventeenth-century romancers finds its parallel in many eighteenth-century novels: as writers turn from Augustus's West to Dido and Cleopatra's East, they forsake familiar geographies in favour of a more expansive heritage, one capable of imagining an increasingly global eighteenth century. Inspired by French romances and especially by Antoine Galland's *Arabian Nights' Entertainments*, tales of the orient had been popular, and had been gaining in popularity, ever since Galland rendered the *Nights* into French at the end of the seventeenth century. Soon translated for English-speaking audiences (1704–17), the *Nights* quickly established its influence over eighteenth-century print culture, and it wasn't long before the heroics of Sindbad rivalled those of Odysseus and Aeneas.[32] At the end of the eighteenth century, for example, Edward Gibbon, in his memoirs and letters, remembered both traditions side-by-side. Despite the predominantly classical bent of his education, he also attested to England's fascination with "Oriental languages" and "Oriental literature": as a boy, he found both Pope's Homer and the *Nights* "books which will always please by the moving picture of human manners and specious miracles"; later, he would write, of a friend's recent visit, that the two men talked "much of books, from my own, on which he flattered me very pleasantly, to Homer and the Arabian Nights,"[33] indicating that the *Nights*, as much as Homer, had become part of England's common patrimony. Perhaps his taste for oriental literature had biased Gibbon against "pious Aeneas"; he was not, at any rate, the only reader to remark on the hero's waning appeal in the presence of more seductive literary pursuits.[34] Indeed, a growing attraction to the East often parallels an increasing disenchantment with the classics, leading Horace Walpole to write to one of his female correspondents, "read Sindbad the Sailor's voyages, and you will be sick of Aeneas's."[35]

Eighteenth-century novelists interested in revising existing narratives thus return to Virgilian epic and Augustan history through the magnified possibilities of romance. Their goal is not to reproduce epic on Virgilian and Augustan terms, or even to counter epic using its own conventions, which would merely, as in the case of Steele's "Inkle and Yarico," affirm the contested model. Instead, their engagements with epic complicate the neoclassical nostalgia of other modes, such as the mock-heroic: conservative appreciation for past models gives way to newfound valorization of dissenting perspectives, foregrounding the voices typically excluded from ancient epic and history. The figures of Cleopatra and Dido, hovering at the margins of Roman and English culture and serving as the obstacles through and against which Rome defined itself, inflect these narratives with their unstable and richly productive foreignness and femininity.

Mirroring the fluidity of generic distinctions, the fluidity of Dido and Cleopatra as narrative figures, combined with the instability of the very category "woman" in the long eighteenth century,[36] intersects powerfully with shifting definitions of "history" to create "romance historiography" as a fictional strategy for eighteenth-century novelists. Even as "history," "novel," "epic," and "romance" often signified similar types of narrative, "history" in particular underwent a further redefinition around mid-century, from the classical subject of the "Great Man" and his political and military actions to a complementary mode that underscored the often private and personal narratives that made classical history possible – what Mark Salber Phillips has called "the invisible movements of economy, custom, or opinion" that "shaped" history in its high, classical form.[37] History's changing fortunes thus paralleled and also structured the evolving status of women in eighteenth-century Britain: for the first time, a newfound emphasis on manners, and on subgenres such as biography and memoir, centralized women as agents of history and gave women writers limited access to certain genres no longer considered beyond the scope of their learning.

A further development, in the rise of Scottish conjectural history from the 1750s onward, reinforced women's prominence in the British historiographic project. That is, the four-stages or stadial view of history that posited progress through various stages of civilization – from hunting and gathering societies to nomadic and herding peoples, to agricultural civilizations and modern commercial society – located women at the forefront of historical progress by "entail[ing] a re-evaluation of history, not simply as a series of political events and military conflicts, but as a civilising process."[38] As the historian Karen O'Brien notes, "In many conjectural versions of history, the figure of the woman functioned as a barometer of social evolution, revealing the deep structure of each stage of development ... Scottish writers almost all (with the exception of [Adam] Smith) equated the sexual and political subjection of women with early, barbarous phases of development, and good treatment of them with the advancement of civilization."[39] Rewriting earlier versions of epic and history thus means enshrining Dido and Cleopatra at the heart of the novelistic project, as "romance historiography" makes legible the ideological underpinnings of Virgilian epic and Augustan propaganda.

In rethinking ancient genres in this way, novelists forge an imaginative link to the past – represented by Dido and her historical counterpart – through contemporary Englishwomen in order to encourage sympathy for Dido's plight. In other words, allusively fostering sympathy for distant historical subjects through modern Englishwomen closes the imaginative gap between past and present, English and foreign. As Phillips has suggested, Englishwomen, in their own marginal positioning, had an affinity with other non-traditional subjects. Although Phillips invokes "the savage Briton" as a counterpart to the eighteenth-century "female reader," the same observation could be made about Dido and Cleopatra as subjects of history: writes Phillips, "the savage Briton and the female reader share their common exclusion from the high ground of classically conceived historical narrative. Neither one, it is fair to say, has a narratable history."[40] At the same time, as Karen O'Brien writes of the latter half of the eighteenth century, "women came to define what was specific and superior about European culture, and represented a point of connection to the best aspects of the past, whether barbarian, medieval or Roman."[41] The female English subject thus closes spatial and temporal distance in her relationship to the past, so that the Dido position comes to signify the possibility of identifying with other potential subjects of history – in this case, the twin queens othered by Roman literature and Augustan historiography.

My first chapter, "'Pulcherrima Dido': Jane Barker and the Epic of Exile," begins with Barker's Jacobite romance *Exilius; or The Banish'd Roman* (written in 1688 and published in 1715). I argue that *Exilius* offers innovative ways of thinking about epic and history – in this case, for the Jacobite supporters of James II who found themselves on the outskirts of official history after the Glorious Revolution that deposed James in 1688. Although the *Aeneid* had come to be inextricably identified with Jacobite interests (the wandering Aeneas a symbol of James II and the ousted Stuart monarchy), Barker's novel reveals the drawbacks of seeking to align oneself with epic's triumphalist version of history. This was especially true for supporters of the Jacobite cause, whose adherents understood themselves as rightful victors forced, after 1688, into the dilatory world of romance. Grappling with the dissonance of James-turned-Dido, *Exilius* seeks to provide heroic alternatives for the Jacobites marginalized by Williamite history. Barker accomplishes this feat by rewriting the conflict that required Dido's dying curse: in *Exilius*, Barker revisits one of the most famous episodes in Roman history, Scipio Africanus's defeat of the Carthaginian general

Hannibal, but omits any trace of the storied hostility between Carthage and Rome, deliberately effacing the longtime enmity between the rival states. In doing so, she rejects epic's treatment of its outcasts by revaluing the Dido position as well as the category of defeat she had come, inevitably, to represent. In *Exilius,* this means embracing North African figures such as the Numidian princess Galecia and Carthaginian Hannibal, and celebrating the story of the Scipios even though their descendant, the Triumvir Pompey, would fail in challenging Julius Caesar for Roman rule. By using putatively historical material that aims, by vying with the *Aeneid,* to rewrite the Jacobite presence into myth and history, *Exilius* foregrounds the value of new modes of representation for Barker's Jacobite readers.

In 1751, Henry Fielding's *Amelia* would build on Barker's legacy by positing a new kind of epic entirely, advocating, in the figure of his titular heroine, a remarkable shift in the subject of national heroism. Fielding turns away, in his final novel, from the mock-epic and burlesque elements of earlier works such as *Joseph Andrews* (1742) and *Tom Jones* (1749), instead seriously blending romance and epic in *Amelia.* Chapter 2, "'What Is There of a Woman Worth Relating?' Revising the *Aeneid* in Henry Fielding's *Amelia,*" builds on feminist discussions of Fielding's work in order to take seriously the modernization of Aeneas in the novel's heroine, Amelia Booth.[42] Like Steele and Barker, Fielding condemns inappropriate uses of Virgilian epic in the present: showing the potential of classical learning to alienate female characters, even the classically trained Mrs Bennet, Fielding condemns Dr Harrison's attempts to intimidate Amelia and Mrs Bennet with his superior knowledge of the ancients. While Barker desires to vindicate Jacobite history, which jars uncomfortably with existing models of mythmaking, Fielding takes aim at systemic patterns of behaviour, especially in Harrison's recourse to classical authority. By staging multiple wronged Didos in the figures of Amelia, Mrs Bennet, and Miss Mathews, Fielding both illuminates the failures of the novel's so-called heroes and advocates new narratives that rework classical models in order to embrace women as epic subjects themselves.

Chapter 3, "'A Pattern to Ensuing Ages': Reinventing Historical Practice in Charlotte Lennox's *Female Quixote,*" functions as the turning point between Parts 1 and 2 as Lennox makes visible the evident slippage between romance and history. Where Arabella's contemporaries remember Cleopatra as the Egyptian "whore," Arabella celebrates her noble qualities, and their legacy in her daughter, Cleopatra VIII.

For Lennox, Cleopatra becomes a symbol of the complicity between generic and ideological battles: it is no accident that Arabella's male companions – despite a professed aversion to the putative fictions of romance – remark quite readily on Cleopatra's scandalous intrigues while revealing their broader ignorance of ancient history. The seventeenth-century French heroic novel that allows Barker to reimagine, by intervening in, early Roman history thus proves equally productive for Lennox in her 1752 adaptation of *Don Quixote*. A more explicit exploration than Barker's of the intersections among ancient and modern histories, *The Female Quixote* underscores the extent to which the traditional categories of "history" and "romance" are, in fact, one and the same. Chapter 3 takes up Arabella's particular reading material, the critically neglected works of Scudéry and La Calprenède, and urges that scholars treat Arabella's romances as alternative histories. Inspired by the Heliodoran novel of late antiquity, the romances reach back to the classical past, especially to Persia and North Africa, championing the narratives of putatively Eastern heroines over Western heroes. Explicitly opposed, yet also indebted, to epic, romance supplements conventional histories rendered unreliable by the bias of the ancients as well as Arabella's contemporaries.

In 1757, Sarah Fielding takes as her subject precisely the Cleopatra whose vilified historical record makes possible the romances I discuss in chapter 3. Building on an increasingly hostile historical tradition, Fielding carries the Cleopatra narrative to its logical conclusion, depicting a Cleopatra of consummate villainy as she parodies the historical prejudices that make romance historiography necessary in the first place. Where Lennox contends with a historiographic tradition that neglects women as writers, readers, and subjects of history, Sarah Fielding's *Lives of Cleopatra and Octavia* shows the process of history making in action. Chapter 4, "Performing Augustan History in Sarah Fielding's *Lives of Cleopatra and Octavia*," argues that Fielding employs a didactic framework to undercut any facile contest between the titular heroines. Blending romance, novel, (auto)biography, oriental tale, and ancient history, Fielding resists and indicts the script of Augustan propaganda, even as Cleopatra and Octavia perform that script with exaggerated obedience. Like Dido, consigned to Virgil's epic with little regard for prior history, Cleopatra falls victim to Octavian's mastery of available narratives. Sharing Lennox's concerns with the power of narrative control, Fielding suggests a competing classical history in her heroines' stories of authority and influence, counting on her readers to recognize the dissonance within and between the women's narratives, between fiction and authorized fact. Stripping away the comical confrontation between the historiographic and romance Cleopatras at the centre of *The Female Quixote*, Fielding reveals the brutality of traditional history for characters as diverse as Cleopatra and the virtuous Octavia.

Finally, chapter 5, "Whose 'Wild and Extravagant Stories'? Clara Reeve's *Progress of Romance* and *The History of Charoba, Queen of Ægypt*," argues that Reeve's literary-critical dialogue (1785) extends the narrative potential of novels such as *The Female Quixote* and *The Lives of Cleopatra and Octavia* by explicitly elevating romance in epic's stead. Appending *The History of Charoba, Queen of Ægypt* to her dialogue, Reeve offers a new historiographic model in the story of a queen who resists narrative and imperial domination. In commemorating Charoba's story alongside the history of the would-be conqueror, Gebirus, Reeve rewrites the triumph of Aeneas over Dido, and Octavian over Cleopatra; subverting the seeming inevitability of Dido's defeat, she emphasizes the stakes of representation by offering the histories of Charoba and Gebirus side by side. In this way, *Charoba* parallels debates about canon formation earlier in *The Progress*, suggesting the fallacy of presenting a single, unified narrative as undisputed fact. Where eighteenth-century moralists hastened to declare the novel's perils for female audiences, *The Progress of Romance* thus echoes *Spectator* 11's denunciation of the Commonplace Talker by demonstrating that classical learning had engendered a completely different class of misguided reader: men like Reeve's champion of epic, Hortensius, whose elite education precludes viewpoints at odds with epic's version of history.

In this way, Reeve demonstrates, in her literary-critical dialogue, how critical attempts to regulate generic categories threaten to efface female writers just as Augustan epic and history had marginalized female characters. If novelists could intervene in the canonizing impulse – something they could the more easily accomplish with the help of classical authority – then they could engage in the process in an unprecedented way. From Barker's heroic novel to Reeve's literary criticism and illustrative oriental tale, "romance historiography" provides a set of tools with which to question concepts of gender and genre, fact and fiction, ancient and modern at a time when the instabilities of "woman" and "fiction" resonated with the rich experimentation that marked the eighteenth-century novel as a new form.

Embracing the varied possibilities represented by Dido's myth and Cleopatra's history, novelists return to English cultural origins in order to posit alternative narratives based in the same epic tradition that had shaped Western civilization and legitimated England's own fabled history. Turning to Dido alongside, and sometimes over, Aeneas, writers like Reeve facilitate a more expansive view of history, one that centralizes female characters and the genres associated with them, while modelling proper interpretive practices for the Aeneases and Gebiruses who resent the fates of so many Didos and Charobas. In thus recovering the ancient pedigree of the novel, *Novel Cleopatras* situates eighteenth-century women writers at the heart of a long tradition of rereading Virgilian epic and, at the same time, foregrounds their participation – at the intersections of "novel," "romance," "epic," and "history" – in neoclassical culture.

PART 1

Demythologizing Dido: Epic and Romance

1 "Pulcherrima Dido": Jane Barker and the Epic of Exile

Bright *Shees*, what Glories had your Names acquir'd,
Had you consum'd those whom your Beauties fir'd,
Had laugh'd to see them burn, and so retir'd:
Then they cou'd ne'er have glory'd in their shames,
Either to *Roman*, or to *English* Dames,
Had you but warm'd, not melted in their flames.
You'd not been wrack'd then on despair's rough coast,
Nor yet by storms of Perjuries been toss'd,
Had you but fix'd your flowing Love with Frost.
Had you put on the Armour of your scorn,
(That *Gem* which do's our Beauties most adorn)
What hardy *Hero* durst have been forsworn.
But since they found such *lenity* in you,
Their crime so Epidemical do's grow,
All have, or do, or would be doing so.

Jane Barker, "To Ovid's Heroines in His Epistles,"
from *Poetical Recreations* (1688)

For Jane Barker (1652?–1732), the foremost Jacobite writer of her day and an early innovator of the eighteenth-century novel, the Glorious Revolution gave added significance to the twin narratives of Dido's and Aeneas's wanderings.[1] As the dominant framework for the epic of national destiny in seventeenth- and eighteenth-century England, the *Aeneid* resonated with the displaced Stuarts and their supporters, known as Jacobites (after James II), who recognized in Aeneas's story the plight of the Stuart monarchy. Thanks to Geoffrey of Monmouth's twelfth-century chronicle, *Historia Regum Brittaniae*, Britain, like Rome, could boast of Trojan origins: according to legend, Aeneas's descendant, Brutus, founded Nova Troia on the site of London, his rule legitimated by the same history celebrated in Virgil's epic. Although James I would later style himself the new Augustus, fulfilling the promise of Brutus's founding, the Glorious Revolution denied James II a similarly triumphal narrative. Unjustly deprived of his throne, James became, like Dido, the Wanderer, displaced from epic and history into the dilatory world of romance.[2] Although the *Aeneid* remained a royalist text, famously translated by Dryden with a Tory slant, its celebratory anticipation of the rise of the Roman Empire could no longer make sense of Jacobite experience, which rendered James, at once, both Aeneas and Dido, victor and vanquished. Driven from the victors' narrative, James and his supporters found themselves relegated to the margins of history, left with an ill-fitting epic model that could only speak to their defeat.[3]

In her poem "To Ovid's Heroines in His Epistles" (published in 1688's *Poetical Recreations*), Barker inveighs against the familiar trope that would cast James and his followers into narrative limbo. Censuring the epic pattern that pits victors against losers, leaving heroines seduced and abandoned, at the mercy of the hero's plot, Barker also locates an originary failure in Virgil's Dido, one of the figures whom Ovid ventriloquizes in the *Heroides*:[4] the "Bright shee's" whose heroes "glory in their shames" mark a dangerous precedent that delimits subsequent narratives, not only for future heroines but also for others – like the Jacobites – consigned to romance's supplemental history. In reimagining a lover's burning – this time, hero for heroine – the opening stanza at once evokes and rewrites Dido's immolation in its invocation of literal and metaphoric fire: if only Dido had "retir'd" while Aeneas "burn[ed]." In this way, Barker's poem trades on a simple inversion in order to challenge the settled trajectory of both Dido's story and Western civilization itself. "Had you but warm'd not melted in their flames," she writes, "They cou'd ne'er have glory'd in their shames, / Either to *Roman* or to *English* Dames[.]" Aeneas's heroic actions furnish the template for present-day English custom, transforming "English Dames" into the affronted and defeated heroines commemorated in Ovid's epistles. Barker's closing lines, emphasizing the crucial stakes of her argument, again link English transgressors with their Roman counterparts: "But since they found such *lenity* in you [Ovid's heroines], / Their crime so epidemical do's grow, / All have, or do, or wou'd be doing so." In condemning Ovid's heroines, Barker defies existing literary hierarchies and the legacy of Western history – the triumph of Aeneas over Dido, and later William over James – in order to foreground the failure of Virgilian analogy for late seventeenth-century England. Even Ovid, that poet of love so invested in the plight of female characters, is complicit: giving voice, however sympathetic, to Dido's suffering ultimately reaffirms the Virgilian narrative that consigns Dido to romance.

In this way, Barker identifies, via Ovid, a larger narrative pattern entrenched in the ancient imagination: naturalizing the hierarchy between epic hero and romance heroine, stories like the *Aeneid* cast Aeneas and Dido in the roles of victor and loser as a *fait accompli*. With the weight of history and the canon on its side, the "epic hero/betrayed heroine" plot appears to justify the apparent lack of alternative possibilities. In the world of the *Aeneid*, Dido exists in order to be abandoned and, finally, to commit suicide, effacing herself from the Romans' epic of national destiny. As Barker's rebuke implies, it is no accident that so many Greco-Roman heroines succumb to a similar fate, a pattern prolific enough to merit Ovid's *Heroides*, an entire work dedicated to the women often silenced by Greek and Roman mythology.

In this chapter, I will argue that Barker's novel *Exilius; or, The Banish'd Roman* (1688) represents an attempt to imagine a Jacobite mythos that at once expands notions of heroism and refutes the limitations of traditional epic and history. Although the Stuarts and their supporters would successfully dominate Virgilian epic, despite Williamite objections, until the 1730s, the *Aeneid* had its shortcomings as a relevant model.[5] James and his heirs may have seen themselves as the dispossessed Aeneas, believing that divine prophecy would one day convey the Stuarts to their rightful homeland, but this vision, however earnestly conceived, contradicted the history actually unfolding.[6] An unlawful usurper, according to the Jacobites who opposed his rule, William nonetheless represented – for some contemporaries, at least – the Greeks' victory over the upstart Trojans, the dutiful Aeneas necessarily abandoning Queen Dido for the common good.[7] From the perspective of Williamite history, the Jacobite James/Aeneas resembles, instead, Virgil's ill-fated queen, permanently exiled from her homeland of Tyre; among the Jacobites, the "optima Dido" was evidently a popular toast. Later, James Boswell would capture, in the slightest of gestures, the problem with embracing the *Aeneid* for the Stuart cause: in the *Journal of a Tour to the Hebrides* (1785), the memoir of his journey with Samuel Johnson, he refers to Prince Charles Edward Stuart as, simply, "The

Wanderer." With the spectre of Charles uncannily out-Didoing Dido – eternally displaced, unnamed, and disguised in women's clothing – the Stuart translation from victor to vanquished, from Aeneas to Dido – that other Wanderer – seemed complete.[8]

For Barker, the circumstances of Stuart exile strained Virgil's template for imperial prosperity, especially for the Jacobites, whose reality required a new script, one that could account for the complexities of exile and the doublenesses of Jacobite experience. Born of the same political spirit that infused much of Barker's writing, *Exilius* relates the fortunes of the Sciplones, one of the most illustrious families of Middle Republican Rome. The elder Scipio's retirement from corrupt Roman politics frames Barker's romance. Publius Scipio, in grief at the loss of his wife, his banished friend, Catullus, and (as he then believes) his two sons, Africanus and Asiaticus, seeks a quiet and virtuous life at his estate in the country. Here, a group of young lovers converge, at various points, and relate their adventures. The principal couples include Publius Scipio's daughter, Scipiana, and Catullus's son, Exilius; the Roman war hero, Asiaticus, and his childhood love, Clarinthia; and Exilius's sister, Cordiala, and Scipio Africanus. The romance draws to a close with the series of revelations necessary to secure the happiness of the Scipio family – the safe return of Asiaticus, Africanus, and Catullus – and the lovers' joyful union. It then concludes by anticipating the couples' marriages and the "Glories of the *Scipio's*."[9]

Taking inspiration from history, Barker sets *Exilius* in the interval between the First (246–241 BCE) and Second Punic Wars (218–201 BCE), yet omits any trace of the fabled enmity between Carthage and Rome. Locating her history at a moment that – counterfactually, at least – predates the *Aeneid*, Barker revisits the Sciplones at the very moment that enables Virgil to link Dido's self-destruction to the wars with Carthage, translating the chaste Dido of Phoenician legend into the sympathetic, yet doomed, queen of Roman epic. Barker's choice, I argue, is deliberate: she returns to this precise moment of Roman history in order to uncouple the interrelated categories that unite Dido, Hannibal, and the Jacobites – the potently linked terms "woman," "foreigner," and "loser." By returning to the prehistory of the Carthaginian conflict, Barker makes possible a rethinking of the hierarchies that the dynamics of Augustan culture would later consolidate. *Exilius* represents a new moment of possibility for Roman – and, by extension – Jacobite history, one with no Dido to thwart in order to forge Rome's identity.

The most celebrated of the Scipiones, Scipio Africanus, won distinction for his victory in the Second Punic War. So called after the Phoenician origins of Rome's challenger, Carthage, the wars dominated Roman politics for more than a century. Pre-dating the legendary founding of Rome and strategically located just south of Corsica and Sardinia in the present-day Gulf of Tunis, Carthage posed a serious economic and military threat to the early Republic. So great was the spectre of Carthage's military ascendency that Marcus Cato, the statesman and censor, seized every opportunity to call for the city's destruction: in the aftermath of the First Punic War, Cato concluded every speech before the Senate – no matter the subject – by exhorting his fellow Romans, "delenda est Carthago" – "Carthage must be destroyed." Of all the conflicts between Carthage and Rome, Scipio's subsequent defeat of the great tactician Hannibal (247–183? BCE) was particularly well known, owing to the stakes of Roman victory. Under Hannibal's command, Carthage invaded the Italian peninsula from the north, traversing Spain, Gaul, and finally the Alps themselves in a terrifying display of military prowess. Scipio arrested Hannibal's triumphant march through Italy, reversing Carthage's fortunes. In the wake of Hannibal's crushing defeat of the Roman army at Cannae (216 BCE), Scipio insisted that Rome take its fight directly to Carthage's shores: with Hannibal still in Italy, the vulnerable Carthaginians quickly surrendered to Roman terms for peace. Resentful of Scipio's tactics, Carthage would make one last bid for freedom in the Third and final Punic War (ca. 146), although there, too, the outcome favoured the Scipiones: Scipio Aemilianus, the adoptive grandson of S. Africanus, sold the citizens into slavery, razed the city to the ground, and reputedly salted the earth, ostensibly ensuring its sterility for ages to come.[10]

Scipio's defeat of Hannibal consolidated the myth of Roman supremacy, quickly recasting Carthage as eternally foredoomed. In hindsight, the image of Hannibal's transalpine march, like the failure, for Barker, of epic's "bright shees," becomes part of a larger pattern: marshalling thirty-eight thousand infantry, eight thousand cavalry, and thirty-eight elephants, Hannibal nonetheless succumbed to Roman domination.[11] Earlier generations of Romans would have recalled an analogue, for example, in the Persian king Xerxes' ill-advised attempts to invade Greece during the Persian Wars: as he bridges the Hellespont, Xerxes' violation of the natural order showcases his otherworldly power even as his hubris forecasts his demise. Starting with Virgil, they would also remember the fate of Hannibal's ancestor and legendary founder of

Carthage, Queen Dido: armed with the knowledge of Scipio's triumph, Virgil's *Aeneid* naturalizes Hannibal's defeat by predicating both his limited successes and his certain failure on Dido's deathbed curse. The first writer to reimagine Dido as Aeneas's contemporary – the "Famous Anachronism" defended by Dryden in his preface to the *Aeneid* – Virgil took advantage of Dido's suicide to "espouse," in Dryden's words, "the Cause and Quarrel of his Country against Carthage."[12] As Dido calls upon her descendants to avenge Aeneas's wrongs, Virgil enshrines Carthage's destruction at the very origins of its foundation story: underwriting Rome's future military success, the glorious founding of Dido's city invokes, at the same time, its subsequent ruins. Imagining Hannibal's rise – "some Avenger of our Lybian Blood" – Dido enjoins Carthage to remember Aeneas's plighted faith: "Now, and from hence in ev'rey future Age, / When Rage excites your Arms, and Strength supplies the Rage: / Rise some Avenger of our Lybian Blood, / With Fire and Sword pursue the perjur'd Brood: / Our Arms, our Seas, our Shores, oppos'd to theirs, /And the same hate descend on all our Heirs" (4.895–904). Dido's curse, in accounting for "the immortal hatred betwixt the two Rival Nations," foresees Hannibal's rise, but cannot anticipate the defeat well known to Virgil's audience (5:298). Her malediction thus fails even before she utters it: thanks to the Scipiones, Carthage has already been destroyed.

Intervening in the history that posits Carthage's inevitable defeat, Barker's *Exilius* attempts to envision a world that pre-dates Virgil's successful reframing of Dido's death as the aetiology for the Punic Wars. By imagining a world in which the *Aeneid* has yet to be written and the Second Punic War, with Scipio's decisive victory over Hannibal, has not yet occurred, *Exilius*, I argue, liberates Dido from her Virgilian context and, in doing so, obviates the self-destruction requisite for Carthage's defeat. Although Scipio Africanus and Hannibal, his future rival, emerge on the cusp of military greatness in *Exilius*, Barker effaces the conflict between Rome and Carthage, and thus undermines the history-as-hindsight that lends prophetic weight to Dido's malediction. Disrupting the teleology that subjects Dido's narrative to Aeneas's while mandating her demise, Barker makes available a new model of epic and history that no longer requires the subordination of epic's losers. When Carthage, in Barker's alternative history, never takes up arms against Rome, Dido needn't be sacrificed to the mandates of Roman mythopoesis. Revaluing forms of history that lack Virgil's confidence, Barker seizes on romance to explore the complicated and shifting identities unleashed by the Glorious Revolution and subsequent Jacobite exile. *Exilius* thus posits an alternative version of the past that accommodates Roman victors and Carthaginian losers by resisting the logic that subordinates Dido to Aeneas and Carthage to Rome.

The "Glories of the Scipios"? *Exilius*'s Romance Rewriting of History

In 1688, the publication of *Poetical Recreations* anticipated *Exilius*'s investments in the generative union between romance and history. I have already argued that Barker's verse epistle, "To Ovid's Heroines," reimagines women like Dido at a crucial moment of possibility: conjuring the prospect of alternative narratives, Barker unsettles the pattern of abandonment at once naturalized and lamented in the *Heroides*. At the same time, *Exilius*'s framing performs a similar feat. Celebrated, in *Poetical Recreations*, as the then-unpublished romance "Scipina," *Exilius*'s own origin story proclaims Barker a new Dido: positing Barker as Dido in the volume's epigraph, and paradoxically comparing her to Scipio in its commendatory verses, *Poetical Recreations* further authorizes *Exilius*'s counterfactual history by celebrating its origins in the alternative versions of Dido and Scipio represented by Barker herself.

Published collaboratively by Benjamin Crayle and Barker's circle of Cambridge friends, *Poetical Recreations* marked Barker's entrance into the world of print. Although we know little about Barker's literary circle – the "Gentlemen of the UNIVERSITIES, and OTHERS" indicated on the volume's title page – Barker originally met these men through her brother, Edward, himself a student at Cambridge. Encouraging Barker's learning, Edward instructed her in Latin and medicine, and introduced her to the intellectual circle that would become her group of literary interlocutors. Although the identities of her Cambridge companions remain largely unknown, *Poetical Recreations* attests to their crucial influence on Barker's career. The collection includes fifty-one poems by Barker as well as the poetry of her circle, with several of the verses – including a poem by Crayle himself – extolling Barker's literary talents, especially in the form of the then-unpublished text of "Scipina," later printed as the Jacobite romance, *Exilius: or, The Banish'd Roman*.[13] The early circulation of *Exilius* prior to its publication in 1715 gives a glimpse of the vibrant manuscript culture that celebrated Barker's engagement with print. Following *Poetical Recreations*, she would continue to shape the early novel in the series of works now known as the *Galesia Trilogy*, after its heroine, a semi-autobiographical version of Barker herself. The first novel in the trilogy, *Love Intrigues*, appeared in 1713, followed by *A Patch-Work Screen for the Ladies* (1723) and *The Lining of the Patch-Work Screen* (1726). "As a coterie and then court poet turned market place novelist," Barker, writes Kathryn King, "exemplifies the emergence of female literary professionalism," transitioning from "an amateur, court-centred manuscript-based literary system to the market-driven culture of print."[14] At the heart of this shift, the manuscript of "Scipina" achieved enough popularity as the published *Exilius* to be reprinted, alongside *Love Intrigues*, in *The Amours of Bosvil and Galesia* (1719, the same year that George Sewell commended Barker's authorship in his *Poems on Several Occasions*), and again in *The Entertaining Novels of Mrs. Jane Barker* in 1743.

Fêting Barker's foray into the world of print, *Poetical Recreations* opens with an epigraph from the *Aeneid* selected by her Cambridge friends. Describing, in the Dryden translation, "The beauteous Dido, with a num'rous Train / And pomp of Guards," as she "ascends the sacred Fane," the Latin epigraph substitutes "virgo" for "Dido": "pulcherrima virgo / Incedit, magna juvenum stipante caterva."[15] In this way, the epigraph reimagines Dido's appearance before her subjects as Barker's ascent to the temple of poetic fame, surrounded by the "train" and "pomp" that herald her literary empire. Recalling Barker's criticism of the "bright Shees" of Ovid's *Heroides*, it might seem odd to align the self-styled virgin poet with the infamous queen she chastises. Yet, in foregrounding Barker's virtue, the epigraph transforms her into an alternative Dido – perhaps that other Dido of pre-Virgilian legend, who remains faithfully devoted to the memory of her husband Sychaeus. This was, after all, the steadfast and uncompromising Dido embraced by Elizabeth I, whose use of female exemplars of virtue would be inherited by the Stuart monarchy.[16] A figure of doubleness from her pre-Virgilian origins, Dido represents the complexities of identity, subjectivity, and genre that fascinated Barker throughout her literary career.[17] The twinned legacies of the pre- and post-Virgilian queen embody the tensions between history and Virgilian poetics, victor and vanquished, epic and romance, resonating with Barker's own fraught identity as a Catholic Englishwoman in a foreign land. Kathryn King has brilliantly characterized this Barker as "Janus Barker," after the two-faced Roman god who looks simultaneously forward and backward, to the future as well as the past.[18]

At once effacing Virgil's queen and underlining her absence, the epithet "pulcherimma virgo" thus prefigures the origins of an alternative trajectory for the Dido story in *Exilius* itself. At this juncture in *Aeneid* 1, Virgil introduces Dido at the Temple of Juno, depicting her as a pious and judicious queen, reminiscent, in her charms, of the virgin goddess Diana (1.700). On the verge of welcoming the Trojan refugees, she has not yet met Aeneas, nor has Cupid, at Venus's behest, poisoned Dido with the fatal passion that will ensure the hero's protection at the cost of Dido's life. At this liminal moment, poised between Phoenician legend and Augustan mythmaking, Dido's appearance in *Aeneid* 1 echoes the setting of *Exilius*'s action between the First and Second Punic Wars. Revisiting the pre-history of Virgil's Dido, just as *Exilius* revisits the storied conflict between Carthage and Rome, the epigraph marks an imaginative crossroads: proliferating Didos, it militates against the *Aeneid*'s teleological mythmaking. Centralizing Dido as a figure of narrative abundance, *Poetical Recreations* lauds Barker as an alternative Dido who at once legitimates, and is legitimated by, *Exilius*'s revision of Roman history.

In championing Dido's descendant, Hannibal, alongside Scipio Africanus, Barker locates new origins for the Jacobite mythos in the strategies of heroic romance. The enormously popular tradition exemplified by Madeleine de Scudéry (1607–1701) and Gauthier de Costes, Seigneur de la Calprenède (1609/10–1663) had already established a familiar framework for fictionalizing ancient history. The seventeenth-century French heroic novel – widely emulated by Restoration and eighteenth-century writers – exploited lacunae in the historical record, offering an imaginative supplement to the well-known histories of writers like Herodotus and Livy. Taken as a tradition, these romances embody the allusive fecundity of the neoclassical impulse: proliferating Romes, Egypts, Persias (and so forth), they take a particular interest in figures, especially women and foreigners, regularly slighted by conventional historiographic practices. Defending their own historicity, these *romans de longue haleine* hybridize history and fiction, profiting from what I call "romance historiography" in order to make available a complementary and competing source for citations of antiquity as they repackage Greek and Roman history for polite society.

Referring to the "unfashionable constancy" of her eponymous hero, Barker self-consciously underlines *Exilius*'s formal and ideological descent from this French romance tradition: she overstates, I argue,

Exilius's antiquated form in order to foreground its origins in the revolutionary possibilities that engendered the heroic novel, at the crossroads of romance, novel, and history.[19] The mid-seventeenth century had been a time of political turmoil for France as well as England. Following the death of Louis XIII, the revolt (known as the Fronde, 1648–53) against Anne of Austria and her counsellor, Cardinal Mazarin, gave rise to a Bourbon challenger, the Prince de Condé. Rallying around Condé, the *frondeurs*, members of the old aristocracy, resented the growing power of the royal family and sought to limit its influence. Although their efforts were unsuccessful – Louis XIV would famously go on to style himself the "Sun King," championing absolutism and centralizing power at Versailles – the Fronde's challenge to monarchic authority and legitimacy would furnish the crucible in which the heroic novel was forged. The dynamic relationship between the Fronde and modes of representation available to women writers and readers has been well documented by critics such as Joan DeJean, and a full discussion of its political valences is beyond the scope of my argument in this chapter.[20] Instead, in recalling the revolutionary origins of the French romance, I wish to illuminate, from a slightly different perspective, Barker's deployment of a seemingly "unfashionable" form. Turning to the French romance, Barker embraces a genre deeply rooted in the imaginative possibilities of history: the heroic novel, politicized from the outset, enacts complementary versions of the past in order to make visible the endlessly proliferating narratives foreclosed by the teleological illusion of history.

Thus adopting a historical framework, *Exilius* – even more so than the "old-fashioned" French romances from which Barker drew inspiration – rewrites Roman history in particularly striking ways: foregrounding the fame of the little-known Asiaticus over the legendary Scipio, it also transforms into friendship the rank hatred between Carthage and Rome. Barker thus creates a story that is not merely complementary, but alternative to, Roman history: *Exilius* depicts one of the most important families, at one of the most crucial moments, in the Roman past, while completely effacing the storied conflict that eventually led to Carthage's destruction. It is a stunning move, given the well-known subject, one made more surprising by the elevation of the relatively unknown Asiaticus over his brother, Africanus, and the explicit introduction of an entirely unthreatening Hannibal, who – in Barker's fiction – commands as his servant the long-lost Scipio Africanus, the same Scipio who won this cognomen by defeating Hannibal and subjecting Carthage to Rome.

Despite *Exilius*'s allegiance to the stratagems of romance, its sharp departure from the patterns typical of romance historiography boldly signals its status as mythmaking: in the fictional world of *Exilius*, the Scipiones become the inheritors of Aeneas's mythological legacy, ensuring – or at least poised to ensure – the future success of the Roman Empire. In this way, Barker's narrative runs parallel to the *Aeneid*, following a similar pattern of heroism, prophecy, and redemption. Yet, like the Stuarts' failure to reclaim Aeneas's role, *Exilius* ends without staging Scipio's greatest triumph, the defeat of Hannibal, whose name would have been synonymous with "Scipio" to Barker's seventeenth-century readers. Indeed, the novel even leaves that triumph in question, giving pride of place to Asiaticus, not Africanus, casting Africanus and Hannibal as mutual admirers, and generally proceeding as though no enmity between Rome and Carthage existed. I therefore argue that, in remapping elements of the *Aeneid* onto the story of the Scipio family, Barker returns to an earlier moment of Roman history in order to reconceive the very meaning of that history. For all Pompey's ill success, *Exilius* demonstrates that Aeneas's is not the only legitimate heroism, and that categories of victory and defeat defy neat classification, both for the Scipiones who begin as Carthaginian victors and for the Jacobites who inherit Roman history. Barker adopts the strategies of romance historiography in order to recall the fame and promise of the Scipiones, regardless of their ultimate fate. At the same time, *Exilius*'s blatant – even, given the famed subject matter, one could even say defiant – fictionality underscores the ideological nature of the *Aeneid*, and of history itself.

Resembling Dido: Reinventing Carthage and Rome

In returning to Roman history just prior to the Second Punic War, Barker returns to Dido, and Dido's Carthage, as figures of new originary possibility. Where Virgil neutralizes the threat of Carthage by requiring Dido's defeat, Barker seizes Dido's story, and later Hannibal's, in order to imagine a world in which the hostility between Rome and Carthage no longer exists. For Barker, Dido is perhaps most conspicuous in her absence: in *Exilius*, Virgil has not yet transformed Dido into the romance heroine whose defeat symbolizes the future antagonism between Scipio and Hannibal. Yet her presence, like a palimpsest, haunts *Exilius*, not only in the figure of the Numidian princess Galecia, but in the Roman heroines who would inherit Virgil's narrative of the defeated queen.

Recalling Dido's story as the archetype of amatory suffering made famous by Virgil and Ovid, Barker's heroines attempt to interpret their experiences through the pattern of Dido's misfortunes. So successful is the originary narrative deployed by Virgil that *Exilius* offers no competing allusion; even in Dido's absence, she becomes the foremost explanatory pattern for Barker's heroines, signalling the extent to which the *Aeneid* had naturalized Dido's fate. When Clarinthia, kidnapped and imprisoned by her amorous half-brother, compares herself to the *Aeneid*'s lovesick queen, she attempts to understand her circumstances through an available model that can only magnify her heartache. Describing her agitated state of mind, Clarinthia relates: "I went out on the Balcony which appertain'd to my Lodging, and jetted, as it were, over the Sea. Here I walk'd many Turns in the greatest Perplexity a Soul cou'd suffer. I fancy I resembled Queen *Dido* (as History describes her) at the Departure of her *Aeneas*, and was as much embarras'd and distracted how to avoid my amorous Persecutor, as she cou'd be how to follow or overtake her beloved Fugitive" (1:47). In order to interpret her circumstances through the example of Dido's experience, Clarinthia must reconstruct the simile entirely, inverting her connection with Valerius: although she describes herself as "resembl[ing] Queen *Dido*," the analogy places Barker's heroine, despite her intent, in Aeneas's position, for she longs to escape captivity at the hands of a criminally impassioned lover. That Clarinthia fastens on Dido even when the allusion proves inadequate suggests the primacy of the Dido position as a naturalized framework for women's amatory experiences; in the absence of other precedents, Clarinthia turns to Dido despite the rhetorical acrobatics her analogy requires.

Affirming the difficulty of defining female suffering beyond the context of Dido's narrative, the wicked Asbella, Clarinthia's stepmother, also calls upon the Virgilian archetype even as she chafes against its limitations. At first more aligned than Clarinthia with Dido's role as abandoned lover, Asbella rebukes her husband, Turpius, for spurning her. "It is very hard," she says, "that I shou'd now be the Object of your Anger, for no other Cause but endeavouring to make you happy, by keeping you within the Reach of my Embrace. Had Queen *Dido* done so by her *Trojan* Hero, Despair and Death had not been her only Refuge" (2:101). Asbella's highly conditional language, like the abrupt turn in Clarinthia's analogy, gestures once again towards the telling inappropriateness of the Dido allusion. She is like Dido only had Dido acted in a completely different way; in other words, she is not like Dido at all, refusing to accept a narrative in which "Despair and Death" might be "her only Refuge." Aware of the fundamental incongruity of the allusion, Asbella, like Clarinthia, recognizes the insufficiency of Dido's example even as she grasps for a familiar template to make legible her experience.

As the narratives of Clarinthia and Asbella suggest, *Exilius*'s spare allusions to the Dido story capture the striking dissonances between her narrative and those of Barker's heroines. As Clarinthia's self-conscious reference to Dido suggests, the *Aeneid* establishes an amatory pattern so virulent that it both transcends generic boundaries and disrupts the temporal logic of Barker's novel. Thanks to Virgil, the fictionalization of Dido's meeting with Aeneas – itself an example of temporal violence – transforms Roman history before the fact, even becoming transhistorical; the narrative power of Virgil's Dido cannot be effaced, even in a history that putatively pre-dates it.

Its conspicuous presence therefore highlights the difficulty of constructing an alternative reality unencumbered by the Roman mythos; Virgil's epic model is so pervasive, for Barker, that it resists temporal confinement, thoroughly redefining the Roman past as it infiltrates even her pre-Virgilian history. Virgilian Dido haunts the margins of the text *avant la lettre*, an anachronistic reminder of the "Bright Shees" whose ominous fates Barker lamented in "To Ovid's Heroines in His Epistles." The shadowy presence of lovelorn Dido and her incompatibility with Barker's narrative realize the obstacles of reinscribing "Dido" as a common allusion for amatory suffering. Encouraging subsequent characters to identify, even wrongly, with her plight, these allusions threaten to assimilate Barker's heroines to a reductive pattern that denies other narrative outcomes.

Having acknowledged the far-reaching influence of Virgil's Dido, Barker sets about uncoupling "Dido" and "amatory suffering" by laying the groundwork for a new point of origin in the Numidian princess Galecia. A rebuke to Dido-as-lovelorn-heroine, Barker's Galecia marks a return to narrative origins by embracing the qualities associated with the legendary Dido rather than Virgil's queen. In this way, Galecia resonates with Barker's poetic persona in the *Galesia Trilogy,* as well as her persona in *Exilius,* "Pulcherrima virgo/Dido." For example, the warrior princess, Galecia, wishes "for ever to be exempt from all human Society, to spend my Days in Study and Contemplation, and praising the Powers divine" (2:37), even though Prince Boccus of Mauretania seeks her hand in marriage. Like Dido, she is a huntress:

fittingly, Asiaticus first meets her in the Numidian forest, seeing "a Panther pursu'd by a Lady on Horseback" (2:31), and we later learn that hunting is one of the particular "Pleasure[s] of the Princess, who delighted in that robust Recreation" (2:32). Having made her acquaintance, Asiaticus expresses admiration for Galecia's "masculine Spirit," noting that she "undervalu'd the little Delicacies of her Sex, making the Study of Philosophy and the Laws of her Country her chief Business, in which she was pleas'd sometimes to entertain me very learnedly" (2:32). Far from being a damsel in distress, she does not shy away from physically protecting Asiaticus from Boccus, ultimately wounding Boccus with Asiaticus's sword (2:39). In her fierce dedication to virginity, her skill as a huntress, and her ability in combat, Galecia also embodies the spirit of the *femme forte* celebrated in the French heroic romance. The *femme forte,* or strong woman, became an archetype of female heroism during the French civil war, as many of the *frondeuses* styled themselves Amazons in the face of the illegitimate authority exercised by Anne of Austria on behalf of Louis XIV. In patterning her own heroine after such storied women, Barker also originates in Galecia a positive source of allusion for future heroines, freed from the weight of Dido's abandonment and loss.

That Galecia is a Numidian princess further underscores the romance geography that enables Barker to rethink the relationship between Rome and Carthage, including Carthage's allies. For Barker's 1715 readers, the geography of Numidia would have conjured romance intrigues: in Joseph Addison's enormously popular 1713 tragedy, *Cato,* the Numidian Juba – a passionate friend to Cato and Rome – plays a starring role. But Juba and his homeland of Numidia would have been best remembered from La Calprenède's heroic romance, *Cleopatra* (1648–58). Taking its inspiration from history, *Cleopatra* follows the twin journeys of Cleopatra's daughter, Cleopatra VIII, and Juba's son, Juba II. It was standard practice in the Roman imperial household to raise the children of Rome's enemies, reinstalling them in client kingdoms as agents of Roman rule: although too dangerous to relocate to Egypt or Numidia, respectively, Cleopatra VIII and Juba II inherited sovereignty, on Rome's behalf, over the neighbouring kingdom of Mauretania. Where La Calprenède's heroes inherit Augustan policy – history dictated by the winners – Barker challenges that legacy by reimagining the relationship between Rome and Numidia: unencumbered by Virgil's providential history, Galecia emerges as a friend and potential ally to Rome. A far cry from Virgil's lovesick queen of Carthage, so suspicious for her lack of *romanitas*, Galecia marks a new narrative beginning that reinterprets North Africa as a place of kinship rather than hostility, underlining the portrait of a Rome unburdened by even the likeliest of Mediterranean foes. If, as I will argue, returning to the enmity between Carthage and Rome means uncoupling "Dido" and "defeat," then returning to Numidia means expanding the narrative possibilities for future Jubas and Cleopatras.

"One Must Loser Be": The Fate of the Scipiones

At the same time, Barker further neutralizes Carthage by rewriting the struggle between Hannibal and Scipio. Indeed, in staging Roman history as though the antagonism between Rome and Carthage never existed, *Exilius* omits the inveterate enmity between the two states. In doing so, it negates the aetiology that assimilates Dido to the paradigm of the abandoned woman – the transformation necessary to recast Dido and Aeneas as emblems of Carthage and Rome. In Barker's alternative history, no less than Scipio himself sings Hannibal's praises. Enslaved in Carthage and unaware of his true identity, Scipio/Ismenus declares that he "enjoy'd as much Happiness by the Favour of *Hannibal*, and his Father, as cou'd be hop'd for in Servitude, for I was on the same footing with his Pages, which were Free Men" (1:53). From Scipio, we learn that Hannibal's public and private conduct alike merit Roman esteem: he describes the future general as "in his Nature Courteous and Civil, and in all his Actions Just and Generous," exhibiting precisely those "Bases on which a great Man ought to build his Glory" (1:54); in rewarding good conduct with such "Eagerness, as if he desir'd to recompence both the Virtue and the Person," Hannibal "makes every Body his Friend" (1:54). Indeed, so noble and generous is Hannibal's disposition that he pleads Scipio's cause. When Hannibal wrongly suspects Scipio of courting Clarinthia and attacks his rival in a jealous rage, Scipio wounds Hannibal "in the Body," a "Crime so brutal" that Amilcar, Hannibal's father, condemns the slave to be "devour'd by wild Beasts" (1:64). Despite the offence – an error so grave that it leads even Scipio to reflect that he "partly deserv'd" to "be made a publick Example" (1:63) – Hannibal nonetheless beseeches Amilcar to pardon him (1:64). In this way, Barker conjures the infamous rivalry between Scipio and Hannibal only to dispel it.

Underlining the peculiarity of *Exilius*'s counterfactual history, Barker thus frustrates narrative expectations, refusing to stage, in Hannibal's friendship to Scipio, the ongoing conflict between Carthage and Rome. Just as Scipio himself lauds Hannibal, Barker profits from Hannibal's first introduction in the novel to augur his future success: as Scipio relates, "his Birth has plac'd him in an exalted Sphere" and "his personal Worth shines there with such Lustre, as from thence [the Carthaginians] calculate coming Glories to their Country" (1:55). Yet those glories remain unspecified, and the description of Hannibal as "Just and Generous" in "all his Actions" (1:54) sits uneasily with the possibility of Carthage attacking Rome. At the same time, *Exilius* ends by foreshadowing Scipio's greatness: Catullus relates a dream, in which "*Africa* should give [Scipio] a Name, as *Asia* had done his Brother"; Asiaticus then "call'd to Mind what the Sybil had foretold him in her Cave, and *Scipiana* remember'd what *Cordiala's* good Genius had sung to her in the Chapel of *Diana*; insomuch that they were almost ready to salute him *Scipio Africanus*" (2:141). However, in the context of the larger narrative, the cognomen "Africanus" points us elsewhere, not to Carthage; despite the official history that pits Scipio and Hannibal against each other, nowhere does *Exilius* prepare readers for the extratextual outcome celebrated by historians.

Yet, as I have noted, the action of Barker's novel takes place at an extremely tense moment in Roman history, between the First and Second Punic Wars. The outcome of the wars would determine whether Rome or Carthage ruled the Mediterranean. Given the extent of this mutual resentment – to say nothing of the fame of Barker's subject, so well known to eighteenth-century audiences – it is especially striking that *Exilius* fails to raise even the spectre of past conflict. Scipio and Hannibal are certainly old enough to remember the First Punic War and its legacy: the image of young Hannibal, merely nine years old, swearing eternal enmity to Rome, had been a popular subject for paintings and engravings since the Renaissance (see Figure 1.1).

To be sure, the war had left an indelible imprint on their fathers, the generals Publius Scipio and Amilcar (Hamilcar Barca). Yet both Hannibal and Amilcar praise Ismenus, the unknown Scipio, for the Roman qualities which they, in turn, attempt to emulate: Scipio relates that they "wou'd sometimes say, there appear'd in me a true *Roman* Genius, which was saying, in one Word, all that cou'd be said on that Subject, the *Romans* bearing the Prize of Renown from the whole Universe" (1:54). The young men's roles in *Exilius* also point to their potential readiness for war: Hannibal is old enough to make a name for himself, and Scipio of an age to engage in romantic intrigues, marrying Cordiala

Figure 1.1. Jacopo Amigoni (c. 1675–1752), *Hannibal swearing eternal enmity to Rome*. Private Collection. Photo © Agnew's, London. Bridgeman Images.

at the end of the novel. Yet, even as they prepare to take their respective places on the political stage, neither man hints at the legacy inherited by his historical counterpart. The one Scipio who has been engaged in military conflict, ostensibly subduing threats to Rome, is the brilliant Asiaticus, whose conquest of Asia brought "the greatest Augmentation of the *Roman* Glory that ever Hero yet acquir'd" (1:3). Historically, Lucius Cornelius Scipio earned the cognomen "Asiagenes" for defeating Antiochus III, the ruler of the Seleucid Empire, at the battle of Magnesia (in modern-day Turkey) in 190. Barker therefore inverts the prominence of the two brothers, changing their birth order and exaggerating the successes of Asiaticus – a figure, unlike Scipio, of almost no import to Roman history.

Diverted almost entirely from Scipio, whose subsequent exploits remain unspecified at the end of the text, we instead focus on Asiaticus, who not only outstrips his brother in prominence but, Aeneas-like, receives a prophecy that foretells the greatness of his house and the future rise of "An Emperor of matchless Pow'r and Worth." When he discovers the cave of the Sibyl following his escape from Numidia, she promises him: "Great as thou art, yet others of thy Name / Shall thee transcend in martial Acts of Fame"; she then predicts the rise of Scipio Africanus and Scipio Aemilianus. The next part of the prophecy looks forward to the struggles leading up to Augustan rule two hundred years later: the Sibyl relates, "For he who shall thy great Attempts compleat, / Deservedly shall gain the name of Great. / Lo! He the Heiress of your House shall take, / But after Fortune shall his Chief forsake." These words identify Gaius Magnus Pompeius (Pompey) as Asiaticus's heir, thanks to his marriage to Cornelia, daughter of Quintus Caecilius Metellus Pius Scipio. Yet the Sibyl also warns Asiaticus of Pompey's defeat: because the combatants cannot share the same fortune, "*one must Loser be; so in this Play / The Senate in thy House falls at* Pharsalia" (2:61). The prophecy then turns from the greatness of the Scipiones to the glory of Rome, and impresses Asiaticus so forcefully that it "shock'd all [his] former Resolutions" to live a retired life in Clarinthia's absence.

Blending history and fiction in this way, and contrasting Asiaticus's legacy with Aeneas's – for Asiaticus's line would give rise to the defeated Pompey, not the victorious Augustus – Barker extends the project she had already begun in reconceiving the Dido figure. Whereas Aeneas's lineage leads directly to Julius Caesar, and thence to Augustus, the Sibyl's prophecy reveals that the Scipiones' greatness dies in Pompey, Caesar's rival. Where Aeneas successfully produces a victor who subdues "Chaos" and causes "all Noise of War" to cease, Asiaticus's descendant becomes a cause of *"great Discord in the State"* (2:61). Yet, the prophecy also indicates that Pompey and Caesar appear equally matched, so that the battle comes down to *"run[ning] the Hazard of one Day,"* and *"stak[ing] their Fortunes at* Pharsalia" (2:61). Naturally enough under these circumstances, "one must Loser be," and the emphasis on "Fortune" at this moment – to describe victory and defeat – empties both categories of moral judgment. The victor could have been Pompey as well as Caesar, and, indeed, the prophecy goes on to relate Caesar's demise, falling *"by cursed Treason's Wounds"* (2:61). Asiaticus's prophecy therefore recontextualizes the very notion of defeat: though the descendants of the Scipiones will not usher in a new Golden Age, *Exilius* challenges the exclusive value of the victor's narrative, creating, at once, a new mythology for the ancestors of Pompey and the followers of James II.

In turn, reimagining the relationship between Scipio and Hannibal enables Barker to disrupt the Dido narrative that, in the context of the queen's deathbed curse, anticipates the fabled enmity between Rome and its North African rival. Put simply, if Dido's curse explains the legendary origins of Carthaginian aggression, but that hostility vanishes from Barker's alternative history, then rethinking history makes possible a reimagining of the mythology – pitting Aeneas against Dido, epic against romance, and Rome against Carthage – that claims to engender it. Reconceived in this way, representations of history expand to include other narratives, such as the story of the North African princess, Galecia, Barker's stand-in for the queens of Carthage and Egypt. Giving equal weight to Galecia's story, as she does to all of the novel's heroines and heroes, Barker foregrounds the multiplicity typical of romance, preserving a space for Jacobite historiographies by rewriting the Roman past that dictates history's terms. If epic forces Dido to become a romance heroine, displacing her into the losers' genre, then rethinking her plight means reconceptualizing loss itself, and the narratives available to subsequent losers – not only to abandoned women, but to anyone meant to occupy a similar position of defeat.[21]

Becoming Roman: *Exilius* and Jacobite Identity

In *Exilius*, Barker eschews the Whig rewriting of history that casts Dido-James as an eternal Wanderer: instead, she embraces romance strategies in order to cultivate a quotidian heroism for the Jacobite exiles – women and men, parents and children, friends and other loved ones – who seemed to have fallen on the wrong side of history, deprived of an appropriate language to express their daily recommitment to the "unfashionable" Stuart cause. At the same time, she explores the difficulties of forging a Jacobite selfhood under the circumstances of exile. Throughout the romance, Barker exploits the dualities of the *Aeneid* as well as Jacobite identity to unleash other kinds of doublenesses, from the rewriting of the Dido and Scipio narratives to the privileging of more complicated identities in the text: in typical romance fashion, characters are not always what they seem, and categories of identity – from gender performance to national allegiance – often remain in flux for the principal characters. Indeed, the novel opens with the disguised Scipiana embracing her affronted cousin, Clelia: "she saw a Youth in the Habit of a Page approaching her; who, coming near, cast his Arms about her Neck ... *Clelia*, both angry and astonish'd, gave him a Reprimand suitable to his Crime and her own Indignation" (1:2). When Scipiana reveals her identity moments later, "pulling off some little Disguise," Clelia then, "quite transported with Joy, embrac'd her with all the Tenderness that Love and Excess of Satisfaction could produce," wondering what has happened to Scipiana to render her "thus metamorphos'd" (1:2). Later, Cordiala dresses as a man in order to escape her persecutor, and even Exilius mistakes a cross-dressed Ismenus/Scipio for Scipio's sister, "whereupon he made me a thousand extravagant Complements, and ... cast himself at my Feet, crying, *Scipiana, Scipiana*" (1:69). Their identities break down in the course of the narrative in response to the characters' estrangement from their homeland and the dangers that attend them: they assume new identities, with help or by chance, to escape their captors.

Throughout *Exilius*, fundamental confusions of identity dilate outward from the individual to the family: from the gendered disguises of Scipiana, Cordiala, and Scipio, Barker moves to the uncertainties of national identity associated with Scipio and Exilius. Relating his story, Exilius begins, "by my Speech I should be a *Roman*; but I never knew any other Place or Habitation, but a certain Rocky Island near *Sardinia*, where, in a Cave, my Father and I liv'd, or rather breath'd, for one cannot call such an Aboad living" (1:89). Only a little earlier in the narrative, Scipio recounts a similar story, but with greater doubt as to his origins: "My name, said he, is call'd *Ismenus*, but of what Country or Family I know not; I suppose a *Roman*, though I never knew any other Being, or State of Life, but that of Slave to *Hannibal*" (1:53). These volatile identities stabilize at the end of the novel when Publius Scipio reunites with Scipio Africanus and Catullus regains Cordiala: the marks of an eagle on Scipio's breast, and a heart on Cordiala's arm, confirm their origins. Even as the rest of the narrative threatens to erode its heroines' and heroes' identities – driving them to disguise, alienating them from their homeland, and depriving them of family ties – the country retreat of Publius Scipio becomes a liminal space, between Rome and the Mediterranean, between old ties and new, where the main characters reaffirm their previous identities while preparing to fashion themselves anew through marriage.[22] What matters, for Barker's heroines and heroes, is not their outward circumstances but the affective ties that bind them in a common cause.

Redefinitions of identity extend from the newly forged affective bonds between lovers and family members to the nature of *romanitas* itself. Despite his misfortunes – and, according to Clelia, "none ever experienc'd the Mutability of human Affairs more thoroughly than my Uncle" (1:12) – Publius Scipio "demonstrate[s] himself a true noble *Roman*" (1:12), a poignant contrast to the senators who condemn Catullus's virtues. At the end of the romance, Catullus finds himself "in great Affliction for the Loss of all [Publius's] Children," and this alone encourages him to return from exile: though he had "intended always to remain" on his rocky island, he nonetheless revisits his "unjust and unnatural Country" "to endeavour to consulate my Friend, and give him what information I could touching his Daughter's Departure from me" (2:140). Publius exudes true Romanness while Catullus rejects it, yet the banished Catullus is no less his equal. In complicating the characters' identities in this way, *Exilius* vests meaning in the familial and interpersonal values associated with romance. Where the threat of banishment presumes that one of the greatest punishments a citizen can suffer is his estrangement from the state, Catullus's "affliction" comes from fellow feeling, not self-pity. Thus alienated by the unjust treatment of the Senate, he honours his relationship with Publius over his obligations to Rome, suggesting that the state, in its corruption, has eroded its own authority. The next hero to rise – Scipio Africanus – will be a hybrid figure, part Roman and part Carthaginian, rejecting not only the enmity between the two Mediterranean powers but also the *Romanitas* represented by Asiaticus.

The shifting relationships of the main characters and their complicated identities echo the complexities of the Stuart position. James, as I have suggested, is both Aeneas and Dido, and his followers slip easily into the Dido role, heralding the moment when their "lost lover" will return. In other contexts, Jacobites actively capitalized on narratives that encouraged plurality and dissonance. For example, James depicted himself as both Roman and highlander, and his followers often suggested the conflicting dualities of his identity, "both human and divine, overturned and inviolable, ruined and venerated."[23] As Paul Monod notes, even the "lost lover" motif "was contradictory – he appeared as a pagan vegetation god, a paragon of Christian morality, a man of sorrows, a triumphant Caesar. He was a pastiche of conflicting features, a motley product of the different strands that ran through the fabric of popular culture."[24] British yet foreign, defeated yet with the expectation of rightful victory, the Stuarts embraced the multiplicity of possibilities engendered by their outcast position. *Exilius*, in turn, enacts a similar process with its heroines and heroes, creating a new mythos out of instability and contradiction.

The oppositions inherent in Jacobite identity, expressed in its iconography and ideology, return us once again to Barker's Cambridge friends and the problem of the two Didos. For even as Barker merits a comparison to Dido in the epigraph to *Poetical Recreations*, those same friends compare her – apparently missing the irony of these contradictory epithets – to *Exilius*'s hero, Scipio Africanus. In the second part of *Poetical Recreations*, where her friends and publisher offer praise for her novel, no fewer than three poems relate Barker directly to Scipio. "To the Incomparable Author, Mrs. Jane Barker, On her Excellent Romance of Scipina" imagines Scipio envying Barker's talents, declaring that the "younger *Scipio* willingly wou'd quit / His *Titles* for your more Triumphant *Wit*" (2:36).[25] In "To My Ingenious Friend, Mrs. Jane Barker, on my Publishing her Romance of Scipina," Benjamin Crayle continues this theme, writing, "How wou'd it please the gallant *Scipio*'s Ghost, / (The bravest Gen'ral th'Elyzian Fields can boast,) / To see his *Battles* acted o'er again, / By thy victorious and triumphant Pen" (2:196). "To Mrs. Jane Barker, on her most Delightfull and Excellent Romance of Scipina, now in the Press" also imagines Barker re-enacting the part of the Roman general: "'Twould please thy *Hero*'s awfull *Shade*, to see / His *Part* thus *Acted* o'er again by *Thee*; / Where ev'n his bare *Idea* has that pow'r, / Which *Real Scipio* only had before" (2:30–1).[26] By enacting Scipio's battles over again, Barker becomes a modern Scipio in her own right. Yet the praise she receives calls into question precisely which Scipio she represents: the historical Scipio Africanus or his romance counterpart in *Exilius*.

All three poems recall the exploits of Scipio Africanus – his successes in war, his battles, the ensuing titles – not, in other words, *Exilius*'s Scipio, whose story ends without any such triumphs. This is the second time in *Poetical Recreations* that her friends' flattering remarks have mischaracterized Barker's role. First, the epigraph compares her to Virgil's Dido, whom she abjures in "To Ovid's Heroines" and *Exilius*, and implicitly in the *Galesia Trilogy*. Then, the laudatory poems identify her with precisely the same Scipio whose legacy she attempts to reinvent. Far less conventional than the allusion to Dido, the comparisons to Scipio carefully highlight Barker's imitative role: the suggestion that she follows a script in *Exilius* neutralizes the potential fear, expressed elsewhere as gallant banter in the poems, that she has overstepped feminine propriety in writing at all. Furthermore, the characterization of Barker-as-historical-Scipio reads *Exilius* against Barker's moral, which aims to create a new romance aetiology for the Scipiones and their place in Roman (and Jacobite) history. That Barker can become, at once, Dido, the legendary originator of the Carthaginian threat, and its destroyer, Scipio, further echoes the quandary experienced in *Exilius* by Clarinthia and Asbella, who turn unthinkingly to Dido's example as a way of interpreting their own circumstances. Thus, although Barker embraces the chaste, pre-Virgilian queen, her friends allude to the *Aeneid*; similarly, although she reimagines Scipio Africanus as the younger brother of the more successful Asiaticus, her companions have recourse to the historical Scipio, even after presumably reading the romance they praise. In short, reinscribing Barker into familiar available narratives, the epigraph and prefatory poems stage the very problems with mythmaking that *Exilius* exposes: they strain to fit Barker into a known pattern even when her own narrative not only thwarts such attempts but provides alternative ways of thinking about history. At the same time, Barker's ability to embody both Dido and Scipio also indicates, if unwittingly, the success of her enterprise. That she can represent both simultaneously, without any apparent irony or contradiction, suggests the extent to which *Exilius* succeeds in uncoupling narratives of victory and defeat. Although Barker's friends envision her as the most traditional incarnation of each figure, she radically reimagines what these figures represent: in rejecting epic and history, *Exilius* upends the categories embodied by Dido and Aeneas, Hannibal and Scipio, Carthage and Rome.

Representing Troy Town: Barker's Jacobite Nostalgia

This tension between readings reflects the friction between an essentially conservative impulse – reading Barker as Virgil's Dido or the historical Scipio – and the more innovative purposes to which she deploys the Dido and Scipio narratives. The poems' investment in the Roman leader and in Barker's apparent re-enactment of his victories points to a counterproductive nostalgia: as *Exilius* searches for a narrative future for its readers, *Poetical Recreations'* epigraph and prefatory poems remain mired not only in the past, but in the very storytelling patterns whose destructive cycle Barker seeks to upend. In this way, *Exilius* represents a paradoxically forward-looking nostalgia, one that embraces the past to modern ends. Outside of *Exilius*'s re-exploration of the Dido and Scipio narratives, its rejection of nostalgic re-enactment is nowhere more striking than at the very centre of the romance. As the lovers Exilius and Scipiana meet secretly in the king of Egypt's garden, Barker commemorates, in botanical form, the glorious palace of the Trojan king, Priam; "Troy Town" unfolds around them in the landscape, part of an immense garden inspired by Greco-Roman designs. It is at once life-sized and miniaturized in that the king of Egypt contains Troy within this larger garden, itself part of a larger city, emphasizing his apparent mastery of the Trojan material. Anticipating objections to her detailed depiction of the scene, Barker notes in the preface to *Exilius* that the reader may "pass ... over [this lengthy description] unread, without any Prejudice to the Substantial Part of the Story" (n.p.). Yet it was evidently an important addition, the only difference, she claims, between manuscript (1688) and published text (1715).

In Exilius's description of the king's garden, elements of the gigantic and miniature collide, disrupting history and unsettling the scene of Trojan nostalgia. In the course of recalling his adventures in Egypt, Exilius devotes a significant portion of his narration to the garden, "certainly," as he says, "the finest in the Universe." The centrepiece of this description is "a Wood, or Grove, which represents *Troy* Town" (1:147). The account is worth quoting in full:

> The Hedges which encompass this Grove are so high, even, and thick, that they may truly be call'd what they represent, *to wit*, the Walls of *Troy*; and not only so, but they have Towers, Ballasters, and Battlements on them, cut out of the Green, admirable to behold. Round these Hedges, or green Walls, are divers Statues of the most renow'd *Greeks* and *Trojans*; one of

white Marble, the other of polish'd Brass; here an *Achilles*, there an *Hector*; here an *Ajax*, there an *Aeneas*; so that one sees the History of that renown'd Siege in Sculpture and cast Statues. Within these green Walls are Walks representing Streets, and little Arbours instead of Houses; and here and there, in proper Uniformity, are larger and high Arbours, representing the Palaces of the *Trojan* Princes. In the Midst is King *Priam*'s Palace, more large, and better adorn'd than all the rest. (1:147–8)

Despite its apparent accuracy – Exilius's assertion that the hedges "may truly be call'd what they represent" – this replica of Troy invariably foregrounds its own artifice, its position as a representation twice removed. Remarkably, from Exilius's description, "Troy Town" appears at once larger than life and also miniaturized: "little Arbours" depict houses, with the "Palaces of the *Trojan* Princes" constructed in "proper Uniformity" according to scale. It is a curious scene, one made more so by the Egyptian interest in publicly commemorating a celebrated moment in Greco-Roman history. Indeed, Exilius notes that "one sees the History of that renown'd Siege in Sculpture and cast Statues" (1:148), so that the representation of Troy Town functions as a static re-enactment, encouraging a dynamic confrontation of geographies and temporalities. The critic Susan Stewart has described the ways in which the miniature creates a rupture between present time and its own time, what Stewart calls "an 'other' time, a type of transcendent time which negates change and the flux of lived reality."[27] The "function of the miniature," she argues, "is to bring historical events 'to life,' to immediacy, and thereby to erase their history, to lose us within their presentness."[28] In threatening to enshrine the past as an unattainable ideal that distorts lived reality, the miniature is powerful precisely because of its accessible and exploitable fixity. As Stewart argues, "The miniature, linked to nostalgic versions of childhood and history, presents a diminutive, and thereby manipulatable, version of experience, a version which is domesticated and protected from contamination"[29] The idealization of Greco-Roman culture in a place so little expected reflects, in turn, on English veneration of Roman antiquity. The displacement of Troy to Egypt defamiliarizes its history, highlighting the ways in which eighteenth-century writers turned to Greece and Rome in order to exalt a "domesticated" and "uncontaminated" version of the past: it is no accident that "[t]he consumerism of the miniature is the consumerism of the classic," with its comfortable but unproductive stasis.[30] The theatrical nature of Exilius's description – and both the miniature and gigantic are theatrical spectacles – underscores the impossibility of nostalgic petrification, the sense that Barker rethinks, in Egypt, her own culture's uses of the past.[31]

For this reason, there is perhaps no better episode of Greco-Roman mythology to depict. A foundational moment, like the tale of Dido and Aeneas, the Trojan War becomes an originary narrative, for the Romans and Britons – including the Stuarts – who invented their ancestors from Trojan ashes. In this way, the world of the miniature can be dangerous, both in its setting of a treacherous precedent and in its capacity, like the Sirens' song, to ensnare its observers in an unreal past.[32] For the world of the miniature holds no future; the relentless presentness of its time frame at once obscures the past even while translating it into an unshakeable present, leaving the observer simultaneously entrapped and unmoored, suspended between past and future. The miniature, which "finds its 'use value' transformed into the infinite time of reverie," provides an escape from reality, the opportunity never to confront the history at odds with the miniature's tableau.[33] Indeed, nothing about "Troy Town" appears to recall the disastrous aftermath of the Trojan War; in this representation, Troy will never fall and has never fallen. The siege-in-progress thus complicates the subject of nostalgia as well as the process of identification – Greeks and Trojans coexist in suspended violence, celebrating Achilles and Hector, Aeneas and Ajax, with no distinction between winners and losers.[34] Just as Barker rewrites Scipio's story (and hence Dido's), creating a new Jacobite mythos, the garden reconceives the past, inscribing a version of history in which Rome, that great threat to Egypt, never exists, at once commemorating and negating Roman origins. In this way, it is significant that Barker depicts Troy in the form of a garden, the product of human cultivation. That the natural landscape resists stasis, requiring regular discipline, demonstrates the wilfulness of rewriting the past-as-present to the exclusion of other possible engagements with history.

The addition of "Troy Town" in the published text appears all the more striking for its relationship to a similar episode in the *Aeneid*, in which Aeneas must leave behind another replica Troy that ensnares Trojan refugees among the ghosts of the past. In Book 3, Aeneas, arriving at Buthrotum, discovers Andromache at Hector's empty tomb. She and her new husband, Helenus, have constructed a new Troy, what Virgil calls "parva Troia," or "little Troy" (3.349–50).[35] Surprised by so unanticipated a visit, Andromache mistakes Aeneas for a shade, and falls into a swoon; the scene thus symbolically aligns all three characters – hero, widow, and deceased husband – with death.[36] Helenus and Andromache appear to take comfort in the illusion. Yet Aeneas meets Andromache at her husband's grave, becoming, if only temporarily, a shade himself: as a double, "inadequacy, a melancholy lack that prevents it from fully replacing the original" forever marks their "little Troy," so that the refugee Trojans, practically shades themselves, relive the past without recognizing its dangers.[37] Like the Buthrotum episode of the *Aeneid*, Barker's "Troy Town" confronts the need to escape the traumatic past, whether Trojan or English; for the Jacobites as for Andromache, "the dead Trojan past of Hector cannot be brought back to life; the Roman future of Aeneas has taken its place."[38] Like Virgil's Aeneas, Barker thus rejects the seductive nostalgia for fixed mythical origins, but not in a bid to forget them: rather than erasing and supplanting the past, *Exilius* depends on the discrepancy between past and present in order to forge a future that accommodates Jacobite agency.[39]

By electing to depict a scene that is at once necessarily miniaturized in its subordination to the surrounding garden and city and also larger than life – where the characters, in interacting with the landscape, disrupt the fixed tableau, conflating Romans with Greeks and Troy with Egypt – Barker thus denies the desire for static re-enactment embodied by "Troy Town."[40] As the text comes to a standstill, embracing ekphrasis in Exilius's description, she renounces what Stewart calls "the still and perfect universe of the miniature" by interrupting it with the gigantic in the form of a life-sized Troy.[41] For, even as it happily recalls the Trojan War, infinitely delaying its disastrous outcome, "Troy Town" comes to represent treachery and death in another, more immediate context. Although Exilius and Scipiana believe themselves safe in the garden, in fact the princess Philometra, fearing some love intrigue, has encouraged her brother to spy on them; he subsequently condemns Exilius to death.[42] The lovers have sought the garden precisely for its stasis and secrecy, its suspension in time, yet the elements of the gigantic – here, the life-sized replica of Troy – make impossible the security of the miniature, disrupting the hopes of heroine and hero as well as the tableau itself: Exilius, Scipiana, and the king alter it with their presence, drawing idealized historical time into conflict with present reality. In this way, the gigantic introduces "the order and disorder of historical forces,"[43] so that we may read this moment as a representation of the tensions staged in *Exilius* at large: the clash between miniature and gigantic, nostalgic past and present/future, embodies the conflicts between epic and romance versions of history, between Virgil's Dido and her chaste original, the historical Scipio and Barker's active rewriting of his narrative. The miniature version of "Troy Town" aligns with the conservative expectations of Barker's Cambridge friends – Barker as Virgilian Dido, as historical Scipio – while elements of the gigantic introduce the prospect of dynamic change. The convergence of categories at this moment creates a rupture in temporalities, disordering history in order to rethink it.

Challenging nostalgia for Roman origins proves essential to Barker's project of rewriting traditional history, for an idealized view of antiquity, with its fundamentally conservative impulse, sits at odds with the story she tells: *Exilius* voices discontent with the same narratives romanticized by her Cambridge friends. In this way, it also proves a necessary aspect of recuperating the Dido figure. If, as Judith Broome has argued, "Nostalgia serves as a reinforcement for male subjectivity" so that "[w]omen, associated with tradition and the past, bear the burden of [and are the objects of masculine] nostalgia,"[44] perhaps no ancient representation bears this burden more explicitly than Virgil's Dido. She becomes a cipher for masculine nostalgia, representing Augustus's victory over Cleopatra, the triumph of Rome over barbarian – of the Roman masculinity that had seen defeat in Antony, but not in Aeneas or Augustus. The *Aeneid* yearns for a Golden Age of sorts, where Dido's death – and Cleopatra's, and the defeat of Hannibal and Carthage – may be enacted over and over again. A nostalgic view of this past watches Dido burn infinitely in order to exorcise Roman anxieties. At the same time, it makes available an economy of allusion that comes to contextualize women's experience, so that, in *Exilius*, Clarinthia and Asbella "naturally" resort to Dido's ill-fitting example.

In this way, Barker repudiates traditional forms of nostalgia in order to revalue the past, making it relevant for her Jacobite audience and a modernity in need of new originary narratives.[45] Although key aspects of *Exilius* – its pastoral element, Publius's retreat to the country, the Roman setting itself – can all be read as nostalgic moves, Barker challenges the very meaning of nostalgia, creating a new space for the defeated, the Jacobites who, though hopeful of victory, find themselves at odds with the very epic meant to reflect their experience of exile. For the fixed tableau of the *Aeneid*, like *Exilius*'s representation of "Troy Town" in miniature, forces the Stuarts and their supporters into a position outside history, a static past that can never be recuperated, leaving no place for them. In rejecting the *Aeneid* as an appropriate model,

Exilius instead replaces epic with romance, and blends public with private history in order to revalue both categories for the Stuarts and their supporters, to whom Williamite victory denied full historical agency. Despite the strong ties between Jacobites and antiquarians, according to whom "change always appeared ... as decline," Barker demonstrates the possibility of deploying the neoclassical impulse to dynamic ends.[46]

In thus returning to Dido – in becoming, at once, both Dido and Virgil – Barker positions herself against the Virgilian queen and historical Scipio invoked by her companions, and also against the Virgilian narrative that requires, for the first time, Dido's unrequited love and subsequent death. Though popularly identified with the Stuart cause, the *Aeneid* proved a difficult template for Barker and her fellow Jacobites, "winners" forced into the "losers'" narrative, unexpectedly Dido and Aeneas at the same time. *Exilius* and the *Galesia Trilogy* offer alternatives designed to grapple with the intricacies of Jacobite experience, creating stories that divorce the Dido position from the category of defeat represented by her presence in the *Aeneid*.[47] For Barker, superimposing Dido's story onto the historical record does violence to legend and history: without the weight of the Dido myth to explain their conflict, Scipio and Hannibal become mutual admirers rather than enemies in *Exilius*'s imaginative corrective to history.

In 1751, Henry Fielding's *Amelia* would go further still, rewriting not only the Dido and Aeneas myth but the *Aeneid* itself. For Fielding, the treatment of Dido's character is emblematic of epic's reception more generally, as Doctor Harrison's views of women, inspired by Homer and Virgil, make clear: drawing on Mercury's famous condemnation of womanly fickleness in Book 4, Harrison uses the *Aeneid* against his interlocutor, the learned Mrs Bennet – herself a Dido figure – in order to silence her challenge to his classical authority. Yet, Mrs Bennet will ultimately prove a better reader than the Doctor, relying on her knowledge of Virgil's epic to protect Amelia's virtue and to right her own narrative of betrayal. Fielding's contemporary *Aeneid* will suggest that, if epic has any viability in the modern world, it is through Dido – not Aeneas – as the subject of national heroism.

2 "What Is There of a Woman Worth Relating?" Revising the *Aeneid* in Henry Fielding's *Amelia*

In the mock-heroic rogue's biography *The Life of Mr. Jonathan Wild the Great* (1743), Henry Fielding satirizes his hero, the notorious underworld personality executed in 1725, alongside the so-called great men of antiquity, especially Alexander the Great and Julius Caesar. In order to demonstrate his devotion to the principles of greatness, the ironic narrator confesses himself to be "of that humble Kind of Mortals who consider themselves born for the Behoof of some GREAT Man or other," adding, "could I behold his Happiness carved out of the Labour and Ruin of a thousand such Reptiles as myself, I might with Satisfaction exclaim, *Sic, sic juvat*."[1] Here, the narrator grounds his abstract pronouncements in the *Aeneid*, alluding to Dido's dying words, "Sic, sic iuvat ire sub umbras," or "Thus, thus I go gladly into the dark" (*Aeneid* 4.660).[2] Imagining great men as Aeneases and their victims as willing Didos, the narrator suggests that Dido justly perishes for the sake of Aeneas's "greatness" and that Aeneas rightfully achieves glory at Dido's expense. Despite the generally topsy-turvy morality of Wild's world, it is a rhetorical position that even the narrator cannot finally bring himself to endorse:

> But when I behold one GREAT MAN starving with Hunger and freezing with Cold in the Midst of fifty thousand, who are suffering the same Evils for his Diversion; when I see another whose Mind is more abject Slave to his own Greatness, and is more tortured and wrecked by it than those of all his Vassals: Lastly, when I consider whole Nations extirpated only to bring Tears into the Eyes of a GREAT MAN, that he hath no more Nations to extirpate [e.g., as was said of Alexander the Great], then indeed I am almost inclined to wish that Nature had spared us this her MASTERPIECE, and that no GREAT MAN had ever been born into the World. (47)

It is one of the rare moments where Fielding's narrator openly undermines the illusion of wholeheartedly supporting the "Great Men" of antiquity and their contemporary counterparts. I begin with *Jonathan Wild* because the narrator's decision to break character at this juncture, while using the specific example of Dido's suicide, underscores the extent to which Dido had come to symbolize the extreme costs of epic heroism. For Fielding as for Barker, Dido escapes the boundaries of Virgilian epic to become shorthand for defeat: stressing the archetypal nature of her position, even the narrator imagines himself becoming a Dido at some great man's behest. Although his primary target is Wildean criminality, Fielding's satire also implicates the *Aeneid*: casting doubt on Dido's role as a necessary sacrifice means calling into question not only Aeneas's heroism but also the entire epic model that subjugates Dido to Aeneas (however reluctantly) and ordinary to "great" men.

Yet even as Fielding finds fault with the Virgilian model, *Jonathan Wild* suggests that Dido's fate, and the fates of subsequent Didos, are far from inevitable. Instead, the very narrative framework that generates these so-called great men forces their inferiors into Dido's position of defeat. Throughout *Jonathan Wild*, Fielding makes clear that opportunistic encounters with ancient writers inspire the hero's misguided version of "greatness": Wild's knowledge of the past is limited to a boyhood acquaintance with classical authors, which he never learned to read because "he would not give himself the Pains requisite to acquire a competent Sufficiency in the learned Languages" (15). Rather, the narrator depicts Wild as three times removed from the actual texts. In addition to being unable to read the ancient languages himself, he does not even appear to know them in translation. Rather, he "readily listen[s] with Attention to others, especially when they translated the Classical Authors to him" (15). Wild, in his limited acquaintance with and misuse of classical learning, thus emerges as a similar type to *Spectator* 11's Commonplace Talker who maliciously appropriates the story of the Ephesian Matron. Relying on scraps of classical narratives about Caesar and Alexander to support his own mercenary version of greatness, Wild proves himself to be a self-interested "reader" of classical culture.[3]

Wild's affinity for ancient authors and the narrator's satirical comment on the Dido narrative show the difficulty of importing classical models into the present: subject to misunderstanding and abuse, history and epic share the limitations of their modern interpreters.

Yet *Jonathan Wild* provides no alternatives. Fielding leaves readers to wonder about the place of epic values in a world where Alexander the Great – so closely identified with the heroism of Homer's *Iliad*, the epic he reportedly kept under his pillow – is praised as a hero for not "cut[ting] the Throat of an old Woman, and ravish[ing] her Daughters whom he had before undone" when he "had with Fire and Sword overrun a whole Empire, and destroyed the Lives of Millions of innocent People" (9). What does epic then mean in the middle of the eighteenth century, especially for a growing audience of diverse readers not necessarily educated in the classics? What place does it leave for women in particular, when the antithesis of the "great man" was so often female, or at least feminine, and predestined, like Dido, for defeat?

In 1751, Fielding returned to these questions in *Amelia*, his final novel and prose *Aeneid*. Departing from his earlier comic-epic style, Fielding's sentimental novel tells the story of the marital trials, and eventual happiness, of Amelia Harris and her husband, William Booth, a half-pay officer who struggles to support their growing family after he elopes with Amelia despite her mother's wishes. Demonstrating the urgency of his project, Fielding championed *Amelia* when, less than a month after its publication on 16 December 1751, it came under attack. Explicitly citing its indebtedness to Virgil, Fielding declared that "he followed the Rules of all those who are acknowledged to have writ best on the Subject … neither *Homer* nor *Virgil* pursued them with greater Care than myself, and the candid and learned Reader will see that the latter was the noble model, which I made use of on this Occasion."[4] Yet the novel's classical pedigree did little to salvage its reputation.[5] Critics missed no opportunity to take the writer of *Joseph Andrews* and *Tom Jones* to task for what could only be perceived as a decidedly Richardsonian turn; after Fielding's burlesque of *Pamela* in *Shamela* (1741), they could not resist denouncing *Amelia* as "Shamelia."[6] In response, Fielding took up arms in his newly begun *Covent-Garden Journal*, published under the name of "Sir Alexander Drawcansir, Censor of Great-Britain." Although he opened his defence by poking fun, as critics had certainly not failed to do, at Amelia's nose,[7] by 25 January 1752, when the abysmal critical reception had not abated, he concluded his defence. "[O]f all my Offspring," Fielding declared, "[*Amelia*] is my favourite Child … I will trouble the World no more with any Children of mine by the same Muse."[8]

Despite the *Covent-Garden Journal*'s earnest defence, few critics have taken seriously Fielding's claim that he modelled *Amelia* after the

Aeneid.[9] Part of this resistance undoubtedly originates in the substitution of Amelia for Aeneas: hesitant to identify Amelia as an epic hero in her own right, scholars have seldom viewed Fielding's heroine, despite her Latinate name and titular position, as an epic figure.[10] This chapter will argue that reconsidering *Amelia*'s indebtedness to the *Aeneid* reveals the important ways in which Fielding radically redefines Virgilian epic. Where traditional Greco-Roman epic minimizes women as characters, writers, and readers, Fielding's reliance on romance narratives and tropes reforms epic for his diverse audience; as a genre, the novel furnishes both an antidote to epic and a more inclusive mode that increasingly rivalled epic's cachet.[11] In rewriting the *Aeneid*, Fielding thus extends Barker's project of revaluing defeat in *Exilius* (1715) by seriously embracing the Dido position: *Amelia* displaces ancient for modern, hero for heroine, recasting "woman" as the subject of national heroism.[12]

In the process, Fielding features no fewer than three major Dido figures, not only Amelia herself but also Miss Mathews and Mrs Bennet-Atkinson.[13] The compulsive repetition of the Dido narrative – as though no other pattern were possible – suggests the enduring legacy of Virgilian epic for contemporary readers. All of *Amelia*'s heroines must reckon with Dido's narrative of loss and defeat: for *Amelia*, only a proliferation of Didos can correct the failures of so many Aeneases. It will take outsiders to the classical tradition – the unlearned Amelia and classically trained Mrs Bennet-Atkinson – to challenge a (neo)classical culture that unites ancient and modern "Great Men," from Caesar and Alexander to Jonathan Wild and men such as *Amelia*'s Noble Peer. That Fielding rewrote the *Aeneid* in this way underscores *Amelia*'s timeliness, the need for countering and expanding a (neo)classical tradition that had evinced so much hostility – as Doctor Harrison, referring explicitly to Virgil, will make clear – towards women, femininity, and female characters.

Harrison's role in the novel emphasizes the dangers of relying on tradition to explain present circumstances. Although Fielding depicts Harrison as a lifelong mentor to Amelia, and a friend and spiritual guide to the Booths, he also complicates Harrison's role by showing how easily even a well-meaning clergyman can succumb to classical stereotypes that obstruct his otherwise sound judgment. Perhaps unsurprisingly, the scholarly failure to take seriously Amelia's heroism finds echoes in the problematic reading practices of the novel's male characters.[14] Booth's reliance on his classical heritage to facilitate male friendships places Amelia in jeopardy, and the novel specifically links the practice of duelling, despite its more immediate chivalric and romance contexts, to Homeric epic. The *Aeneid* also features prominently at a key moment when Harrison attempts to silence the classically learned Mrs Bennet-Atkinson by quoting Mercury's famous line from *Aeneid* 4.569, "varium et mutabile semper femina": woman is a various and changeful thing. Even if the *Aeneid* directs us to sympathize with Dido, Harrison's successful deployment of Mercury's warning to Aeneas suggests more than an opportunistic interpretation of Virgil's text: it highlights how the *Aeneid* itself makes available Harrison's reading. Of course, Mrs Bennet-Atkinson's surprise at this moment – it has never occurred to her that Virgil might be considered hostile – raises the possibility of dissenting interpretations. Yet Harrison's reliance on the *Aeneid* remains troubling because, as a clergyman formally educated in the classics, he has the cultural power to enforce his reading. Although Mrs Bennet-Atkinson later turns to the *Aeneid* in order to effect her revenge against the Noble Peer who has raped her (and similarly schemed to rape Amelia), Fielding suggests that Harrison, and figures like him, have so thoroughly dominated the discourse around ancient epic that a decisive break with the epic model is necessary.

At the same time, *Amelia* implies that only the *Aeneid*, with its dedication to Dido's plight, can establish a new model for contemporary readers. Here again, Fielding profits from the conflict between Harrison and Mrs Bennet-Atkinson to make his case: throughout the novel, the twin presences of Homer and Virgil show, at once, how restrictive and yet generative epic can be. Where Harrison uses his knowledge of the *Aeneid* largely to censure Mrs Bennet-Atkinson – whose preference for Virgil signals its potential for female characters – he repeatedly prefers Homer to his Roman counterpart. Harrison registers his preference by turning regularly to the *Iliad* in order to castigate Mrs Bennet-Atkinson and even – despite her unimpeachable virtue – Amelia herself. In doing so, he self-consciously embraces the strictest of epic models: of the ancient epics, the *Iliad* was also the most alienating, for the language – Greek being less accessible than Latin, even for Mrs Bennet-Atkinson – and subject matter – the vicissitudes of the Trojan War – were likely to marginalize female readers. As Harrison hectors Amelia with the figures of Helen and Andromache, the *Iliad* emerges as an untenable model that works to condemn more than Harrison's unfair treatment of Fielding's heroine. Fielding uses Homer, as he had used Caesar and Alexander in *Jonathan Wild*, to indict contemporary models of masculinity. Where Homer thus furnishes an outmoded template allied with a vexed, hypermasculine military ethos and the marginalization of female characters, Virgil becomes a champion of women in the figure of Dido, who, though sacrificed to Aeneas's divine imperative, is nonetheless his heroic equal with epic promise of her own. Although *Amelia* will ultimately advance a new model, the *Aeneid* also makes possible the heroic potential Fielding represents.

"A Fortress on a Rock": New Epic Foundations in *Amelia*

In shifting the focus from hero to heroine, Fielding upends the values of Virgilian epic by establishing Amelia's quotidian model of domestic virtue as an alternative to Booth's investment in masculine honour and military success. Fielding's emphasis on the site of the cottage – Amelia's symbol of domestic felicity eventually embraced by Booth himself – further displaces Booth's worldly priorities with the more fulfilling goal of familial happiness, privileging the importance of small domestic scenes over the bustling world of London's "Great Men." In doing so, Fielding profits not only from romance, with its equal emphasis on heroine and hero, but from the mid-century redefinition of history as a genre appropriate to private life.[15] Heralding *Amelia*'s departure from the larger scope of his previous novels, Fielding promises to relate the "various Accidents which befell a very worthy Couple, after their uniting in the State of Matrimony,"[16] but also describes the work as a "History." More than a rhetorical move common to the early novel, with its emphasis on the blurred boundaries between history and fiction, Fielding's characterization of *Amelia* foregrounds the new legitimacy emerging around subgenres of history at mid-century. Biography and memoir at once complemented the narratives of "Great Men" celebrated by classical history in its highest form and made history more accessible to a wider variety of readers.

In order to establish the need for a new heroic model in Amelia, Fielding censures the flawed neoclassical culture that produces Doctor Harrison and the novel's other male characters. Especially in the figure of the heroine's husband, William Booth, *Amelia* depicts classical learning as an exclusive instrument of male bonding and, elsewhere in the novel, as inspiration for the deadly practice of duelling. In rebuking Booth's priorities, and notions of military honour more generally, Fielding makes clear that modern uses of the ancients are to blame: we see this in Booth's partiality for Roman literature and, later, in specific references to Homeric and Virgilian epic as precedents for the unchristian practice of duelling. Like Jonathan Wild, Booth is classically trained, and the values he imbibes from the ancients align him with a milder version of Wildean masculinity. For example, in the course of a satire on authors, in which Fielding's narrator mocks an inept translator, we learn that Booth "was a pretty good Master of the Classics: For his Father, tho' he designed his Son for the Army, did not think it necessary to breed him up a Block-head. He did not perhaps imagine that a competent Share of *Latin* and *Greek* would make his Son either a Pedant or a Coward" (324). Knowing that the "Life of a Soldier is in general a Life of Idleness," Booth's father seems particularly concerned with his son's moral education, and finds, in the ancients, a useful tool for keeping him free of trouble: he thought that "the spare Hours of an Officer in Country Quarters would be as well employed with a Book, as in sauntring about the Streets, loitering in a Coffee House, sotting in a Tavern, or in laying Schemes to debauch and ruin a Set of harmless and ignorant Country Girls" (324). The narrator further qualifies Booth's knowledge by stating that he is "therefore what might well be called, in this Age at least, a Man of Learning" (324). In the same chapter, Booth later demonstrates his classical learning when he exposes a fraudulent author by asking his opinion on grammatical details and translations, or his estimation of certain ancient poets. However, even as classical learning – opposed to "sauntering," "loitering," "sotting," and "debauching" – emerges as a virtuous alternative for a man of Booth's stature, it also takes on a parallel significance: if Booth's time "would be as well employed with a Book" as in less savoury activities, the narrator suggests an equivalence that renders Booth's education suspect from the outset, and specifically links classical learning to sexual predation.

Indeed, the consequences of Booth's education exceed mere grammatical quibbling. Early in the novel, Fielding introduces Monsieur Bagillard, a Frenchman whom Booth meets during his military service abroad, to highlight the dangers of elite male friendships; the rapport between the two men, strengthened by their shared knowledge of ancient literature, blinds Booth to Bagillard's sexual interest in Amelia. In fact, Booth's friendship with Bagillard is so centred on classical texts that it leaves little room for Amelia to join their company: He observes, "our Conversation turning chiefly upon Books, and principally upon *Latin* ones (for we read several of the Classics together) she could have but little Entertainment by being with us" (125). Even as Booth acknowledges Amelia's alienation, he enjoys Bagillard's conversation so much that he repeatedly exposes his wife to the man who would seduce her. Though the only friendship explicitly identified with classical learning, Booth's engagement with Bagillard typifies his other relationships in the novel. In addition to leaving Amelia vulnerable to his French companion, Booth will later insist that she attend a masquerade in order to placate his good friend Colonel James, who similarly plans to betray Booth by seducing his wife. Only an outsider to this tradition – the classically educated Mrs Bennet-Atkinson – will discern that homosocial bonding often masks illicit heterosexual desire.[17]

Booth's insistence on conforming to notions of masculine honour also leaves him at the mercy of the Noble Peer who, like James, schemes to rape Amelia. The Peer is only too eager to exploit Booth's circumstances in order to seduce his wife. He vows to help Booth find a commission, but only by separating him from Amelia: "it will be very difficult, I am afraid, to get you a Rank at home. In the *West-Indies* perhaps, or in some Regiment abroad it may be more easy; and," he concludes, "when I consider your Reputation as a Soldier, I make no doubt of your Readiness to go to any Place where the Service of your Country shall call you" (197).[18] For the Peer, granting a commission becomes a convenient way to prey upon Fielding's heroine. He capitalizes on Booth's sense of dignity by emphasizing his "Readiness to go to any Place" for "the Service of [his] Country," and thus exploits Booth's desire to preserve his reputation and his family. At the same time, the Peer's calculated proposal underscores the hollowness of Booth's values in their social context, for the Peer has no personal interest in the cause to which he pays lip service. It is merely a convenient stratagem for raping another man's wife.

In choosing to make Booth a soldier, Fielding further links classical learning and military culture in order to reveal the destructiveness of classical analogues for contemporary notions of masculine honour. *Amelia* features a number of duels: Bath fights Monsieur Bagillard on Booth's behalf; Booth duels Colonel James's brother-in-law, Colonel Bath, and nearly, at the end of the novel, James himself. Although the custom of duelling might recall the world of chivalric romance, Fielding associates it firmly with Greek and Roman epic in *Amelia*, suggesting that the use of classical models in Booth's social milieu imports pagan values into a Christian world. The bellicose Colonel Bath, for example, invokes Homer and Virgil in order to justify the masculine code of honour that requires duelling. When Doctor Harrison asks, attempting to uncouple the terms "Honour and Fighting" (364), "What were all the

Greeks and *Romans*? Were these Cowards; and yet did you ever hear of this Butchery, which we call Duelling, among them?"[19] Bath answers, with perfect comic timing, "Yes, indeed … What else is all Mr. *Pope's Homer* full of, but Duels? … Nay, and in *Dryden's Virgil*, is there any Thing almost besides fighting?" (365). Even Harrison, who attempts to distinguish between military and civilian duels in his conversation with Bath, later admits, in a discussion with Amelia, to sharing Bath's point of view. In displacing blame for Booth's adherence to masculine notions of honour onto Amelia – outrageously blaming "the Nonsense of Women" (504) – he introduces Menelaus and Paris as "duelist[s]" while denouncing women who, "out of heroic Vanity," "hazard" the "Li[ves]" and "Soul[s]" of their "Husband[s]" (504). Although Bath's characterization of Homer and Virgil as "full of … Duels" may easily appear humorous in light of his comical character, Harrison's description of Greek and Trojan heroes as "duelists" nonetheless highlights the troubling model of masculinity cultivated by ancient epic.

Like Booth's friendship with Monsieur Bagillard, Colonels James and Bath represent, for Fielding, the drawbacks of a classically fuelled, hypermasculine ethos that posits masculinity and femininity as mutually exclusive. James, a "perfect Libertine with regard to Women" (174), says first of Miss Mathews, "Pox of her Inclination; I want only the Possession of her Person" (177), and later, the narrator characterizes James's lust for Amelia as a desire "to lead this poor Lamb, as it were, to the Slaughter, in order to purchase a Feast of a few Days by her Final Destruction" (339). Bath's opposition is even more exaggerated, for he comically avoids commerce with women altogether. As the narrator says, he "would at any Time have rather fought with a Man than lain with a Woman" (431), and so rigid are his standards of masculine honour that even James cannot forbear joking to Booth that he "sometimes apprehend[s] [that Bath] will insist on my [cutting his throat], as a Return for my getting him made a Lieutenant-Colonel" (228). Underscoring his destructive inclinations, Bath's honour will ultimately prove fatal, for we learn in the epilogue that he "was killed in a Duel about six Years ago, by a Gentleman who told the Colonel he differed from him in Opinion" (531).

Bath's satirical insistence on masculine heroism requires the deliberate disavowal of so-called feminine weakness, even if that means suppressing the natural tendencies of his character. When Bath's sister falls ill, it drives him to distraction; he dotes on her, acting as her nurse, but also experiences great shame for professing so much love for a woman. When Booth surprises him in his duties, Bath proclaims, "I know how much it is beneath a Man to whine and whimper about a trifling Girl as well as you, or any Man; and if my Sister had died, I should have behaved like a Man on the Occasion. I would not have you think I confined myself from Company merely upon her Account" (129). Marking his potential for conversion to Amelia's model, Booth maintains, by contrast, that "Tenderness for Women is so far from lessening, that it proves a true manly Character" (130). Booth's reflections – which also include the "manly" examples of Brutus, the king of Sweden, and Xerxes – seem to mollify the Colonel, but Bath continues to profess shame, conceding that "nature will get the better of dignity" (130). In this way, Fielding condemns the unnaturalness of the classical values – revealed in Bath's discussion of epic heroes and in the narrator's comparison of Bath to Achilles (416) – that bolster Bath's version of heroic dignity, a model of masculinity that must be rigorously learned, implemented, and policed.[20] Ultimately, Bath feels "shame" for his brotherly affection, not guilt; contradicting Harrison's claims that women goad men into perpetrating heroic violence, Bath worries about *Booth's* perceptions of his manhood. As evidenced by Bath's investment in duelling as the legacy of Greco-Roman culture (364), his concerns reveal an unsettling allegiance to the heroes of Pope's Homer and Dryden's Virgil, despite the contradictory demands of Christian virtue.[21]

By contrast, *Amelia* – both the novel and its heroine – represents a new model of domestic virtue, one available to men and women alike, that signals a sharp break from the classically inspired masculine codes of honour privileged elsewhere in Fielding's novel. The narrative that introduces Amelia sets the stage for her hybrid role. A mixture of epic and romance, it follows closely the opening of the *Aeneid*, for Booth and his old acquaintance, Miss Mathews, take turns in telling their stories of love and adventure while imprisoned in Newgate. Fielding imports additional romance conventions, from the star-crossed lovers theme of Booth's courtship and the numerous obstacles to their marriage, to the stratagems that Booth employs in order to woo Amelia: in an episode borrowed from medieval and early modern romance, he even conceals himself in a wine hamper in order to be conveyed into the Harris household.[22] Although his scheme fails when the servants betray him to Amelia's mother, Booth and Amelia run away to the cottage of her nurse, to whom they pretend to be married. In Booth's relation, Amelia softly whispers, "*that she perceived there might be Happiness in a Cottage,*" leading Miss Mathews to exclaim, "A Cottage! ... [A] Cottage with the Man one loves is a palace" (86).[23]

The epic context of the novel encourages the reader to give serious weight to Amelia's character and aspirations. Thanks to Fielding's heroine, the cottage becomes an important symbol throughout the story, creating a pastoral alternative to war and to the corruptions of London society. It is nobler, in the world of *Amelia*, to invest in family over misguided notions of masculine honour. Even Booth eventually longs for Amelia's model: he relates to Miss Mathews that his departure for Gibraltar caused him to "[repent] my Resolution, and [wish] … that I had taken her Advice, and preferred Love and a Cottage to all the dazzling Charms of Honour" (110). As he tells his story to Miss Mathews, he regrets, in similar terms, his past refusal to exchange commissions with another soldier: this opportunity would have allowed Booth to avoid serving in Gibraltar and, instead, would have enabled him to remain close to his family. Booth laments, "I found Love was not so over-matched by Honour as he ought to have been" (93), suggesting, in hindsight, the hollowness of traditional martial values. Comparing Amelia to a "fortress on a rock," Harrison makes clear that Booth has defended Gibraltar abroad to the detriment of his obligations at home.

In embracing the cottage as a symbol of domestic felicity over military glory, *Amelia* posits an especially feminine and eighteenth-century form of heroism centred on the private world of the rural idyll rather than the public world of London's corrupt urban landscape. Of course, the idea of living the retired life had held its attractions since antiquity, but the special appeal of the cottage – with its noble, rustic simplicity, quiet gentility, and idealized rural happiness revolving around family and home life – was a peculiarly eighteenth-century invention. As one scholar notes, invoking the cult of sensibility that came to signify "the faculty of feeling, the capacity for extremely refined emotion and a quickness to display compassion for suffering," "a refined sensibility coupled with a never to be requited longing were the prerequisites for cottage love."[24] The fantasy of rural life offered a respite from class-based burdens of city living: "The great man's freedom is curtailed by a complex network of social exchanges. Rather than a private retreat where he might be free to express his intimate self, the mansion is a public space in which the great man must maintain his image. Conversely, the cottage embodies a happiness that rests on privacy, personal liberty, and wealth regulated by simple necessity, not public display."[25] As Amelia and Booth seek refuge with Amelia's childhood nurse, and as they elaborate their longing for a model of domesticity to challenge the "dazzling Charms of Honor" (110), Fielding signals their allegiance to the eighteenth-century cult of sensibility. At the same time, he contrasts their virtuous longing with the novel's scathing depictions of the so-called Great Men whose favours Booth initially attempts to earn.

In this way, Booth's attraction to the cottage's symbolism heralds his nascent understanding of the superiority of Amelia's noble model, for Booth must learn to value love in a cottage over honour on the battlefield in the same way that he must learn to identify, as I will argue in the next section, with the domestic virtues of Andromache over the public prowess of Hector and Achilles. Fielding thus anticipates the late eighteenth-century vogue for cottage symbolism, best represented, in the visual arts, by William Gainsborough's cottage door paintings; echoing the shift from political and military to social history, Gainsborough preferred these small rustic scenes to the grander history painting favoured by Sir Joshua Reynolds (see Figure 2.1). If Gainsborough's paintings represent a version of "Adam's paradise,"[26] with their well-fed babes and attractive young women clustered around cottage doors, then *Amelia* offers a version of Eve's paradise – and the novel, at one point, compares Amelia's beauty to that of Milton's Eve (230) – that unites mother, father, and children in one cozy tableau. Because this model of heroism privileges affective bonds between individuals and the feminine world of the home, it provides Booth with a much-needed alternative to conventional modes of masculine self-definition.

In the figure of his heroine, Fielding thus domesticates and democratizes the heroic ideal: Amelia's is the heroism of everyday life. The novel makes this point by introducing a variety of female characters who mirror Amelia physically and in their narrative trajectories. First there is Blear-Eyed Moll, whose syphilis-eaten nose provides an uncomfortable parallel to the results of Amelia's carriage accident; Miss Mathews, who also runs away from home with her would-be husband, to disastrous, rather than happy, consequences; and Mrs Bennet-Atkinson, a previous victim of the same Peer who schemes to rape Amelia. At an important moment in Book 6, the narrator also suggests appropriate poetic counterparts, variously describing the heroine as Milton's Eve, a sweet nymph, and even Cupid (230).[27] These associations, in turn, suggest the resemblances shared among the trio of main female characters: if Amelia can recall Miss Mathews as well as Milton's Eve, associated with *eros* through the invocation of nymphs and Cupid, then Fielding suggests a rich complexity to Amelia's character often obscured by her wifely role. Indeed, the comparison to Cupid, with his "pleasing Fires," "his taking Smiles," and "all that inflames Desires," is especially provocative,

Figure 2.1. Thomas Gainsborough, *Cottage Door* (c. 1780) / Huntington Library and Art Gallery, San Marino, CA, USA / © The Huntington Library, Art Collections and Botanical Gardens / Bridgeman Images.

suggesting that Amelia's robust sexuality coexists with her virtue. At this moment, Fielding depicts Amelia as a fully embodied heroine, even noting, at her entrance, that "Exercise had painted her Face with Vermilion" (230). In humanizing her character – to the point of ridicule in the critical outcry over Amelia's nose – Fielding insists that Amelia's complexities, though atypical of novelistic heroines, should offer no impediment to her virtue.

Indeed, even Amelia, that paragon of virtue who loves Booth so dearly, finds herself flattered, like Miss Mathews, by the attentions of Colonel James (337), and also permits the newly married Serjeant Atkinson, her longtime admirer, to kiss her hand, reflecting afterward that her heart "was yet a little softened by the plain, honest, modest, involuntary, delicate, heroic Passion of this poor and humble Swain; for whom, in spite of herself, she felt a momentary Tenderness and Complacence, at which *Booth*, if he had known it, would perhaps have been displeased" (482–3). Amelia is not a perfect beauty (Helen) or grief-stricken wife (Andromache); she is not an obstacle for Booth (Dido) or threatening Amazon (Camilla), all roles that would reduce her to a predictable type. Instead, Amelia enacts a dynamic, quotidian heroism probably familiar to many of Fielding's eighteenth-century readers.

For Fielding, the novel works hand in hand with the new historiographic interest in manners and customs to make possible a revaluation of women's experiences: the strategies of romance historiography, which puts fiction and history in dialogue with one another, enable Fielding to retell the *Aeneid* through *Amelia* in order to retrieve a rich legacy of female heroism that can be traced, in epic, back to Dido herself, but without recapitulating Dido's position of defeat. In this way, it is important that Fielding sets *Amelia* against the backdrop of the 1727 Siege of Gibraltar, invoking recent British history and not just the distant spectre of the Trojan War. By making his Didos into plausible contemporary figures – by showing that the consequences of the *Aeneid* are not merely literary – Fielding highlights the stakes of generic inclusiveness for female subjects typically subordinated by epic's priorities. In designating Amelia a "Fortress on a Rock" (415) – recalling both Gibraltar and the famed labours of Hercules – the novel embodies, in its heroine, new heroic values that rival, and eventually supersede, Booth's devotion to classical models.

In thus describing Amelia as a "Fortress on a Rock" (415), Doctor Harrison invokes a similar image of mythic foundations while suggesting that Fielding's heroine transcends mere symbolic status to achieve personal autonomy. He describes her chastity as "so strongly defended, as well by a happy natural Disposition of Mind, as by the strongest Principles of Religion and Virtue, implanted by Education, and nourished and improved by Habit, that the Woman must be invincible even without that firm and constant Affection of her Husband, which would guard a much looser and worse disposed Heart" (415). In this way, Harrison transposes the features of the Rock of Gibraltar onto – or rather into – Fielding's heroine: her "natural Disposition of Mind" supplants the landmark's strategic geography, while her strength is metaphorical – "Principles of Religion and Virtue" – rather than literal. So great are these advantages that Amelia needn't rely, in Harrison's formulation, on her soldier-husband to protect her.

For a story that anachronistically recounts the 1727 siege of Gibraltar, the comparison of Fielding's heroine to a "Fortress on a Rock" is particularly halting. Although critics have recently begun to pay more attention to the contemporary political contexts of novels like *Tom Jones*, there has been comparatively little discussion of such events in *Amelia*, despite the historical relevance of the novel's background. As Martin Battestin has noted, "*Amelia*, to a greater degree than any other of Fielding's novels, is a story rooted in the history of its time."[28] The events take place between April and June of 1733, recalling the siege six years earlier. The British conquered the Rock in 1704 during the War of the Spanish Succession, and the Treaty of Utrecht (1713) formally redesignated Gibraltar for Great Britain. Gibraltar, however, had been a Spanish territory since 1462, and Spain periodically attempted to recapture the Rock throughout the eighteenth century. From a strictly economic and military standpoint, the retention of Gibraltar often proved more trouble than it was worth. Public sentiment, however, prevented Britain from ceding the territory to Spain. Despite the military resources necessary for its upkeep and minimal returns on trade, Gibraltar served a powerful symbolic function: as an outpost of the empire at the Western entrance of the Mediterranean Sea, it gave Britain a strategic foothold in the Mediterranean, one with significant classical resonance in Gibraltar's close identification with the fabled labours of Hercules.[29]

Fielding himself called upon the symbolism of Gibraltar when, in a 1745 pamphlet, *A Serious Address to the People of Great Britain*, he inveighed against the evils sure to attend the possible return of the Stuart monarchy: at the moment of publication, the Young Pretender was preparing to invade England with political support from his French and Spanish allies. Among other grievances, Fielding cites the potential restoration of Gibraltar as one of the unthinkable outcomes of Prince Charles Edward Stuart's allegiance to Spain. As Fielding wrote, "If the *Chevalier* succeeds to the Crown, he can do no less, consistently with the Principles of Gratitude and Justice, than to restore to his Benefactor the King of *Spain*, the important Fortresses and Ports of *Gibraltar* and *Mabon*."[30] Fielding's characterization highlights Gibraltar's significance for the British people: "Thus all the Trade to the *Mediterranean* would, in a Manner, depend upon the Pleasure of the *Spanish Court*, and become uncertain and precarious; Neither would it be in the Power of the *British* Nation to rule with her Fleets, as she doth at present, to awe her Enemies, and succour her Friends."[31]

In this way, anxieties about Amelia's well-being radiate outward from the centre of the novel to its margins. By staging repeated predations and comparing Amelia to an impregnable fortress on a rock, the novel at once highlights the importance of England's possession of Gibraltar and also the perils for its female inhabitants at the moment of its conquest. In other words, *Amelia* suggests the troubling nexus of Englishwomen, their colonial counterparts, and the imperial project. During the British victory in 1704, "discipline deteriorated very quickly, and the wretched civilian residents of the Rock had to endure a sack of the place by the victorious soldiers and marines, who broke open the wine-shops and were soon, in many cases, roaring drunk."[32] Unsurprisingly under the circumstances, "[m]any females suffered insults and outrages, whence arose numerous sanguinary acts of vengeance on the part of the inhabitants, who murdered the perpetrators and threw their bodies into wells and sewers."[33] This is the sacrilegious sack of Troy revisited, in which the Greeks – too self-assured of their success – perpetrated similar "insults and outrages" on the Trojan inhabitants, and through their recklessness forfeited their homecoming. However, even as the novel's reminders of English corruption at home and abroad underscore the high costs of traditional heroisms, Fielding also uses the image of Gibraltar to forge a new path in Amelia. Her description as a "Fortress on a Rock" (415) evokes the Mediterranean geography of Cleopatra and Dido, and the Rock of Gibraltar is also one of the Pillars of Hercules, reportedly erected by the hero after his Tenth Labour, in which he stole the cattle of Geryon. The classical association confers an unexpected heroism on Amelia's chastity and conventionally domestic role: it is no accident that the novel ends with the restitution of Amelia's fortune, that we learn virtually nothing of Booth's family and history, and that the child distinguished as Harrison's favourite is the heroine's namesake, suggesting a matrilineal legacy that self-consciously complicates the patrilineal focus of classical epic.

Though the comparison of Amelia to a "Fortress on a Rock" may initially appear reductive – especially coming from Doctor Harrison, whose primary point is Amelia's impenetrable chastity – the complexity of Fielding's heroine complicates Harrison's portrait of Amelia as a mute symbol of virtue. The parallel between Amelia and Gibraltar, playing on the common personification of land-as-woman, at once marks Amelia as Hercules' equal and repudiates the heroic model, represented by Harrison's characterization, that requires her assimilation to an inanimate object because no suitable exemplar exists. The primary figures to which Harrison frequently has recourse – Helen, Andromache, and Dido – fail to suggest appropriate alternatives, demonstrating the paucity of available models; Harrison cannot imagine Amelia's active virtue in classical terms because the epic template will not permit it. Although Harrison is left, then, to describe Amelia in more conventional language, Fielding invents "Amelia" herself as a heroic category for his readers. In locating heroism in Amelia, Fielding in turn recalls the women who enter the novel through her and her counterpart Mrs Bennet, those foreign Didos whom the English appropriation of Gibraltar seeks to repress.

"A Good Woman and Yet": Harrison and Epic Precedents

The presence of Doctor Harrison – a lifelong friend and counsellor of Amelia's family – highlights the harmful nature of classical models, especially for women typically denied heroic agency. On the one hand, Harrison is a faithful guide, one of the few people willing (for the most part, at least) to stand by the Booths in the course of their struggles. Even when Amelia's mother and sister forsake her, Harrison remains a staunch supporter of the couple's union, shepherding them through adverse circumstances. On the rare occasions when he chooses to leave the Booths in distress, Harrison's unusual lapses in decency merely underscore, in the dark world of *Amelia*, the difficulty of making sound judgments. In other words, it is not necessarily a personal failing that Harrison cannot, in spite of his best intentions, reliably determine right from wrong, and he is hardly alone in this dilemma. Yet demonstrating how seductive, because naturalized, classical exemplars can be, Harrison's character also represents the institutional – in this case, religious – forces that Fielding contests in Amelia's quotidian heroism. As I will argue in this section,

Harrison's continued recourse to epic models as exemplars of femininity – especially to Dido, but also to Helen and Andromache – suggests that the *Iliad* and *Aeneid* still act as standards of feminine propriety, however ill-fitting their examples may be. In this way, Amelia at once surpasses Doctor Harrison, whose Christian ideals remain compromised by his classical education, and also comes to serve as a model for Booth's conversion: at an important moment in the novel, Booth will become more like Andromache than Hector, ultimately signifying his readiness to embrace Amelia's model even as Fielding eschews the restrictive binaries suggested first by the *Iliad* and later by Harrison himself.

Signifying the extent to which classical and Christian ideals collide, even the exemplary Doctor Harrison appears conflicted; caught between pagan and Christian principles, he at times unfairly imposes classical models onto Amelia's character. Demonstrating his allegiance to martial ideals, Bath expresses his contempt for femininity and domesticity when he declares that he prefers the laws of honour to the laws of religion, for "Women and the Clergy are upon the same Footing" (364). Harrison does nothing to recuperate the term "honour" at this moment. Instead, he acquiesces in Bath's terms: insisting that "some Clergymen ... would fight as bravely as yourself, Colonel; and that without being paid for it" (364–5), he thus affirms the divide between "honour" and "women" that neglects traditionally feminine – and, indeed, Christian – values. To be sure, Harrison's views on honour prove inconsistent throughout the novel. First he declares Amelia an enemy to Booth's reputation because she wishes to compromise his honour by preventing him from going to war (100–1); then he compares her, unfavourably, to Helen and Dido, declaring her an enemy to Booth's reputation because she desires to protect his public honour as an officer (501–6). In the same way that Harrison's views on honour shift inexplicably throughout the text, so too do his standards of femininity, suggesting the impossibility of conforming to existing classical models. In precisely the scene where he condemns Amelia for being an irresponsible Helen who encourages Booth's duelling, he lauds Andromache as an exemplar of female tenderness (504). But when Amelia objects to destructive notions of military honour earlier in the text, in a scene reminiscent of Hector and Andromache's parting on the Skaian Gates in *Iliad* 6, Harrison condemns her in the strongest possible terms. Even when she acts the part of Andromache, she is never "Andromache" enough; Harrison's excessively strict standards of feminine propriety leave no positive classical model available to her.

In the first instance, Fielding invokes Hector's wife only obliquely: Amelia's concern for herself and her family recalls the anxiety of the Trojan princess, the enormous price paid by Trojan women for the so-called honour of their husbands (101–3). Fielding dedicates this chapter, entitled "Containing a Scene of the tender Kind," to Booth's farewell, and, as Martin Battestin notes in his edition of the novel, the meeting between Hector and Andromache in *Iliad* 6 is the "*locus classicus* of the parting of a soldier and his wife on the eve of battle."[34] In the second instance, Harrison makes explicit the model Amelia should emulate by chastising her failure to do so. Here, he praises Andromache for "dissuad[ing] [Hector] from exposing himself to danger, even in a just cause" (504), precisely as Amelia had done with Booth previously (102–3). "This is indeed a Weakness," he continues, "but it is an amiable one, and becoming the true feminine Character" (504). By contrast, the Doctor claims that "a Woman, who out of heroic Vanity (for so it is) would hazard not only the Life, but the Soul too of her Husband in a Duel, is a Monster, and ought to be painted in no other Character but that of a Fury" (504).

Astonishingly, he classifies Amelia in this group, even after admitting her virtue. "I know," he concedes, "you are a good woman; *and yet I must observe to you*, that this very desire of feeding the passion of female vanity with the heroism of her man, old *Homer* seems to make the characteristic of a bad and loose woman" (504; emphasis added). As Harrison stands face-to-face with Amelia under the direst of circumstances, confessing, "I do know your meaning [that you desire only to protect Booth's reputation]," he nonetheless "rall[ies] [her] so unmercifully" (505) that he cannot help but have recourse to classical stereotypes. With a flesh-and-blood woman in front of him – a woman whom he has known since her infancy – he not only falls back on insulting canards about female character, but paradoxically criticizes Amelia for having fallen short of exactly the same model she had so well emulated as to merit his contempt and disapproval earlier in the text (100–1). Indeed, Harrison's rigid ideals – his uncompromising adherence to a nonsensical classical template that renders Amelia at once Helen and her antithesis, Andromache – bring him unmistakably closer to the blustering and untrustworthy Colonel Bath: he embodies a milder version of the heroic ethos caricatured in the Colonel. If the relationship between Booth and Bagillard reveals the dangers of classical learning at the local level, in private friendships between men, then Harrison's learning reveals its dangers in the context of real institutional and social power.[35] Because Harrison is an otherwise sympathetic figure in the novel – a devoted ally of the Booths and a sincere well-wisher to their happiness – Fielding demonstrates, in his character, how even a fundamentally good man can succumb to harmful classical stereotypes that, in turn, distort his perception of the more complicated reality in front of him. Far from making sense of Amelia's situation, Harrison's recourse to Helen and Andromache unfairly dismisses Fielding's heroine as she actively attempts to protect her family from ruin.

Highlighting the importance of Harrison's misinterpretation of Amelia's motives, Fielding uses the narrator, elsewhere in the novel, to expose the stakes of misreading at the level of narration. The narrator attempts, albeit humorously, to bias the reader against Miss Mathews by invoking classical models of femininity, even when it means doing violence to her story as another wronged Dido. Like Harrison's castigation of Amelia's character, the narrator's unusual intrusion shows the deployment of classical narratives in action: when even the narrator resorts to the examples of Medea and Cleopatra as the most immediate and effective way to condemn Miss Mathews, a former acquaintance with whom Booth reunites in prison, then the novel illustrates the extent to which such models have become a naturalized frame for interpreting female character. Despite Booth's apparent devotion to Amelia, he commits adultery with his new companion, and, in light of Booth's transgression, the narrator profits from allusion to imagine the readers who would magnify Miss Mathews's faults:

> It may be necessary to whisper a Word or two to the Critics, who have perhaps begun to express no less Astonishment than Mr. *Booth,* that a Lady, in whom we had remarked a most extraordinary Power of displaying Softness, should the very next Moment after the Words were out of our Mouth, express Sentiments becoming the Lips of a *Dalila, Jezebel, Medea, Semiramis, Parysatis, Tanaquil, Livilla, Messaline, Agrippina, Brunichilde, Elfrida,* Lady *Macbeth, Joan* of *Naples, Christina* of *Sweden, Katharine Hays, Sarah Malcolm, Con. Philips,* or any other Heroine of the tender sex, which History sacred or prophane, ancient or modern, false or true, hath recorded. (44–5)

In thus humorously exploiting the archetype of the infamous woman, the narrator momentarily invites the negative reading practices that Fielding seeks, in *Amelia,* to correct. That is, while the narrator counts on the reader to vilify Miss Mathews by reducing her to a vulgar type,

Fielding temporarily aligns the narrator with other characters, from Colonel Bath to Doctor Harrison, who deploy sexist myths with the authority of classical culture. In effect, the narrator imagines how certain "Critics" might ungenerously render Miss Mathews's story non-narratable through recourse to reductive allusions, however comical, and Miss Mathews's question to Booth – "[W]hat is there of a woman worth relating, after what I have told you?" (48) – reflects her understanding of her own position at the narrative margins.

Later, the narrator's comparison of Miss Mathews to Cleopatra – "*cast*[ing] [on Booth] *a Look as languishingly sweet*, as ever *Cleopatra* gave to *Anthony*" (151) – will further underscore his allegiance to narratives of female transgression, be they "false or true" (45). The narrator refers to the Cleopatra not of history but of romance, for he relates that "Mr. *Booth* had been her first Love, and had made those Impressions on her young Heart, which the Learned in this Branch of Philosophy affirm, and perhaps truly, are never to be eradicated" (151). Though a mere aside in the context of the larger story, the narrator's allusion stages the aftermath of the Augustan propaganda campaign that at once created Dido as the lovesick queen of Carthage and recast Cleopatra as a lover and, of course, adulterer; in this configuration, Amelia comes to play the role of the virtuous Octavia, faithfully tending to domestic matters while Cleopatra seduces her husband. There is simply no positive role for Miss Mathews to play when the narrator casts Booth as hero and the Booth family as the subject of his epic. Indeed, this is the very point Fielding employs the narrator to make: transforming Cleopatra into a seductress and assimilating Miss Mathews to the "Cleopatra type" underscores the same troubling aspects of neoclassical culture seen in Booth's notions of friendship and masculine honour.

In contrast to Harrison, with his quick reliance on classical models of feminine (im)propriety, Amelia, that "Fortress on a Rock" (415), helps to establish the novel's new moral genealogy. An outsider to the classical education enjoyed by Harrison and Booth, Amelia avoids the problems such an education engenders: the conflict between pagan and Christian values; the preconceived, seemingly immutable, stereotypes that condition Harrison's and Booth's often limited thinking. Jill Campbell has rightly described Booth's conversion as a change in reading practices, from the classical materials that formed the basis of his relationship with Monsieur Bagillard to the Christian books, particularly Doctor Barrow, that he shares with Amelia.[36] What I would like to add to Campbell's formulation is the way Fielding characterizes this shift through classical allusion, marking Booth's transformation from a traditionally masculine heroic figure, Achilles, to the Andromache model that Fielding (positively, 101ff) and Harrison (negatively, 504) associate with Amelia. Highlighting Booth's potential allegiance to Colonel Bath's brand of heroism, the narrator refers to Booth and his men as "*Booth* and his Myrmidons," positioning Booth as Achilles (as he had Bath, 416), the Myrmidons' leader.[37] At the same time – and in a move that allies Fielding with Homer, whose reverse similes in the *Odyssey* identify Odysseus with Penelope and vice versa, suggesting the importance of a feminine heroic ethos for men and women alike – Fielding aligns Booth with Andromache at a key moment when his fate and Amelia's hang in the balance.[38] After receiving aid from Colonel James, who has promised that he "will advance [Booth] a sum of money to pay off all [his] debts" and that he will seek a commission for him in the West Indies, Booth "returned to Amelia in that kind of disposition which the great master of human passion would describe in *Andromache*, when he tells us she cried and smiled at the same instant" (368–9). The allusion recalls Hector's leave-taking in *Iliad* 6 – the same scene that had previously identified Booth with Hector and Amelia with Andromache (101–3). Just before this description, Hector expresses his personal reluctance to fight, his duty to uphold his public honour, and his grief for Andromache's fate at enemy hands. As Andromache holds their son, the young Astyanax, she at once smiles and grieves for his future. For the only acceptable outcome is to follow in his father's footsteps: despite the wartime reality that will shortly tear Hector's family asunder, he wishes for Astyanax to perpetuate this destructive cycle in the next generation, bringing tragedy to future Astyanaxes and Andromaches, a fantasy of the future that causes Andromache to "smile in her tears" (6.482–4).[39]

The unexpected resemblance of Booth – on the cusp, as he believes, of military success – to Andromache, rather than to Hector or Achilles, marks at once a reversal of his earlier position and the gradual acknowledgment – and, hence, eventual rejection – of the seemingly necessary, yet thoroughly destructive, heroic code that motivates him throughout the novel. At this late point in the story, it identifies him not only with Andromache but with Amelia, indicating the extent to which he has come to sympathize with Amelia's position. It also demonstrates an evolution away from the hypermasculine ideals encouraged by his culture towards the natural sweetness of Booth's character: just as Colonel Bath attempts to cast off feminine weakness during his sister's illness, protesting his manliness, Fielding suggests that Booth's masculine persona is sometimes at odds with his native temperament.[40] This cross-identification, like Booth's insistence, despite convention, on actively assisting his wife during childbirth, roundly refutes Harrison's prescription of separate spheres, in which he mocks Mrs Bennet-Atkinson's unfeminine learning by quoting Hector's lines to Andromache, "Go home and mind your own Business. Follow your Spinning, and keep your Maids to their Work" (427).[41]

In upending Harrison's reductive views of masculine and feminine propriety, Fielding in fact calls on the complexities of Homeric epic evidently lost on Harrison. Instead of realizing, for example, that Hector embraces heroic masculinity because he has no other choice, Harrison wrongly assumes the fundamental incompatibility of Hector's and Andromache's worlds. However, as the *Iliad* makes clear, Hector fights because of enormous social pressure; fearing the shame of his people, he cannot defy expectation.[42] Later, in the *Odyssey*, Achilles will explicitly regret choosing martial glory over a long but unmemorable life in the country, yearning for a version of the pastoral existence that captivates Amelia (86).[43] Here again Booth echoes Achilles: as I have shown, too late does Booth "[repent] my Resolution, and [wish] … that I had taken [Amelia's] Advice, and preferred Love and a Cottage to all the dazzling Charms of Honour" (110). Because of the epic nature of the *Iliad*, Achilles never seriously considers forsaking personal glory; it takes the romance commitments of the *Odyssey* and confinement to the Underworld for him to confess his regrets to Odysseus. However, because of *Amelia*'s hybridity, Booth needn't follow the same heroic path, and neither Amelia nor Mrs Bennet-Atkinson need become a Helen, Andromache, or Dido.

Fielding's use of the *Iliad* therefore serves a threefold purpose in the novel. It shows how constraining the epic model can be, even for its heroes; in doing so, it undermines Harrison's deployment of epic discourse to enforce gendered standards of behaviour recognized, even in the *Iliad*, to be socially constructed; and, finally, it reveals Harrison's willingness to resort to the most austere of ancient epics – older, more venerable, and less inclusive than Virgil's *Aeneid*, which fuses epic and romance elements from the *Iliad* and *Odyssey* – in order to wield cultural authority over other characters, especially women. Indeed, the *Iliad* gives him the upper hand against even the learned Mrs Bennet-Atkinson: the point at which she confesses that she "do[es] not pretend … to be a Critic in the *Greek*" and can only "read a little of *Homer*, at least with the Help of looking now and then in the *Latin*" is the point at which Harrison recites, without translating, from Homer (427); he then alludes to the section of Juvenal's infamously misogynist Sixth Satire in which the Roman poet condemns women's learning, especially when it comes to mastering Greek (427). Because, as I will argue shortly, Mrs Bennet-Atkinson can compete more effectively with Harrison on the subject of Virgilian epic, he resorts to Greek in order to maintain his dominance as a man and clergyman.

On the one hand, Harrison's superimposition of the Hector and Andromache model onto Amelia's narrative highlights his stark black-and-white view of Amelia's character – either vain "monster" (504) or passive helpmeet – and the arbitrary distinction between masculine and feminine roles. On the other, it also foregrounds the problematic nature of an epic template that offers no alternative to martial glory or feminine "weakness" (504), both for Hector and Achilles and for most of Fielding's characters. As Mrs Bennet-Atkinson will show, the Dido model succeeds where the Andromache model fails because Dido offers a parallel and competing originary narrative. More than Aeneas's wife, Dido is his heroic counterpart, the famed queen of Carthage who, were it not for Virgil, would have escaped the fate of *Aeneid* 4.[44] Because she exists prior to the *Aeneid,* and as one of the chief protagonists within the romance framework of the first six books, Dido becomes the originator of a competing epic tradition, inflected by romance, that makes possible a more expansive definition of heroism.

In this way, Fielding structures "Dido" – and, especially in the passage above, "Andromache" – as categories meant to close sympathetic distance between characters with different, sometimes conflicting, backgrounds and experiences. Here, too, Harrison's allusions are instructive: by referring to Helen, for example, he attempts to enact distance, recalling Amelia to her senses by invoking a figure with whom she should fail to identify. Triangulating their relationship through an allusion to Helen in turn estranges Harrison from Amelia and vice versa: for Harrison, "Helen" is a negative category that represents his inability to sympathize with Amelia's circumstances. However, in characterizing Amelia and Booth as "Andromaches," the narrator emphasizes the strength of their similarities rather than differences; Fielding suggests that, in closing the emotional gap between heroine and hero, such allusion fosters an imaginative union that joins the Booths together rather than driving them apart. The ability to sympathize with the Dido position – the position of the marginalized female subject – not only marks Booth's conversion to Amelia's model of heroism but also signifies the appropriate sensibility that enables Dido to become a heroine in her own right.

"All the Fortune given her by her Father": Mrs Bennet-Atkinson

Fielding's most fascinating revision of the Dido story comes in the tragic narrative of Mrs Bennet, later Mrs Atkinson (Mrs Bennet-Atkinson), whose classical training and familiarity with the *Aeneid* allow her to interrupt predictable narratives of female loss and victimization: she both rewrites her betrayal by the Noble Peer and prevents him from enacting the same script with Amelia. Though initially reluctant to reveal the story of her rape, she confesses the Peer's crime after noticing his suspicious interest in Amelia; it turns out that he has a habit of befriending women in distress. Mrs Bennet-Atkinson relates how, in order to execute his scheme, he sent her then-husband, Mr Bennet, away on business while Mrs Ellison, the man's procuress, persuaded her to attend a masquerade at Ranelagh. This news causes Amelia to turn "pale as Death" (294), owing to the similarities with her own story. Though flattered, as she relates, by the Peer's attentions, Mrs Bennet desired nothing more than an evening of innocent conversation. Instead, she explains, he drugged and raped her: although she drank not "a Drop more than [her] usual Stint" (295), she quickly found herself "giddy" and "intoxicated" (295). Determined to spare Amelia a similar fate, she concludes, "I am convinced, by what I have lately seen, that you are the destined Sacrifice to this wicked Lord; and that Mrs. *Ellison*, whom I no longer doubt to have been the Instrument of my Ruin, intended to betray you in the same Manner" (303). As the resemblance between the women's stories suggests, the Peer follows a pattern of predation that enables Mrs Bennet-Atkinson to prevent the repetition of that pattern with Amelia.

In the friendship between Amelia and Mrs Bennet-Atkinson, Fielding thus maps romance elements onto the epic structure represented by the *Aeneid* in order to unsettle the patterns so familiar in traditional epic.[45] In Mrs Bennet's story, Fielding raises the spectre of an epic teleology that seems to require the "destined sacrifice" (303) of so many female characters, but ultimately subsumes it to romance by foregrounding the relationship between heroines against the backdrop, as I have suggested, of competitive friendships between men. Patricia Parker notes that "it is the female characters – Dido, Allecto, Amata, Juno (and their agents) – who are the chief perpetrators of delay and even of obstructionism in relation to the master or imperial project of the completion of the text"; women can "delay the fated ending but cannot indefinitely forestall or finally alter it."[46] *Amelia* challenges this characterization: Mrs Bennet-Atkinson's narrative and its influence on Amelia's demonstrate that, in Fielding's new kind of epic, women can "forestall" and, indeed, "finally alter" the "fated ending."

Essential to Fielding's rewriting of Virgilian epic, Mrs Bennet-Atkinson's ability to thwart the Noble Peer's designs derives, in part, from her classical learning. She is unique in the novel in that she is the only character who directly ventriloquizes Dido and self-consciously revises the Dido narrative (407). From the outset, Fielding casts her as the learned lady and establishes her allegiance to the *Aeneid* in general and to Dido in particular. The narrator relates that her classical knowledge is "all the Fortune given her by her Father, and all the Dower left her by her Husband" (258). In the moment that occasions this revelation, Mrs Bennet-Atkinson has been discussing the validity of second marriages with Booth. She quotes – in Latin – from *Aeneid* 4.24–9, in which Dido swears fidelity to her deceased husband. The figure of the learned lady or Amazon was a popular negative stereotype throughout the eighteenth century because of the masculine associations of intellectual activity and especially classical learning.[47] Yet Mrs Bennet-Atkinson appears to be an exception to this rule. Unlike Aunt Western of *Tom Jones*, whose party politics Fielding consistently satirizes, Mrs Bennet-Atkinson's learning is criticized not so much by the narrator as by other characters, her aunt and Harrison in particular, both of whom are made to seem ridiculous, incompetent, or narrow-mindedly judgmental at other moments in the novel. In Harrison's case, for example, Nancy Mace has shown that his "occupation with minor points ... is the hallmark of his interest in the classics,"[48] and – as I have already argued about his relationship to Amelia – his use of classical learning often amounts to outright bullying. Indeed, as he questions the usefulness of learning to a woman's education (407), he cannot help but rally Mrs Bennet-Atkinson on her love of Latin, mockingly fearful that it might disrupt an otherwise happy marriage by giving the wife an unwarranted claim to superiority over her husband (408).

To the extent that Mrs Bennet-Atkinson's learning is problematic, it has nothing to do with displeasing Serjeant Atkinson. Instead, Fielding suggests, epic – as one of the legacies of classical culture inherited by

Booth and Doctor Harrison – is dangerous because of its hostility to women and female characters. Even as Fielding posits his allegiance to the *Aeneid* in the *Covent-Garden Journal* and names Virgil as Mrs Bennet-Atkinson's favourite author, he nonetheless stages the antagonistic relationship between Harrison and Mrs Bennet-Atkinson as a clash between hostile epic authority, represented by the very Virgil whom she admires, and marginalized female readers. During a heated discussion on the merits of her favourite poet, Harrison reminds Mrs Bennet-Atkinson of Virgil's famous expression from *Aeneid* 4.569–70, "Varium et mutabile semper Femina" ("Woman is always a various and changeable thing/animal"), the final words of Mercury's speech as he ushers Aeneas from Carthage. Mrs Bennet-Atkinson acknowledges that the Doctor has "quoted the severest Thing that ever was said against us" (409), what Dryden called the "sharpest Satire in the fewest words that was ever made on Womankind."[49] "And yet," the Doctor continues, "this is the *Virgil* ... that you are so fond of, who hath made you all of the Neuter Gender; or as we say in English, he hath made mere Animals of you: For if we translate it thus; *Woman is a various and changeable Animal,* there will be no Fault, I believe, unless in point of Civility to the Ladies" (410).

The controversy surrounding Mercury's speech, as the Doctor implies, is that the adjectives modifying "femina" are both neuter, forcing the addition of a neuter noun in order to make grammatical sense. Either Virgil made a mistake, an idea Harrison briefly entertains, or the passage requires adding a generic neuter such as "thing" or "animal" to complete the sentiment.[50] The line serves as a calculated response to the perceived failure of Aeneas's heroic masculinity. Mercury reproaches Aeneas on two separate occasions, the first having been insufficiently motivational. Emphasizing, for a contemporary Roman audience, the depths to which Aeneas has sunk, echoes of an enamoured Antony dallying with Cleopatra in Egypt tinge the first rebuke: "Degenerate Man," Mercury begins, "Thou Woman's Property, what mak'st thou here, / These foreign Walls, and *Tyrian* Tow'rs to rear, / Forgetful of thy own? ... What means thy ling'ring in the *Lybian* Land?" (4.390–5). Aeneas's subordination to the Dido narrative just won't do; Mercury rewrites falling in love with and helping Dido as degeneracy and unmanly enslavement to a woman. The second warning then plays on stereotypes about wild and vindictive femininity in order to expedite Aeneas's departure. Mercury claims that Dido "harbours in her Heart a furious hate; / And thou shalt find the dire Effects too late; /

Fix'd on Revenge, and Obstinate to die: / Haste swiftly hence, while thou hast pow'r to fly" (4.810–13). The casual misogyny of his parting question – "Who knows what Hazards thy Delay may bring? / Woman's a various and a changeful Thing" (4.818–19) – reflects the power of Mercury's characterization of Dido as crazed ex-lover, the presumption that a woman scorned is capable of anything. Eager to usher Aeneas from Carthage, his concluding words forestall objection by offering the force of common knowledge – surely, having agreed that "Woman's a various and a changeful Thing," no further comment is necessary. The phrase becomes an easy maxim, passed from Mercury to Aeneas and from the *Aeneid* to subsequent generations of men.[51]

Mercury's strategy expresses a twofold problem. The first is the point articulated by Harrison. Superficially, the success of Mercury's argument depends on the reduction of women to "things" (or "animals") as a class distinct from, and decidedly inferior to, men. Yet it also suggests that assigning Dido her full human value can only be at odds with proper heroic action. In this way, there is more at stake than the conflict between Aeneas's private desires and public duties. Rather, Mercury's characterization suggests that epic heroism relies on Dido's necessary and inevitable dehumanization, and the expendability or interchangeability of Virgil's other female characters confirms this reading. In repositioning love and compassion as degeneracy and emasculation, in suggesting that Dido and Aeneas were never compatible and never can be, and in requiring the dehumanization of Dido's character as an essential component of epic heroism, Mercury shrugs off Dido's death as a logical consequence of her own unpredictable and barbaric femininity. Aeneas's failure – the failures of the epic model more generally – escape censure. Blaming the victim for her own demise, for being forced to inhabit a role that can entail nothing but victimization, Mercury, and the Roman culture he embodies, emerge triumphant at the expense of Dido's very presence, and of the potentially heroic trajectory her presence represents.

Fielding thus capitalizes on Harrison's slight against Mrs Bennet-Atkinson in order to effect a twofold critique. Harrison's bullying, bolstered by the *Aeneid*, allows *Amelia* at once to show the problems with contemporary reception of Virgilian epic and, through Mercury's response to Aeneas, to illustrate the problems inherent in epic heroism itself. In the mouth of Doctor Harrison, and deployed against Mrs Bennet-Atkinson in a bid to humiliate her, the continued relevance of Mercury's speech becomes clearer. It is no coincidence that Harrison introduces the quotation in the first place because of his irritation at Mrs Bennet-Atkinson's impressive command of classical texts; he asserts his superior authority over her, and his "natural" relationship to classical authority, by quoting Mercury in order to remind Mrs Bennet-Atkinson that she, like Dido, is an outsider. Even as he attempts to mock her for her devotion to a seemingly hostile text, Harrison becomes Mercury, justifying Mrs Bennet-Atkinson's formal exclusion from a tradition so inimical to female readers. Mrs Bennet-Atkinson is so taken aback by the implications of Mercury's speech that she "protest[s] [she] never thought of it before" (410), a response that suggests the potential for alternative readings even as it emphasizes the treacherous nature of received wisdom. But in the face of Harrison's formal training, she must accept his interpretation of Virgil's poem.

At the same time, Mrs Bennet-Atkinson's continued admiration of Virgil, coupled with the eventual triumph of her narrative, suggests the possibility that Dido's story of betrayal can be revised when female characters discipline it to their own ends. In this case, her knowledge of the *Aeneid* as a potential frame of reference proves crucial. Despite Harrison's insistence that Virgil reduces women to things and animals, Mrs Bennet-Atkinson's familiarity with Dido's story allows her to intervene in, and disrupt, the Peer's plans: in inviting Amelia to the masquerade, he signals his intention to execute the same script of seduction and violence that he had earlier used with Mrs Bennet. To this end, Mrs Bennet-Atkinson, as she lays the masquerade trap for the Noble Peer, explicitly recasts him as a Dido-figure, declaring to the Doctor that "two Women surely will be too hard for one Man" (407), playing on *Aeneid* 4.95: "Una dolo divum si Foemina victa duorum est" ("If one woman [Dido] is conquered by the guile of two gods").[52] Her reconstruction explicitly alters the dynamics of the original context, elevating the women to the level of "gods" who determine their own destiny. No tractable Dido, she seeks to punish the Peer for his abuse and to protect Amelia at the same time. She therefore seizes the opportunity of the masquerade, taking advantage of her resemblance to Amelia to promise (in her stead) to fulfil the Peer's desires should he provide a commission for Serjeant Atkinson.[53] Despite her rape, Mrs Bennet-Atkinson ultimately emerges from her ordeal in good spirits, having proceeded to live a happy life after the first masquerade and, after the second, having regained power in the wake of her violation by imposing on the Noble Peer in the figure of Amelia. Despite Harrison's reductive use of Virgil, Fielding links Mrs Bennet-Atkinson's success to her reading of the *Aeneid*: reimagining the Dido story enables her at once to entrap the Noble Peer and to escape the narrative of misery and ruin so typical for abandoned heroines.

However, Mrs Bennet-Atkinson employs the *Aeneid* as a frame of reference for her actions only to turn that model upside-down. In transferring the source of power from "gods" to women, she mirrors the larger interests of *Amelia* itself: the blending of epic and romance, the ongoing attempt to find alternatives to a (neo)classical culture that compromises women, femininity, and female characters. In this way, Mrs Bennet-Atkinson's use of Virgil offers a competing model of reading that serves as a point of contrast to the classical training enjoyed by the novel's aristocratic and military classes. Importantly, this model is only possible when employed subversively, and may only be accessible to female characters: Harrison's half-mocking but mostly serious ventriloquization of Mercury's speech dramatizes the difficulty of thoughtlessly embracing a tradition so problematic for its female readers. Mrs Bennet-Atkinson's ploy succeeds because it allows her, in turning the tables, to cast off the Dido narrative of betrayal and self-destruction. But the Dido position is still the position of defeat, the role relegated to the loser: when the only options are "Dido" and "Aeneas," success means recasting the Peer as Dido and affirming Dido's outcast status. This strategy works for Mrs Bennet-Atkinson because the story of Dido and Aeneas, of female victims and male betrayers, shapes the world she navigates; she operates within the narrative constraints allotted her to make meaningful – especially to the Noble Peer, who has clearly internalized the victor/loser binary – the nature of her revenge.

Yet the very existence of Mrs Bennet-Atkinson's character argues for a more complicated approach to the Dido narrative, one that revalues her outcast position. By creating modern-day Didos in Miss Mathews, Amelia, and Mrs Bennet-Atkinson, Fielding insists on escaping the reductive victor/loser binary that had been so lethal to the queen of Carthage in her original epic context. As I have argued, simply remapping classical narratives proves insufficient: Steele's *Spectator* 11 illuminates the helplessness of Arietta's position, for – in turning the tables on the Commonplace Talker, with his story of the Ephesian Matron – her reframing of the Dido-Aeneas episode as Inkle and Yarico still results in Yarico's enslavement, just as Mrs Bennet-Atkinson recasts the Noble Peer in a culturally legible position of defeat. However, Mrs Bennet-Atkinson – and even the transgressive Miss Mathews – experience failure and victory; structurally and figuratively, rape and seduction mark the beginnings, not the ends, of their subplots, and they both go on to live happy lives, thwarting narrative expectations. Although Amelia emerges as perhaps the most traditional heroine in the text – virtuous through and through, capable of heroic agency but also rescued in the nick of time (by a fellow woman, no less) from the Noble Peer's predations – Fielding complicates the notion of a fixed, passive feminine ideal by offering a more expansive vision of female heroism. Miss Mathews anticipates Amelia, who, in turn, anticipates her look-alike, Mrs Bennet-Atkinson, thwarting the reader's attempts to take refuge in reductive binaries of female character.

The narrator's scapegoating of Miss Mathews, Mercury's characterization of Dido in *Aeneid* 4, Booth and Harrison's continued willingness to underestimate Amelia's character, and Harrison's inability to take seriously Mrs Bennet-Atkinson's learning, all reveal the problems of grappling with a legacy that at once precludes the possibility of female heroism and renders predatory and dehumanizing the masculine heroic ideal. Only by fundamentally re-envisioning epic can *Amelia* evade and rewrite the categories of the *Aeneid*: romance provides not only an antidote to epic, but an inclusive, polyglot medium that encourages revision of epic tropes, the creation of a hybrid genre that can accommodate Dido instead of requiring her violent demise. For Fielding, this hybrid takes the form of the novel, a genre closely allied to epic as well as history. Where the *Aeneid* inspires ceaseless Didos, however sympathetic, romance (as Barker's *Exilius* demonstrates so brilliantly), by encouraging repetition with variation in its fundamental structure, can imagine a way out of the Dido problem and into a world where the logic of Virgil's epic (Aeneas vs Dido, Rome vs Carthage) no longer need obtain. The stakes are high: because epic functions as a national genre, *Amelia* at once centralizes Dido's story, women's narratives, and romance historiography at the heart of the eighteenth-century novel as it insists on women as the subjects of national heroism.

Fielding thus advances, in *Amelia,* a new epic model, no less sceptical of the neoclassical element of English culture than of the classical legacy of ancient Rome. Far from requiring the rejection of its heroines, this model places them at the core of the epic. Their inclusion heralds a fundamentally modern and progressive template that self-consciously denies – no doubt rankling *Amelia*'s critics – the masculine aristocratic elitism of the *Aeneid*. In *The Female Quixote* (1752), Charlotte Lennox would continue Fielding's project in the adventures of her heroine, Arabella, whose dedication to the principles of seventeenth-century romance enables her to rewrite defeated heroines into history. For Lennox, too, Cleopatra becomes an emblematic figure, for her originary narrative – the story of the exotic, irrational woman justly defeated by Rome – had consequences not only for her literary incarnation, Dido, but for the subsequent women who would be maligned as Cleopatras in turn.

PART 2

Mythologizing Cleopatra: Romance Historiography and the Queens of Egypt

3 "A Pattern to Ensuing Ages": Reinventing Historical Practice in Charlotte Lennox's *Female Quixote*

In her short-lived periodical venture, the *Lady's Museum* (1760–1), Charlotte Lennox's eidolon – the ironically named Trifler – makes it her mission, as she says, to teach philosophy and history "to the ladies."[1] Mocking women's exclusion from traditionally masculine spheres of knowledge, she deems her female readers better suited to the study of such disciplines. After all, she notes slyly, they are "[u]ndisturbed by the more intricate affairs of business, unburthened with the load of political entanglements; with the anxiety of commercial negotiations; or the suspense and anguish which attend on the pursuit of fame or fortune" (29). According to the Trifler, women – "not being tied down by wearisome attention to mathematical investigations, metaphysical chimeras, or abstruse scholastic learning, are more at liberty to observe with care, see with perspicuity, and judge without prejudice, concerning the amazing world of wonders round them" (130). Her goal is thus to render readers "learned not pedantic, conversable rather than scientific," so that "[i]f therefore we treat of philosophy," she explains, "it shall be polished from the rust of theoretical erudition, and adorned with all those advantages which a connexion with the politer arts and sciences can throw upon it. If of history," she continues,

> a pleasing relation of the most interesting facts shall be endeavoured at, the movement of the grand machine of government shall indeed be set before our readers, and the influence of each apparent wheel be rendered visible: but we shall think it unnecessary to look into every secret spring whereby these wheels were actuated; and shall dispense with entering into the never to be discovered causes of the rise and fall of nations now no more, to make room for the more useful knowledge of those movements of the human heart on which depend the happiness or ruin of individuals. (130–1)

I begin with the *Lady's Museum* because it records, for Lennox's audience, her nonfictional ideas about the nature of history and invites readers to revisit Lennox's historical project elsewhere in her oeuvre. In staking a claim for the "movements of the human heart" in opposition to the subjects of political and military history, the Trifler, I suggest, recalls Arabella, the heroine of Lennox's *Female Quixote* (1752), whose beloved seventeenth-century French romances foreground the "happiness or ruin of individuals" in order to supplement conventional histories. *The Female Quixote* prefigures the objectives of the *Lady's Museum* by giving centre stage to Arabella's romances, which furnish the heroine with an alternative historiographic model that allows her, at once, to expand the canon of classical history and to celebrate a feminocentric republic of letters inspired by the famed Madeleine de Scudéry and the salonnières, and salon culture, of the previous century.

The *Lady's Museum* offers only a glimpse into Lennox's longstanding interest in history.[2] In addition to her translation of the duke of Sully's memoirs (1755), which saw fifteen editions by 1856, Lennox translated *The Memoirs of the Countess of Berci* (1756) and *Memoirs for the History of Madame de Maintenon* (1757); she also produced the first comparative study of Shakespeare's historical and romance sources in *Shakespear Illustrated* (1753–4). In 1759, Lennox was even contemplating an original history of Elizabeth I, for which she consulted the well-known Scottish historian William Robertson. Though not usually considered an appropriate subject for women writers, history was a lucrative genre in the eighteenth century – much more so than the emerging novel – and, as the *Lady's Museum* suggests, was often recommended for readers of both sexes. Though Lennox never styled herself a historian, her astonishing command of the characters and plots of heroic romance, a genre so invested in legitimate history, suggests an abiding interest in questions of gender and genre that exceeded her career as a translator and critic. Even as Lennox established her reputation as a translator, she was also making a name for herself as a novelist, finally achieving fame as author of *The Female Quixote*. No less than the celebrated Samuel Johnson fêted her inaugural work, *The Life of Harriot Stuart, Written by Herself* (1751); Samuel Richardson served as Lennox's literary mentor; and Henry Fielding – no stranger to Cervantes' legacy – favourably praised *The Female Quixote*, her sophomore debut. As a testament to her artistic fame, Lennox would later be commemorated by Sir Joshua Reynolds (1775) and hailed by Richard Samuel as one of the *Nine Living Muses of Great Britain* (1779) alongside Anna Letitia Barbauld, Elizabeth Carter, Elizabeth Griffith, Angelica Kauffman, Elizabeth Linley, Catharine Macaulay, Elizabeth Montagu, and Hannah More (see Figure 3.1).

Figure 3.1. Richard Samuel, *Portraits in the Characters of the Muses in the Temple of Apollo*, 1778. © National Portrait Gallery, London. From left to right: Elizabeth Carter, Anna Letitia Barbauld, Angelica Kauffman, Elizabeth Linley, Catharine Macaulay (seated), Hannah More, Elizabeth Montagu (seated), Charlotte Lennox, Elizabeth Griffith (seated).

In Lennox's most popular novel, she tells the story of a young gentlewoman named Arabella who, like her namesake Don Quixote, is made delusional by romance reading. Raised amid scenes of pastoral fantasy thanks to her father's banishment from court to country, Arabella spends her time sequestered in the marquis's "large and well-furnished" library, where she finds books of legitimate history, such as Temple Stanyan's *Grecian History*, and also her preferred reading material (in very bad translations, laments the narrator), the heroic romances made popular in the previous century by Madeleine de Scudéry and Gauthier de Costes, Seigneur de la Calprenède.[3] Taking refuge in these stories, she resists a life of proper domesticity by aligning herself with the "heroines of antiquity" (44, 186, 277) and touting romance precedents for her unruly behaviour; in a grand display of "heroic disobedience" (27), she refuses, for example, to marry her cousin, Glanville.[4] However, the destabilizing force of Arabella's romances does not proceed unchecked for long.[5] In an abrupt ending, one that sits uneasily with the rest of the novel, we are left with the image of Arabella humbly yielding to Glanville after her conversion at the hands of a learned Divine.[6]

It is fitting that Arabella should discover the legacies of her mother and father side by side, for the relationship between history and fiction had been potent since antiquity: Herodotus's well-regulated universe and Thucydides' long set speeches introduce fictional elements while still laying claim to historical accuracy. The categories of "history" and "fiction" remained entangled, even in some cases indistinguishable, through much of the eighteenth century, first as the properties of "fiction" began to stabilize with the advent of the novel and later as historiographers often borrowed novelistic techniques.[7] As one scholar notes, comparing the historians William Robertson and David Hume to Samuel Richardson and Henry Fielding, the "*History of Scotland* [1759] contained more sensational incidents – kidnappings, disguises, explosions, and poisonings – than all of Lovelace's exploits combined, while Hume's Mary, Queen of Scots, was more promiscuous than Tom Jones."[8] Although, by 1752, Arabella's inability to distinguish between history and fiction furnishes the source of Lennox's satire, Arabella, in taking her romances for historical truth, becomes not unlike "the contemporary [seventeenth-century] reader [who] would not always find so striking a difference between the novels and histories at his disposal."[9] Making matters more complicated, novels such as Scudéry's *Grand Cyrus* referred to contemporary people and events – there is famously a key, now lost – and Scudéry took care to insist on the historical accuracy of her representations and (though not learned in the ancient languages herself) had more than a passing acquaintance with classical literature and history.

In the course of this chapter, I will argue that Arabella's heroic romances become part of a complementary classical canon that at once recovers a variety of heroines from Greek and Roman antiquity and allows Arabella to construct herself, via the intercession of seventeenth-century salon culture, as a potential subject of history. The representational vicissitudes of such heroines, especially the contested figure of Cleopatra, suggest the extent to which history conspires with fiction, and fiction becomes history when culturally authorized. In turning to romance historiography and wholeheartedly embracing the foreignness of her heroines, Arabella unearths the silent corollary to standard histories of Greece and Rome: the experience of empire's so-called losers whom "high" political and military history had largely effaced. In this way, the romances represent a hybrid historical genre, part traditional history – with plenty of battles, sieges, the rise and fall of republics and empires, and the feats of "Great Men" – and part social history, with its emphasis on manners (a favourite subject of seventeenth-century salon culture), affective relations, and the seemingly minor figures who appear only briefly, if at all, in the context of "high" history.[10]

I note this hybridity because it is crucial to Lennox's project of trying to imagine a genre that can commemorate female heroism without violating standards of feminine propriety. This is the objection, of course, of the Countess, one of the characters who fail to effect Arabella's cure and whose conformity to the dictates of domestic realism sits at odds with romance's drive towards adventure. Social history constructed itself against high history by offering a different point of access to the past, one that was often seen as more appropriate for and attractive to female readers.[11] Yet even social history, with its ostensibly more feminine concerns, cannot accommodate Arabella's desire for heroic glory: almost all of Arabella's elite classical heroines participate in the alternative high history of romance, with military and political sway of their own. In her discussion of *The Female Quixote*, Catherine Gallagher makes a compelling case for the novel's attempts to stabilize its identity by, in part, defining itself against "a rival genre with a claim on the 'real' – scandal," so that scapegoating scandal in turn allows Lennox to depict "the innocent romance writer" as "merely insufficiently attentive to the distinction between history and fiction."[12] I suggest, by contrast, that this formulation misses the attractions of romance for Lennox, Arabella, and the reader.[13] Instead, I argue that Lennox, in turning to a genre that had legitimate claims to historical truth, actively embraces an intermediary form – part high political and military history, part social history – that provides Arabella with a frame for achieving the renown she desires, and that the elision between fiction and history is necessary, given the available generic options, to conceive of such a form.

Of course, in following in the footsteps of its namesake, *Don Quixote*, Lennox's novel is manifestly satirical, finding humour in Arabella's delusions while also casting her contemporaries in an unflattering light. Yet Lennox similarly follows Cervantes in giving serious weight to the quixote's romance ideals, however incompatible they may be with present circumstances. For Arabella's romance exemplars, available historiographic models have failed. Tradition has reduced the poet Sappho to a symbol of tragic love, and Julia, the daughter of Augustus, to a figure of scandal. It has transformed Clelia and Lucretia into ciphers for the Roman Republic, divesting their acts of personal agency. It has altogether obscured the lives of Statira and Parisatis, and has done nothing but propound the infamy of well-known figures such as Cleopatra. Thus anticipating the condemnation of historiographic practices dramatized so compellingly in Sarah Fielding's *Lives of Cleopatra and Octavia* (1757), Arabella emphasizes romance's historicity even as other characters insist on their own versions of historical "truth." Unsurprisingly, for Arabella as for Fielding, Cleopatra becomes an important symbol in the conflict between romance and history: identifying not only with the notorious queen, but with her daughter, Cleopatra VIII (Cleopatra Selene II), Arabella herself becomes a metaphorical child of the unruly woman who threatened the Roman Empire. In this way, the allusive presence of Cleopatra in the novel fully realizes the stakes of Arabella's romance reading. Even as she attempts to invoke Cleopatra as a model heroine, male characters recognize only the Egyptian "whore" (105), revealing the limits of historical discourse for all women, not simply Arabella. Because returning to Cleopatra – as Barker and Henry Fielding had returned, in *Exilius* and *Amelia*, to her fictional counterpart, Dido – is to return to narrative origins, romance celebrates an offshoot of the existing historical tradition that makes possible other kinds of history. Relying on the seemingly fabulous, yet historical, texts made popular by the seventeenth-century heroic novel, Lennox distinguishes between men's romance – the scandalous tales of women that become legitimate history – and the correctives that Arabella inherits from Scudéry and La Calprenède, thus highlighting the blurred boundaries between fiction and the emerging discipline of history. For these reasons, it is important to note, as I argue later in this chapter, that

Arabella's achievement relies on her allegiance to the Moderns, not the Ancients: only modernity can celebrate heroines like Statira and Cleopatra as proper subjects of history.

In evoking the Augustan mythology that transforms Cleopatra from the politically savvy ruler of Egypt to an exotic and seductive queen, Lennox's male characters draw, if unwittingly, on the afterlife of Virgil's epic. The *Aeneid* had similarly transformed Dido – the star of her own foundation narrative – into the lovesick queen of Carthage whose legacy would prove so fatal to ancient Rome; it similarly inscribed Cleopatra as a barbarian ruler doomed to succumb to Roman supremacy. In this way, the translation of Dido from Phoenician myth to Virgilian romance echoes the translation of Cleopatra from history to propaganda, and at the same time naturalizes the history that marked Cleopatra's defeat. According to the logic of the *Aeneid,* long before Egypt's subordination to Rome, Dido's mythic capitulation to Aeneas's narrative makes inevitable Augustus's triumph and attendant rewriting of history. In seizing on the figure of Cleopatra, Lennox thus makes explicit the historical stakes of the Dido narrative already grasped so well by Barker and Fielding. Where Barker and Fielding take up the mythmaking potential of Cleopatra's literary counterpart, *The Female Quixote* stages Cleopatra's legacy at the crossroads of fiction and history, romance and classical reception. The circulation of multiple Cleopatras – at once virtuous heroine and artful gypsy – allows Lennox and her readers to rethink the very meaning of history, especially for marginalized subjects. In doing so, she anticipates not only Sarah Fielding's exploration of the limits of biography for female characters, virtuous and scandalous alike, but also Clara Reeve's vindication of romance in her 1785 literary history. *The Female Quixote,* in staging the antagonism between romance and history, between male authorities and feminine genres, offers its own literary history in novel form, one that registers the hostility to romance even as it highlights romance's centrality to the developing novel, making visible the debates that authorize both history and fiction.[14]

In this way, Lennox's turn to Cleopatra, from epic mythology to history, demonstrates the fundamental complicity of both genres. Insofar as epic and history are synonymous categories, both Dido and Cleopatra must be consigned to defeat and to the dilatory world of epic's losers. Although the ancient collusion between epic and history may have been uncoupled by the Moderns, the damage to Cleopatra – and to women like her – had already been done. In *The Female Quixote*, the seventeenth-century romance provides an antidote to the Virgilian narrative that reduces Dido to a star-crossed lover, and Cleopatra (and Arabella's other heroines) to subsidiary figures whose narratives can only be accommodated as sexual scandal at the margins of history. The heroic romance establishes a liminal space between literature (Dido) and history (Cleopatra), a conscious blending of fact and fiction that counters a series of well-known stories encoded as cultural truths. The romances of Scudéry and La Calprenède, as inheritors of the Heliodoran tradition that positioned itself against Homeric epic, thus furnish a stepping-stone to the eighteenth-century novel in the form of *The Female Quixote* itself. Indeed, to the extent that Arabella's romance world view fails, unable fully to escape the same hierarchies that render classical epic and history so problematic for *The Female Quixote*'s readers, Lennox's literary endeavour suggests the comparative success of the novel as a viable form. If, for the seventeenth-century romances of Scudéry and La Calprenède, there can be no truly radical rewriting of history, romance and the eighteenth-century novel combine to exceed romance's limitations. If Arabella's response to traditional narratives is at times too conservative, invoking familiar paradigms in a romance context, then Lennox's is far more radical, suggesting the potential for a new literary-historiographic legacy in the novel itself.

"But for the famous Scudéry": Reviving Classical Precedents

The heroic romances that Arabella inherits from her mother rival the histories enshrined in her father's library. Like earlier texts, suppressed or erased, the works of Scudéry and La Calprenède compete with "legitimate" history, bleeding through a palimpsest of officially authorized narratives that attempt to discredit alternative accounts as irrational and absurd. From its origins, the French romance insisted on its historicity, exploiting lacunae in the historical record in order to foreground narratives silenced by traditional histories. Based, for example, on texts such as Herodotus's *Historiae* and Livy's *Ab Urbe Condita*, the seventeenth-century French romance at once traced its lineage to the very inception of history itself, and also to the Greek romances of Heliodorus (third century CE), whose *Aithiopika*, or Ethiopian Story – a genre that competed with Homeric epic – enjoyed enormous popularity in the early modern era, as well as in the eighteenth century, thanks to the rediscovery and revival of Heliodorus's novel.[15] In France as in England, fiction took shape alongside the emerging genre of history in ways that underscored the inextricability of history and fiction: as a result, Thomas DiPiero notes, the "comparison of different forms of prose incited critical reflection on the ideological stances adopted in history, a genre which most people had considered virtually above reproach because it had been handed down from the ancients." From this perspective, "the new novel form explicitly revealed the narrative construction of truth, and it suggested in the process new means for fashioning it."[16]

Of course, to someone as well versed in her father's books as in her mother's, the supplementary nature of Arabella's beloved romances would have been self-evident. It is little wonder, then, that Arabella finds herself constantly vexed by her companions' apparent poverty of understanding (though, aside from Glanville, their knowledge of antiquity is no better). She takes umbrage at Sir Charles's cursory denouncement of the "finest Productions in the World" (61) when he classifies romances as mere "fairy tales," relegating them to children's literature (and aligning women with children). She politely insists, "we are infinitely obliged to these Authors, who have, in so sublime a Style, delivered down to Posterity the heroic Actions of the bravest Men, and most virtuous of Women," continuing, "But for the inimitable Pen of the famous *Scudery*, we had been ignorant of the Lives of many great and illustrious Persons" (61). The "illustrious Persons" of whom Arabella speaks are forgotten heroines, "those fair and chaste Ladies, who were the Objects of [heroes'] pure and constant Passions, [and] had still been buried in Obscurity [were it not for Scudéry]; and neither their divine Beauties, or singular Virtue, been the Subject of our Admiration and Praise." She then goes on to name specific women worthy of emulation and commemoration:

> But for the famous *Scudery*, we had not known the true Cause of that Action of *Clelia*'s, for which the Senate decreed her a Statue; namely, Her casting herself with an unparalleled Courage, into the *Tyber*, a deep and rapid River, as you must certainly know, and swimming to the other Side. It was not, as the *Roman* Historians falsly report, a Stratagem to recover herself, and the other Hostages, from the Power of *Porsena*; it was to preserve her Honour from Violation by the impious *Sextus*, who was in the Camp. But for *Scudery*, we had still thought the inimitable Poetess *Sappho* to be a loose Wanton, whose Verses breathed nothing but unchaste

> and irregular Fires: On the contrary, she was so remarkably chaste, that she would never even consent to marry; but, loving *Phaon*, only with a Platonic Passion, obliged him to restrain his Desires within the Compass of a Brother's Affection. Numberless are the Mistakes he has cleared up of this Kind; and I question, if any other Historian, but himself, knew that *Cleopatra* was really married to *Julius Caesar*; or that *Caesario*, her Son by this Marriage, was not murdered, as was supposed, by the Order of *Augustus*, but married the fair Queen of *Ethiopia*, in whose Dominions he took Refuge. The prodigious Acts of Valour, which he has recounted of those accomplished Princes, have never been equaled by the Heroes of either the *Greek* or *Roman* Historians: How poor and insignificant are the Actions of their Warriors to *Scudery*'s, where one of those admirable Heroes would put whole Armies into Terror, and with his single Arm oppose a Legion! (61–2)[17]

All of the women whom Arabella mentions – Clelia, Sappho, Cleopatra VII – are historical figures left largely in obscurity until valorized by romance. Whereas, in traditional Roman histories, Clelia's daring escape from her captors is met with orders to return as a hostage to Porsenna so as not to tarnish the reputation of Rome,[18] Scudéry presents a different picture, in which Clelia does not scheme to devise a "stratagem to recover herself" but to protect her virtue from a tyrant. As we will see, her story serves as a parallel to the unfortunate Lucretia's, whose history Scudéry magnifies beyond Livy's brief relation, where it serves primarily to engender outrage against the Tarquins rather than admiration for Lucretia's virtue. Just as Arabella defends Clelia, she also champions the chaste reputations of Sappho and Cleopatra: these women were not wantons and whores, but virtuous matrons whose desires were circumscribed by an ennobling and completely respectable love. Arabella's defensiveness reveals her awareness of the heroines' treatment in traditional histories, and of the bias that reproduces such narratives with remarkable predictability. Issuing a direct challenge to classical heroism, she pits the warriors of romance antiquity against those of ancient historians, claiming that the actions of "*their* Warriors" are "insignificant" by comparison (61–2; emphasis added). In this way, Arabella redefines proper heroic action as motivated by love, not martial glory, and, in turn, opens the possibility for extending heroic respectability to female characters whose association with *eros* had traditionally consigned them to the realms of scandal.

In doing so, she credits Scudéry for this historical intervention, conflating Scudéry (*Clelia*, *The Grand Cyrus*) and La Calprenède (*Cassandra*, *Cleopatra*), thanks, no doubt, to Scudéry's mastery of the heroic novel and, in particular, the feminocentric legacy of her literary career. A point often overlooked by critics because of their understandable lack of familiarity with Arabella's reading, "romance" is not a static category but a complex signifier: from 1640 to 1660, Scudéry's works evolved as a result of La Calprenède's success, and vice versa, illustrating the dialogic creation of an expansive, inclusive tradition that actively sought to reinvent itself in response to changing social and economic circumstances and to the desires of its readership.

Despite their similarities, these romances espouse very different ethical systems, for the values of heroic romance change over time, thanks to the feminizing impulse of French salon culture and the accompanying popularity of Scudéry's refined depictions of heroic love that privileged the art of conversation over military prowess. The enormous success of the fiercely militaristic *Cassandra* (1642–5) influences Scudéry's *Grand Cyrus* (1649–53), whose popular refinement of heroic love in turn softens La Calprenède's *Cleopatra* (1648–58) and reaches its finest expression in Scudéry's subsequent romance, *Clelia* (1654–60, known as *Clélie* in French and *Clœlia* in Latin). In this way, it becomes possible to chart the evolution of Arabella's understanding of heroic romance from the essentially epic model of La Calprenède, with its fundamentally inequitable relationship between heroines and heroes, to the more familiar, egalitarian romance template crafted by Scudéry;[19] from "aristocratic individualism rooted in love and pride" to "those virtues in the heroic spectrum that raise the hero above his fellow men to those that bind him more closely to them – kindness, loyalty to friends, sympathy" as well as "liberality and modesty."[20]

Following in the footsteps of Homeric and Virgilian epic, the *Cassandra* advances glory over love: not unlike Hector and Achilles, La Calprenède's heroes devote themselves to their heroic reputations first and foremost, despite their romantic entanglements. Yet La Calprenède alters this model in the *Cleopatra*, where love takes centre stage, superseding heroic glory in importance, with a corresponding softening of the heroes. Responding to historical circumstances, the *Cleopatra* thus "reflects," as Mark Bannister has noted, "the less warlike atmosphere of the period following the end of the Fronde, [or] when the virtues of the warrior were coming to be less highly regarded and when strongly feminist views were being heard in the salons."[21] The success of the

Grand Cyrus makes possible this shift between the *Cassandra*-like opening books and subsequent volumes. In her famous novel, Scudéry created "an alternative interpretation of the values of heroism, redefined in accordance with the kind of world in which the stories are set, namely a refined circle of courtiers, dominated by the female characters, in which the encounters are verbal and emotional rather than physical," where "[s]ocial graces" are "more important than a martial air."[22] As Bannister remarks, "In *Clélie*, the process reaches its completion: the form is still retained but little attempt is made to hide the fact that the heroic element has become an empty convention."[23] In less than a decade, Scudéry reshaped the romance landscape, ushering in a new brand of heroism – and a new relationship between heroine and hero – that challenged and supplanted earlier models.

Renowned throughout Europe, Madeleine de Scudéry (1607–1701) was one of the most famous writers of the seventeenth century; although she published anonymously or under the name of her brother, Georges, her true identity was an open secret. One of the first women writers to earn her living by the pen, Scudéry enjoyed translation into English, Italian, Spanish, German, and Arabic and, to the chagrin of male critics, remained popular well into the eighteenth and even nineteenth centuries. As Karen Newman writes in her introduction to the scholarly edition of *The Story of Sapho*, a crucial episode from *The Grand Cyrus* that stages the importance of female authorship and mentoring in Scudéry's work,

> Contemporary readers were apparently willing to pay for single sheets before an entire print run was completed, booksellers inflated their profits by dividing her ten-volume *Clélie* into even smaller sections and selling them separately; English readers across the channel managed to secure the last volumes of perhaps her most popular novel, *Artamène; ou, Le grand Cyrus*, (1649–53) within weeks of its publication even in the midst of the French civil uprising known as the Fronde.[24]

Praised (and later reviled) for her heroic romances, especially the magisterial *Grand Cyrus* and the notorious *Clélie*, Scudéry also championed women in *Les Femmes illustres* (1642), otherwise known as *Famous Women, or Heroic Speeches*, and further argued for women's equality in *Conversations morales* (1686) and *Nouvelles conversations de morale* (1688), which revolutionized the form of the conversation by showcasing women's social and rhetorical power. By 1654, her fame was such that she inaugurated her own salon, known as *les Samedies*, and thus joined the ranks of other famous salonnières, including the Marquise de Rambouillet (whose salon she had also frequented), Mademoiselle de Montpensier, Madame de La Fayette, and the inner circle of Anne of Austria, the queen regent. Described as "an important voice in countering the misogyny of the period through her portraits of strong, intelligent, talkative women in her novels, speeches, and conversational dialogues," Scudéry provoked controversy among the critical establishment.[25] No text was more controversial than *Clelia*, with its infamous *Carte de Tendre*, a visual record of the amorous landscape Clelia's companions must navigate. "[R]epeated, and amplified, for decades," these attacks "prov[ed] with each reformulation that French society was still able to conceive of Scudéry's new woman as a social ideal."[26] So popular was Scudéry's romance that Perdou de Subligny wrote the *Mock-Clelia*, translated into English in 1678; after Scudéry's death, the French critic Nicolas Boileau (both royal historiographer and "lawmaker of Parnassus") staged the ritual killing of her heroes in his *Dialogue des héros de roman* (1710); and the Jesuit Father Porée condemned *Clelia* as the consummate example of the dangers of novel reading (1736).

Scudéry achieved fame at an unusual moment in history, during a time of political upheaval in which the disintegration of the social fabric during the civil war enabled women to carve a place for themselves as the New Amazons and *femmes fortes* of French culture. Although salon culture, inspired by Castiglione's *Book of the Courtier*, first began to take shape in the sixteenth century, under Catherine de' Médicis (the queen mother and regent of France), Queen Marguerite de Navarre, and other members of the nobility, it gained traction in the seventeenth century during the regency of Anne of Austria (1643–61) while Louis XIV was still in his minority. As Marianne Legault notes in *Female Intimacies in Seventeenth-Century French Literature*, this historical moment "witnesses the blossoming of a lexical, intellectual, and social movement in which women became the sovereign rulers: the *précieux* movement." "The *précieux* movement," she explains, "emerges partly out of the need of a few women to react against the vulgar mores of the French court by using a new lexicon, and also from the necessity to fight patriarchal oppression both philosophically and through literature. It is most definitely a grouping created by women and for women – a true feminocentric movement."[27] Legault goes further still, proclaiming it "first and foremost feminist in its essence since its goal was for women to regain full recognition of their merit that, since the start of the *Querelle des femmes* [or the debate surrounding the "woman question"] around 1400, had been strongly under attack, even literally derided, in various misogynistic literary discourses."[28] Although the first part of the century saw a tradition of literary heroism dominated by male romancers, the political upheaval of the Fronde (1648–53), in which aristocrats sought to restore their traditional privileges and to limit the power of the monarchy, engendered a kind of new world order. As Joan DeJean reminds us, "Both the modern French novel and the French tradition of women's writing came into existence during and just after a period of the kind of extreme political turbulence in which extraordinary things become possible." Aristocratic women took on active, even military roles: "At the end of the 1640s, the *femme forte* was surpassed in history, and amazons actually did seem to walk the earth in France."[29]

The figure of the *femme forte* – the so-called strong or heroic woman – rose to prominence in the 1640s, celebrated in numerous biographies and catalogues of illustrious women from antiquity through the present time. These biographies featured women "distinguished by their capacity for political or military leadership," adapting a vocabulary "created to characterize a nearly legendary foreign past to the depiction of contemporary French women."[30] Of these, Pierre Le Moyne's *Galerie des femmes fortes* (1647) enjoyed unprecedented popularity.[31] Prior to this incarnation of the "heroic woman," the Amazons of the 1620s through 1640s served as male projections of female heroism – much as they had in antiquity, where the Amazon poses an alien threat to the Greek male citizen, and exists only to be defeated in an Amazonomachy. The craze for Amazons gave way to real-life representations, designed to celebrate female aristocrats such as the Comtesse de Saint-Baslemont, represented triumphantly on horseback, outfitted in masculine costume, by Claude Deruet (c. 1640). As Joan DeJean explains, Saint-Baslemont takes centre stage because of the reproducibility of her image. *Le Mercure français*, one of the first French periodicals, mass-produced an engraving of her portrait, so that, "For the first time ever in France, representations of a real-life Amazon had been put into a type of circulation that was as public as it was conceivable at that time." The Amazon then became a prolific symbol in the "new iconography of female heroic daring," one that transcended the visual arts and became a print phenomenon, collecting portraits of women in "galeries" such as Le Moyne's.[32]

Here, too, Scudéry proved herself a generic innovator: although Le Moyne's compilation was the most famous of its kind, Scudéry had already helped to fashion the discourse of the heroic woman with *Les Femmes illustres, ou les harangues héroique* in 1642 (see Figures 3.2–3.4).

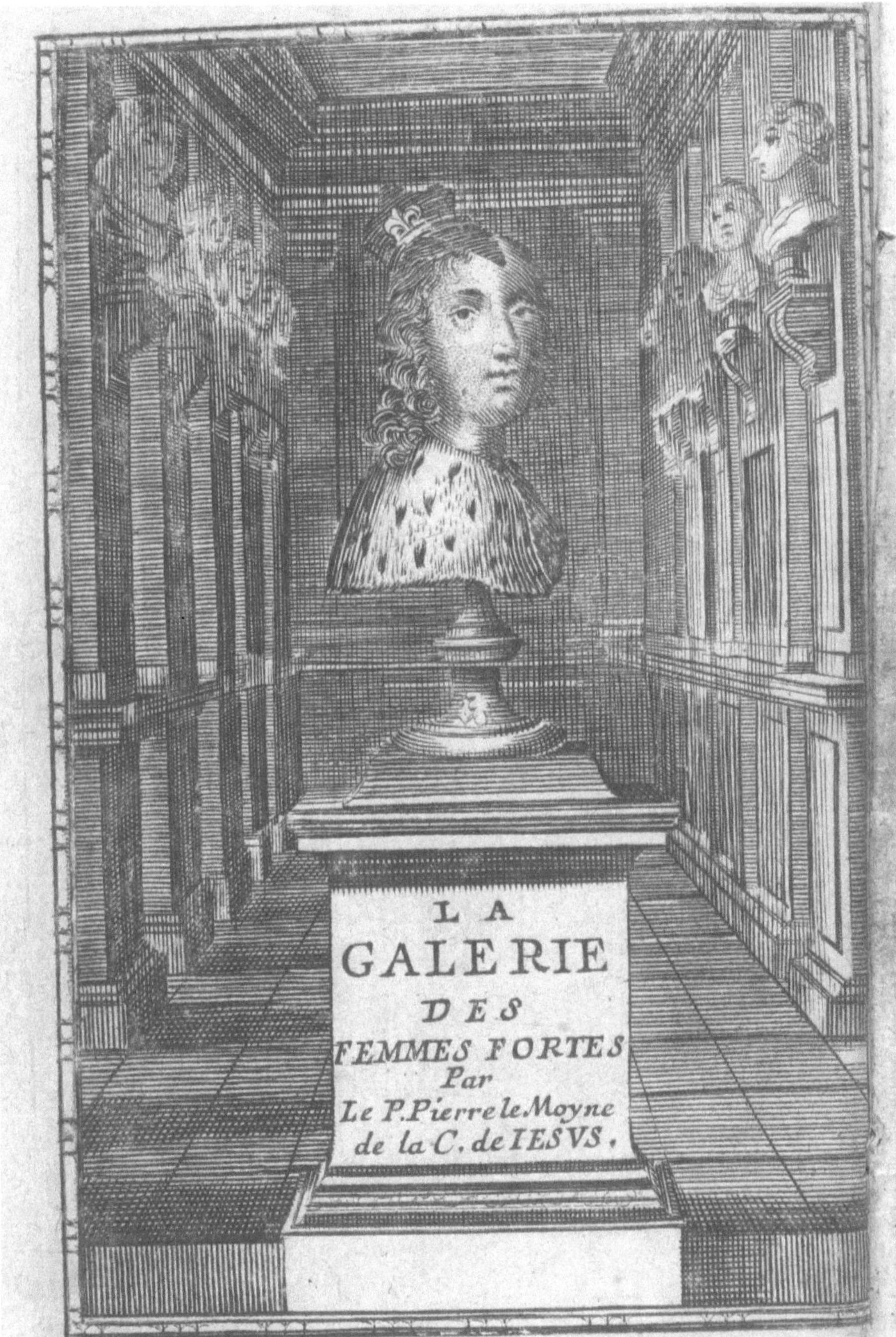

Figure 3.2. From Pierre Le Moyne's *Galerie des femmes fortes* (1647). Image courtesy of the Henry E. Huntington Library and Art Gallery, San Marino, California.

Figure 3.3. From Pierre Le Moyne's *Galerie des femmes fortes* (1647). Image courtesy of the Henry E. Huntington Library and Art Gallery, San Marino, California.

Figure 3.4. From Madeleine de Scudéry's *Femmes illustres*, inscribed "To the Glory of the [Female] Sex" (1642). Image courtesy of the Henry E. Huntington Library and Art Gallery, San Marino, California.

In her study of famed women from history, she sets forth the examples of twenty different heroines, ten in each volume, each example consisting of an opening argument, a speech by the heroine, and a concluding effect. Scudéry's presentation is unusual in that she privileges the first-person narration of the women themselves. These are no Ovidian heroines, lamenting, as they do in the *Heroides*, their pitiful mistreatment and abandonment at the hands of male heroes. Instead, Scudéry's *femmes illustres* provide a series of factual correctives that, like the romances themselves, supplement traditional history: the harangues "do not seek to reproduce the historical narrative, but rather to explore its gaps and fissures, to give voice to silent interstices. The shift in point of view, favouring women, brings to the foreground what history unusually confines to the background, or ignores altogether."[33] Taking advantage of her heroines' position on the cusp of public and private life, *Les Femmes illustres* amounts to nothing less than "an action-oriented call to contemporary women to repeat the glorious exploits of their predecessors."[34] Scudéry returned to many of these heroines in her romances, unfolding, over the course of thousands of pages – in some of the longest works ever written in any language – the heroic possibilities they represented.

Amazons and Cleopatras

Following the exile of real-life Amazons after the Fronde, women writers like Scudéry turned their attention towards the literary endeavours of salon culture. In doing so, part of Scudéry's project was to translate the heroic conversations of novels like *The Grand Cyrus* for the new, feminocentric republic of letters known as the salon. Published in works such as *Conversations sur divers sujets* (1680) and *Nouvelles conversations sur divers sujets* (1684), these conversations served as models for polite and egalitarian sociability. Inherited from humanism, the form of the conversation, like the form of the oration represented in *Les Femmes illustres*, created a space for "women writers across Europe [to argue] for the equality of women's intellect and the necessity of education for women. These forms, as humanists practiced them, were especially amenable to these purposes because of their position straddling the boundary of private and public."[35] Scudéry teaches that "Reading is necessary to refine intelligence, regulate morals, and strengthen judgment," and Lennox showcases the extent to which Arabella owes her own conversational excellence to Scudéry's works.[36] Though Glanville assumes, without having read Arabella's romances, that they are written "upon the most trifling Subjects imaginable" (49), these are the very texts that nurture her superior understanding: her censure of "the ill-judged Raillery of the young Beau [Tinsel]" as "very dangerous and unpleasing" (267) earns Sir Charles's admiration and the compliment that she "speak[s] like an Orator" (269); Sir Charles declares that "she would have made a great Figure in Parliament, and that her Speeches might have come to be printed in Time" (311), and similarly acknowledges that she "was a very sensible young Lady, and sometimes talk'd as learnedly as a Divine" (314).

At these moments and others, Lennox involves Arabella in her rhetorical project: in her critique of indifference, for example, she echoes Scudéry's conversation on the same topic; in her declamation against raillery – which earns so much praise from her companions – Arabella owes an obvious debt to *The Grand Cyrus*, whose speech on the same subject also appeared in *Conversations sur divers sujets*.[37] No less a model conversationalist than an aspiring heroine, Arabella learns from her romance reading how to excel in social discourse in ways that become a potential model for participating in a larger republic of letters. Scudéry's discourse on the art of conversation, "On Speaking Too Much or Too Little, and How to Speak Well," explains that a "rational woman" should speak "agreeably." In other words:

> [A]ll her expressions are at once noble and natural; she does not hunt around for something to say; there is no hesitation in her words; her discourse is clear and easy; there is a gentle turn in her manner of speaking, no affectation in the sound of her voice, a great deal of freedom in her movement, and a wonderful coherence between her eyes and her words that contributes a great deal to making her speech more agreeable.[38]

Like Scudéry's heroines, Arabella values a "pleasing Variety of Conversation" (149). She enjoys such "rational Entertainment" as discussing the ancients with Glanville (83); indeed, her interest in antiquity is so reliable that Glanville can purposefully mention Greek history in order to "engross her Conversation, for two Hours, wholly to himself" (83). Impressing Glanville with the strength of her understanding, she speaks eloquently of the Olympic Games (81–3), indicating her familiarity with Temple Stanyan's *Grecian History*.[39] Yet, more often than not, Arabella finds herself "disgusted" by the "insipid Discourse" (361) of her contemporaries, especially her female companions, a lament also voiced in Scudéry. If "the usual Topicks of Conversation among young Ladies" amount to "their Winnings and Losings at *Brag*, the Prices of Silks, the newest Fashions, the best Hair-Cutter, the Scandal at the last Assembly, &c." (361), Arabella longs for the art of conversation perfected in heroic romance. Extolling its virtues to a sceptical Glanville, she "beesech[es]" him:

> [R]eflect a little upon those numerous and long Conversations, which these Subjects [of Beauty and Love, in this case] have given Rise to in *Clelia*, and the *Grand Cyrus*, where the most illustrious and greatest Personages in the World manage the Disputes; and the agreeable Diversity of their Sentiments on those Heads affords a most pleasing and rational Entertainment: You will there find, that the greatest Conquerors, and Heroes of invincible Valour, reason with the most exact and scrupulous Nicety upon Love and Beauty. (149–50)

For Arabella, conversational excellence is a necessary characteristic of the model hero: "What room, I pray you, does a Lady give for high and noble Adventures, who consumes her Days in Dressing, Dancing, listening to Songs, and ranging the Walks with People as thoughtless as herself? Nor can I persuade myself," she continues, "that any of those Men whom I saw in the Assembly, with Figures so feminine, Voices so soft, such tripping Steps, and unmeaning Gestures, have ever signalized either their Courage or Constancy; but might be overcome by their Enemy in Battle, or be false to their Mistress in Love" (279). Miss Glanville, aghast, replies, "Do you expect that Persons of Quality, and fine Gentlemen, will go to the Wars? What Business have they to fight? That belongs to the Officers" (279). "How," Arabella responds, "would so many glorious Battles have been fought, Cities taken, Ladies rescu'd, and other great and noble Adventures been atchiev'd, if the Men, sunk in Sloth and Effeminacy, had continually follow'd the Sound of a Fiddle, saunter'd in Publick Walks, and tattled over a Tea-table?" (280).[40] In this way, Arabella's reading elevates her concerns above ordinary talk of "Fashions, Assemblies, Cards, or Scandal" (68), causing Glanville to reflect that "the Strength of her Understanding; her lively Wit; the Sweetness of her Temper, and a Thousand amiable Qualities ... distinguished her from the rest of her Sex," so that even her "Follies, when opposed to all those Charms of Mind and Person, seemed inconsiderable and weak" (117).

Turning the keen judgment encouraged by her romance reading to the defence of maligned heroines such as Thalestris, Cleopatra, and Julia, Arabella challenges the scandalous perceptions of these women that appear to serve as legitimate history's stock in trade. For example, Arabella's debate with Glanville over the fate of Thalestris, queen of the Amazons, brings into stark relief the necessity of advancing romance alternatives to the familiar tales enshrined by classical learning. Glanville epitomizes the conflict between classical and romance traditions when he asks Arabella, "But, Madam ... pray what became of this Queen of the *Amazons*? Was she not killed at the Siege of *Troy*?" Arabella replies, "She never was at the Siege of *Troy* ... But she assisted the Princes who besieged *Babylon*, to recover the Liberty of *Statira* and *Parisatis*: And it was in the opposite Party that she met with her faithless Lover" (126). Whereas Glanville takes his history from Apollodorus and the *Iliad*, a tradition that essentially silenced the Amazon myth, Arabella refers to the *Cassandra* to bring that myth to life again.[41] Where epic commemorates the powerful queen's death at the hand of Achilles as she fought against Greek oppressors during the Trojan War, the romance version offers a different legacy, marked by victory and faithful sisterhood. Glanville's "history" is no more reliable than Arabella's, but it illustrates the costs of preferring a tradition that enshrines a masculine, martial ethos incompatible with heroic femininity.

Despite the ends to which writers historically deployed the figure of the Amazon – and, as I noted earlier, Amazons existed, as figments of the Greek imagination, only to be conquered – Arabella exalts Thalestris as a heroic and virtuous queen: where men create Amazons as ciphers for difference and imperial violence, Arabella lauds Thalestris' exemplarity. Moreover, like the romances that tell the Amazons' stories, she reclaims the queen's potential historicity – a stark contrast to Greek culture, according to which "the Amazons could not be accommodated in the regular realm of history, where men were unquestionably assumed to be the agents of culture and politics." Instead, the classicist Josine Blok argues, "they were assigned a space of their own, a niche carved out from the past, beyond the boundaries of history and myth."[42] Arabella recovers the Amazons as ancient representations of femininity, insisting on their existence as models inside culture and history – even for well-bred Englishwomen like herself. Indeed, one of the senses of a "female quixote" was "a woman daring enough to tilt at the landmarks of masculine authority or educational privilege and, in the process, to become a person neither entirely masculine nor traditionally feminine."[43] Although Miss Glanville shudders at the thought of encountering such "a very masculine Sort of Creature" (125), Arabella argues that a woman's ability to equal – or surpass – the skills, honour, and bravery of the best of men is still entirely feminine. Thalestris serves as a female exemplar who confounds easy distinctions between men and women, "high" history and social history, and therefore enlarges the available template for subsequent heroines.[44]

Lending support to Arabella's defence of the "famous Scudéry," Lennox foregrounds the figures of Cleopatra (VII and VIII) and Julia, the daughter of Augustus, throughout her heroine's "adventures"; they play crucial, though nearly invisible, roles in the text, symbolizing the narrative fate of women who cannot relate their own histories. For example, when Arabella attempts to justify, to an anonymous gentleman, her surprising appearance so far from home, she cites Parthenissa and Cleopatra as precedents. Although he has never heard of Parthenissa, he confesses, "nor do I remember to have heard of any more than one *Cleopatra*: But she was never ravished, I am certain; for she was too willing" (105). When Arabella, taken aback, responds, "How! ... Was *Cleopatra* ever willing to run away with her Ravisher?" he replies, "*Cleopatra* was a Whore, was she not Madam?" Arabella, in turn, commands him to hold his peace, and "profane not the Memory of that fair and glorious Queen, by such injurious Language: That Queen, I say, whose Courage was equal to her Beauty; and her Virtue surpassed by neither." According to codes of heroic sisterhood, the gentleman's betrayal of Cleopatra's memory functions as a betrayal of Arabella: "Good Heavens!" she exclaims, "What a black Defamer have I chosen for my Protector!" (105). Arabella knows too well that a man who believes a woman "willingly ravished" will either not defend her or believe her unworthy of defending; either way, his harsh judgment of Cleopatra signals a heroic failure.[45] Just a short while later, Arabella will explicitly articulate this failure in her rebuke: "by the Calumnies you have uttered against a Person of that Sex which merits all your Admiration and Reverence ... I hold you very unfit to be a Protector of any of it" (107). As it turns out, he does not even recognize the Cleopatra to whom Arabella refers; she invokes Cleopatra VII's daughter, not the infamous lover of Antony and Caesar, but it is all the same to the gentleman and, indeed, to Glanville, who clumsily attempts to defend Cleopatra's reputation while making the same mistake.[46] In this way, romances celebrate stories that can only be told in such a capacious medium, for – as long, at least, as current generic definitions prevail – Arabella's heroines will never be commemorated in epic or valorized in history, the genres reserved for history's victors.

Arabella's interchange with the historian Mr Selvin follows a similar pattern, demonstrating the translation of casual prejudice into (un)official history. When Arabella appears wearing a dress fashioned after the style of the Roman Julia, Selvin exclaims that she injures herself by the comparison, yet Arabella contends, "I never heard Licentiousness imputed to the Daughter of *Augustus Caesar*," and denies his hyperbolic statement that she was "the most abandon'd Prostitute in *Rome*" (272–3).[47] Selvin finally admits defeat, "not daring to contradict a Lady whose extensive Reading had furnish'd her with Anecdotes unknown almost to any Body else" (273). Even as Selvin's deferential response to Arabella's learning furnishes much of the moment's humour, it also raises a number of serious questions that prevent the reader from too long amusing herself at Arabella's expense. Lennox uses the debate between Arabella and Selvin to contest basic understandings of fiction and history, without necessarily ridiculing Arabella's romances. Selvin emerges as a foolish character not because of his rigorous adherence to the "masculine" ancients, but because of his desire to "collect" bits of ancient history, to show off his scholarly knowledge of antiquity, and to affect far more learning than he comprehends or possesses. Arabella, by contrast, exhibits none of these boastful qualities. Nor is the quality of her knowledge the same as Selvin's, for, as I have argued, she is apparently well read in history in addition to her fictionalized romances.

In this way, it is significant that, in the Battle of the Books, Arabella falls on the side of the Moderns, not the Ancients. Although critics often place her in the latter category, thanks to her interest in reviving "past" manners, the position that Arabella occupies can only be articulated from within a place of modernity, with the full knowledge of the subjectivity she seeks through (modern) romance precedents.[48] Those precedents, though they recall the works of historians such as Herodotus, Livy, and Plutarch, are emphatically not classical texts; hence Arabella's pointed turn to the heroic romance to complement her knowledge of Greco-Roman antiquity. Although the romances relate classical histories, their ability to do so is entirely contingent on the specific circumstances of their seventeenth-century production. To the extent that Arabella expresses nostalgia – another common error in the criticism – she expresses nostalgia, more properly, for the French salon culture of the previous century, a culture that foregrounded women's literary talents and interests; precisely the tradition, in other words, whose legacy the Divine attempts to efface at the end of the text. This distinction is crucial. There can be no nostalgia for a classical past that never existed, and can only exist, in modernity, through the medium of romance; traditional political and military history would render Arabella, no less than Julia or Cleopatra, a scandalous figure at the margins of history, if it bothered to represent her at all. To be sure, this is exactly the dynamic – inherited from classical history – that *The Female Quixote* replicates, as we have seen: recasting Arabella as "mad," it seeks to "cure" her, and, should that fail, entertains the prospect of confining her to a madhouse where her multiplicity of perspectives will no longer threaten to reveal the high price, for women and other outsiders, of traditional histories. Arabella's historiographic model, though inspired by Scudéry, represents an innovative neoclassicism that emphatically breaks with past narratives, both romance and historical. It is worth remembering, too, that Scudéry herself was roundly criticized in the Battle of the Books, known in France as the *Querelle des Anciens and des Modernes*: Boileau saw Scudéry's novels as an attack on the ancient heroic mode, and – much like Arabella's detractors – contended that her fictions amounted even to a symptom of madness.[49]

By contrast, Selvin, with his classical pretensions, emerges as one of the text's main objects of satire, suggesting the fallibility of certain historiographic models as well as a blind admiration for the ancients. Selvin's presence as the representative historian in the text serves to illuminate questions about the boundaries between, and the nature of, truth and fiction, classical and romance narratives, reputable and disreputable history. We learn when we first meet him that he "affected to be thought deep-read in History, and never failed to take all Opportunities of displaying his Knowledge of Antiquity" (264). Yet at one point he concedes that Scudéry is more ancient than Herodotus, Thucydides, and Plutarch (266–7), and then assumes that Arabella's favourite historian must be Roman. She finally corrects him, and, upon learning that Scudéry was French, Selvin responds, "with a look of Self-applause," "Oh! then, 'tis not surprising, that I have not read him: I read no Authors but the Ancients, Madam … I cannot relish the Moderns at all: I have no Taste for their Way of Writing" (267). Selvin's empty allegiance to the Ancients closely mirrors the limited knowledge of other characters, rendering suspect his particular assessment of Julia's reputation: with such a flimsy acquaintance with the classics, he certainly seems to know a good deal of Julia's private life, just as the other men – including Sir Charles, despite his startling inability to recognize classical geography and history – are familiar with Cleopatra's sexual exploits. Such details imply that so-called genuine histories, accepted as true, are based on the very same kind of scandal liberally satirized elsewhere in Lennox's novel. Indeed, it is no coincidence that the notorious gossip Mr Tinsel is described as another kind of historian of the scandal-mongering variety.

Given the close association between scandal, romance, and history, it is certainly intentional that Lennox criticizes scandal throughout *The Female Quixote* and repeatedly emphasizes Arabella's aversion to it. Rather, it is the novel's male characters who relish opportunities to disclose the secret histories of Cleopatra, Julia, and Thalestris, demonstrating that even so-called history is subject to romance fictions. Reassured by his faith in the "known Facts of History," Glanville secretly mocks Selvin's capitulation to Arabella, yet her victory undermines her cousin's smug satisfaction as she and Selvin reach an impasse. Observing the outcome of their conversation, Glanville, "who knew all these Anecdotes were drawn from Romances, which he found contradicted the known Facts in History, and assign'd the most ridiculous Causes for Things of the greatest Importance; could not help smiling at the Facility with which Mr. *Selvin* gave into these idle Absurdities" (273). Glanville cannot see that these seemingly indisputable "facts" result from political and cultural bias because he himself belongs to the social hierarchy that produces and naturalizes them. For even the "known Facts in History" depend upon their sources: it is unsurprising, for example, that Cleopatra, as a threatening Eastern queen, would be subjected to reinterpretation by the Roman historians who, in attempting to rewrite and tame her, trumpeted her reputation as a "gypsey" and a "whore."[50]

Clelia and the Quest for Glory

Both historical and extra-historical, Arabella's romances paradoxically offer her the potential to escape the kind of history that rewrites Cleopatra, one of her role models, as the Egyptian "whore," and also reaffirm her place, particularly through the "cure" at the end of the novel, in that history: Arabella's will ultimately be a story authorized by the men around her, who determine her "madness," desire her "cure," and label dangerous her beloved romances. In this way, her failed attempts to imitate the noble actions of the Roman Clelia become emblematic of the failure to credit women's actions in history, for how many moderns – other than romancers – still celebrate Clelia's heroic virtue? These events, recorded not only in romance but also in Livy's *Ab Urbe Condita*, relating the history of Rome from its origins, lay claim to history and fiction, and come from presumably the same type of work the Divine encourages Arabella to consult instead of romance histories. Clelia's prominence at the end of the novel thus undermines the Divine's claims for the superiority of history, for Livy and Scudéry – history and romance – intersect in the figure of Arabella's heroic exemplar, suggesting the speciousness of the Doctor's arguments.

Of all the Amazonian heroines that Arabella emulates, none were more controversial than Scudéry's Clelia. The central controversy revolved around the inclusion in *Clelia* of a map, the *carte de tendre* (see Figure 3.5) devised by Clelia, that allowed her companions to understand where they stood in relation to her *inclination*, a term synonymous with female desire made popular by Scudéry and embraced by Lennox's Arabella. As Joan DeJean reminds us, "inclination" in *Clelia* suggests an emotion far more radical than passive esteem: it has the power to reshape society and the outlines of human history through its emphasis on female desire. "In *Clélie, inclination* is defined as a force of attraction that works against prearranged marriages and encourages women to rebel against the authority and values of the patriarchal system ... Scudéry is asserting such fundamental concepts as a woman's right to choose for herself and merit rather than family status as the measure of an individual's worth."[51] For Arabella, freedom of inclination is paramount: she agrees to receive Glanville "with that Civility and Friendship due to so near a Relation" because her father, she believes, "would never attempt to lay any Force upon her Inclinations" to the contrary.

At issue was rebellious female inclination in particular: Father Porée inveighed against *Clelia* by demanding, "'What do we see [in novels]? a daughter in her father's house busy drawing up the map of her infamous exploits.'" As Joan DeJean argues, "Unlike love at first sight, which strikes both partners simultaneously, *inclination* is consistently described from the woman's perspective as the force that makes her lean in the direction of one suitor over all others."[52] Jeffrey Peters thus foregrounds the stakes involved in Clelia's enterprise, accounting in no small part for the critical backlash: according to the geography of the *carte de tendre,*

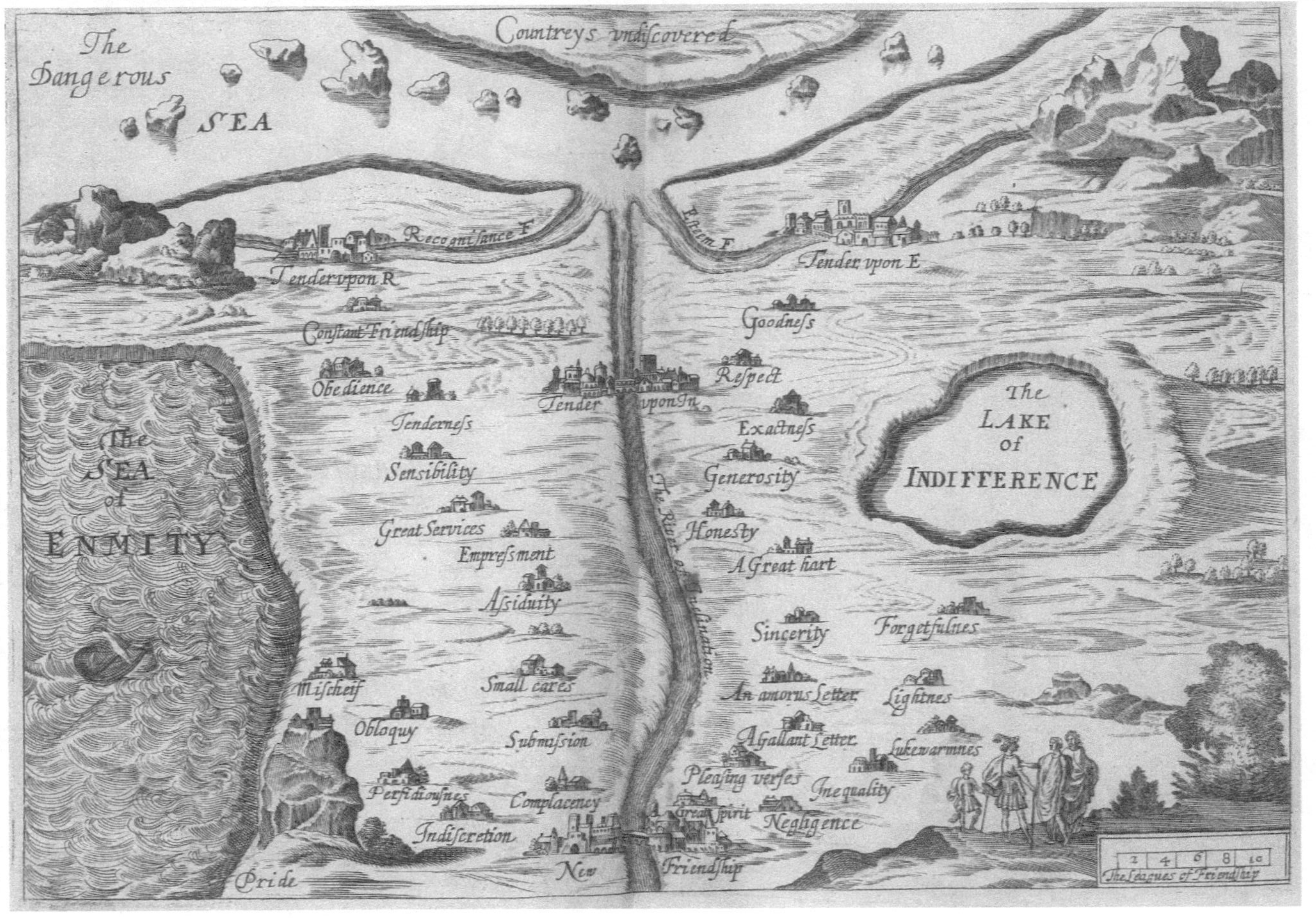

Figure 3.5. The *Carte de Tendre*, from Madeleine de Scudéry's *Clelia, ou histoire romaine* (1654–60). Image courtesy of the Henry E. Huntington Library and Art Gallery, San Marino, California.

> Clélie makes it clear that her admirers may move forward or backward, slide laterally, stay in place, or turn in circles, interrupting the uniquely forward movements of an older model of amorous possession found in the medieval *romance*. No longer the passive goal of a knight proceeding upon a linear path of inevitable sexual fulfillment strewn with temporary obstacles, the women of Scudéry's novel have at their disposal a cartographic vocabulary with which they may define both the shape of the space in which men move and the nature of their movements.[53]

The *carte de tendre*, in other words, documents the centrality of Clelia's authority in determining the amorous alliance she will eventually make.

I would like to return here to the portraits of female worthies celebrated by Le Moyne and Scudéry, since Clelia appears prominently as an exemplary figure in each work. (Figure 3.6 depicts Clelia as represented in Le Moyne's original French and subsequent English translation.)

In Le Moyne's *Galerie des femmes fortes*, the engraving that accompanies Clelia's example depicts the heroine having triumphantly forded the Tiber. Otherwise unarmed, she holds aloft a quill in her right hand. The scene behind her sketches her escape in action. Clelia leads her fellow hostages to the possibility of safety on Roman shores, a hail of arrows from the enemy camp at their backs. Of course, there is no mention of Clelia emerging, pen in hand, in Livy's canonical account of her story in the *Ab Urbe Condita*, or *History of Rome*; Livy's Clelia (Latin, *Clœlia*) remains a mute symbol of female virtue. Even Le Moyne, who celebrates her valour and initiates the possibility of Clelia as a writing subject, finds his limits in third-person narration about, rather than by, his unusual heroine. Instead, it falls to Scudéry to commemorate Clelia's heroic agency, distinguished, like the other heroines in *Les Femmes illustres*, by her unwavering eloquence in the face of tyranny. Indeed, as Jane Donawerth and Julie Strongson note in their introduction to Scudéry's *Selected Letters, Orations, and Rhetorical Dialogues*:

> In *Famous Women*, Scudéry pulls out all the stops and produces resounding oratorical style … Scudéry's style in these orations is fully oratorical: long, often periodic sentences, frequent exclamation, interjection, and heroic epithets … [she displays] metaphor, personification, irony, vivid description, catalogues, hyperbole, and all the other resources of figurative language, and clever, well-formulated arguments, drawing on all the commonplaces of rhetorical training (arguments from cause, effect, definition, comparison, opposites, names or etymology, associations or adjuncts, etc.).[54]

Figure 3.6. Engraving of Clelia, from Pierre Le Moyne's *Galerie des femmes fortes* (1647). Image courtesy of the Henry E. Huntington Library and Art Gallery, San Marino, California.

Figure 3.7. Engraving of Lucretia, from Pierre Le Moyne's *Galerie des femmes fortes* (1647). Image courtesy of the Henry E. Huntington Library and Art Gallery, San Marino, California.

Where Lucretia bears the knife of her suicide in her right hand, eyes futilely supplicating the heavens (see Figure 3.7), Clelia takes charge of her destiny, reminding us not only of the future equestrian monument to her heroism – almost unheard of in ancient Rome – but of her personal desire for glory and the real possibility, in the engraving in Le Moyne's gallery, that female eloquence has triumphed over male tyranny, and that Clelia has already seized (and may well seize again) the means of self-representation for herself and for the honour of her country.

In this way, Clelia marks a different point of origin for the archetype of the imperilled heroine: unlike other well-known exemplars from Roman history, Clelia survives the threat to her virtue and achieves public recognition for her heroism. The most famous female ciphers of Roman virtue in the early books of Livy's *Ab Urbe Condita* are the matron Lucretia and the maid Verginia. Lucretia, believed to be the most virtuous woman in Rome, unwittingly attracts the lascivious Tarquin with her untarnished reputation. After he rapes her, she commits suicide lest she inadvertently serve as a future example for unchaste women. Her suicide in Book 1 provides the catalyst for the overthrow of the Tarquins, just as Verginia's near-rape instigates the ouster of the Council of Ten later in Book 3. In Verginia's case, the corrupt judge, Appius, seeks to prey on her unguarded virginity by claiming her as his household slave; however, her father, the general Verginius, returns in time to avert Verginia's dishonour by stabbing her to death before the Roman people. In this way, both women exist as part of a larger pattern, "successive reenactments of a historical cycle" that requires a female sacrifice in order to consecrate and ensure the virility of the new republic in the face of unspeakable tyranny.[55] As Melissa Matthes writes in *The Rape of Lucretia and the Founding of Republics*, "the process of founding is recalled and repeated as an exemplar of moral virtue[;] the rape of the Sabine women, the rape and suicide of Lucretia, the slaughter of Verginia – in other words, the role of women as themselves founders, as *pharmakons* who make possible the very movement of history – is neglected and forgotten." These stories become "myths that stabilize the Roman foundation but are simultaneously erased as evocations that threaten the very male republican citizens they have helped to beget."[56] Despite the Divine's argument to the contrary, it is no romance fantasy that civilizations have been founded, both really and symbolically, on violence against women.

Yet Clelia disrupts this pattern of instrumental female sacrifice: crucially for Scudéry's purposes, Clelia marks an alternative heroic lineage, one that evades the effacement required of her more famous counterparts. Although Livy's account of Clelia's virtue is predictably slim, the *Roman History* itself acknowledges the potential for radical heroism in Clelia's actions. At the end of Book 2, Livy offers the following summary of Clelia's noble deeds and their reception by the Romans and the rival Etruscan king, Porsenna: "Porsenna proposed terms of peace and, having taken hostages, relinquished the war. One of the hostages, the maiden Clœlia, evaded the sentinels and swam across the Tiber [with the other female hostages] to her people. She was given up to Porsenna, but was restored by him with marks of honour, and was presented with an equestrian statue."[57] In other words, the Romans return the escaped Clelia as a hostage because of their pledge to Porsenna; the conflict is between Clelia's attempt to preserve her honour as a maiden and the Romans' attempt to honour their word with the Etruscan king. However, Porsenna, equally impressed by Clelia's daring, so much admires her bravery that he releases her to the Romans once again. Unlike Lucretia and Verginia, whose sacrifices merit no commemoration, Clelia signals the dawning of a different kind of heroism: as Livy describes the aftermath of her return in Book 2, "When peace had been established the Romans rewarded this *new* valour in a woman with a *new* kind of honour, an equestrian statue, which was set up on the summit of the Sacred Way, and represented the maiden seated on a horse" (emphasis added).[58]

In Scudéry's *Femmes illustres*, Clelia takes centre stage at a critical moment *in medias res* to defend her honour before the enemy king: Porsenna desires to know who conceived of the Roman maidens' bold escape, and all of Clelia's companions remain silent, fearing to incriminate their beloved leader. Nonetheless, Clelia emerges from the crowd to challenge Porsenna: she acknowledges that both she and her parents have acted from a sense of duty – she, to preserve her virtue; her parents, to honour their pledge to Porsenna – and insists that she cannot be culpable for so virtuous an action as to defend her, and her companions', chastity. Describing her actions as "having too noble a cause not to be glorious," she further declares that she is "uncapable of fearing anie thing, if it be not the loss of my honor."[59] So thoroughly possessed of the heroic spirit, she further exhorts her companions to "love better to put yourselves in hazard of dying gloriouslie then of living with infamie" (182), insisting "that whatsoever is done for honour, cannot but be glorious" (192). Honouring the pledge of her parents, she declares that they "will not break the peace; we will not cheat

Porsenna; we will onlie shun shame and infamie, or die with the same glorie wherein we lived" (192). So powerful is Clelia's speech that her companions "looked death in the face with constancie, and quitted the banks of the river with joy, though according to all liklie hood, they almost saw their death assured" (193). Brazen in the face of death, she is likewise unyielding in her appeal to Porsenna: she describes herself as "defend[ing] her cause" and reasons through the arguments on both sides (194) in order to prove the justness of her position. Moreover, Clelia is not concerned for her honour merely: she and her companions seek nothing less than "the preservation of their honour, and that of their countrey" (195), and she underscores the public heroism of her action by invoking the comparable deeds of other Roman statesmen whose heroism remains unquestioned. Finally, she defiantly puts the onus of judgment on Porsenna himself, forcing him to a decision, declaring, "It belongs now to you, to consider if you will treat us like fugitives, like enemies or like *Romans*" (196), and urging him to "Resiste not ... the glorious title of our Liberator, because we earnstlie desire to give it you" (198). Negotiating on her own behalf for her freedom, Clelia takes on the role of the wise foreign counsellor, a fixture since Herodotus; she exhorts Porsenna to behave honourably and to pardon them, reminding him that "the vertue of Women should be scrupulous and timide, They should almost look upon all People, as if they were their enemies: And because by custome armes are forbidden to them, fear must serve in stead of prudence: And it was more worthie for them to flee, or to have died a little too soon, then to have lingered, or to have lived a little too long" (198).

In his version of Clelia's story, Le Moyne leaves no doubt as to the justice of Clelia's actions by concluding her example – as he does with every *femme forte* narrative – with a question for debate, a so-called Moral Question, which asks, in this case, "Whether the Vertue of Women be as beneficial to the Publick as that of Men?"[60] Here, he argues for the equality of men and women on the subject of virtue, suggesting that women have been too circumscribed in their actions and have therefore been unable to contribute as virtuously to the good of the republic. Indeed, he concludes that women's virtue is "more conducing to the Publick Good" (28) and insists that "the generosity of *Clœlia* effected more alone then all the heads of the Senate, and all the arms of the Camp: And that which is very strange, a virtuous Woman and a bold Maid were the Foundresses of the Republick, and the principal causes of the Roman Liberty. A more famous proof cannot be brought, concerning the utility of the Vertue of women" (24). He further reminds readers, "The Republick, which received its Birth from the Vertue of a Woman, was conserved by the boldness of a Maid: And the Camilli, Fabricii and the Cato's inherited from Lucretia and Clœlia, Courage, Glory, and Liberty" (23–4).

With very little inspiration from Livy, Le Moyne – and especially Scudéry – dilate Clelia's narrative, foregrounding the political significance that only tangentially interests Livy's history. In doing so, they recover Clelia's story – only instrumental for Rome's foundation narrative – in order to celebrate Clelia on her own terms. The story's emphasis on proactive female virtue and public recognition for female heroism at once makes Clelia the perfect model for Scudéry's eponymous romance and the ideal exemplar for Arabella's emulation: under the perceived threat to her honour, Arabella doesn't recall Lucretia (who also makes an appearance in *Clelia*) or Verginia, and instead boldly insists on her desire to merit the praise celebrated by Scudéry's heroine. She exhorts her fellow "heroines," "'Tis now, my fair Companions … that the Destinies have furnish'd you with an Opportunity of displaying in a Manner truly Heroick, the Sublimity of your Virtue, and the Grandeur of your Courage to the World" (362). She continues,

> The Action we have it in our Power to perform will immortalize our Fame, and raise us to a Pitch of Glory equal to that of the renown'd Clelia herself.
>
> Like her, we may expect Statues erected to our Honour: Like her, be propos'd as Patterns to Heroines in ensuing Ages: And like her, perhaps, meet with Sceptres and Crowns for our Reward …
>
> Fortune, which has thrown us into this Exigence, presents us the Means of gloriously escaping: And the admiration and Esteem of all Ages to come, will be the Recompence of our noble Daring (363)

Like Clelia, Arabella seeks to achieve heroism by defending her person as well as the subsequent representation of her virtue. Essential to her desire is the power to "display" "the Sublimity of [her] Virtue, and the Grandeur of [her] Courage" before the entire world, gaining the "admiration and Esteem of all Ages to come." She ambitiously intends to "immortalize [her] Fame," twice invokes the glory inevitable to such actions, and anticipates "Recompence" for such "noble Daring" not only in the form of "Statues" but even in the currency of "Sceptres and Crowns," translating personal into political sovereignty. All the while, she demonstrates her complete awareness of the stakes of her actions, as she exhorts her female companions to follow her example. Arabella expects nothing less than to serve as a pattern to present company and the "Heroines in ensuing Ages," suggesting that she recognizes Clelia's potential to rupture the existing pattern of sacrifice, silence, and loss represented by Lucretia and Verginia. Just as returning to Dido or Cleopatra amounts to a return to narrative origins, expanding the possibilities for alternative histories of female heroism, Clelia makes available the same transformative potential in the world of romance.

Herein lies, I argue, Arabella's fear of rape, consistent throughout the novel: othered by her family and society, and aligned with subjected romance heroines who frequently resist or succumb to imperial domination, Arabella's apprehension of sexual violation also expresses anxiety about men's narrative control, about the usefulness of rape narratives for the writing of history.[61] The classicist Carol Dougherty argues that rape, "As a literary and artistic motif ... powerfully and persuasively represents military and political domination as erotic conquest, with women's bodies as symbols for a land and its people, and this motif is not at all restricted to ancient Greece and Rome."[62] Yet, as Dougherty reminds us, rape is not a motif merely: noting its real possibility in antiquity, she then extends her discussion to the programmatic rapes in modern Bosnia, writing, "These are not isolated acts of wartime violence – they are part of a larger discursive framework that unites women's bodies and the land to express political domination of the latter as sexual conquest of the former."[63] Living in a country almost perennially at war, Arabella has a right to be afraid. Nor were the English exempt from such atrocities. As the historian Carol Berkin notes of the colonial American context, "women knew that the presence of the military always meant the possibility of rape or physical humiliation" – even if that military were English, as it was in the American colonies.[64] The classically trained Arabella guards her person as a way of protecting a narrative that rape would at once silence and also wrest from her control. Arabella fears succumbing to men's histories, but has no respectable options for telling her own story.[65]

At the same time that Arabella expresses admiration for Scudéry's *Clelia* and the possibility of heroism that Clelia suggests, she exposes the myths – indeed, romances – that constitute Roman history. Although the Divine argues for the absurdity of Arabella's jumping into the Thames, he never broaches the subject of Clelia, a figure familiar from Livy, if not from Scudéry. Instead, he dismisses history along with Arabella's fears, and therefore denies the violence behind foundation myths, even as England mythologizes – as Steele's "Inkle and Yarico" poignantly demonstrates – its own expansion. Although Lennox undermines the Doctor's version of historiography and fiction, one determined by self-interested and appointed arbiters of cultural truth, she thus suggests its relevance for contemporary readers. Unable to tell her story, or to have a story to tell, Arabella and women like her will face the same defeat as the Amazon Penthesilea: not at the hands of a mighty Achilles, but at the cold pens of historians who vilify their strength, manipulate their courage and virtue, and quietly reinscribe their lives, for better or worse, in the service of good, valiant, and brave-hearted men.

Just a few years later in 1757, Sarah Fielding's *Lives of Cleopatra and Octavia* would dramatize with chilling clarity the erasure of women from history, engaging one of Arabella's favourite heroines in the context of the unforgiving historical record that had driven Cleopatra into romance. In embracing that record, Fielding offers a stark contrast to the romance tradition, producing a reading that more closely mirrors the corrupt understanding of Arabella's contemporaries, always eager to identify Cleopatra as the Egyptian "whore." Yet, supporting Arabella's defence of romance, the virtuous Octavia hardly fares better. Earning her nothing but heartache and a subordinate role to her far more powerful brother, Octavia's virtue secures her footnote to Rome's history, but ultimately affirms Pericles' infamous declaration that "the greatest glory of a woman is to be least talked about by men."[66] The story of Cleopatra reminds us that the prejudices of Arabella's companions boast an ancient pedigree, one that Fielding traces to the origins of Augustan – and, some might say, Western – history itself, born in no small part of the Cleopatra legend. Disappearing from history into propaganda, Cleopatra – like Clelia – was always fiction, the product of romance and history.

4 Performing Augustan History in Sarah Fielding's *Lives of Cleopatra and Octavia*

> Characters, which are drawn up by Historians, are often perplexed and confused by Party Spirit; Prejudice or Partiality too often swaying the Authors, either to lash them with unreasonable Satire, or to smooth them over with a kind of glittery Varnish, so that it is as difficult to trace the real Features of the Man, who is transmitted to Posterity in a Figure perfectly different from what he really bore in his Life-time, as it would be to discover a Roman Senator dressed like a modern fine Gentleman.
>
> From Fielding's Introduction to *The History of the Countess of Dellwyn* (1759)

> *Cleopatra* presents us with the abandoned Consequences, and the fatal Catastrophe, of an haughty, false, and intriguing Woman; whose only Views were to exert her Charms, and prostitute her Power, to the Gratification of a boundless Vanity and Avarice, without Regard to the Ruin of her Country, or the Sufferings of others.
>
> The amiable and gentle *Octavia* gives us, on the reverse, an Example of all those Graces and Embellishments, worthy the most refined Female Character ... Such was the accomplished Character of *Octavia*!
>
> From Fielding's Dedication to *The Lives of Cleopatra and Octavia* (1757)

In *The Lives of Cleopatra and Octavia* (1757), Sarah Fielding's fictional biography of the infamous queen and her Roman rival, Fielding explains in the Introduction that she specifically chooses biography in order to combat the "Knight errantry" attendant upon fiction, which encourages readers, against their better judgment, to "draw ... fictitious Characters into a real Existence."[1] Although Fielding recommends "the Lives of Persons who have really made their Appearance on the Stage of the World" (55) as a method of "balanc[ing]" the seductive lure of fiction, she also underscores the theatricality of history by explaining that *The Lives* will make use of fictional strategies, introducing "some Mixture of Romance" (55), in order to appeal to contemporary readers. In advancing the superiority of biography while maintaining an allegiance – however superficially reticent – to fiction, Fielding implicitly concedes that *The Lives* may encourage such "Knight errantry" as well. Like other novels, it may potentially leave her readers "pleasingly deluded" (54). By framing *The Lives* in this way, Fielding draws attention, I argue, to the "Knight errantry" involved not merely in the production of fiction, but of history: where Arabella's infatuation with romances reveals the possible dangers of novel reading, especially for a young and sheltered heroine, *The Lives of Cleopatra and Octavia* stages the potential for delusion in another, more venerable, context. Fielding takes as her object of satire the quixotic historians whose fantasies of Cleopatra's vice and Octavia's virtue come to structure authorized history.

Decades after the publication of *The Female Quixote* and *The Lives of Cleopatra and Octavia*, the translation of Arnaud Berquin's popular children's book, *L'ami des enfans* (Englished as *The Looking-Glass for the Mind; or, Intellectual Mirror*), would extend Fielding's project, illustrating the enduring success of Augustan propaganda, the ease with which fiction comes to be taken for history and immutable fact.[2] First published in English in 1783, *The Looking-Glass* boasts a series of vignettes worthy of the *Spectator*: it "constantly represent[s] [Virtue]," the translator avers, "as the Fountain of Happiness, and Vice as the Source of every Evil," exhibiting only "such Scenes … as come within the Reach of the Observations of young People in Common Life," with nothing "extravagant or romantic" to excite their imaginations. Recommended to every Youth, "whether Miss or Master," "it is a Mirror that will not flatter them, nor lead them into Error"; instead clearing "the Way to the *Temple of Honour and Fame*" (preface, np).

Although Berquin assigns generic or allegorical names to most of the characters in the thirty-six stories, two tales in particular depend, for their respective morals, on a specific historical context: "Antony and Augustus; or, a Rational Education Preferable to Riches," followed shortly by "Cleopatra; or the Reformed Little Tyrant." In the former tale, we learn that "Nothing can be more injurious to the health and happiness of children, than using them to excess of delicacy, and, under the idea of pleasing them, to indulge them in their whimsical and obstinate humours" (162). In this way, long before Antony can ever fall prey to the wiles of a manipulative lover, he falls "victim to the misguided indulgence of his parents, while Augustus lived to be happy by the prudent management he received in his infancy" (166). Later, "Cleopatra" champions proper femininity by explaining that "a girl, who set up her own opinion against that of every one else, would soon become intolerable and insupportable to all her acquaintance" (194).

These stories simplify the tradition of didactic historiography by reducing Antony, Augustus, and Cleopatra to easily identifiable types whose foremost purpose is moral instruction. The narrative of Antony and Augustus tells the story of these "almost inseparable companions" (158) from the time of their childhood to their departure to study law at university. The spoiled Antony comes from a wealthy family, Augustus from less "affluent circumstances" (159). Where the "healthy and robust" Augustus "enjoyed a tranquil chearfulness," the effeminate Antony, on the other hand, "was continually eating without being hungry, drinking without being dry, and slumbering without being sleepy," which naturally "brought on a weak habit of body, and frequent head-achs" (159). Despite his best intentions, Antony's father, Mr Lenox, indulges his son "in the most excessive delicacy" (160). Eventually, we learn, "he became so whimsical and imperious, that he was hated and despised by every one in the house, excepting his parents" (160–1). Mr Lenox, eager to learn the secret of Augustus's happiness and success, discovers that the boy's father has taught him the importance of industry, and of balancing work with pleasure. Resolved to reform his son, Mr Lenox finds that it is too late for the fourteen-year-old Antony, whose mother, "as weak as himself," allowed him to persist in his "destructive effeminacy" (162–3). When the two boys go off to university, Antony quickly becomes jealous of his friend's accomplishments and application, forsaking him in order to let "loose ... his vitiated taste, and wander[ing] from pleasure to pleasure in search of happiness" (164); "he at last returned home with the seeds of a moral distemper in his bosom, and after languishing a few months, expired in the greatest agonies" (164). Augustus, by contrast, remains the joy of his parents, friends, and family, a moral exemplar for present and future generations.

Naturalizing the relationship between "Augustus" and "virtue" and "Antony" and "vice," the story thus caters to fears of effeminacy and women's influence. Antony's taste for luxury and excess, though indulged by his parents, is a specifically feminine trait, ultimately encouraged and protected by his mother. Finally unmanned by his wife's pleading, Mr Lenox abandons his plans for reform. A similar anxiety pervades the story of "Cleopatra," the so-called "reformed little tyrant." Although her parents attempt to correct Cleopatra's temperament, they have little success until a visiting gentleman rebukes her aggressive manners. "I was lately in France," he explains, "and, as I was fond of being present at the soldiers exercise, I used to go … to see their manoeuvres on the parade … Among the soldiers there were many I observed with whiskers, which gave them a very fierce and soldier-like look. Now, had I a child like your Cleopatra," he declares, "I would instantly give her a soldier's uniform, and put her on a pair of whiskers, when she might, with rather more propriety than at present, act the part of a commander" (195). Having been chided by so authoritative a figure, Cleopatra stands admonished, "covered with confusion! She could not help blushing and was unable to conceal her tears … [T]his reproach," we learn, "perfectly reformed her, and she became sensible how unbecoming was a tyrannizing temper"; "with the assistance of her mother's prudent counsels, [she] became an amiable girl" (195–6). Berquin thus concludes, "[I]t is much to be wished, that all young ladies, who take no pains to conquer their passions, would at last imitate Cleopatra, and wish to avoid being told, that a soldier's dress and a pair of whiskers would better become them than nice cambric frocks and silk slips" (196).

It is the image of herself dressed as a soldier, acting "the part of the commander," that leaves Cleopatra "blushing," crying, and "covered with confusion." The visitor's suggestion makes manifest her transgressive behaviour, revealing the silliness of female heroism: Cleopatra is better suited to "nice cambric frocks and silk slips," and should worry about being "amiable," not authoritative, and certainly not "fierce and soldier-like" – though, presumably, neither should she exercise her newfound love of finery in the service of cultivating feminine wiles. The story reduces powerful femininity first to vice ("tyranny," 195–6), then to caricature. The historical Cleopatra, once a serious threat to the Roman Empire, has found her representational limits in Berquin, rendered a universal (and universally transgressive) character type for the admonishment of children.

In this way, Berquin's retelling of the Cleopatra myth highlights the narrative bias that marks the earliest introduction to ancient history for the young "misses" and especially "masters" who will go on to receive a formal education in Latin language and literature. Indeed, that these popular children's tales would likely figure as one of a child's first exposures, at least obliquely, to the Roman past suggests the success of Augustus's reinterpretation of history, the degree to which he so thoroughly vanquished Antony's reputation that "Antony" and "Cleopatra" exist outside history as recognizable types, the negative complements to "Augustus." *The Looking-Glass*'s authoritative, didactic model does not suggest parallel or alternative readings: Augustus *is* strength and virtue; Antony, weakness and effeminacy; Cleopatra, haughtiness and tyranny. For Berquin, the story of Antony and Cleopatra has advanced, almost imperceptibly, from fiction to history and, in turn, to incontrovertible (if fictionalized) fact.

I begin with Berquin's *Looking-Glass* because it offers a more banal expression of a historical trend begun nearly two thousand years earlier, when Augustus's contemporaries advanced the first rewritings of the Cleopatra myth in history and literature. As I have demonstrated in previous chapters, the Augustan period marks the inauguration of Dido-Cleopatra as an exotic foil for Aeneas's *romanitas*. Responding to the instabilities unleashed by so threatening a figure, the *Aeneid* at once rewrites Cleopatra as the far more tamable Dido, driven mad by love, and dismisses her to the margins of epic where her influence could be contained with safety. The effusive romance Dido of Books 1–4 gives way, in Book 8, to the captive Cleopatra whom Virgil relegates to an inert image on the shield of Aeneas, where she symbolizes the final obstacle to Octavian's imperial success.[3] As Virgil depicts her surrounded with "Barbarian Aids, and Troops of Eastern Kings" (6:8.908), it is hard to imagine that she ever posed a serious threat to Roman dominance. Ineffectually "rich in gaudy Robes," she is simply Antony's "ill Fate," "th'*Egyptian* Wife" (6:8.911–12).[4] History and Virgil have already condemned her, thus magnificently ranged against Octavian's forces, to defeat. An unwitting "Fool," she has "not yet divin'd / Her cruel Fate"; "Her Country gods, the Monsters of the Sky" are no match for Apollo, "pour[ing] down his Arrows" as Bellona "shakes her Iron Rod above their Heads" (6:8.933–6). With seeming inevitability, the "trembling *Indians*, and *Egyptians* yield," and Cleopatra flees: "Aghast she looks; and heaves her Breast, for Breath: / Panting, and pale with fear for future Death." The "fatal Mistress," she is both doomed and dooming as she abandons the luckless Antony in her wake.

Octavian, of course, escapes this fate, resisting, like *pius* Aeneas, the allure of North African charms. Thanks to Cleopatra's resemblance to

Dido, Octavian's victory takes on epic as well as historical significance. Indeed, following Egypt's defeat, Augustan defiance would gain iconic status for historians like Cassius Dio. Exulting in Roman superiority, Dio asserts that "By love she gained the title of Queen of the Egyptians, and when she hoped by the same means to win also that of Queen of the Romans, she failed of this and lost the other besides."[5] Surpassing his predecessor, Julius Caesar, and his rival, Mark Antony, Octavian alone exhibits an unassailable resolve in the face of Cleopatra's allure: "She captivated the two greatest Romans of her day, and because of the third she destroyed herself."[6] What began as a battle between Rome and Egypt became, rhetorically at least, a matter of man against woman, West against East, civilization against barbarism, so that Octavian's victory over "the ideal national foe" quickly took on symbolic significance.[7] By the time he declared war on Cleopatra, she had come to embody everything the Romans feared, and his triumph ensured that the unnatural image of a seductive, haughty, and luxurious queen would be forever enshrined in Roman cultural memory. That same narrative would consign Cleopatra to certain defeat, the inescapable fate of a woman and Egyptian.

On Pleasing Delusions: Reading *The Lives* as Satire

Sketching her approach in the Introduction to *The Lives*, Fielding explains the allure of fictionalized autobiography: it "promise[s] to entertain, captivate, and enchant the Mind" while showing readers "Originals ... taken from Life," in order to encourage "juster Notions of ourselves" (55). The grand prospect of biography – its ability to depict "the Lives of Persons whose superior Talents, Power, and Station; or whose uncommon Turns of Fortune, have diversified their Characters, and distinguished them from the rest of our Species" (54) – soon dwindles to the narrower compass of Cleopatra's vice and Octavia's virtue. From the "Manners of human Nature, and Customs of the World; the Intrigues of Policy, the Arts of Lovers, and the Exploits of Heroes; [as well as] the secret Springs and Motives of their Actions" (54), we at length arrive at "the fatal Consequences of a mad intoxicated Lover, and a false insinuating Woman," both ranged against the "Distresses of a virtuous *Octavia*" (55). Here, Fielding recalls the characterizations of the Dedication, where she claims that her heroines "form, perhaps, the strongest Contrast of any Ladies celebrated in History" (41). The predictably negative portrait of Cleopatra, who represents "the fatal Catastrophe, of an haughty, false, and intriguing Woman," gives way to the "amiable and gentle *Octavia*," who serves, she argues, as "an Example of all those Graces and Embellishments, worthy the most refined Female Character" (41). In this way, Fielding's recourse to "some Mixture of Romance" (55) seems not to have spared *The Lives of Cleopatra and Octavia* from her criticism of history two years later in the Introduction to *The History of the Countess of Dellwyn* (1759). There, Fielding would argue that "Characters, which are drawn up by Historians, are often perplexed and confused by Party Spirit; Prejudice or Partiality too often swaying the Authors, either to lash them with unreasonable Satire, or to smooth them over with a kind of glittery Varnish, so that it is as difficult to trace the real Features of the Man, who is transmitted to Posterity in a Figure perfectly different from what he really bore in his Life-time, as it would be to discover a Roman Senator dressed like a modern fine Gentleman."[8] Given Fielding's critique of historians' "Party Spirit," we might expect *The Lives* to reject the "Prejudice or Partiality" that, like the pleasing delusions of fiction, encourages a kind of "Knight errantry" among historians. Yet *The Lives* appears to renounce *Dellwyn*'s injunction against authorial prejudice, making Cleopatra the object of "unreasonable Satire" and, superficially at least, "smooth[ing]" over Octavia's character. Fielding's approach to *The Lives of Cleopatra and Octavia* emphasizes the power of biography to "balance" the entertaining strategies of fiction even as it foregrounds the complicity between fiction and history, the counterfeit image "transmitted to Posterity" (what she also calls, in the Introduction to *The Lives*, the "false Coin" of fiction) and so-called "real Features of the Man" (the "current Gold" of history and biography).

I argue that, by presenting *The Lives of Cleopatra and Octavia* as a fictionalized autobiography at odds with the view of history she articulates in *The Countess of Dellwyn*, Fielding ironizes the novel's claims to representational authority. The artifice of the frame narrative raises further suspicion: nothing less than necromancy enables "her Interview with those Heroines" (55) as Fielding imagines herself conducted by an "Eastern Sorcerer or Magician" to the land of the dead. The magician's "Interest at Court" allows him to persuade Pluto to "command those celebrated Shades" to "give [Fielding] a faithful Detail of their Lives," an injunction they cannot refuse because there is "no disrupting his Orders." Claiming an ancient pedigree for her novel, Fielding similarly exposes the collusion between epic and history as she aligns her fictional approach with an epic discourse that shapes the

Cleopatra narrative. Relying on a conceit familiar to readers of "*Homer, Virgil, Aristophanes, Lucan,* and others," she invokes the journey "to the gloomy Realms of *Pluto*" necessary to the hero's quest (55). This conceit, in turn, suggests the limits of Fielding's project. For Homer and for Virgil, the Underworld visit is a triumphalist revelation of the hero's future. Odysseus and Aeneas, for example, each receive news of conquests yet to come; the Underworld journey portends future victory for the living – presumably, in Fielding's case, for the reader, the *nouvel héros/nouvelle héroïne* whom she guides into a realm at once strange and familiar. Fielding styles herself a neo-Virgil, the privileged witness of these lives: when Cleopatra concludes her tale, Fielding notes how the queen "retired, like *Dido,* with a gloomy Countenance" (126). Yet the references to Aristophanes and Lucan complicate this trajectory by invoking its parody in Athenian comedy and its impossibility for writers like Lucan, whose unfinished *Pharsalia* tried to reimagine epic, post-Virgil, in the context of the Roman Civil Wars. Fielding's dissonant set of precedents both recalls the Dedication's easy moral – the "good" Octavia will supplant the "bad" Cleopatra – and gestures towards the over-determined simplicity of that moral. In its various significations, the Underworld journey embodies an ethos of history-as-hindsight that justifies Fielding's putative didacticism and, at a further remove, acknowledges the conditions of its production.

To the "false Coin" of fiction-as-history – the Roman and English fictions that define Octavia and especially Cleopatra – Fielding offers, in her fictional biography, the "current Gold" that will destabilize and add satiric weight to her heroines' narratives. Put another way, Fielding, like Lennox, benefits from the strategies of romance historiography in order to highlight – and ultimately to deconstruct – the discursive processes that determine "Cleopatra" and "Octavia" for Fielding's audience. The layers of fictional mediation required to tell Cleopatra's and Octavia's stories shift the focus from self-scrutiny to scrutiny of the discourses that produce the self: the "autobiographer's 'fiction,'" Patricia Meyer Spacks reminds us, "is stronger and more telling than his 'truth.'"[9] In profiting from a genre that unites history and fiction, *The Lives of Cleopatra and Octavia* reveals the sleight of hand that first associates Fielding's heroines with romance (or, at least, with the amatory realm) and subsequently justifies their exclusion from history.

In order to fashion this critique, Fielding read widely in primary and secondary materials, demonstrating her command of the literary and historiographic traditions that had constructed "Cleopatra" and

"Octavia" for eighteenth-century readers.[10] Given the depth of Fielding's research, what fascinates about *The Lives* is the extent to which she departs from conventional histories, especially Plutarch, in her biographical practice. Indeed, in telling her heroines' stories, Fielding ignores her source material to a remarkable degree. In order to explain the discrepancy between Fielding's extensive reading and the histories she constructs, I will argue that Fielding relies on her research precisely in order to showcase the discursive processes that cemented Augustan supremacy. *The Lives of Cleopatra and Octavia,* in actively rejecting a more even-handed approach to the Cleopatra legend, extends an increasingly vitriolic historiographic trajectory already verging on self-parody. Indeed, it is important to note, here, that Octavia's brother and Cleopatra's rival, Octavian, emerges from the history relatively unscathed, suggesting that *The Lives of Cleopatra and Octavia* represents no challenge to his world view. Hence Fielding's ironic celebration of Octavia's virtue and Cleopatra's vice: parodying available accounts, Fielding reimagines history savagely dominated by its victors.

Fielding was especially well equipped to undertake such a project. Observing the contours of Fielding's literary pursuits, Betty Schellenberg notes that her "rough progression from miscellaneous pieces, to the relatively demotic fictional and familiar letter genres, to the more prestigious forms of criticism, educational writing, historical biography, and classical translation" exemplifies "the eighteenth-century version" of "the classical and Renaissance trajectory of the poet's career."[11] Fielding's interest in ancient languages and literature marked her as a female version of the gentleman scholar: like Henry, she was a proficient student of the classics, and apparently bested him in Greek. Dr Arthur Collier, the sibling of her lifelong friend and collaborator Jane, instructed Sarah in the ancient languages and described her as "an able Scholar both in the Latin language and in the Greek."[12] According to Jane, it was this proficiency that occasioned a sometime strain on Sarah's relationship with Henry; Collier imagined that "Sarah's growing competence in the classics had soured her relationship with her brother,"[13] a perhaps unsurprising outcome given the monopoly men held on formal classical learning. Whatever antagonism it may have engendered, her facility with ancient languages was nonetheless a source of pride for Fielding: her 1762 translation of *Xenophon's Memoirs of Socrates, with the Defence of Socrates before his Judges,* was the first and final work she published under her full name.[14]

The Lives of Cleopatra and Octavia is the only other work Fielding acknowledged as her own, signing her dedication to the Countess of Pomfret "S. Fielding." Published under the auspices of her mentor, Samuel Richardson, the first edition of *The Lives* had 441 subscribers and made a "handsome book. Richardson collated *The Lives* in quarto, printed it on royal paper, used a large Caslon type, and decorated the text with display capitals and several stock ornaments."[15] The unusual biographical approach sits in tension with Fielding's educational pedigree: she was the first female author to offer, in English, an account of Cleopatra via first-person narration, and also "the first to concentrate not on the love affair between Cleopatra and Antony but on the contrasting characters and fortunes of Cleopatra and Octavia."[16] In doing so, she followed Plutarch (about whom, more below), whose own historical practice in the *Parallel Lives* establishes a model that frustrates a straightforwardly didactic interpretation of Fielding's novel. Choosing a form at once traditional and innovative, Fielding in turning to history in 1757 was making a savvy move for economic as well as ideological reasons. Although history was a lucrative enterprise, the mid-century market for novels was less certain. As Susan Carlile explains, "the cost of producing two- and three-hundred page novels was much higher [by the 1750s] than many of the other popular texts at the time ... Publishers were specifically hesitant to take a risk on a novel, unless the title was certain of success."[17] Although *The Lives of Cleopatra and Octavia* benefits from the traditional expectations associated with a conservative genre like history, Fielding's infusion of romance textures her didactic project by embracing a medium, in the form of fictional (auto)biography, that enables her to foreground the fictive strategies that deny historical agency to her heroines.

Donna Landry has recently observed that Fielding was "a paradoxical writer, at once almost unimaginably radical for her time and yet extremely popular,"[18] and a growing body of criticism continues to move beyond the impulse to view Sarah Fielding as a proper mid-century woman writer motivated by predictable moralistic ends. These arguments represent a renewed interest in resituating Sarah Fielding as an innovative author at the very heart of mid-eighteenth-century fiction. Although the critical fortunes of Henry Fielding and Samuel Richardson have long eclipsed her formerly illustrious status, Sarah Fielding was "among the most popular of all English novelists," nearly matching Henry and Laurence Sterne in popularity, and ranked only behind Eliza Haywood and Marie Jeanne Riccobini as the third most popular female novelist of the century.[19] Schellenberg describes her as "easily among the ten most prolific British producers of new fiction titles" from 1744 through the 1760s, so popular that the name "Sarah Fielding" "achieved [the status of] an author function."[20] In this context, Fielding's experiment with fictional (auto)biography in *The Lives of Cleopatra and Octavia* typifies a literary career that was not only remarkably varied, but also consistently experimental. Over a decade earlier, Fielding's first novel, *The Adventures of David Simple* (1744), debuted the man of feeling for eighteenth-century readers, *The Governess, or The Little Female Academy* (1749) inaugurated the genre of children's literature, and *The History of Ophelia* (1761) anticipated the birth of gothic fiction later that same decade. Fielding experimented with satire in *The Countess of Dellwyn* (1759) – a character whose divorce made her a rather curious subject for a heroine – and her delightfully eccentric novel *The Cry: A New Dramatic Fable* (1754), written in collaboration with Jane Collier, not only foregrounds her commitment to generic experimentation but also her dissatisfaction with familiar classical tropes and their mobilization in eighteenth-century culture.

I join Landry in urging new approaches to Fielding's oeuvre – especially her less studied and more experimental novels – that recover the inventive nature of her fiction. Following earlier work by Deborah Downs-Miers and Carolyn Woodward, Christopher D. Johnson has lately argued that Fielding's novels engage "questions of authority and responsibility, which are themselves connected to questions of gender," allowing "form and genre to define – and sometimes limit – [Fielding's] own narrative authority and to teach the reader, especially the female reader, to become intellectually independent."[21] Other critics go even further. For example, observing that Fielding's "tough-minded, satirical use of Shakespeare" often results in a "black comedy" that "challenges critical assumptions about the way that she, and other female novelists, related to the dramatist," Kate Rumbold argues that *The History of the Countess of Dellwyn* "reveals a less earnest side to an author long categorized as the devoted mentee of Samuel Richardson and Henry Fielding."[22] Landry contends that "Fielding pioneered a kind of fiction that was at once sentimental and utopian, backward-looking in its evocations of ideas of commonwealth and Christian charity, yet radically emancipatory if compared with later eighteenth-century writing."[23] She argues that the "English Enlightenment's revolutionary origins remain legible in Sarah Fielding's work. Through the language of benevolence, she perpetuates the vision of economic redistribution associated with the most radical voices raised during the Civil War and Interregnum." Landry concludes that Fielding's benevolence "should be read as communist, or proto-communist in the light of nineteenth-century developments."[24] Daniel Gross, noting, like Landry, Fielding's engagement with the broader intellectual movements of her time, links *David Simple* to the characterization of the passions in David Hume's *A Treatise on Human Nature*, published only a few years earlier in 1740. Arguing that Fielding "tells a sophisticated story of humility-in-action that points directly to the paradox of agency vexing someone like Hume and works out in fine detail what might happen if a particular subculture imagined property relations very differently," Gross makes a case for "analyz[ing] with greater acuity how patriarchy as a psychic form of government and subordination is imagined in mid-century England and how authors such as Hume and Fielding characterize it with different degrees of resistance."[25]

Arguments of this nature at once enrich the interpretive possibilities of Fielding's work by attending carefully to its literary and historical contexts, and adopt the scepticism that Fielding herself encourages of her readers. Warning, as it does, of the seductions of "Knight errantry" while deploying the strategies of history and fiction, *The Lives of Cleopatra and Octavia* unsettles, from the start, the host of assumptions mobilized by its title.

Recovering the Significance of *The Lives*: Fielding and Plutarch

For a novel invested in the intersections between fiction and history, biography offered an ideal genre for deconstructing familiar portrayals of Cleopatra and her rival. Unlike the masculine dignity of high military and political history, the status of biography was more ambiguous. Although men were "the sole authorized vendors of the private biographical subject and its ideology of genre," biography's emphasis on private matters and domestic affairs allied it with stereotypically feminine concerns.[26] Even as she capitalizes on the authority of ancient writers, Fielding thus centralizes figures relegated to the peripheries of Roman history. In particular, *The Lives of Cleopatra and Octavia* takes its inspiration from Plutarch's *Life of Antony*, what Michael Grant, one of Cleopatra's modern biographers, has called "[p]erhaps the most important single source for Cleopatra that we possess, and far the most alluring."[27] First translated into English by Thomas North in 1579, with a new translation supervised by John Dryden between 1684 and 1688, Plutarch's *Parallel Lives* (written sometime in the late first century CE) was extremely popular throughout the seventeenth and eighteenth centuries. Given Fielding's knowledge of Greek, it's possible that she may have even read Plutarch in the original (a critical edition had appeared in Paris in 1572), but North's and Dryden's translations were the gold standard in the period. As its title indicates, Plutarch's *Lives* appear largely in pairs (twenty-three, in all) and follow a particular format: Plutarch presents the biography of a Greek statesman alongside a Roman counterpart, a single book emerging from the resulting pair.

Most crucially for its application to *The Lives of Cleopatra and Octavia,* Plutarch's parallel structure would have been entirely familiar to Fielding and her eighteenth-century readers. In the twentieth- and twenty-first centuries, by contrast, individual lives have tended to be extracted from their original coupling, ignoring the structure of Plutarch's text in order to produce editions suitable for classroom use. In recent years, classicists have returned to the centrality of the *Parallel Lives'* organization and its bearing on the themes of Plutarch's work. Among many others, critics such as Christopher Pelling, Tim Duff, and Philip Stadter have demonstrated the necessity of reading each life in tension with its partner, and even across pairings, in order to appreciate Plutarch's historiographic practice and didactic intent.[28]

Like the paratexts of Fielding's *Lives of Cleopatra and Octavia,* with its Dedication, Introduction, and framing remarks by the narrator, Plutarch linked individual pairings via a prologue and concluding *synkrisis,* or comparison of the lives, a structure that encourages readers to move beyond each individual example. Fielding's appropriation of Plutarch's parallel format thus attests to her broader knowledge of his work: she produces *The Lives of Cleopatra and Octavia* knowing, as an eighteenth-century writer, that one life is inextricable, rhetorically, from its pair and, as an eighteenth-century reader, that her primary source – *The Life of Antony* – was intertwined with the *Life* that preceded it, a biography of Demetrius, the Macedonian king who saw himself as the heir to Alexander the Great, just as Antony saw himself as the heir to Julius Caesar. Readers of *Demetrius* would know, of course, that both lives were meant to be negative exempla, illustrating the Platonic idea that "great natures produce great vices as well as great virtues."[29] Given Fielding's characterization of Antony, this is hardly a surprise, and yet the recollection of Antony's pairing with Demetrius prevents easy moral conclusions. Although Fielding's Dedication – and Plutarch's prologues and *synkriseis* themselves – acknowledge the temptation to simplify biography towards moralistic ends, both texts nonetheless encourage readers to recognize the flaws of their protagonists, however attractive or sympathetic they may otherwise be. This includes, for Fielding, the figure of Octavia, no matter how pitiable. In following Plutarch's structure, Fielding at once adopts the Greek-Roman order of narration and deploys Cleopatra's narrative to recontextualize Octavia's. "Important here," as Tim Duff notes, "is the principle of pattern and variation: the first Life sets a pattern which is then exploited and varied in the second."[30] The same may be said of the historiographic pattern in which Fielding herself participates by writing *The Lives*.

This is the proper literary and historical context from which to approach *The Lives of Cleopatra and Octavia*. Resituating Fielding in relation to her indebtedness to Plutarch foregrounds the novel's textual dissonances in order to recover its interpretive challenge to the reader. This is true not only of the individual lives, paratexts, and narratorial intrusions, but also of Fielding's heavy-handed use of biography (a genre typically used with more didactic restraint), her decision to retell histories already well known to her readers, and her reduction of "Cleopatra" to "vice" and "Octavia" to "virtue." In this way, rereading *The Lives of Cleopatra and Octavia* in the context of Fielding's source material helps to make evident the overly simplistic moralizing of its Dedication. While "Plutarch seems to promise" "easily extractable moral lessons," Tim Duff notes that the structural complexity of the *Parallel Lives* in fact resists the urge to read one biography as superior to the other: "the attempt to classify Lives as being either negative or positive is not only difficult but probably misguided."[31] Even, he concedes, in the case of "those few pairs of Lives whose prologues suggest that the Lives which follow should be seen as exemplars of virtue or vice, it is impossible in practice to see the protagonists as wholly good or bad. Few protagonists live wholly blameless or blameworthy Lives; *they are not stock examples of virtue or vice*" (emphasis added).[32] Plutarch's comparisons between lives do not serve, from this standpoint, as "unconvincing afterthoughts" or "summaries of the content of the Lives themselves," but as an interpretive tool "designed to make the reader ask new and rather challenging moral questions."[33] If Fielding's aim is to teach the reader, especially the female reader, "to become intellectually independent" – a viewpoint that has engendered much support in recent years – then bald didacticism seems an insufficient strategy for the task.[34] As Pelling observes of Plutarch's moralism, "Are we to assume an audience which really needed telling these things, all agog for any Cleopatra which came along, all arrogantly proud of their lack of education or their class-bound inflexibility? These, surely, were morals which everyone already knew all too well."[35] In this way, I argue that *The Lives of Cleopatra and Octavia* relies precisely on Cleopatra's infamy and Octavia's fame in order to complicate the literary and historiographic traditions inherited by Fielding and her readers. The novel is indeed didactic, but not in the ways critics have heretofore assumed.

Imagining Power: Fielding's Cleopatra and the Construction of History

Promising to present the "true Picture of [her] self" (56) – the real and authentic queen of Egypt – Fielding's Cleopatra complicates, from the outset, the stated aims of *The Lives'* fictional (auto)biogaphies. In offering her audience the "Picture" of Cleopatra, Fielding reminds readers of the levels of mediation that distance the audience from the historical queen, even in her own purportedly first-person narration. Savvy to her position as spectre and spectacle, Fielding's Cleopatra constructs herself as a repentant spirit at the mercy of the Underworld king, Pluto, making a show of her obedience – the vain, prideful queen, conquered – while vowing to "obey [the] irresistible Command" to relate her history. She thus begins dramatically, seductively, raising and fulfilling expectations; the opening to her narrative has the tone of a confession, the assurance of a scandalous memoir. She vows to honour the "hard task" of recounting "with Impartiality and Faithfulness the History of my own Life," but does not neglect to pique the reader's curiosity by promising "to reveal" the "secret Motives of [her] Actions" – motives, indeed, so secret that they were "little known [even] to [her]self," rendering Cleopatra the very "Object of [her] own Deceit" (56). Yet Cleopatra's stance of submission gives way to boastful reminiscences of her former character: once she has properly framed her story, she discards that frame altogether. Confessing that she "looked on *Anthony* as my Prey" (60), she gloats over the success of her strategies, playing the whole "artillery of love" against him, and revels in the "Glory of [her] Conquest" (60), the ease with which she rules Antony "by Tricks and Deceit" and will continue to do so "for the Remainder of his Life" (62). Although she concludes by affecting to regret the "Spirit of Pride and Vanity" that "had produced far more Misery than Happiness," acknowledging that she "breathed [her] last, [while] sadly imposing on [her]self" (125), her brief sentiments of regret do little to counterbalance the self-satisfied catalogue of conquests and victories.

Of course, Fielding would have known, thanks to her extensive reading, that Cleopatra's alliance with Antony could be attributed to motives other than pride and its near relation, vanity. By characterizing pride as Cleopatra's predominant passion, Fielding exploits controversial ideas about human morality that had been circulating since the seventeenth century. Most relevant for my discussion here are the figures of Alexander Pope, who popularizes the concept of the "ruling passion" in Epistle II of the *Essay on Man* (1734), and the moralists Samuel Johnson and Henry Fielding, who rejected Pope's "pernicious doctrine" (to use Johnson's words). Summarizing the *Essay on Man*'s unique contribution to ongoing reflections on the passions, Bertrand Goldgar explains that, in Pope's psychology, "passions arise from sense perception, but different objects make greater impressions on different senses, so that one dominant passion rules over all the rest in each individual. This passion is stronger than reason and comes to us at birth as part of our very nature. Its power is increased by nature, habit, and reason itself, which can only treat it as a friend and a guard, since it comes from 'A mightier Pow'r.'"[36] So offended was Johnson by the idea of a passion "innate and irresistible" that he took Pope to task in his literary biography of the poet (1779). Objecting to the influence of an "ascendant planet or predominating humour," he calls Pope's doctrine not only "pernicious" but "false": as Johnson writes, "its tendency is to produce the belief of a kind of moral predestination, or overruling principle which cannot be resisted; he that admits it, is prepared to comply with every desire that caprice or opportunity shall excite, and to flatter himself that he submits only to the lawful dominion of Nature, in obeying the resistless authority of his 'ruling passion.'"[37] Even closer to the publication of *The Lives of Cleopatra and Octavia*, Henry Fielding's *Amelia* (1751) took a similar view. Lamenting those "Men of Sense" who quit "the Directions of Prudence" by "following the blind Guidance of a predominant Passion,"[38] Fielding's "Exordium" sets the stage for the reformation of his hero, William Booth, an otherwise admirable character led astray by a doctrine that nearly leads him to ruin.

On the one hand, Sarah Fielding's organization of *The Lives* according to each heroine's predominant passion makes it possible to view Cleopatra, sadly imposing on herself until the end, as an object lesson, like *Amelia*'s Booth: she falls victim to her vanity and pride, understanding the logic of her actions only in hindsight. Yet this formulation of a potential moral also foregrounds its difficulty: liberated from her body, in which she was formerly "blinded by Passion" (56), Cleopatra gains an insight that is still a form of blindness. Fielding's heroine, reinterpreting her history through the lens of pride, discursively reproduces her former self as if that self were inevitable.

The trajectory of Cleopatra's narrative thus appears to corroborate Johnson's fear that the doctrine of the ruling passion might "produce the belief of a kind of moral predestination, or overruling principle which cannot be resisted." The dangerous fatalism of such a doctrine provides, in turn, an instructive parallel to the teleological narratives that inform the Cleopatra myth. It is no wonder that, once Cleopatra concludes that "Pride" motivated her earthly aims, the rest of her autobiography falls seamlessly into place. The same pattern will repeat itself in *The Life of Octavia*. By employing the conceit that her heroines retrospectively narrate their own autobiographies, Fielding demarcates the limitations of each history. That the sublunary self becomes legible only in hindsight suggests its limited didactic potential for the living and the dead. In adopting the discourse of the ruling passion, with its easy moralizing, Cleopatra's reinterpretation of her life, from the vantage point of the passion that dictated it, invites readers to reconsider *The Lives'* own didactic claims.

In deliberately flattening Cleopatra's character by organizing the biography around a capitulation to her predominant passion, Fielding underscores the over-determined nature of the Cleopatra narrative. From a public figure – the queen of one of the most important countries in the ancient Mediterranean – Fielding's Cleopatra becomes a private heroine undone by her own conceit. That Fielding reduces the complexity of Cleopatra's character indicates the extent to which subsequent historians had strategically effaced the nuanced sympathy of Plutarch. Profiting from the vitriolic accounts that would furnish plenty of damning material for *The Lives'* portrait, Fielding transposes the extravagancies and delusions of Plutarch's Antony onto a Cleopatra all too eager to affirm them. In transforming *The Life of Antony* into *The Life of Cleopatra*, Fielding appropriates Antony's flaws – namely, his inability to remember and honour his political goals – and thus vividly demonstrates the convenient act of displacement that allowed Octavian to scapegoat Cleopatra for Antony's failures. Plutarch's Antony, far more than Cleopatra, emerges as a slave to his desires, forsaking ambition in order to satisfy his amorous appetites. For example, he bestows Roman lands on Cleopatra when he returns to Egypt after his marriage to Octavia – "nothing stung the Romans like the shame of these honours paid to Cleopatra" (1124–5; 1133) – and bungles the Parthian war because of his desire to reunite with the queen (1125); she, feeling threatened by the strength of his ties to Rome through Octavia, "feigned to be dying for love of Antony" (1134) and encouraged further military delays through her "creatures," who, in reproaching Antony, sought to "melt and unman him" (1135).[39] Conquered by Cleopatra's irresistible charms, Antony becomes a "mere appendage to [her] person" (1139) by the outbreak of civil war. He defers to her military counsel to fight at sea, an engagement from which she notoriously flees while "the day was still undecided, and the battle equal" (1141): "Here it was," writes Plutarch of Antony's decision to follow her, "that Antony showed to all the world that he was no longer actuated by the thoughts and motives of a commander or a man, or indeed by his own judgment at all" (1142). Thus, when Fielding's Cleopatra proudly boasts – playing on eighteenth-century anxieties about women and their pets, particularly the unholy triumvirate of the monkey, the parrot, and the lapdog – that she has domesticated Antony in the worst possible sense, she conveniently divests him of responsibility for his actions while happily taking the blame: "having it in my Power thus to make a Man, a *Roman* General, one of the Three Lords of the Universe, a Monkey for my sake, was such exulting Pleasure, such rapturous Joy, as is not to be described" (*Life of Cleopatra*, 98).[40] In this way, Fielding continues the practice, first begun by Roman historians, of displacing Antony's failings onto the Egyptian queen: in transforming "civil war" to "war against Egypt," and declaring war on Cleopatra rather than Antony, Octavian could safely scapegoat Antony's Egyptian proxy for his own lack of allegiance to Rome.

Further augmenting the negative details furnished by the historical record, Fielding takes inspiration from a number of subsequent historians, including the Romano-Jewish writer Josephus (first century CE), the most vituperative of Cleopatra's ancient critics.[41] Far exceeding Plutarch's already unflattering picture of a lovesick Roman and his manipulative mistress, Josephus describes a Cleopatra who goads Antony into "tak[ing] away the dominions" of other rulers; a woman who "had a great influence over him because of his passion for her," so that Antony, "already demoralized by his love for Cleopatra, was becoming wholly enslaved to his passion" (*JA*, 15.88; *WJ*, 1.359). According to Josephus, "there was no lawless deed which she did not commit" (*JA*, 15.89); even the assassination of her brother and sister could not sate her lust for power: "Now Cleopatra had put to death all her kindred, till no one near her in blood remained alive, and after that she fell a slaying those no way related to her" (*WJ*, 1.359). Naturally of a sacrilegious temperament, "For the sake of any money which there was the slightest hope of getting, both temples and tombs were violated. No sacred place was considered so inviolable that it did not suffer every kind of forbidden treatment" (*JA*, 15.90). Unsatisfied with the immense presents Antony has bestowed, Cleopatra insists that he hand over Judaea and attempts to seduce its king, Herod, behind his back. According to Josephus, she thus emerges as a supremely disruptive force, upending familial and religious institutions – and hence social and political hierarchies – with a penchant for fratri- and sororicide coupled with sacrilege. Fielding borrows much of Josephus's characterization, from the planned seduction of Herod (125–6) to Cleopatra's desire to obtain Judea (125) and her use of Antony as an instrument to secure additional lands (92).

In addition to incorporating some of the least flattering anecdotes from among the most hostile ancient authors, Fielding's *Life of Cleopatra* emphasizes the fiction behind the Cleopatra myth by inventing details where the historical record is found wanting. For example, contradicting ancient historians, Cleopatra claims that she aided both sides in the civil war in order to "keep in Favour with both Parties," hedging her bets with Cassius and Brutus on one side and Antony and Octavian on the other (59), when in fact she remained loyal to Antony from the start. At the same time, she does not relate, despite historical precedent,[42] how she defended herself to Antony against charges of aiding their mutual enemy, the rebels in Egypt; instead, she claims responsibility for the perfidious actions of Serapion, the general of Cyprus, who had decided, given the political unrest in Rome, to support Cassius and Brutus, ousting Cleopatra and installing her sister Arsinoe on the throne. From outside Egypt, the appearance of such an action could certainly be construed as treachery, and Fielding's Cleopatra is happy to let this interpretation stand. At the same time, Fielding's dissimulation serves to divorce Arsinoe's death from its political context – it was essentially capital punishment for treason – and thus further indicts Cleopatra's tyrannical character. Although Cleopatra's request that Antony execute Arsinoe stemmed, in reality, from her sister's rebellion against her, Fielding's Cleopatra transforms this act into yet another proof of Antony's subjection to Cleopatra's will, a further instance of gratuitous cruelty. Fielding's Cleopatra thus actively builds on, and luxuriates in, the rhetoric of previous histories in order to enact the very historiographic model that had produced "Cleopatra" for eighteenth-century audiences.

Modern histories adopt the same predictable pattern. When *The Lives of Cleopatra and Octavia* appeared in 1757, an increasingly one-dimensional Cleopatra had continued to emerge: popular histories such as John Lockman's *New Roman History, by Question and Answer* (1737) and Charles Rollin's *Ancient History* (1738) and *Roman History from the Foundation of Rome to the Battle of Actium* (which he finished with the help of Jean Baptiste Louis Crevier, 1739) depicted Cleopatra with the simplicity of a stock character, relegating her to the role of villain. Lockman, for example, prefigures the language of Fielding's heroine by depicting a Cleopatra, contra Plutarch, eager to bind Antony's will: "to captivate [him] still more, [she] never suffered him to be out of her Sight; but made it her whole Study to divert him, and bind him the faster ... Her only Care was, to amuse him agreeably, and not to give him time to feel the Weight of his Chains" (cf. Fielding's *Cleopatra*, 63).[43] Lockman never allows the reader to forget that she was "the only Cause of all [Antony's] Misfortunes" and that, despite her keen intellect, she was a stereotypical woman through and through: when news of Antony's marriage to Octavia renders her jealous and angry, he must "pacify her" by handing over Roman territories (*NRH*, 330; 332); following in the footsteps of ancient historians such as Dio, Lockman declares that Cleopatra flees Actium because she was "terrified at the Noise" (*NRH*, 328).[44] Christopher D. Johnson credits the Rollin-Crevier history, in particular, with inspiring Fielding's description of a thoroughly manipulative Cleopatra who appears pathologically incapable of feeling the least regret upon Antony's death.[45] Rollin avers, "if she could have fallen upon any method of saving herself without him, or even at his expence[,] there is no question but she would have done it with joy" (*RH*, 16:71).

The heavy-handed didacticism of modern historians such as Lockman, Rollin, and Crevier anticipates the binary moral of Fielding's Dedication and Introduction even as the parallel structure of *The Lives of Cleopatra and Octavia* complicates the novel's didactic objective. Unequivocally condemning Cleopatra, Lockman exclaims, "What a Monster was this Queen! The most odious Vices were complicated in her Person; an absolute Renunciation of all Modesty; a violent Propension to Fraud, Injustice and Cruelty; and, what is worst of all, a most detestable Hypocrisy" (*NRH*, 329; 332). Crevier concludes the *Roman*

History in similar terms, lambasting her "foolish ambition," the "fruit of [her] audacious project" to rule the Roman Empire, which resulted in nothing but the "ruin both of Antony and of her," a symptom of the "[h]aughtiness [that] attended her even to her last moments" (*RH*, 16:97). Rounding out his condemnation, he adopts the type of hyperbole that Fielding would later imitate: describing Cleopatra as the single "most disdainful woman that ever lived" (*RH*, 16:98), Crevier reduces her to a superlative exemplum that anticipates Fielding's claim that "The Lives of *Cleopatra* and *Octavia* form, perhaps, the strongest Contrast of any Ladies celebrated in History" (41). The success of histories like those by Lockman, Rollin, and Crevier meant that Fielding could count on an audience familiar with the trajectory of the Cleopatra story, from its sympathetic treatment in Plutarch to the Rollin-Crevier caricature. Because histories like Lockman's were schoolbook standards – so much so that copyright on his similarly successful *History of England by Question and Answer* "was worth over £100 in 1787 and its twenty-fifth edition appeared in 1811" – Fielding, like Plutarch, had little need to tell her readers what they already knew.[46] The very first line of Fielding's novel thus resonates with the interpretive potential engendered by the romance historiography of her hybrid fiction: even as she declares that the historical lives of her heroines may form the "strongest Contrast," she also suggests that *The Lives of Cleopatra and Octavia*, the object itself, "form[s], perhaps, the strongest Contrast of any Ladies celebrated in History." The opening words enact an illocutionary declaration, performing the same tautology that enables Fielding's source material. In presenting *The Lives of Cleopatra and Octavia* to the Countess of Pomfret, she recommends the fiction's moral while underscoring the artifice of history itself; the duality invoked by *The Lives*/the Lives at once legitimates the opposition of "Cleopatra" to "Octavia" and calls upon her readers to deconstruct it.

"A perpetual and disgraceful Monument": The Spectacular Cleopatra

As the Cleopatra of the eighteenth-century historiographic tradition becomes increasingly villainous, so too does she become transparently performative, at least in the hands of her historians. For Lockman, her "detestable Hypocrisy" is "worst of all" (*NRH*, 329; 332), while Rollin declares her an "artful princess, who knew how to excite love, without suffering herself from that passion" (*RH*, 15:217; cf. Fielding's *Cleopatra*, 64);

he later insists that she was "the more capable of counterfeiting outward appearances, as she felt nothing within" (*RH*, 16:74). Although Plutarch had drawn different conclusions about Cleopatra's motives, he nonetheless made available the dramatic vocabulary that would inspire Lockman, Rollin – and later Fielding herself – as well as no fewer than seventy-seven plays, forty-five operas, and five ballets between 1540 and 1905.[47] Critics have long observed the especially theatrical nature of *The Life of Antony*, from Plutarch's own metaphorical characterizations to the religious and political performances orchestrated by Cleopatra and Antony as the new Isis and Osiris of the ancient Mediterranean. Fielding, in turn, self-consciously foregrounds the theatricality of her novel from the Introduction onward: conflating history and fiction, she acknowledges the value of biography, with its "true Coin," because it represents the "Lives of Persons who have really made their Appearance on the Stage of the World" (55). Even before she arrives at the justification for including some "Mixture of Romance" in her fictional (auto)biographies, Fielding follows Plutarch by characterizing history as fundamentally performative.

Pursuing the hints by Lockman and Rollin, Fielding's Cleopatra emerges as artifice through and through. Always aware of the part she must play to manipulate Antony, she transforms his death into the scene of her most powerful performance. In the events surrounding Antony's suicide – a time when even the most hostile writers tend to treat Cleopatra with sympathy – Fielding's heroine flatly insists that earlier historians are wrong. Whereas most histories remain silent on her retreat from Actium, or at least attribute her flight to womanly fear, Fielding's Cleopatra, after making Antony "shew his Followers how much he was [her] Slave" by compelling him to fight at sea, quickly deserts him, "being full of the Scheme of making [her] Peace with *Caesar*" (113). She soon determines that, if Antony's ruin is inevitable, it might better suit her, in her negotiations with Octavian, to betray him; she considers, but without "any Horror," the sometime fate of Pompey, whose assassination her brother had arranged: "The *Egyptian* Shore," she claims, "seemed to me destined for the Grave of the *Roman* great Men, and for the freeing successive *Caesars* of their Rivals" (114–15). Indeed, she maintains, seemingly echoing Rollin, "Had I been sure of *Caesar*, I had made no Scruple of giving up *Anthony*." But Fielding's Cleopatra succumbs to pride, fearing that Octavian will "le[a]d [her] in Triumph" (117). Anticipating her historical reception, she "glor[ies] in the Appearance of being faithful" to Antony (120), as if to impose upon future historians.

In this way, Fielding most aggressively contradicts the historical record when the stakes are highest, in the final act of the tragedy. Recommitting to her portrait of an irredeemable, self-serving seductress who never loved Antony at all, the resulting fiction at once mirrors the allegations of historians like Lockman, Rollin, and Crevier and corroborates their basest suspicions. As the end approaches, Fielding's Cleopatra callously relates how she actively hoped that Antony would kill himself, how she gave out false information of her own death to that purpose, and how she abruptly changed her mind: the "[m]oment I apprehended he might be further useful to me, quick as Lightning I dispatched a Messenger" to rouse him (121). When Antony finally comes, dying, to her tomb, Cleopatra remains largely unmoved by his plight. Although she admits feeling "[a] little Compassion for *Anthony*," she owns experiencing "a good deal for myself" (122). "In reality," she states, "I mourned for myself," and reveals that, "had *Caesar* been amorous enough to have been ensnared by my Charms, *Anthony's* Fate might have remained for ever unlamented by the perfidious *Cleopatra*" (124). Here, at the one moment when, in most histories and theatrical productions alike, Cleopatra – no matter how villainous – usually gives vent to sorrow for Antony, expressing her love for and devotion to him, Fielding's heroine insists on seeing him as an "Object of [her] Power" to the end (122).

Well aware that "faithful lover" will be the only positive role available to her, this Cleopatra is a thorough hypocrite in both senses of the term. She confesses that self-interest alone motivated her expressions of love, and revels in being perceived as a faithful lover while secretly professing otherwise, as if to augment her crimes. Perhaps no moment in Fielding's novel better reveals Cleopatra's awareness of the historical tradition that will impugn her than her calculated response to Antony's death. Convinced of Octavian's betrayal, she explains that "the only Refuge left me to die with the least Shadow of Honour, was imposing on the World my violent and faithful Love of *Anthony*," and boasts that, "in order to set forth that Love," the semblance of her "Affectation displayed all its Extravagance, and forced me to put on a thousand theatrical Postures, which Reality and Truth would scorn to appear in" (122). Knowing that historians (the "World") would measure her earthly "Honour" by the extent to which she convincingly feigns love for Antony, Cleopatra attempts to play the game by their rules, conceding to be commemorated as a "faithful Love[r]," since "theatrical Postures" are clearly preferable to "Reality and Truth." Yet, even by these standards, she fails, gaining only the "Shadow of Honour," not honour itself, an achievement reserved for the victors. Fielding thus demonstrates the lengths to which Cleopatra must go in order to become a mere footnote to Octavian's victory, either a mute image on Aeneas's shield or, in the form of Dido, the self-destructive queen of Carthage whose very madness justifies her demise.

Fielding goes so far as to make explicit the connections between "Cleopatra" and artifice at key points in the novel, as she does when Cleopatra wonders what will become of her if Antony's successes ennoble his wife, Fulvia:

> Not even Cicero could describe my Agonies. Apelles could not have painted my convulsive Anguish: It would have baffled the Power of his utmost Art: Nor could Roscius himself, in the Height of all his Glory, when crowded Theatres panted for Breath in the Contest which should get foremost to behold him, have represented to the Life the various Passions that would have agitated my Soul, and destroyed my Peace; never to have been healed, nor restored again. (72)

Cleopatra envisions her translation from fact to fantasy – or, more particularly, her untranslatability – at the hands of the greatest artists of antiquity. Yet even these men, with their skill, cannot portray her; in the strength and depth of her emotions and, no doubt, in her sheer inscrutability as a woman and Egyptian, she exceeds the limits of their art, a process that she enacts even in her relation of it: at this moment, allusions stand in place of potential outrage, substituting rhetoric for emotion. Already, Cleopatra imagines the (im)possibility of future representation. In this tableau, she exceeds and becomes rhetorical artifice (Cicero), a consummate actor (Roscius), no match even for Apelles, the only artist permitted to render a portrait of Alexander the Great. What hopes does she have from history, Fielding seems to ask, when even her own contemporaries, these venerable ancients, lack the terms to describe her, and when the recognized geniuses of her example are either long dead or Roman enemies? Certainly, it is no accident that she conjures the silver-tongued Cicero, Antony's inveterate foe, to confront the limits of representation.

The theatricality of Fielding's Cleopatra thus emphasizes her self-awareness as an object of history; she both resists and yet mockingly complies with the historical project that seeks to stabilize her meaning. Magnifying the ever-present disjuncture between signifier and signified, Fielding assuages, by exploiting, the anxiety that Cleopatra is not what she appears. To be sure, "Cleopatra" functions, in this way, as the emblem of a more basic interpretive problem. Her role as queen of Egypt (an actual person) intersects with her position as subject of history (the representation of that person), making her a striking example of the instabilities that signs proliferate. Given the distance between the person known as Cleopatra VII and her subsequent representations, how can we ever hope to recover "the secret Springs and Motives" (54) of her actions if those springs are altogether too secret and the motives easily mistaken? Rollin's *Roman History* resolves this dilemma by advancing obvious speculation as decided fact, declaring, once and for all, that Cleopatra "had never had a true and sincere love for Antony" (*RH*, 16:71). Avowing the "truth" with as much confidence as if Cleopatra had told it to him directly, he leaves no room for interpretive doubt: "there is no question but she would have [sacrificed Antony] with joy" (*RH*, 16:71). In this way, Rollin articulates precisely the anxiety that Fielding's narrative conceit appears to satisfy: the world will know Cleopatra's motives, even if she must be conjured from the dead.

Showcasing her theatricality, Fielding's Cleopatra suggests that the lost subjectivity Rollin seeks to recover is irrelevant to his history. After all, Fielding's heroine can still be read, from another angle, as Plutarch's: even as she supplements the narrative with invented details, promising to divulge her secrets, she reminds readers that "Cleopatra-as-faithful-lover" and "Cleopatra-as-false-insinuating-woman" are indistinguishable to the naked eye. In this way, the Cleopatra of *The Lives* is not only a skilled actress but an exemplar of the craft, anticipating Diderot's unfinished essay, "The Paradox of Acting" (1769), over ten years later. Insists Diderot, "All the actor's talents consist not in feeling, as you imagine, but in rendering so scrupulously the external signs of feeling, that you are taken in."[48] He continues

> Reflect a little as to what, in the language of the theatre is being true. Is it showing things as they are in nature? Certainly not. Were it so, the true would be commonplace. What is the truth for stage purposes? It is the conforming of action, diction, face, voice, movement, and gesture to an ideal type, invented by the poet and frequently enhanced by the player.

For Diderot, the titular paradox is that an actor must be "a cold and tranquil spectator," in control of the sensibility he performs: "If there is anyone sure to give and present this sublimity, it is the man who can feel it with his passion and genius and reproduce it with complete self-possession." Inviting us to view her theatrical postures, Fielding's Cleopatra appears, in this light, a superb actress in a two-act play. Yet there is no intermediary, no actress who underscores, by drawing attention to, the fiction. Fielding's heroine is almost purely discursive, recalling Nancy Armstrong's characterization of Samuel Richardson's *Pamela*: this "Cleopatra" – indeed, every Cleopatra – is nothing but words.[49] This uncomfortable realization, in turn, drives Rollin and other historians to claim privileged access to the contours of her mind – the "Soul" that Fielding teasingly presents to the reader, liberated from the body's "prison" (56). Though he makes the observation to different ends, Fielding's early twentieth-century editor, R. Brimley Johnson, articulates the source of this anxiety: Cleopatra "is not a human being," he writes in his Introduction to *The Lives*, "but a malignant machine, of devilish cunning, callous cruelty, and untiring hate; drunk with worship of self, wholly governed by vanity and pride; never, for one moment, relaxing her role, lifting her veil, exposing her sin."[50] In this way, Fielding's lexicon of "Soul" and "Body" at once disguises and discloses the perpetual narrative machine beneath. Set in motion by the novel's Underworld frame, Fielding's Cleopatra has all the raw materials she needs: with the details of previous histories at her disposal, she awaits only a ruling passion to animate her performance.

Although Fielding's Cleopatra makes a final bid to be commemorated as the devoted lover of Antony, the role of "faithful lover" – no less than the part of "consummate villainess" – remains circumscribed by Cleopatra's defeat and Augustan mastery of available narratives. The eighteenth-century stage, inspired as it was by Plutarch's account, trades on the double-bind that Fielding's Cleopatra also seeks to exploit. The transformation of Plutarch's Cleopatra from politically savvy queen of Egypt to lovelorn heroine reaches its apotheosis in Dryden's *All for Love; Or the World Well Lost* (1666). Performed 123 times throughout the century, Dryden's play eclipsed Shakespeare's and helped to define Cleopatra for Fielding's readers.[51] Although Dryden frequently reprises Augustan rhetoric through the character of Ventidius, he also softens Cleopatra's image, eulogizing the faithful lover over the savvy queen – the very process of transformation that Fielding's Cleopatra appears to anticipate. In Dryden's recasting of Plutarch's narrative, Cleopatra's love equals Antony's: she is possessed of a "noble madness" and "transcendent passion" (2.1.17; 20), claiming precedence, in suffering, over his lawful wife, because "the world contemns poor me, / For

I have lost my honor, lost my fame, / And stained the glory of my royal house, / And all to bear the branded name of mistress" (3.461–4). Antony, vacillating between despair and passion, admits that he values Cleopatra "[b]eyond life, conquest, empire" (1.424), and fears that they have loved each other "[i]nto [their] mutual ruin" (2.244–5). This sense of mutuality is crucial, for it depicts a Cleopatra as pitiable – but also as incompetent – as her Roman lover: when Antony, believing Cleopatra to be false, attempts to expel her from his sight, she replies, "My joys, my only joys, are centered here: / What place have I to go to? My own kingdom? / That I have lost for you" (4.42–4). By the time the play concludes, Serapion is able to commemorate the royal couple with little sense of irony: "Sleep, blest pair, / Secure from human chance, long ages out, / While all the storms of Fate fly o'er your tomb, / And fame to late posterity shall tell, / No lovers lived so great, or died so well" (5.515–19). Dryden's Cleopatra at once ensures the queen's consignment to romance and further legitimates romance-as-history.

Just as Dryden's Cleopatra leaves audiences hard pressed to envision a ruler whose influence extends beyond her ability to win Antony's love, Fielding follows a similar path, constructing a Cleopatra who, divested of actual power, continually falls prey to her imagination. In this way, *The Lives* shows how the same Augustan narrative that displaces Antony's failings onto Cleopatra also substitutes imaginary for actual influence by a neat sleight of hand, recasting Cleopatra as a victim of her own fancy, just as Plutarch had cast Antony as a slave to lust. This version of history, like Virgil's description of Actium, precludes Cleopatra's success from the start, blaming her for certain failure: challenging Rome, whatever the actual circumstances, can only mark Cleopatra as self-deluded, a thrall to her wild imagination. Led astray by the chimeras of her fancy, even before Cleopatra meets Antony she confesses that she delights in allowing her "Imagination [to] rove through the Variety of Pleasures the extensive Power [of Anthony] could invest me with" (60). Later, when Antony assassinates a king in order to hand over the spoils to Cleopatra, she exults now that "*Cyrene*, *Cyprus*, *Caelo-Syria*, *Iturea*, and *Phenicia*, with great Part of *Cilicia* and *Crete*, were all added to my hereditary Dominions," but declares that she looks upon them "as a mere Trifle, in comparison of that unbounded Power, and immense Treasure, my Fancy had bestowed on me" (92). So powerful is Cleopatra's imagination that she "indulged [her] Fancy to such an Excess, in the Thoughts that [she] should, by *Anthony*'s Means, become Mistress of the World, that [she] could sit whole Hours and entertain

[her]self with the Prospect of being at the Capitol of *Rome*" (104). In stressing the imaginary nature of this power, Fielding's Cleopatra incriminates Roman history while paradoxically affirming its assessment: so obviously deluded about the scope of her influence, she can hardly be threatening at all.

In *The Lives*, the extremity of Cleopatra's vanity and pride augments the destructive force of her imagination as she continually undermines her efforts to control Antony and advance Egypt's claims against the Roman Empire. Although Octavian would seem to be her primary enemy, Fielding's Cleopatra fixates on Antony's first wife, Fulvia, and especially on Octavian's wife, Livia, and sister, Octavia, venting misplaced anger towards the Roman women who have little control over her fate. Even as she faces humiliating defeat, Cleopatra twice fears being "led in Triumph" not, as readers might expect, because of Rome's treatment of foreign powers, who were typically executed at the Triumph's close, but because "*Livia* and *Octavia* should behold my Dishonour, and exult in my Misery" (117). Where Octavian's "Triumph" consists of establishing himself as sole ruler of the Mediterranean, Cleopatra's amounts to besting his women: she relishes the prospect of subduing him only because "by that Means I might triumph at *Rome* over *Livia* and *Octavia*" (117). For Cleopatra, the "unbounded Desire of Empire" shrinks from dominion over Egypt to control of Antony, and then to "insolently triumphing over *Livia* and *Octavia*" by "making *Caesar* my Slave" (118). "*Caesar*'s Power" and "the Triumph of *Livia* and *Octavia*" exist in apposition to one another in Cleopatra's thoughts, "croud[ing] my Mind with such various and bitter Reflections, as almost hurried me to Distraction" (125). In impotently focusing Cleopatra's energies on her Roman rivals, Fielding transforms them into surrogate threats to the queen's power: Cleopatra's self-deceiving pride leads her to recast the war as a manipulative struggle among women, thereby lessening its significance and conveniently disguising the danger posed by her true enemy, Octavian. Yet again, her willingness to succumb to the seductions of imagination – itself associated with the luxurious allure of the East – marks Cleopatra as always and already defeated.

In the same way that her vanity and pride distract Cleopatra's focus from Octavian, they leave her fixated, to the couple's mutual ruin, on the narrow goal of enslaving Antony. Presumably, Antony and Cleopatra desire similar outcomes – the ouster of Octavian and their own installation as rulers of the Empire – yet there is little sense of a joint, concerted effort in their narrative. At one point, she even declares that "I was very sensible nothing but blinding Anthony to his own Interest could keep him in my Power" (71), as if they did not share mutual goals. At first, Cleopatra states that her "Design was to be Mistress of the Kingdoms or Empires which Anthony could conquer" (67); subsequently enlarging her intentions, she adds that "Power was my Pursuit": "nothing," she says, "could gratify me more than such Instances as proved that I could rule and turn Mark Anthony's Mind with a Look, a Word, or any the least Sign of Resentment" (69). At this point, Cleopatra's desires begin to come into conflict unproductively with one another: "Avarice and Ambition," she explains, "both united in my Desire of *Anthony*'s gaining new Kingdoms, because I knew he would lay them at my Feet; yet," she continues, "his being my Slave, and the World's seeing he was the Dupe of his Passion for me, were my principal Points of view" (97). There is, she insists, no sense of equality between them; she does not plan to rule the Empire with Antony, but to "make him lay at my Feet whatever Part of the Universe fell to his Share" (82). Although she initially joins with him because her "Fate depend[s]" on it (60), positioning her to regain the glory of the Ptolemaic Empire and, eventually, to unite East and West under one rule, she quickly forsakes real-world influence in favour of "imaginary Power" (82).

Signalling her final capitulation to Augustan propaganda, Fielding's Cleopatra eventually crosses the line between controlling Antony for the sake of political expediency and doing so for private pleasure. Although his defeat at Octavian's hands is a severe blow to her position, she nonetheless "looked on [Antony's] Disgrace as [her] Triumph, and exulted as much in [her] Imagination as if [she] had gained a Victory" (114). "Besides," she adds, as though defeat were a mere inconvenience, "I still flattered myself, that whilst *Anthony* was so much my Slave, I needed not despair of commanding the World; for I had joined those Two Ideas so strongly together, that it was very difficult to separate or disunite them" (114). It is at this moment of confessed self-delusion that we learn Cleopatra has indeed been "baffling [her] Designs" (67), acting in ways that "by no means answer[ed] [her] Purpose" (72). In hindsight, Cleopatra has thwarted her own success: "The Strength of my Imagination, by assisting to place before my Eyes … charming Pictures of what I would do when I was Mistress of the World, was the Cause of all my future Misfortunes" (104). *The Life of Cleopatra* thus cautions against conjuring unprofitable fictions, at once reminding the reader of the frame narrative, with its Eastern sorcerer, and of the historiographic tendencies – the "Knight errantry" of fiction-as-history – that Fielding scrutinizes. Succumbing to pleasing delusions, Cleopatra represents imagination run wild – not only, as it turns out, in her irredeemable pride, but also in her mocking appropriation of the lurid fantasies she embodies for Fielding's readers.

Being Made a Sacrifice: Octavia and Roman Virtue

In Donatus's *Life of Virgil*, he relates how Octavia, listening as the poet reads to Augustus from Book 6 of the *Aeneid*, faints at Virgil's praise of her son, Marcellus.[52] A potential heir to her brother's throne, Marcellus had died unexpectedly, in the flower of youth, with every promise of an accomplished life ahead of him. It was a subject that lent itself to artistic representation. At the end of the eighteenth century, for example, Angelica Kauffman's *Virgil Reading the Aeneid to Octavia and Augustus* (1788) would depict the poet temporarily distracted from his masterpiece as Octavia swoons; her brother and two waiting women (one looking reproachfully at the poet?) rush to her side (see Figure 4.1). Virgil holds a scroll revealing the following line: "Tu Marcellus eris," part of Anchises' address to Aeneas in the Underworld, thus translated by Dryden, "Ah, cou'dst thou break through Fates severe Decree / A new *Marcellus* shall arise in thee!" (5:6.1220–1). These lines explicitly align Aeneas with Octavia's son, another in a long line of illustrious Romans whose subsequent glory Virgil's hero would make possible. The image of an Octavia rendered senseless by Virgilian mythmaking neatly highlights the narrative dilemma of *The Lives*, no less than the *Aeneid* itself: the problem of escaping a teleological trajectory that casts both Cleopatra and Octavia as silenced actors in Octavian's history. A bystander to her brother's glory, Octavia relives her son's death as a virtual outsider to Virgilian epic: although Marcellus's mother, she becomes a spectator to, instead of an actor in, contemporary events. Octavia's immobilizing swoon, recalled against the static portrait of Cleopatra on Aeneas's shield, invites readers to view her as a participant in the same paradigm of feminine propriety, one of two sides of the same "false Coin" represented, in Fielding's Introduction, by fiction rather than truth. Her brother deploys the "Octavia" narrative as effectively as he does Cleopatra's: as the perfect Roman matron, she becomes a suitable counter-example for his rallying cry, a virtuous, obedient woman who could demonstrate the ideological stakes of waging war against a masculine queen.

Figure 4.1. Angelica Kauffman, *Virgil Reading the Aeneid to Augustus* (1788). Image courtesy of the Heritage Museum.

Yet following Cleopatra's narration, Octavia's appears almost as an afterthought: *The Life of Cleopatra* dominates the novel in its length – nearly four times *The Life of Octavia* – and dictates the events of Octavia's story, as well as its historical value. After all, Cleopatra needs no Octavia to be remembered, but Octavia needs Cleopatra in order to achieve her symbolic potential. As I argued at the beginning of this chapter, the structure of Plutarch's *Parallel Lives* further informs Octavia's *Life* in relation to Cleopatra's. "Important here," to recall Duff's observation on the correct interpretation of Plutarch's didactic intent, "is the principle of pattern and variation: the first Life sets a pattern which is then exploited and varied in the second."[53] Repeatedly throughout the *Life of Octavia*, key elements of Cleopatra's narrative recur, providing a ready-made context for interpreting their resurgence in Octavia's account.

From the beginning, Fielding depicts an Octavia susceptible to her own ruling passion, in this case the passion of love (126). This is not the first time that Octavia, in a first-person defence, would lay claim to the logic of love to frame her earthly actions: Madeleine de Scudéry's *Les Femmes illustres; ou, Les harangues héroïques* (1642), that series of speeches so central to Lennox's project in *The Female Quixote*, likewise foregrounds an Octavia motivated by love. Although beyond the scope of this chapter, it is worth noting that *Femmes illustres* also depicts, among its twenty "harangues" (or orations) by famous – and sometimes infamous – women, a Cleopatra who vindicates her reputation by explaining to Antony that she flees Actium with no thought more self-serving than the preservation of his life. Yet Fielding's Octavia is a far cry from Scudéry's: while, in *Femmes illustres*, both Cleopatra and Octavia stand as model heroines, they transform into more complicated, even negative exempla in *The Lives of Cleopatra and Octavia*, illustrating the dangers of self-aggrandizement and self-delusion.[54]

From the outset, the pattern of Octavia's marriage to Marcellus mimics the pattern of Cleopatra's marriage to Antony: Cleopatra's tactics of seduction anticipate the circumstances that will lead Octavia to her union, a match as political as it is companionate. Seeking to ensure that Antony will desire her long before their first encounter, Cleopatra hopes that the artist Dellius will "represent and paint me in such amiable Colours to *Anthony*, as would make him impatient to behold the Original of so fair a Picture" (60). Later, it is the fair picture reported of Marcellus that inspires Octavia to visit him, eager to see if he will match the portrait of an ideal husband long cherished in her mind. At the beginning of her *Life*, she claims that "the highest Notion I could form of Happiness, was a private Life, with a Husband who was agreeable to my Inclinations, and capable of a reciprocal Affection" (126). She thus refuses to marry unless "Considerations of State" require it, twice affirming that she will "live single" should it prove "impossible to meet with the Counter-part of the Picture which dwelt in my Imagination" (127). *Mirabile dictu*, she soon hears the praises of Marcellus and insists on meeting him for herself: wasting no time, she "took the first Opportunity" to visit him, affirming that he "exceeded my Picture, as much as the hand of Nature excels that of Art." Instead of describing Marcellus, she "describe[s] [for the reader] the Picture I had long before drawn by my own Fancy" (127), since the two are one and the same. By the time she invokes "the story of *Pygmalion* and his Statue" as a model of her relationship with Marcellus – "he was the Portrait I had drawn, animated with Life and Motion" (128) – her "good Fortune" indeed seems too good to be true.

In fact, just as Cleopatra invents anecdotes to enhance the viciousness of her character, Octavia breaks with history in order to magnify her virtue. Though she doesn't hesitate to call attention to a genealogical "Mistake in Plutarch" (126), indicating her apparent familiarity with *The Life of Antony*, Octavia is less scrupulous in noting deviations that work to her advantage. For example, she idealizes her marriage to Marcellus by characterizing it as a love match that occurs only after Pompey rejects an alliance with Julius Caesar, and credits her brother, Octavian, for "destin[ing]" Marcellus to be her husband (127). In reality, by the time Octavia was useful to Caesar in his negotiations with Pompey, she was already married to Marcellus, and certainly would have divorced him at her uncle's behest, had Pompey wished to strengthen his ties with Caesar. In keeping with Octavia's status, the marriage to Marcellus was arranged; she was fifteen at the time and her new husband was approximately twenty years her senior. Fielding's Octavia makes no mention of Marcellus's attempts to defy Caesar, for which he was later pardoned, thereby neatly omitting a detail that aligns the historical Marcellus with Antony: Marcellus's unsuccessful opposition to Julius Caesar anticipates Antony's unsuccessful opposition to that later Caesar, her brother.

The inventions of Fielding's Octavia would be less striking were it not for the incredulity they inspire. In this Octavia's version of history, her marriage to Marcellus becomes a retreat into fantasy. Absorbed by their mutual infatuation to the point of distraction, the couple appear untouched by the strife that dominates the beginning of the narrative. Having attained her utmost happiness by finding the picture of her fancy completed in Marcellus, Octavia describes the dreamlike cast of their time together: "whether we staid at home, or went abroad, were serious or disposed to Mirth, still by our Sympathy and Love, every Trifle made a Pleasure, and every Pleasure was heightened into Joy by our mutual Participation of it; our Hearts exulted with that Rapture which is built on the strong Foundation of undissembled Love" (130). So powerful is this rapture that it transforms otherwise unexceptional experiences into the marvellous: "Every Tree and Bush, every common Object produced by Nature, became, by our Observations, and giving way to our delighted Imaginations, Matter of the most agreeable Entertainment" (130). As their shared fancy enlivens the ordinary beauties of the natural world, Octavia declares, with a note of triumph, that they successfully "banished all tumultuous Passions from our Breasts," left "with no other Thoughts but those of Peace, Tranquility, and Joy" (130). Yet "Peace, Tranquility, and Joy" give way, abruptly, to a gruesome scene, as Octavia concedes: "The public Calamity, in the Time of the famous Proscription by *Caesar*, *Anthony*, and *Lepidus*, did indeed interrupt our Composure, move our Compassion, and fill us with Terror" (130). The sudden intrusion of the Proscriptions, in which the Triumvirate mutually agreed to have their enemies executed, quickly forecloses additional rhapsodizing. Have Octavia and Marcellus been indulging "mutual Love," transported by "their delighted Imaginations" as Rome burns (130)?

Following *The Life of Cleopatra*, Octavia's withdrawal from current events into a kind of timeless pastoral recalls Cleopatra's seduction of Antony, complete with the numerous pleasures, delights, and entertainments that similarly isolate Antony and weaken his judgment. Motivated by her ruling passion of love, Octavia emerges more "Antony" than "Cleopatra." Her passion, like Antony's, assumes a distinctly erotic cast: she desires a husband who is "agreeable" to her "Inclinations" (126), explaining that her "Judgment and Inclination" both encouraged her to become Marcellus's wife (127); although she imagines her future husband in terms of "Character," she nonetheless envisions him as a pleasing picture (127). Lest there be any doubt of the erotic significance, Octavia's own "Remembrance" of "the Story of *Pygmalion* and his Statue" (128) performs a reverse transformation, in which Marcellus becomes the nude and desirable sculpture, now incarnated – with Octavia's imagination taking the place of Aphrodite – for their mutual pleasure and delight. The point, here, is not that virtue and sexual desire are mutually exclusive for a heroine like Octavia; the mere existence of Octavia's desire is beside the point. Instead, the repetition of the pattern established in Antony and Cleopatra's narrative suggests that Octavia's love for Marcellus transports her into a cloistered imaginative world reminiscent of the retreat that leaves Antony (in Fielding and in Plutarch) vulnerable to his passions. Thus succumbing to the passion of love, Octavia exits the public sphere at the precise moment when her public virtue is most valuable.

Of course, Fielding's Octavia (no less than Plutarch's) is also an exemplar of reason: just as her judgment tempers her inclination in the decision to marry Marcellus, she obeys Marcellus's dying injunction to "calm [her] Mind" (131), mastering her grief in order to care for their children. In the initial "Agony" of her "Sorrow," Octavia reasons with herself: "Shall then the dying Command of my beloved Husband be the only one in which I ever disobeyed him? Is there any the most trying Proof of Regard I would not grant him? Shall Octavia give a Loose to Sorrows (which, as they are the present Bent of her Nature, would be her greatest Indulgence) till they sink her to the Grave?" (132). These reflections moderate Octavia's grief, "prevent[ing] its preying too deeply on [her] Heart" (132). The subsequent death of her son similarly affects her, leaving her with "a kind of Melancholy" that "became [her] greatest Relief," though it does not "prevent [her] from exerting [her]self to perform what [she] thought [her] Duty" (143). Octavia's exertions, accompanied eventually by her retirement from Rome, enable her to end her days "with a Mind steady, serene, and calm" (144), her soul "as clear as a limpid Stream" and "as unruffled by perplexing Sorrow, as a smiling Infant" (143). Although finally enabled by her retirement, absolute solitude, and continued exertions, Octavia's is an otherworldly virtue. Just as she is eminently reasonable, she describes Roman society as superlatively corrupt, emphasizing her own exceptionalism: "My Station," she laments, "unavoidably threw me into the Conversation of Women of the first Quality and Distinction; but I accounted every Moment spent in their Company as so much Loss of Time. Their Infidelity to their Husbands, and the general Profligacy of their Manners, raised in me the utmost Abhorrence of their Conduct" (131).

Although Marcellus enjoins Octavia, on his deathbed, to remember that her "Station may demand [her] Hand as a Sacrifice to the public Peace" (131), her ruling passion dictates the remainder of her narrative: unable to achieve happiness without Marcellus, Octavia finds that "Glory" becomes "Misery" when the "Name of Wife" unites her with Antony (133). News of the alliance leaves Octavia "shocked much more than if [her brother] had decreed [her] Death as the Means of the public Good" (133). As much as her imagination once fired her with the desire to meet Marcellus, it now baffles Octavia: she confesses that she "could form no Conception how it was possible for me to live with [Antony]" (133). From the moment of the proposed match, Antony is that "Dupe both of *Fulvia* and *Cleopatra*" and that "Slave to Two such Women" (133). There is no suggestion that Octavia has a more intimate knowledge of his character, yet her imagination fills her with apprehension: she has already determined that Antony will view her "Meekness" as

"Meanness of Spirit," her "Disposition inclined to forgive" as a "Want of Resolution" and "a wavering unsteady Temper," her "Openness of Heart" as "Artifice," and her "Simplicity and Honesty" as "Perfidy and Cunning" (133). Having constructed herself as perfectly opposite to Fulvia and Cleopatra, Octavia expects Antony to misread her.

In mobilizing an array of antonyms around Octavia's character, Fielding returns to the crisis of legibility that transforms Cleopatra into such a cipher. Cleopatra manipulates this crisis to her advantage, knowing that the appearance of truth supersedes truth itself. Octavia attempts to do the same: "resolv[ing] to be as cautious in all [her] Deportment to make *Anthony* a good Wife, as if he had been the Object of [her] Choice," she redoubles her efforts to please him precisely because her motives have changed. As "Duty" now "supplie[s] the Place" of "Inclination," she acknowledges that "I was the more watchful over my Behaviour, as fearing the Want of that Affection I had indulged for *Marcellus*, might tempt me to be careless of my Conduct to a Husband for whom I had not the same Inclination" (134). However, Octavia's exceptionalism dooms her to failure: seemingly the last virtuous woman in Rome, there is no available standard by which to read her model of virtue.

The fastidiousness of Octavia's virtue thus calls to mind the distinction between practicable and impracticable virtue that Dryden makes in the dedicatory epistle to *Aureng-Zebe* (1675), the tragedy that immediately predates *All for Love* and anticipates many of its themes. For Dryden, such "practicable virtue" represents a mean between Stoic mastery of the passions and excessive sensibility: it "mix[es] with the frailties and imperfections of humane life" – an active, adaptable, dynamic virtue that eschews the model, superficially endorsed in Fielding's Dedication and Introduction to *The Lives*, of virtue-as-set-piece.[55] The most devoted character in Dryden's play is the heroine, Melesinda: she is "a Woman passionately loving of her Husband, patient of injuries and contempt, and constant in her kindness to the last."[56] Yet it is precisely these qualities that make her virtue impracticable; she commits suicide at the end of the play, willing to immolate herself for the sake of her dead husband. Dryden envisions Melesinda's sacrifice according to a Roman model of female virtue: such "loving Fools" belong with the "*Arria's* and *Portia's* of old *Rome*"[57] – and, perhaps, the Octavias, too. It is this kind of impracticable virtue that leads Octavia to sabotage her marriage to Antony: echoing Cleopatra's confession that she "baffl[ed]" her "Designs" (67), acting in ways that "by no means answer[ed] [her] Purpose" (72), Octavia recognizes that she has "destroyed [her] own Purpose" (137) in redoubling her conformity to the Roman model of wifely obedience. Although she professes to love Antony, she refuses to honour him as she had Marcellus; she therefore withdraws from her new husband under the guise of feminine propriety, affecting to be least capable of performing her duty to Rome when her duty is most required.

In this way, Octavia resigns herself to the discourse of martyrdom that will at last make her virtue legible. No less aware than Cleopatra of her position as spectacle, Octavia describes how she musters the strength to effect her union with Antony by imagining herself as an unwilling actress cast in a noble role: called back to Rome from her retirement, Octavia describes herself as "destined to appear again on the public Stage; and the Part allotted me was both difficult and painful to perform" (132–3). The prospect of being a sacrifice haunts Octavia's story from the outset: "I dreaded from my Youth," she says, "that I should be sacrificed to political Views, and be disposed of in the solemn Tie of Matrimony to some Man, whose Ambition alone would lead him to take me as a Pledge of Friendship" (126). Indeed, in the course of *The Lives*, Octavia refers to herself as a sacrifice no fewer than seven times. In each case, she obscures agency: she fears that she "should be sacrificed" for the good of Roman politics; that "Considerations of State obliged me to be a Sacrifice" (127); that "it was necessary to make me a Sacrifice" (127); that her "Station," in the words of her dying first husband, Marcellus, "may demand [her] Hand as a Sacrifice to the public Peace" (131); and three times refers to "being made a Sacrifice to prevent the Effusion of Blood" (133–4; 137–8) or "for the Sake of Peace" (141). Although Octavia perfectly understands the delicacy of her position, in each case she avoids naming her brother as the author of her misfortunes. Setting the limits of her role in Octavian's history, she understands that she does not, and cannot, sacrifice herself, but submits instead to "being sacrificed" at her brother's behest.

The crucial opposition between "sacrificing" and "being sacrificed" ultimately characterizes Octavia's narrative as a whole: the difference between acting and being acted upon, between legitimate authority and passive influence. It is true that Plutarch acknowledges her reputation as "quite a wonder of a woman" (1121), distinguished by "beauty, honour, and prudence" (1122). But she enters into history for the sake of political expediency, married to Antony "because it was found convenient for the affairs of her brother that it should be so" (1134). Fielding also attempts to enlarge this limited characterization in her Dedication. Octavia, she argues, is "a sincere Friend, an affectionate Sister, a faithful Wife, and both a tender and instructive Parent." Yet, despite these accomplishments, Octavia's "*Roman* spirit" still comes down to "sacrificing her private to the public Good" (41). Fielding positions this outcome as a noble goal for women, yet Octavia's subsequent narrative gives the lie to the Dedication's positive framing of sacrificial female virtue.

Although Octavia – following Marcellus's dying injunction – fancies herself an important agent of the public good, Fielding suggests that she, like Cleopatra, has fallen victim to her imagination; centralizing her importance to the future of Rome, Octavia recasts passive sacrifice as a form of active virtue. Such moments abound in *The Lives*, as Octavia attempts to mitigate her brother's policies, ameliorating the bloodthirsty climate precipitated by civil war. But, outside of the scenes carefully orchestrated by her brother, *The Life* affords little room for Octavia's benevolent nature and, in a striking episode, even suggests how ridiculous her aspirations to heroic agency may be. Recalling the "general Misery" of the Proscriptions that interrupts her reverie with Marcellus, Octavia describes the extraordinary feats of compassion inspired by extraordinary circumstances. She explains how "[e]ven Slaves, habiting themselves like their Masters, met Death in their Stead: Sons, unaccustomed to disobey their Fathers … were resolute to die the first: Women in Numbers fled, bearing their Husbands, as Aeneas did his Father Anchises, on their Shoulders; with whom they secreted themselves in distant Caverns" (130). But these "Instances of Fidelity and Love," remarkable as extraordinary testaments to the Proscriptions' horrors, reveal at once the futility of setting herself against her brother's rule and the potentially comic – and hence admonitory – possibilities of doing so. For the image of female heroism that Octavia witnesses recalls Aeneas fleeing Trojan ashes with Anchises on his back, ushering onward his father and his son, Ascanius, even at the expense of his wife, Creusa, who, falling behind, next appears to Aeneas as a consoling shade, urging his continued *pietas*. In its unmistakable allusion to Aeneas's filial devotion, the tableau emphasizes, by contrast, a model of heroism properly suited to men: the women carrying their husbands on their backs serve as a reminder of the extent to which Octavia can never achieve the standard of Virgilian heroism, the heroism – to read Octavia against Virgil in hindsight – of the new Empire. It establishes, at the same time, her circumscription by that very template, the narrative of her brother's glorious conquest that relegates even Dido to the realms of romance.

In addition to Fielding's immediate evocation, given the Augustan context, of Aeneas's heroic flight from Troy, avid readers of the *Spectator* would perhaps have recalled another familiar allusion, drawn from *Spectator* 499 (1712), in which the gallant Will Honeycomb takes advantage of a similar story of virtue in order to satirize women as vain, material creatures. He does so under the guise of a dream he had, inspired by the legend of the *Weibertreue*, or loyal wives, of twelfth-century Hensburg, Germany. During a siege, the women "petitioned the Emperor [Conrad III, the duke of Bavaria's rival] that they might depart out of [the city], with so much as each of them could carry." Each chooses to take her husband, leaving the emperor "so moved at the sight, that he burst into Tears."[58] Will's dream, however, has quite the opposite ending. Rather than saving their husbands, Will's women "stagger" under the "burden" of "China-Ware," a "Favourite Monkey," a "huge Bale of Cards," a "Lap-Dog," and a "Bag of Gold," mocking contemporary objects of affection among fashionable eighteenth-century ladies. An already perverse image thanks to its inversion of the *Aeneid*'s heroics, the idea of a woman rescuing her husband appears even more ludicrous in Will's narration. Although Fielding implicitly refutes Will's cynical view in Octavia's account, the women's evident desperation, alongside their grouping with slaves as another example of unnatural valour, undermines the possibility that any such active female heroism can exist.

Perhaps no moment better juxtaposes Octavia's personal helplessness with her naive idealism than her request to meet Antony with reinforcements for the Parthian war, a gesture superficially intended to reunite her with her husband and to reaffirm his partnership with Octavian. An incident of central importance in the histories because of its precipitation of civil war, it also reveals the nature of Octavia's symbolic function. Fielding takes advantage of this moment to showcase Octavia's powerlessness to participate in her own self-fashioning, and the futility of the very peace her sacrificial marriage was intended to effect. For although Octavian gives his sister leave to play peacemaker, historians tend to agree on the emptiness of Octavia's hopes: Plutarch writes, for example, that Octavian gave her leave to see Antony, "not so much … to gratify his sister, as to obtain a fair pretence to begin war upon her dishonourable reception" (1134). He hoped, in other words, that "Antony would use her ill, and that thereby she would become the occasion, though innocently, of exciting against her faithless, and ungrateful spouse, an universal discontent in the minds of the people, by whom she was very justly held in the greatest esteem" (Rollin-Crevier, *RH*, 16:8). Octavian thus employs his sister, however "innocent" her intentions, as a pawn. Her symbolic function as the peace between Antony and Octavian translates instead to a function of "war" when, yet again, her brother finds it "convenient for [his] affairs ... that it should be so" (Plutarch 1134).

In sabotaging Octavia's mission from the outset – for "the derisory smallness of her escort" was far short of the twenty thousand he had promised Antony[59] – Octavian renders her a liability to his enemy, instead of an asset to her husband. As Michael Grant has noted in his biography of Cleopatra, Octavia's "honest efforts" were not only "of no value to Antony," they were, in terms of "their propaganda effects," "positively harmful" if "Octavian had no intention of keeping his side of the agreement."[60] While, a short time earlier, the Octavia of *The Lives* thinks herself fortunate that, "by my Prayers and Tears, I so pacified and softened my Brother, that I had the Pleasure of once more seeing myself the Cause of Harmony between him and my Husband" (138), she does not realize that her brother's desires for sole imperial rule militate against her allegiance to her husband and her own desires for peace. Her brother dictates history so thoroughly that Octavia fails to recognize his puppeteering; instead, she blames herself, miserable "at the Consideration, that although I had been made so great a Sacrifice for the Sake of Peace, I should now be deemed one of the principal Causes of a bloody War" (141).[61] Even as she laments Antony's suicide, when she "was yet ready to receive him, and use her utmost Endeavours to crown him with Peace and Empire" (142), Octavia believes, until the last, that she will be able to exert her sisterly influence on his enemy; she never concedes that neither peace nor empire is hers to give. Fielding thus reveals Octavia, no less than Cleopatra, to be a victim of wishful thinking: even in her own first-person narration, she has only as much agency as Octavian permits.

Armed with histories ancient and modern, Fielding thus mocks the twin scripts of female vice and virtue by carrying them to their ultimate, vengeful conclusion, creating a self-destructive Cleopatra utterly possessed by ambition, an Antony whom she misses no opportunity to betray, and an Octavia so attendant to the dictates of wifely submission that she destroys her own marriage. Certainly, Octavia would stand for virtue and innocence had she merited a place in Berquin's *Looking-Glass*, but she remains curiously absent, suitably mirroring her symbolic fate as Octavian's sister and Antony's wife, the so-called pledge of peace and cause of war between great men. In the end, both women are ciphers, not just Cleopatra; each becomes, in her own way, the emblematic sacrifice on which Octavian rhetorically, and in fact, built the Roman Empire. Meanwhile, Octavian himself receives little censure, much as he thwarts Octavia's purposes: Fielding writes nothing less than history imagined by the victors. By deliberately turning to the most defamatory accounts available, Fielding makes explicit, through her novelization of Cleopatra's and Octavia's lives, the prejudices – invisible because naturalized – that shape conventional histories. In this way, she harnesses and redirects the charges typically levelled against novel reading: where, in *The Female Quixote*, Arabella appears deluded thanks to romance precepts, Fielding's heroines undermine the claims of Lennox's Divine – that history is superior to romance – because they have imbibed their delusions from history itself. In short, both Cleopatra and Octavia become the dupes of the fictionalized discourses that produce them for future audiences. Fielding thus unsettles – precisely by satisfying and exceeding – the revisionist history that transforms Cleopatra and Dido into vain and lovesick queens, plots that neutralize their power and influence.

5 Whose "Wild and Extravagant Stories"? Clara Reeve's *The Progress of Romance* and *The History of Charoba, Queen of Ægypt*

In 1798, the writer Walter Savage Landor inspired the beginnings of Romantic Orientalism with the publication of his poem *Gebir*.[1] Landor's epic details the hero's loss of love and empire: the titular prince, seeking, at once, to woo Queen Charoba of Egypt and reclaim ancestral lands, instead suffers defeat at the hands of Charoba's nurse, a powerful enchantress. Her lethal intervention brings to an end Gebir's imperial ambitions, and also his star-crossed love for the young queen, the hapless victim of her nurse's stratagems. Five years later, Landor would explain the purpose of his poem in a new edition: "In the moral are exhibited the folly, the injustice, and the punishment of Invasion, with the calamities which must ever attend the superfluous colonization of a peopled country."[2] Yet the poem idealizes Gebir, leading even Charoba – his intended conquest – to lament his tragic fall in Egypt. Landor's version of the Charoba story marks a reversal of Charoba's original history, in which the queen of Egypt recalls both Dido, entertaining a foreign suitor, and another historical queen, Cleopatra, but upsets the patterns of the *Aeneid* and Augustan historiography by avoiding Dido and Cleopatra's fate.

Although Landor's tale of the exotic East would influence writers such as Robert Southey, Percy Shelley, and Lord Byron, he himself found inspiration for his epic in the work of the eighteenth-century novelist Clara Reeve. Landor based *Gebir* on Reeve's *History of Charoba, Queen of Ægypt*, the oriental tale she appended to her 1785 literary-critical dialogue, *The Progress of Romance*, in which Euphrasia, Reeve's mouthpiece, aims to convince epic's champion, Hortenisus, of romance's superior merits, finally encouraging him to renounce epic at the end of the dialogue. In *The History of Charoba*, Reeve tells a story very different from Landor's, one inherited from the thirteenth-century Arabic *Egyptian History* of Murtada ibn al-Khafif, first translated into French by Pierre Vattier (1666) and into English by John Davies in 1672. In Reeve's version, Charoba is a mighty Egyptian queen, beloved by her people and foreign kingdoms alike; with the help of her nurse (whom Landor conflates with her successor, Dalica), she rebuffs Gebirus's advances by meeting his threats of violence with the gift of a poisoned cloak. Landor's Preface to the 1798 edition credits Reeve, but forbears ever mentioning her by name. Disavowing her influence through his use of the passive voice and suggesting the mere "shadow" of her example, Landor claims that "The subject was taken, or rather the shadow of the subject, from a wild and incoherent, but fanciful, Arabian Romance," noting only that he had come across the work in a circulating library, and that it "had nothing remarkable in it, except indeed we reckon remarkable the pertness and petulance of female criticism."[3] Yet Reeve was no novice in the Republic of Letters. She was a prolific novelist whose works included *The Two Mentors: A Modern Story* (1783), *Castle Connor: An Irish Story* (1787, lost), *The Exiles: or, Memoirs of the Count de Cronstadt* (1788), *The School for Widows* (1791), *Memoirs of Sir Roger de Clarendon* (1793), *Destination: or, Memoirs of a Private Family* (1799), and *Edwin, King of Northumberland: A Story of the Seventeenth Century* (1802), in addition to *Original Poems on Several Occasions* (1769) and her educational treatise, *Plans of Education* (1792). Her best-known work, *The Old English Baron* (1777), is the first gothic novel to appear after Walpole's *Castle of Otranto*; it was often reprinted, and Anna Letitia Barbauld included the *Baron* in her *British Novelists* series in the early nineteenth century (1810).

Yet, unwilling to let Reeve's "pertness and petulance" stand, Landor domesticates Charoba: although he faithfully depicts Gebir's defeat, he divests the queen of her fortitude and political acumen, recasting her as a tragic heroine undone by love. *Gebir* thus follows in the footsteps of the same Augustan propaganda that reduces Dido and Cleopatra to symbols of romance: in elevating Gebir over Charoba, despite Reeve's original history, Landor takes advantage of the template established by the *Aeneid* – the dashing hero who inspires love in his hostess-queen – in order to mythologize his hero at Charoba's expense. Where Reeve's *Progress of Romance* makes a point of challenging epic in order to suggest romance's superiority as a national literature, Landor's poem resolutely ignores Reeve's conclusions, rewriting *Charoba* as *Gebir* and substituting epic for romance. In light of Landor's modifications, it is difficult not to read *Gebir* as a calculated corrective. He not only dismisses *The Progress*'s conclusions but shifts the focus to its villain, reinscribing Charoba as a fragile and childlike queen, deeply enamoured of Gebir but at the mercy of her nurse-enchantress. Apparently missing the point entirely – or, perhaps, grasping it but too well – Landor at once exalts Gebir's status and extols his hero in an epic poem occupying seven books of florid blank verse, which, in 1803, he translated into Latin, implicitly aligning his efforts with Virgil's. Nothing could better embody the astonishing contrast between *Gebir* and *Charoba*: where Reeve seeks to embrace foreign traditions, introducing romance's complex lineage to her readers and appending a translation as an example of her argument, Landor's insistence on Latinizing *Gebir* anticipates a much smaller audience of elite male readers and, in its exclusivity, forestalls potential criticism. Where Reeve desires to expand her readers' horizons, Landor wishes to restore order, reinstating the generic hierarchy.

It is a testament to the pioneering nature of Reeve's argument that Landor found her work so provoking. *The Progress of Romance*, both in its structure and in its elevation of an oriental tale to epic status, positions Reeve as a literary innovator, offering to the Republic of Letters one of the first critical histories of its kind, and the first to be authored by a woman.[4] The full title of the dialogue heralds its singular and far-reaching nature: *The Progress of Romance, Through Times, Countries, and Manners; With Remarks on the Good and Bad Effects of it, on Them Respectively; In a Course of Evening Conversations*. Over a series of twelve evenings, Reeve's mouthpiece, Euphrasia, explains romance's history to her audience, the sympathetic Sophronia and sceptical Hortensius, and shows how the novel springs from romance's "ruins" (172). With the help of earlier critics, Euphrasia traces romance back to antiquity, claiming for it an equal footing with epic – that much more reputable Greco-Roman genre – through Homer, whom she describes as the "parent of Romance" (176). Despite Hortensius's objection that Euphrasia degrades epic by repositioning it in this way, she persuasively refutes his claims, illustrating the essential similarity between the two forms.

This chapter will demonstrate that, in challenging epic by the same standards Hortensius uses to decry romance, Euphrasia formulates a serious critique of classical education and the critical practices that endorse it. Reeve suggests that prejudice in favour of ancient texts works hand in hand with ignorance of romance fiction to enshrine classical authors as literary authorities. In this way, *The Progress of Romance* both models and exposes the process of canon formation: Euphrasia's debate with Hortensius casts light on the often invisible work performed by male critics, and reveals the ideological choices involved in such debates. None of the hierarchies that Hortensius takes for granted are written in stone, suggesting the malleability of literary merit and critical practices.[5]

It is likely no coincidence that Reeve felt the extremity of epic's failure in 1785, positioned between the American and French Revolutions. A staunch Whig raised by her father on classical republican values, Reeve had previously intervened in politics with her 1772 translation of John Barclay's Latin romance, *Argenis* (1621).[6] Shortly after *The Progress*, in the 1790s, Reeve wrote in favour of the French Revolution, declaring herself a "friend to liberty, and the security of property, and the rights of man," and saw her dedication to these principles as the specific legacy of her education in ancient history. She had read, she writes, "the Greek and Roman Histories, and Plutarch's lives when quite a child, [and] from them I imbibed principles that can never be shaken. – A love of liberty, a hatred of Tyranny, an affection to the whole race of mankind, a wish to support their owners rights and properties."[7] Reeve scholar Gary Kelly explicitly links *The Progress*'s themes and concerns to the failure of English militarism in light of the American Revolution: Reeve's dialogue charts a progression, Kelly notes, "from masculine culture and literature, foregrounding martial feats and glory, to a specific form of feminised culture and literature, [that] promot[es] love, domesticity, social conciliation, and the arts of [prosperity and peace]."[8] This chapter will argue, moreover, that Reeve accomplishes this shift by the specific substitution of romance for epic, and completes it by appending to *The Progress* the story of *Charoba*, an oriental tale that reworks classical elements in order to cull better contemporary values from the same venerable tradition that continued to corrupt English schoolboys.[9]

For Reeve, as for Lennox, the dangers of epic are not merely narrative and rhetorical, confined to a distant romance past, now outmoded and forgotten. Like the act – dramatized so effectively in Sarah Fielding's *Lives of Cleopatra and Octavia* – of sanctioning fiction as history, the process of literary canonization threatens to exclude women writers in ways that limit their contributions to the larger culture: critics denounce romance fiction and female authors in an attempt to dictate merit and taste at women's expense. In this way, the generic hierarchy Reeve seeks to undermine is political as well as literary. By the time she reaches the end of *The Progress of Romance*, it will be clear that romance's subordination to epic reinforces other kinds of submission: not only female to male (and feminine to masculine), but foreign to English and East to West, and that – even when such conflicts are enacted in an entirely discursive sphere – they still have the power to influence history. As England becomes an increasingly cosmopolitan nation, it needs, Reeve implicitly argues, a suitably cosmopolitan genre, one that embraces the expansive possibilities of romance.[10]

In resisting the process of generic fixing that begins to take place at mid-century, Reeve thus offers an alternative genealogy for romance, and its daughter the novel, that focuses on the instabilities and continuities of familiar categories. *The Progress* and *Charoba*, taken together, demonstrate that debates about canonicity – far from being self-evident, as Hortensius assumes – are always subject to reinterpretation. During the course of the dialogue's evening conversations, Reeve shows that canonization is an evolving narrative like any other: Euphrasia and Hortensius each have ways of thinking about critical success, and the metaphors they choose define its attainability. For Hortensius, thinking about merit means reaching the heights of Parnassus (250), where Euphrasia prefers the model of a joint romance quest (e.g., 210). The differences between a classical model that suggests its allegiance to epic, verse, and male writers and a romance model available to a variety of authors and readers understandably alters the very premises that underlie discussions of literary value. In championing romance as, at once, a narrative of canonization and a national genre potentially superior to epic, Reeve attempts to undermine Hortensius's distinctions between masculine and feminine categories, epic and romance, by demonstrating that all literature, from the elitist to the popular, owes its debt to the romance, and its origins to the East. Indeed, *The Arabian Nights' Entertainments*, Euphrasia argues in *The Progress*, are ultimately little different from the epics of Homer; only prejudice causes critics to evaluate them negatively.[11] Even the unstable genre of *The Progress* emphasizes generic continuities, as Euphrasia engages her companions in a dialogue form reminiscent both of classical philosophical texts and of *The Arabian Nights* themselves.[12]

Epic in Prose: Redefining Romance Fiction

Although Reeve's heroine, Euphrasia, often draws on other authorities, she offers more than a mere compilation of critical assessments:

The Progress marks an attempt at a mode of literary historiography that actively seeks to rewrite literary history by promoting the work of women writers and the feminine genres associated with them.[13] Mounting a scholarly challenge to contemporary criticism, Euphrasia demonstrates the extent of her credentials by employing techniques traditionally available to male critics: contrasting her systematic approach with Hortensius's uncritical rejection of romance, Euphrasia explains that she has "made extracts from different Authors, and collected materials of various kinds" (170), with the intent of methodizing them "one time or other" (170), and even expresses her desire to furnish her debate to the world (179, 261).[14] However, eschewing the bias evidenced by her male counterparts, Euphrasia insists that she selects works according to a standard of "truth, candour and impartiality" (236, 260), emphasizing that she "oppose[s] opinions long received, and but little examined" (169). Accordingly, she denounces "self-elected censors of books" (200), men who, like Hortensius, have venerated classical literature and male authors while declaring that certain kinds of writing are only "proper furniture for a lady's Library" (165).

Hortensius's reactionary stance and uninformed comments on fiction, however humorous, suggest his allegiance to the class of insensible critics whom Reeve exposes and condemns. Hortensius's gallant defence of epic serves to validate one of Euphrasia's principal claims: namely, that he is mistaken in supposing fiction "to be appropriated to [the female] sex" (225). Venting his grievances in the language of chivalry, Hortensius demands an explanation for Euphrasia's critical judgments, which "seemed to degrade Epic poetry, and to place it on an equality with the old Romance" (169). No sooner has she greeted him than he asks, "What, Madam, do you think you can give a challenge, and go off with impunity?" (169). Yet Hortensius is all bluster and bravado. He even confesses as much, declaring that Euphrasia's papers and extracts are "Artillery and fire-arms against the small sword, the tongue" (170). In this way, Hortensius's playful challenge typifies the very class of critics who have made "mistakes" by conferring "indiscriminate praise or blame" (164); uninterested in the merits of so low a genre as the "old Romance," he erects simplistic strawmen that substitute for actual argument.

Undermining, from the outset, the critical bias that denounces romance as an inferior mode, Euphrasia reveals the difficulty of even defining the terms of debate. None of the dialogue's participants agree on romance's meaning, stressing the often arbitrary nature of generic categories and, by extension, of critical judgments.[15] In challenging the supremacy of epic over romance, Euphrasia explains that "Mankind in general are more biassed by names than things; and what is yet stranger, they are biassed by names to which they have not affixed an absolute and determinate meaning" (170). In drawing attention to critical biases, Euphrasia insists on the fluidity of generic categories: although critics may seek to impose order, distinguishing romance from epic, *The Progress* suggests that such distinctions, however tempting, oversimplify the critical debate and remain open for renegotiation. Even as Hortensius finds inconceivable the prospect of associating romance with epic, declaring that epic is a "very superior composition" (173) and adding, a short while later, that "I cannot with any patience see *Homer* and *Virgil* degraded into writers of Romances" (175), Reeve shows that he cannot define romance with any authority. Euphrasia's simple request to furnish a definition reveals how fraught the prospect of definition happens to be. Where Hortensius describes "romance" as "a wild, extravagant, fabulous Story" (171), Sophronia characterizes it as "all those kind of stories that are built upon fiction, and have no foundation in truth" (171). The contrast between Hortensius and Sophronia suggests their respective experiences: it is unsurprising that Hortensius, with his allegiance to the ancients and ignorance of romance, would resort to such dismissive terms, while Sophronia – an actual reader of romance – describes it as simply another variety of fiction. Euphrasia offers still another definition, one that polemically challenges the categorizing impulse altogether. She declares that she would call romance "simply a *Heroic fable*, – a fabulous Story of such actions as are commonly ascribed to heroes, or men of extraordinary courage and abilities. – Or if you would allow of it, I would say an Epic in prose" (173; see also 174 and 188). In this way, Euphrasia profits from Hortensius's uncritical bias against romance to craft a definition that redefines epic and romance at the same time.

Euphrasia's eagerness to redefine romance in light of the negative critical discourse embodied by Hortensius demonstrates Reeve's investment in the process of canon formation. Even as Reeve structured her argument, a national canon, modelled after the "precedent example of the classical canon," was taking shape.[16] The new English canon "carried with it much of the aura of antiquity: difficulty, rarity, sublimity, masculinity."[17] It was not a canon, in other words, that favoured women's writing. Instead, it was centred on Shakespeare, who, in the preceding decades, had already developed into "*the* national poet," widely admired for his "perennial humanity."[18] Reeve herself enacts this process as Euphrasia occasionally has recourse to Shakespeare's authority to support her own judgments: in *The Progress*, Shakespeare is as legitimate a source as the other critics whom Euphrasia admires (e.g., 196, 203). Yet what many critics praised was really Shakespeare's masculinity as a reaction against the "reading habits of women and effeminate men."[19] Shakespeare's supposed uncanny universality, praised by writers as diverse as Johnson and Montagu, thus allowed his work to take centre stage in a way that Euphrasia's romances and novels could not – that is, at least as long as Hortensius's attitudes remained typical.[20] Genres that appealed only to women, imbued with the same irrational and frivolous characteristics which, in the popular imagination, also dominated the female sex, remained far too specialized, and fell too short of "sublimity," to achieve the same critical status.

Beginning at the end of the eighteenth century, additional economic and social motives – especially changes in copyright law and a strong desire, in light of the French Revolution, to distinguish England from its continental neighbour – conspired to ensure the supremacy of certain British writers, and of British over foreign literatures. As William St Clair explains, "By 1780, the publishers of Great Britain were free, both legally and in practice, to reprint any texts they chose from the hundreds of thousands which lay outside the copyright restrictions of the 1710 statute."[21] In short, the House of Lords determined in 1774 that perpetual copyright was illegal, despite the practices that had been in effect since the early part of the century. As a result, "the public domain now included everything first printed in England or Scotland before 1746, and some even more recent publications. For the first time, English publishers … could choose the text, format, design, print run, and price, and attempt to sell their books in competition with any others who had already entered the same market or who might choose to do so."[22] Although author biographies and commentaries had been growing in popularity since the end of the seventeenth century, the easy availability of works previously regulated by the print trade facilitated the process of canonization. Thanks to shifts in the legal landscape, publishers "could also use materials from out-of-copyright texts to prepare and sell anthologies, abridgements, and adaptations."[23] The emerging canon became decidedly narrow: "Quite suddenly, in the course of a few years from about 1780, English literature became the principal source of texts for English education, aiming to associate learning with reading, reading with pleasure, pleasure with beauty, and beauty with virtue."[24] Thus appearing at a crucial juncture of British literary history in 1785, *The Progress* anticipates and attempts to forestall the canonizing efforts that would eventually distinguish the early nineteenth century from Reeve's own historical moment. As April London notes, "By the end of the Regency period, after the political crisis of Peterloo and with the ascendancy of literary criticism assured, literary history begins to assume its modern contours as a genre centered on consolidating a fixed canon of transcendent works."[25] Put another way, Hortensius prefigures the "conservative effort to standardize literary history writing," while Euphrasia insists on "its potential," still so potent in the eighteenth century, "to unsettle traditional boundaries."[26] Reeve's intervention in the critical debate demonstrates her awareness of the changing literary-critical landscape, and the associated costs – despite substantial gains – for late eighteenth-century readers.

In questioning Hortensius's sentimental attachment to ancient writers, Euphrasia thus highlights the inflexibility of the emerging canon: Hortensius echoes the critical practices that replicate the cultural values of male reviewers, who unfairly "despise and ridicule Romances, as the most contemptible of all kinds of writing, and yet expatiate in raptures, on the beauties of the fables of the old classic Poets, – on stories far more wild and extravagant, and infinitely more incredible" (176). Because Euphrasia seeks to underscore the resemblances between romance and epic, "Homer" becomes the very symbol of entrenched critical prejudice thanks to his unshakeable position among the ancients, his definitive authority over the epic model, and the unwillingness to undermine Homer's position at the pinnacle of generic hierarchies – or, as Hortensius puts it, his placement, alongside Virgil, "at the top of *Parnassus*" (250). The case of Homer illustrates how bias works to crown certain authors as much as it seeks to condemn others. Although "*Homer*," Euphrasia says, "must always claim our respect and even veneration," she also censures critics "who strive, with all their strength, to allegorize away his absurdities," asking Hortensius, "can you forbear smiling at the extravagant sallies of his imagination, can you approve his violent machinery, in which he degrades his deities below his heroes, and makes deities of men?" (176). Appropriating Hortensius's vocabulary of degeneration, and invoking Homer's extravagance alongside other terms frequently associated with romance, Euphrasia maintains that critics make unjust distinctions between the two forms: "*Homer*," she argues, "was the parent of Romance; where ever his works have been known, they have been imitated by the Poets and Romance writers" (176). In order to demonstrate the strong affinity between epic and romance, she even draws on the similarities between the *Odyssey* and the *Arabian Nights' Entertainments*, whose writer also profits from "Machinery" but "is by far the most modest in the use of it" (177). Later, in explaining the flaws of ancient writers in greater detail, Euphrasia will also take issue with "*Virgil* – the modest and delicate *Virgil*, [who] informs [readers] of many things, they had better be ignorant of" (255), effectively undercutting Hortensius's veneration of the ancient poets. "It is astonishing," Euphrasia argues, "that men of sense, and of learning, should so strongly imbibe prejudices, and be so loth to part with them" (176). Hortensius, she implies, should know better.

As Euphrasia demonstrates, the fixity of this model both excludes subsequent writers and precludes innovation. For Euphrasia, the canon exists as an object defined by schoolboy nostalgia and received wisdom rather than by active critical engagement. She wryly relates how, in her youth, some "verses placed before the first editions of *Milton*" convinced her that "there never were but three Epic poets, and that it was impossible there could ever be a fourth" (250). This is her reply to Hortensius's assertion that Ariosto, Tasso, Guarini, Camoens, and Milton are merely "successful imitators of the great Ancients" (250) rather than celebrated poets in their own right. Euphrasia's childhood tale humorously demonstrates how the canonization of Homer and Virgil creates the impression that "there are no other Epic poets" (250), even when subsequent writers fashion works indistinguishable from epic poetry.[27] The canon thus ossifies familiar categories – not only "epic" but also "Homer" and "Virgil" – and resists the possibility of a dynamic tradition. When Euphrasia insists that Pope's plans "for an Epic Poem … might have equalled him to [Hortensius's] great Ancients" (250), Reeve suggests that even so formidable a rival would have been denied epic status by contemporary critics.

In addition to challenging the bias that informs the canonization of Homer, Virgil, and the "great Ancients," Euphrasia also highlights the negative values obscured by an early education in classical authors. As late as the end of Evening XI, Hortensius claims that Euphrasia has "done justice to every body, but the Ancient Poets" (252), still unwilling to concede that his judgment, rather than Euphrasia's – despite her consistently sound and persuasive arguments – is to blame. *The Progress* thus ends where it began, with Euphrasia defending romance against epic on Evening XII, in order to reveal the immoral consequences of a classical education. Questioning Hortensius's twin assumptions that fiction is harmful to female readers and that epic furnishes naturally salutary material for young boys, Euphrasia states, "It seems to me that you are unreasonably severe upon these books, which you suppose to be appropriated to our sex, (which however is not the case): – not considering how many books of worse tendency, are put into the hands of the youth of your own, without scruple" (255). Euphrasia need "not go far" for examples, "fetch[ing] them from the School books, that generally make a part of the education of young Men" (255). Invoking the "History – the Mythology – [and] the Morals – of the great Ancients, whom [Hortensius] and all learned Men revere," Euphrasia lists the undesirable qualities transmitted through classical learning: "their Idolatry – their follies – their vices – and every thing that is shocking to virtuous manners" (255). As Euphrasia explains, even the worst novels and romances have never taught what Lucretius teaches, "that *fear* first made Gods – that men grew out of the earth like trees, and that the indulgence of the passions and appetites, is the truest wisdom." In fact, Euphrasia says, "*Juvenal* and *Persius* describe such scenes, as I may venture to affirm that Romance and Novel-writers of any credit would blush at" (255). If anything, Hortensius should defend romance and decry epic, but his long-cherished assumptions blind him to epic's deleterious effects.

That Hortensius begins by expressing doubt in Euphrasia's arguments and concludes by agreeing wholeheartedly with her criticism suggests the extent to which an irrational allegiance to the ancients has shaped his prior judgments. When Euphrasia first avers the dangers of ancient writers, Hortensius exclaims, "Indeed! – how will you bring proofs of [your] assertion?" (255), as though any such proofs would be impossible to muster. Yet, immediately following Euphrasia's characterization of Juvenal and Persius, Hortensius concedes, "I am astonished – admonished – and convinced! – I cannot deny the truth of what you have advanced, I confess that a reformation is indeed wanting in the mode of Education of the youth of our sex" (255). Despite the suddenness of his conversion, it is unlikely, of course, that Hortensius was ignorant of Euphrasia's examples; the very effectiveness of her argument relies on his familiarity with ancient texts. Instead, Reeve suggests that an inherited preference for the ancients prevents recognition of their faults. As Euphrasia argues earlier in *The Progress*, "Mankind willingly adopt the prejudices of their ancestors, they embrace them with affection, they quit them with reluctance. One of them is to decry Romance, and venerate Epic Poetry" (175). Indicating the strength and uniformity of critical opinion, Hortensius, at one point, describes Euphrasia's characterization of Homer and Virgil as "heretical" (250), implying that the canonization of ancient writers amounts to a kind of religious orthodoxy. Euphrasia similarly imagines herself facing a tribunal (163) of critics who will determine *The Progress*'s fate, an image that not only suggests a judicial body but, specifically, the tribunal of ancient Rome.[28] Defining critics as a "tribunal" and the height of literary achievement as "Parnassus" reveals the standards, inherited from and inspired by the ancients, that set the parameters of canon formation. As long as "Parnassus," "epic," "Homer," and "Virgil" delimit the terms of success, then of course critics will ignore writers who fail to embrace their prescriptions.

By using Euphrasia, Hortensius, and Sophronia to stage the process of canon formation in action while, at the same time, enacting its critique, Reeve suggests that the narrative of canonization is a story like any other, and therefore subject to revision. The antagonistic model represented by Hortensius, in which the trio's evening gatherings must produce a victor and loser, is not the only model available. Eventually, Euphrasia's emphasis on cooperation and collaboration will reform Hortensius's stance, encouraging him to assist Euphrasia in her literary explorations. Where Hortensius repeatedly approaches Euphrasia as an opponent on the battlefield of criticism, employing a vocabulary that emphasizes the hostile nature of the critical enterprise, Euphrasia makes clear that she views their discussions as a mutually rewarding series of conversations. In Evening I, Euphrasia explains to Hortensius that she "shall depend upon your assistance, and since you have opened my mouth upon the subject, you are bound in honour to correct my redundancies, and to supply my deficiencies" (172). Although Hortensius responds warily, asking, "What to furnish you with weapons for my defeat?" (172), Euphrasia wins him to her model in the end: by Evening IX, when Euphrasia mentions the difficulties in discussing "present times," Hortensius insists that she "[c]ommunicate [those difficulties] to your friends, and depend upon our best assistance, to obviate, or at least to abate them" (225). Just as Euphrasia encourages the collaborative effort of the trio's evening visits, she refuses to set herself up as an expert, not only inviting her companions' knowledge and opinions, but relying on other critics, where appropriate, while nonetheless insisting on her own knowledge and discernment (179). In tracing the vicissitudes of romance, Reeve makes clear that canonization is as much a matter of fashion as of critical judgment (196), thus implying that even Euphrasia's opinions are subject to change. The dialogue represents her thinking at a particular moment, based on specific critical extracts and a particular library of books. But *The Progress* characterizes Euphrasia as a good critic, in part, because of her willingness to modify arguments based on available evidence.

Foregrounding the narratives behind canon formation, Reeve figures the trio's journey as a story that Euphrasia self-consciously fashions at every step of the way. By imposing a romance framework on Euphrasia's evening conversations, Reeve stresses the subjective process that shapes critical debate. Euphrasia imagines their discussions as a progress through the regions of romance, telling her companions, "In this fairy land are many Castles of various Architecture. – Some are built in the air, and have no foundation at all, – others are composed of such heavy materials, that their own weight sinks them into the earth, where they lie buried under their own ruins, and leave not a trace behind, – a third sort are built upon a real and solid foundation, and remain impregnable against all the attacks of Criticism, and perhaps even of time itself" (210). She returns to the metaphor as the trio passes from romance to the novel, explaining to her companions that they "have hitherto traveled through these enchanted regions of fiction with tolerable ease and safety. – But as we advance further, new dangers await us every step we set. – We may tread upon serpents that may rise and sting us; or, we may rouse a hornet's nest that may stun us with its noise, or wound us with its deadly weapons" (225). Later, as they move to oriental tales, Euphrasia promises, "I will lead you into enchanted palaces, – delicious gardens, – and endless labyrinths. – We will put ourselves under the protection of the good genii" (244). Couching their investigations in the language of romance thus allows Euphrasia to author a story that at once reinforces her argument and points to its nature as a construct. On the one hand, structuring canonization as a romance journey neatly underscores Euphrasia's attempts to rehabilitate romance, and later the novel, for an audience sceptical of its value. On the other hand, it also reveals the "romance" – that is, the fiction – of canon formation, a point Euphrasia makes when referring to critics who "deal in Romances, though of a different kind" (211). Thanks to the severity of such critics and the difficulty of rendering judgment, it is a process fraught with "dangers"; attempting to discern the absolute truth of literary merit is indeed a fairy tale – a just-so story created, in this case, by critics unwilling to recognize the potential value of marginalized genres.

To make this point, chivalric romance is only one of the modes Reeve incorporates in the narrative structure of *The Progress*. Demonstrating the variety of frameworks available, she also imagines the trio's gatherings as an epic journey, a move that both hints at the mock-heroic nature of critical ventures and signals Euphrasia as a worthy challenger to an entrenched discourse that values epic above other forms. The twelve-evening scope of *The Progress* loosely recalls the twelve books of the *Aeneid*, but the similarities extend beyond the dialogue's form.[29] As Euphrasia begins her discussion of novels, she wonders what epic invocation will suit a critical project of this kind: "What Goddess, or what Muse must I invoke to guide me through these vast, unexplored regions of fancy?" (210). Later, as they turn towards the oriental tale, Hortensius promises Euphrasia, "I shall follow you as *Aeneas* did the *Sybil*, with the same confidence, that you will guide me through in safety" (245), to which she replies, "The allusion is not amiss. – Oh that you could realize the golden bough!" Although Hortensius fears that "the tree does not grow in this country," Euphrasia insists, "Yes it does, but is guarded by Hesperian dragons, and there are a thousand dangers and vexations in the way of those who adventure for the prize" (245). Reeve's rhetoric at once positions Euphrasia as epic poet (invoking the muse), expert guide (leading Hortensius), and valiant hero (challenging, like Hercules, the Hesperian dragons); inviting Hortensius into the heroic project, Euphrasia also imagines him as Aeneas, seeking, with her help, the "golden bough" of literary criticism. Even as Reeve's epic language lends a mock-heroic cast to literary-critical debates – and there is surely a sense of playfulness to Hortensius's back-and-forth with Euphrasia – it also appropriates and expands the category of epic heroism, replacing Aeneas's essentially solitary journey with a collaborative model that owes much to romance. It is no accident that Reeve's epic allusions reinforce the language of romance adventure: by employing metaphors – romance quest, epic journey – that are virtually indistinguishable from one another, Reeve parallels the redefinition of romance as epic in the formal levelling of distinctions between epic and romance.

That Euphrasia's turn to the Eastern tale merits an allusion to Aeneas's underworld journey further complicates generic distinctions, recalling her characterization of Homer as the very parent of romance (176) and the numerous affinities between Homer and the *Arabian Nights* (177). In addition to resembling a romance quest and epic journey, *The Progress* also evokes the *Arabian Nights' Entertainments*: in this formulation, the well-spoken Euphrasia emerges as a modern Scheherazade, mollifying Hortensius's critical ire in a series of evening conversations and, with the help of Sophronia, eventually winning him to her point of view. Sophronia becomes a stand-in for Dinarzade, the often-overlooked sister and companion of Scheherazade, whose gentle promptings fuel the Sultan's curiosity and postpone her sister's execution.[30] As the trio's moderator, she regulates their visits, declaring that the company should meet every Thursday evening (172) until Euphrasia has made her case, and, as a fellow romance reader, regularly supports Euphrasia's assessments in the face of Hortensius's professed ignorance. Because of the serial structure of *The Progress*, the evenings also echo the *Nights'* storytelling tensions, in which Scheherazade nightly leaves her companions in suspense. For example, Hortensius thanks Euphrasia, at the end of Evening I, for her "readiness to gratify [his] curiosity," avowing that he "expect[s] next Thursday with some impatience" (172, 184, 202). Sophronia similarly declares that she "shall reckon the hours 'till our next meeting" (179) and is "impatient to proceed," despite being "in no haste for the end" (223). When Euphrasia anticipates the conclusion on Evening X, even Hortensius will exclaim, "I hope you are not serious? – Your plan is by no means compleated" (242). Like Reeve's allusions to epic, her evocation of the *Nights* might appear comical given the discrepancy between the trio's friendly meetings and Scheherazade's more urgent attempts to save her life and the lives of her countrywomen. Yet Reeve's superimposition of the *Nights'* framework also underscores the seriousness of constructing critical hierarchies that attempt, like the Sultan's violence, to silence female voices. By *The Progress*'s end, Euphrasia's persuasive arguments have lured Hortensius into a collaborative enterprise superior to the militaristic pose he initially adopts, with its mock-chivalric violence reminiscent of the murderous Sultan.

Realizing the stakes of Euphrasia's arguments about the "old" romance, Reeve spends the final evenings of *The Progress* discussing the merits of a much more contemporary form: the novel. Reclaiming romance is therefore not merely an end in itself, but part of a larger rehabilitative project. Although Euphrasia is careful to distinguish the formal characteristics of the novel from romance (210–11), she also explains that the new genre "sprung out of [Romance's] ruins" (172); the progress of romance polemically culminates, in Reeve's literary-critical history, in the newer form. The state of the critical debate demonstrates the urgency of Euphrasia's argument. As she explains to Hortensius, critics have deliberately confounded romance and the novel, "insidiously ... endeavour[ing] to render all writings of both kinds contemptible" (211). Unsurprisingly, the stakes for women writers and readers were particularly high, especially as reviewers distinguished between good novels and bad, which often meant distinguishing men's novels from women's. The trio's attentiveness to the sex of authorship reflects the gendered language that pervaded contemporary debates: the same battle-of-the-sexes rhetoric that first appears in their discussion of romance returns in Euphrasia's consideration of the novel, which inherited much of romance's negative legacy. Euphrasia's observation to Hortensius – that he "condescend[s] to read novels sometimes, especially when they are written by men" (228) – reveals the predicament faced by women writers: critics not only maligned the novel as a feminine genre, unsuitable for male readers (and, in general, Hortesnsius's ignorance of novel writing parallels his ignorance of romance), they also embraced male authors in order to legitimate the emerging form.[31]

Underscoring Euphrasia's arguments about bias against women writers and feminine genres, Eliza Haywood's reputation epitomizes the consequences of enshrining personal prejudice as critical fact. Although Hortensius knows nothing of Haywood's work, he seizes on her name as an opportunity to highlight her infamy. Reminiscent of Lennox's indictment of readers who know little of history, but plenty about Cleopatra's amorous intrigues, Reeve employs Hortensius's prurient curiosity to show the ease with which critics conflate women writers' bodies with their bodies of work. By contrast, Euphrasia cites Haywood as an important innovator whose later writings deserve considerable praise, despite the "infamous immortality" unfairly conferred on Haywood in Pope's *Dunciad* (214). Sophronia's relation – "I have heard it often said that Mr. *Pope* was too severe in his treatment of this lady, which he resented publicly as was too much his way" (215) – exposes the uneasy relationship between personal prejudice and critical judgment. As Pope uses his status as an illustrious poet and respected critic to publish his resentment towards Haywood, the repetition of excess in Sophronia's characterization – "too severe," "too much" – and the apparent popularity of the sentiment – it has been "often said" – suggest the unseemliness of Pope's attacks. The blurring of Pope's public and private feelings makes clear the potentially inappropriate ways in which male critics rely on public platforms to enforce personal judgments.

In this way, Reeve demonstrates how the same process that consigns romance to inferior status also threatens to circumscribe women's contributions to the novel. For Euphrasia, virtue supplies an evaluative category that allows her to embrace men's and women's novels alike: if a novel's didactic potential, rather than the sex of its author, determines its usefulness, then women stand an equal chance of success in the literary marketplace. As a result, Euphrasia ably defends Haywood against Hortensius's attacks by reminding him of Haywood's later works; using the same argument that she applies to romance – that the "female cause is the cause of virtue" (220) – Euphrasia recuperates Haywood as one of the very progenitors of the novel whose legacy Pope had unfairly tarnished. At the same time, Euphrasia's standard of virtue allows her to cast doubt on prominent male authors whose canonicity Hortensius takes for granted. Where Hortensius describes Samuel Richardson as "a writer all your own," adding, "your sex are more obliged to him and *Addison*, than to all other men authors" (220), Euphrasia takes issue with the immorality of Fielding's fiction, and forbears to discuss *Tristram Shandy* at all (221, 235). In reproducing, in the trio's conversations, the same critical tensions that shaped contemporary debates about the novel, Reeve at once highlights critics' dependence on gender as an irrational category of critique and suggests that virtue is a more reasonable and beneficial standard by which to judge prominent and obscure novelists alike. Euphrasia's paradigm not only encourages Hortensius to rethink his harsh judgments of the novel – and especially women novelists – but upends existing hierarchies: even as she stresses the dangers of *Tom Jones*, she advances the novels of Sarah Fielding, arguing that "if they do not equal [Henry's] in wit and learning, they excel in some other material merits, that are more beneficial to their readers" (222). By adhering to expectations of literary propriety, Fielding earns a place in Euphrasia's egalitarian literary history. Where *The Lives* makes visible the historiographic practices that construct Cleopatra as an Egyptian whore, Reeve similarly illuminates the critical tendencies that attempt to efface the literary contributions of female writers like Haywood.

In staging *The Progress* as a series of conversations that enact multiple perspectives and modes, Reeve constructs a polyvocal narrative that invites readers, using – like Euphrasia – their own knowledge and judgment, to participate in the critical debate. Resisting the process of generic fixing that begins at mid-century, as well as the critical consensus that would enshrine the English novel, largely divorced from foreign influences, as a superior prose genre, Reeve celebrates authors both ancient and modern, drawing on her knowledge of Greek, Latin, French, German, Arabic, and English literatures. In this way, *The Progress*'s form reflects Euphrasia's inclusiveness, her willingness to see English writers in a larger global context that highlights debts to other cultures, not just to the "great Ancients" so admired by Hortensius. In "shew[ing] how the modern Novel sprung up out of [Romance's] ruins" (172), Euphrasia reclaims the feminine tradition that makes the novel possible and, in supplanting epic with romance, paves the way for championing the novel's feminine legacy. If, for Hortensius, epic sits atop the lofty regions of Parnassus, then prose fiction is at least as worthy of critical merit, and – in challenging epic – of a similar claim to national status.

Revising Origins: The Bible as Oriental Tale

Representing a potential union of romance and novelistic elements, with its combination of oriental fantasy and realistic, historical events, *The History of Charoba, Queen of Ægypt* completes Reeve's challenge to epic by furnishing an example of Euphrasia's arguments. Incorporating aspects of the biblical and classical traditions, including epic itself, Reeve's oriental tale embraces a range of cultures and generic modes, fulfilling the Preface's intention to map the antiquity of romance and the polyglot origins of the English novel. By the end of the eighteenth century, the oriental tale had become the perfect medium for challenging generic hierarchies. It at once signalled a reaction against classicism and offered a parallel narrative, one made possible by the translation into English of Antoine Galland's *Arabian Nights' Entertainments* at the beginning of the century (1704–17).[32] Although other genres such as biblical scholarship, history, and epic were, as masculine discourses, formally closed to most eighteenth-century women writers, the oriental tale, as a subgenre of romance, offered a potent supplement to available modes,[33] one that was embraced by many of the period's leading writers: from Eliza Haywood's *Eovaai* (1736) and Samuel Johnson's *Rasselas* (1759) to Frances Sheridan's *Nourjahad* (1767) and William Beckford's *Vathek* (1786), the oriental tale was one of the most popular genres of the eighteenth and early nineteenth centuries.

Like Barker's *Exilius* and Lennox's *Female Quixote*, which embrace geographies of resistance by locating revisions of classical epic and history in the romance East, Reeve also turns from England, and English tradition, as she translates and adapts Charoba's story. Where epic recalls the classical West, the geography of Greco-Roman victors, Reeve identifies romance with the ancient East, a land repeatedly associated, by Greek and Roman authors, with subject and defeated peoples. Reeve pursues Barker's project of recuperating defeat, this time in the figure of a successful, putatively historical queen who both conjures and supplants Cleopatra's legacy: in selecting *The History of Charoba*, Reeve presents a story that diverges sharply from traditional myths, the inverse of Aeneas-Augustus's triumph over Dido-Cleopatra. Sanctioned from the outset by its context as an extra-biblical narrative, *Charoba* suggests that its eponymous Egyptian queen, having been blessed by Abraham, rightfully defends her kingdom from Gebirus, a descendant of the Gadites, and establishes Charoba as an ingenious matriarch well equipped to defeat her enemy. Similarly, the classical allusions that identify Charoba with the faithful Penelope and the hero Achilles, as well as her anonymous nurse with the sorceress Medea, and Hercules' wife, Deianeira, help Reeve to champion Charoba's position as an independent leader who relies on female community to effect her prosperous rule. In this confluence of genres, the oriental tale allows Reeve to yoke together seemingly disparate discourses in order to reveal their underlying similarities. If, like Greco-Roman epic, the oriental tale is a national genre, as Reeve argues by prescribing romance for the good of the nation, then *Charoba* – by collapsing the differences between past and present, between biblical, classical, and oriental – emphasizes the importance of an inclusive national narrative that allows a multiplicity of voices to be heard.

By ending *The Progress of Romance* with an apparent reversion to biblical narrative, Reeve returns to the beginning: to the inception (and intersection) of Islam, Judaism, and Christianity; to Egypt, the so-called cradle of civilization; and to Alexandria, a kind of crossroads between East and West, taking advantage of a historical moment when such artificial boundaries were especially fluid and blurred.[34] The very title reflects generic openness and productivity. *Charoba* is not only a biblical story but a "history," the title page tells us, from an alternative – and in some ways, opposing – tradition: *The History of Charoba, Queen of Ægypt. Taken from the History of Ancient Ægypt, According to the Traditions of the Arabians* (265). Reeve adapted Charoba's story from the *Egyptian History* of Murtada ibn al-Khafif, a thirteenth-century Islamic historian living in Cairo. In 1666, his text (now lost) had been translated into French with a thorough introduction by the Arabic scholar Pierre Vattier, and from French into English by John Davies in 1672. Reeve follows closely the Vattier-Davies translations, undoubtedly attracted to the story – as its translators had been – for its similarities to familiar classical material. Yet, as I will argue, Reeve also departs from her source texts in a number of key ways that augment the power of *Charoba*'s retelling.

Charoba's story begins with the advent of Sarah and Abraham in Egypt, where they have come to escape famine in their land. Fearing that the Pharaoh, King Totis, will kill Abraham to obtain his beautiful wife, Abraham claims Sarah as his sister, whereupon Totis assimilates her into his harem. God punishes Totis, who then liberates Sarah and Abraham, and encourages the king's wise and virtuous daughter, Charoba, to show them kindness and generosity during the remainder of their stay. Abraham, in turn, calls on God to bless Charoba's generosity and craftiness. On Totis's death, Charoba soon becomes queen, though not without some misgivings on the part of the nobility, who object "to the government of a woman" (267); the absence of this objection in the Vattier-Davies source texts emphasizes the particularly gendered struggle in Reeve's version. Having prevailed, Charoba sets about improving Egypt for the good of her people. "After a long time," we learn that Gebirus, advised by his physicians to find a more hospitable climate, has brought five thousand Gadites, bearing stones on their heads, to take over Egypt; Gebirus has also heard of Charoba's fame, and intends to force her to marry him. The alternative biblical context established at the beginning of the story works diligently to endorse Charoba's eventual reign, including her triumph over the traditionally heroic-epic figure represented by Gebirus.[35] Because the history of her rule runs parallel to the founding mission of the patriarch, Abraham, who explicitly confers his blessing on Charoba, the text also implies that Charoba's rule and lineage merit divine sanction. Prefiguring the demise of her unwelcome suitor, Abraham says, "Great God give her subtilty to deceive her enemies, and to vanquish all those who shall arise to do her harm, and to strive with her for her land! – Bless her in her country, and in her river, and make that country a place of plenty, safety, and prosperity!" (266). Abraham's blessing thus prophetically marks Charoba's eventual deception of Gebirus as a heroic action that ensures the happiness of Egypt.

Because of the constructive space opened by the generic blending of biblical and oriental tales, Charoba enters Western history as an ideal queen against a background of flawed patriarchs. For, at the same time that Abraham's blessing affirms Charoba's reign, Abraham's actions also undermine the authority of his mission. Although God protects

Sarah's virtue, Abraham's self-interest in claiming his wife as his sister emphasizes, even in light of his benediction to Charoba, Sarah's perilous position: on the one hand, the harem represents a particularly Eastern kind of extravagance and licentiousness, the threat of despotic foreign men to virtuous women like Sarah. On the other, it exposes Abraham's own threat to Sarah, since he risks the possibility of his wife's sexual violation in order to avoid angering King Totis. In this way, Reeve disrupts a simplistic identification with Abraham over Totis, emphasizing instead the proximity of the two patriarchs in the grammatically confused structure of *Charoba*'s opening lines: "In the reign of *Totis*, *Abraham* the beloved of GOD came into *Ægypt*; and it is written, that he would have corrupted *Sarah* the wife of *Abraham*, but GOD punished the king, and delivered his servants" (265). Although we know, by concluding the sentence, that Totis "would have corrupted Sarah," the closest grammatical subject is Abraham himself.[36]

Charoba, by contrast, exhibits every mark of a just and virtuous monarch. Early in the narrative, we learn that she "was of a mild and gentle disposition, always endeavouring to prevent the shedding of blood. She was also of a great capacity and ingenuity," described by the Vizier as "a woman of great understanding" and "of a mild and merciful disposition ... beloved by all that are acquainted with her noble qualities" (267). Although the Old Testament makes no mention of Charoba's crucial aid to Sarah and Abraham, the "Traditions of the Arabians" foreground her pivotal role. Knowing that Abraham will reject her generosity, she cleverly conceals riches among other necessities she provides him, allowing him to spend "those gifts in pious works" (266). No less important, Charoba bestows Hagar on Sarah, so that she enters biblical history, and Islamic history in particular, as the Egyptian queen who makes possible the birth of "our Father Ishmael" (265), the product of Hagar and Abraham's union.[37] In profiting from romance to depict Charoba working alongside Abraham as an able and virtuous matriarch, Reeve presents, in *Charoba*, a counter-epic positioned against – yet built upon – biblical as well as classical elements, one whose radical shift in perspective requires an accompanying generic redefinition that goes back to the origins of narrative itself.

Penelope, Medea, Deianeira: Classical Heroism Revisited

In appending *The History of Charoba* to *The Progress of Romance*, Reeve creates a hybrid genre – part epic, romance, history, oriental tale – that prevents Charoba from sharing the fate of so many of her forebears. Following Euphrasia's persuasive arguments about epic's failures in *The Progress, Charoba* suggests a possible alternative to traditional heroisms by revisiting figures such as Penelope, Medea, and Deianeira. The contrast between their fortunes and Charoba's argues for the levelling of romance and epic that Euphrasia seeks earlier in the dialogue: where epic marginalizes female characters as diverse as Penelope and Medea, romance at once foregrounds such stories and sympathizes with their heroines, rejecting the denunciation of female heroism represented, as I will argue, by Gebirus's deathbed speech. Of course, Reeve was not the first, in her 1785 adaptation of *Charoba* from the Vattier-Davies translations, to notice similarities between *The History of Charoba* and familiar classical narratives. The Vattier-Davies Prefaces note that Homer's *Odyssey*, Virgil's *Eclogues*, and Ovid's *Metamorphoses* all suggest striking parallels from Greek and Roman mythology, and Reeve benefits from additional echoes not explicitly named by either of the translators.[38] The existence of similar narratives across cultures and time periods implies a particular cultural indebtedness, and perhaps even a shared literary past, that further complicates Hortensius's defence of epic and male-authored novels.

Though Reeve would have known the reference to Virgil from Vattier and Davies, she instead centralizes the *Odyssey*, and especially Ovid's *Metamorphoses*, over Virgil's *Eclogues* in her own Preface, a rhetorical move that advances *The Progress*'s denunciation of epic values by citing an Augustan poet critical of martial ideals, including the pervasive violence against women that serves as a dominant motif in epic narratives. Ovid, known primarily as a love poet, consciously situates his verse against Homeric and Virgilian epic: as he relates in *Amores*, he will not celebrate Augustus or imperial glory, but rather seduction and the arts of love.[39] Even the *Metamorphoses* represents a kind of anti-epic. Singing of "new forms," Ovid constructs a slippery, hero-less text, one whose narrative constantly turns upon itself, transforming endlessly, blurring generic boundaries.[40] Yet, revealing the limits of epic for figures like Charoba, Ovid's world is one of danger and annihilation for its shapeshifting women, leading one scholar to remark that "Ovid understands male sexuality at its most savage."[41] One might characterize such masculinity as "epic" in kind, the sort affiliated with gods and heroes, from Zeus to Hercules, figures known for their sexual violence. According to this view of epic masculinity and sexuality, Gebirus happily attempts to meet expectations, and believes that history – as he makes Charoba promise to record his story – will sympathize with his own untimely end.

However, although Reeve adopts the generic inclusiveness of Ovid's work, its self-conscious deconstruction of boundaries, she ultimately dismisses epic as a viable mode; even when read against Homer or Virgil, the *Metamorphoses* is still a text that depends, at least to a certain extent, on the violation of women's bodies. Only a decisive turn towards romance can preserve Charoba's rule from the generic violence inherent in epic: with the help of her nurse, Charoba jealously guards the bodies politic and natural, refusing Gebirus's attempts to transform her into an unwilling bride. Put simply, her achievement requires a genre that can envision her success. Reeve's allusions to the *Odyssey* and *Metamorphoses* in her Preface therefore reject traditional epic as a mode inimical to women's narratives, even in its most "romantic" and "feminine" forms.

As Reeve revisits classical epic in her Preface and in the allusions that appear throughout *Charoba*, she thus turns to a variety of ancient heroines in order to recuperate positive values from epic and history. Through the various intertexts functioning around and through *Charoba*, Reeve invites readers to redefine familiar stories. Using Charoba to reclaim frequently monstrous figures, such as Medea and Deianeira – and, as I will argue in the next section, Dido and Cleopatra – she also highlights the cleverness of typically docile women, such as the virtuous Penelope. By strengthening the continuum between classical mythology and Eastern tales, this matrix of allusions helps to establish Charoba as a kind of romantic-epic figure in Gebirus's stead, a heroine for contemporary English audiences. The purpose of these intertexts is twofold: allusions to Odysseus's wife celebrate the classical heritage of "subtilty" that links the heroine of the *Odyssey* to *Charoba*, while the stories of Medea and Deianeira subvert the kind of masculine storytelling that depicts women, because of their sex and/or nationality, as dangerous figures whose presence fundamentally threatens the hero's quest.

Although Reeve replaces the Vattier-Davies reference to Virgil with an allusion to his antagonist, Ovid, she maintains the reference to the *Odyssey*, affirming Euphrasia's characterization of Homer as the very "parent of romance" (176). Like the crafty figure of Penelope, Charoba creates an indefinite delay to postpone her suitor's violence: she instructs Gebirus to build a city, and vows to marry him once the task is complete. Gebirus toils in vain as his efforts continually vanish overnight, but eventually he learns the queen's secret. Charoba's stratagem recalls Penelope's: Odysseus's wife also promises that, having finished the shroud she weaves for Odysseus's father, Laertes, she will choose a suitor in her husband's absence, but she similarly undoes the work by night. The figure of Penelope, as a model of the faithful and ingenious woman, positively informs the virtuous and shrewd Charoba, who successfully keeps her enemy at bay. In displacing stereotypically feminine work onto Gebirus, Charoba acknowledges the binary he seeks to impose while, at the same time, maintaining more traditional forms of power, in her rulership of Egypt, for herself.

If Charoba recalls Penelope, then Charoba's nurse, as the author of the poisoned cloak that will kill Gebirus, resonates with the darker figures of Medea and Deianeira. *Charoba* thus invites readers to reconsider the narrative bias that transforms Medea and Deianeira into murderers. Like the allusions to the *Odyssey* and *Metamorphoses*, textual echoes of the Medea story work to subvert conventional models of heroism and femininity. In order to effect her revenge on Jason, Medea designs a poisoned robe for his new wife and even, in Euripides, murders their children in an act of heroic vengeance.[42] From Jason's unrepentant point of view, she is a barbarian princess fortunate to have helped so illustrious a Greek hero, while Medea rages at the disrespect Jason has shown for her heroic commitments. Jason's blindness to the reasons behind Medea's anger – he routinely attributes her wrath to romantic rather than ethical concerns – becomes a metaphor for epic's blindness to female heroism. Medea's desire to maintain the power she enjoyed in her Eastern homeland, and to be recognized as Jason's heroic equal, consigns her to tragedy.

Where Medea is monstrous because she oversteps the bounds of feminine propriety, Deianeira's desperate attempts to revive Hercules' love are no less deadly. Deianeira's defeat of Hercules thus posits romance and epic as antithetical – and romance as the more dangerous of the two modes. In Deianeira's case, her love for Hercules takes a misguidedly lethal turn in the shape of the poisoned cloak she hopes will regain his lost affection. Tricked by the centaur Nessus into believing that his blood is a powerful love-charm, she unwittingly becomes the instrument of Nessus's revenge on Hercules. In this way, Deianeira enters literary history – as Gebirus would have Charoba – as the final obstacle the great Hercules could not overcome.[43] Deianeira's recourse to the poisoned cloak implies that even faithful, virtuous women are dangerous, for, unaware that Nessus has duped her, she has no control over Hercules' murder.

In appropriating aspects of Medea's and Deianeira's stories, Reeve's *Charoba* at once reminds readers of the limited plots available to such diverse female characters and undermines prejudicial distinctions between epic and romance: the poisoned garment that kills Gebirus translates a symbol of romantic love and revenge into one of epic triumph. Together, Charoba and her nurse, like Euphrasia and Sophronia, make a formidable team, illustrating the power of female community, an image that contrasts starkly with the discord depicted in the Medea and Deianeira narratives, where competition between women leads even to murder. In an ironic reversal of expectations, Gebirus's unlawful encroachment justifies Charoba's actions, just as the image of the poisoned cloak encourages the reader to view *Charoba*'s allusions with a more critical eye: in condemning Medea and Deianeira, classical narratives have unjustly allowed heroes to escape their share of the blame. By virtue of romance, Charoba avoids the reductive categories reserved for Deianeira and Medea, just as she escapes the epic teleology that circumscribes their stories. Because of the position of women and foreigners in Greek culture, such characters may be nothing *but* monstrous; when "Deianeira" literally means "man-killer" or "she who destroys her spouse," her narrative fate reveals the blunt impediments to female heroism.[44]

Reeve's Charoba thus offers a corrective for the heroic values associated with epic earlier in *The Progress of Romance*. Instead, Charoba fulfils the part of a "reformed" Achilles as Gebirus's dying words echo those of Hector to Achilles in the *Iliad*.[45] By reversing our expectations at this pivotal moment, Reeve implies that Charoba does not resemble the wrathful hero of Homer's epic – even as Gebirus still represents the old standard – but rather an improved heroic ideal for a new and modern age. Gebirus says, "Oh *Charoba*! – triumph not in my death! – for there shall come upon thee a day like unto this, and the time is not very far distant. – Then shalt thou reflect on the vicissitudes of fortune, and the certainty of death" (274). Similarly, in the *Iliad*, Hector says to Achilles, "I know you well as I look upon you, I know that I could not / persuade you, since indeed in your breast is a heart of iron. / Be careful now; for I might be made into the gods' curse / upon you, on that day when Paris and Phoibos Apollo / destroy you in the Skaian gates, for all your valour" (22.355–60). To this potentially damning speech, Achilles replies only, "Die: and I will take my own death at whatever time / Zeus and the rest of the immortals choose to accomplish it" (22.365–6).[46] Later, he desecrates Hector's body. To Gebirus, Charoba behaves more kindly, "renew[ing] her promise to [commemorate] him" in the moments leading up to his death, and later order[ing] Gebirus's body "to be honorably interred in the city which he had builded" (274). When a serpent, reminding us of the old guard of critics of whom Euphrasia must beware, later bites Charoba and she loses her sight, the queen says only, "The day is come with which Gebirus threatened me: – a day which all the great ones of the earth must meet and submit to" (275). Having condemned the failure of epic in *The Progress*, Reeve uses *Charoba* to suggest romance's potential to transform epic's values for future audiences. Charoba's refusal to glory in Gebirus's defeat reveals the problems with one-sided epic narratives that reduce Achilles and Hector to victor and loser, celebrating a heroic code that requires one hero to triumph at another's expense.[47] Though *Charoba* marks Gebirus as justly defeated, it also records his story in his own words, making available both Charoba's response and the biased history that requires it.

Seizing Narrative Control: Lessons from Cleopatra and Scheherazade

Reeve's inclusion of Charoba's story underscores Euphrasia's claim in *The Progress* that the construction of generic hierarchies is politically motivated. *Charoba* reworks classical elements and stages the queen's conflict with Gebirus in order to foreground the ways in which a more basic struggle for narrative control shapes the process of canonization. *Charoba*'s history thus parallels *The Progress*'s literary-critical dialogue: the trio of Charoba, her nurse, and Gebirus replaces Euphrasia, Sophronia, and Hortensius as Gebirus becomes a stand-in for the epic and historiographic models that shape narratives such as Medea's and Cleopatra's. By depicting an embattled Egyptian monarch who recalls figures as diverse as Penelope and Deianeira, Cleopatra and Scheherazade, Reeve centralizes the far-reaching stakes of Euphrasia's discursive battle: as Gebirus's dying words suggest, generic hegemony can easily serve as a script for other kinds of domination.

Reproducing, in his dying wish, the univocal perspective represented by Hortensius in *The Progress*, Gebirus attempts to impose on Charoba his own version of history. He expects Charoba to eulogize his seemingly unjust fate, and – vividly illustrating the problems of authorial bias – bitterly extrapolates a condemnation of the female sex from his conflict with the queen of Egypt. In a speech worth quoting at length, Gebirus invokes his patrimony, listing his transitory accomplishments:

> I *Gebirus*, the *Metaphequian*, the son of *Gevirus*, that have caused marbles to be polished, – both the red and the green stone to be wrought curiously; who was possessed of gold, and jewels, and various treasures; who have raised armies; built cities; erected palaces; – who have cut my way through mountains; have stopped rivers; and done many great and wonderful actions; – with all this my power, and my strength, and my valour, and my vices: I have been circumvented by the wiles of a woman; weak, impotent, and deceitful; who hath deprived me of my strength and understanding; and finally hath taken away my life: – Wherefore, whosoever is desirous to be great and to prosper ... let him put no trust in a woman; but let him, at all times, beware of the craft and subtilty of a woman. (274)

Overwhelmed, for the moment, by Gebirus's version of events, Charoba's fate is temporarily unclear. To her country, she is still a wise and virtuous queen, hardly "weak" and "impotent," as much as Gebirus would like to rewrite and contain her. Yet to Gebirus and his people, who cannot comprehend his wrongdoing, Charoba's "deceitful" "wiles" are surely to blame; from Gebirus's perspective, the problem is not that he has repeatedly overstepped his bounds – by his own admission, Egypt is not the first time he intended to "stop rivers" – but that he "put ... trust in a woman."

Charoba has the power to dismiss Gebirus's request, as she evidently does in the Vattier-Davies source texts. However, Reeve's Charoba honours Gebirus's dying wish, faithfully recording his words for posterity. At the same time, she also inscribes her own history, ensuring the commemoration of Gebirus's interpretation of his defeat alongside the celebration of her victory. In this way, just as *The Progress* profits from a series of evening conversations to present the varied opinions of its participants, *Charoba* enacts a historiographic model that accommodates multiple perspectives. Offering, in Charoba's romance legacy, a corrective to Gebirus's model of conquest and appropriation – a model that links him with Augustus and Aeneas – Reeve's oriental tale stands as a monument for future historians, literary critics, and writers of fiction alike. In immortalizing Gebirus's dying words alongside her own, Charoba at once unearths narrative bias and prevents it from dictating her history. Just as Reeve reworks allusions to Greek heroines in order to recover figures traditionally marginalized by epic, she provides a competing historiographic model in order to reimagine women as agents of history.

Charoba's decision to commemorate Gebirus's dying words appears all the more remarkable because of its peculiarity to Reeve; the Vattier-Davies translations differ substantially in their relation of Gebirus's demise. At the moment, in the source texts, of his death-by-poisoned-cloak, the nurse taunts Gebirus before inquiring after his dying requests; although he asks that his final, self-serving boast be recorded for posterity, the text offers no hint that Charoba or her nurse takes seriously his demands. In fact, as soon as Gebirus expires, "Charoba thereupon commanded his head to be cut off, and that it should be set upon the gate of the City of Memphis; which was put in execution by her people. After that," we learn, "she caused the Tower of Alexandria to be built, and to be graved thereon her own name, and that of Gebirus, and what she had done to him, and the time when the City had been built."[48] By contrast, Reeve's Charoba promises to honour Gebirus's request, even "comfort[ing] him, and renew[ing] her promise to him" (274) as he slips in and out of consciousness. Although Gebirus characterizes her actions as "triumph[ing] in [his] death," there is no indication that Charoba is insincere, and – in a striking innovation upon the source texts – she immediately executes his request as promised, without the accompanying violence. Yet Charoba also attests to her own version of history: in the new city, where she orders Gebirus's body "honorably interred" rather than decapitated, "she built an high tower … and caused to be engraven upon it her own name, and that of *Gebirus*: and an history of all that she had done unto him, and also those his last words" (274). Although her name and history precede her enemy's, Charoba presents both sides of their struggle and allows readers to determine for themselves the justness of Gebirus's fate.

Charoba's resemblances to Dido and to her historical counterpart, Cleopatra, make her an apt figure for exploring the intersections between fiction and history. In imagining Charoba's triumph over Gebirus, Reeve presents one possibility for successfully reimagining the Dido story, combating both the famed Virgilian model, in which Dido succumbs to love for Aeneas, and the earlier mythic tradition in which she immolates herself to avoid remarriage. Reeve's framework, in always foregrounding the political demands of Charoba's situation, repudiates the role of lovesick queen so attractive to Virgil and to subsequent shapers of the Antony and Cleopatra narrative. Reeve also rejects the alternative suggested by the original Dido story, in which Dido, having fled to Libya, commits suicide in order to escape marriage to the overbearing king, Iarbas. Whereas the generic clash between romance and epic results in immolation for Virgil's queen, this same tension in Reeve – subordinating, this time, epic to romance – allows Charoba to thwart Gebirus, and ensures her lasting fame in the process. In positioning itself against the epic heroism represented not only by Iarbas but by Gebirus-Aeneas, *Charoba* rejects the imperialistic narrative of the *Aeneid*, in which Dido falls victim to Aeneas's success. Affirming the superior possibilities of romance, Reeve commemorates both Charoba and Gebirus at the same time.

From Gebirus's dying curse to Charoba's position as queen of Egypt, the vicissitudes of the Cleopatra narrative further inform Reeve's story. Where Charoba's resonances with the Dido myth subvert the epic narrative that makes inevitable Aeneas's success, her similarities to Cleopatra resist mythmaking-as-history. Unlike Gebirus, Cleopatra never has the opportunity to relate her own story; her premature death and Octavian's invasion of Egypt seal her narrative fate.[49] The resulting contrast between Gebirus's fortunes and Cleopatra's suggests an alternative model for constructing histories of defeat, just as it highlights the historiographic process that produces Roman history. Indeed, Gebirus's tactics – first denouncing Charoba, then generalizing from Charoba to all women – fit into an established historiographic pattern. For example, the ancient historian Cassius Dio relates – in a moment reminiscent of Gebirus's deathbed curse – Octavian's proclamation that he is fighting "to conquer and rule all mankind, [and] to allow no woman to make herself equal to a man."[50] In surpassing the conflict between Rome and Egypt, Dio's characterization – like Gebirus's – reveals the stakes of Octavian's historiographic project: "Cleopatra" becomes, at once, a monument to the just inequality between Rome and other empires ("all mankind") and to the just subordination of women to men; in this formulation, the moral exceeds Cleopatra, and even other figures like her, to become a global narrative of domination that naturalizes the parallel between Roman rule and male supremacy. Of course, Reeve's Charoba also has an agenda, but one narrowly limited to Egypt's welfare. Forbearing claims to the rulership of mankind, and refusing to extrapolate from Gebirus to the category of "men" more generally, Charoba draws from Gebirus's fate a moral that applies only to "such men as would compel Queens to marry them, and kingdoms to receive them for their Kings" (274). By presenting Gebirus's account alongside her own, and by enshrining his words in the context of their utterance – the city she ordered him to build – Charoba foregrounds the contrast between Gebirus's relation and her own version of events, thus rendering transparent the motivations that create "Charoba" – or "Cleopatra" – for various audiences. If "Cleopatra" is a byword for the narrative fate of history's losers, then "Gebirus" represents the subsistence of authorial bias, and "Charoba" the prospect of a dialogic historiography capable of disrupting the patterns that produce Gebirus's narrative.

By seizing narrative control, Charoba enters history through romance geography as an illustrious queen in a long line of potent rulers, including her figurative descendants, Alexander the Great and Cleopatra. By establishing the foundations on which Alexander will later build the city bearing his name, Charoba assumes an important role, closely associated with epic, as the founder of the future Alexandria, the most important city of the Hellenistic age. Fittingly for Charoba's narrative, it is a city known for its cosmopolitan inclusiveness, situated at the crossroads of East and West, a polyglot centre of art and learning that would become home to a number of exceptional women – not only Cleopatra, but figures like Arsinoe, Berenice II, Zenobia, Hypatia, and Olympias, Alexander's mother.[51] In this way, Charoba's Egypt reflects a specific kind of feminine excellence and virtue, distinguished against the reign of Charoba's father, King Totis, and against the violent advent of Gebirus. Indeed, Reeve's version highlights a specifically feminine lineage by making Charoba's successor, Dalica, definitively female – an important departure from the indecision that marks the Vattier-Davies source texts, in which Dalica's sex remains unclear.[52]

In modifying *The History of Charoba* from its source texts, Reeve thus highlights the narrative choices that construct subsequent histories. Like the critical bias that produces canon formation, the prejudices of individual historians will either condemn or exonerate the Egyptian queens. In the Vattier-Davies translations, for example, Charoba's death represents a fulfilment of Gebirus's dying words. Suggesting the serpent's retributive function, Charoba recalls Gebirus's prophecy at the very moment of her snakebite. By contrast, Reeve omits Charoba's recollection of Gebirus's curse, and further supports Charoba's judgment by describing how Gebirus's death causes her "fame [to go] forth, and c[o]me to the ears of many Kings, and they feared and respected her" (274), resulting in "many offers of friendship and alliance; but *Charoba* remained a virgin to the end of her life" (274). Even the facts of Charoba's death – the snakebite and resulting blindness – yield conflicting interpretations that either herald Charoba's defeat or celebrate her queenship. Although, in their Christian context, snakes represent evil, sin, and temptation, they also symbolize health, fertility, intelligence, and ingenuity. For the ancient world, the snake was a symbol of salvation and redemption in addition to its associations with the Fall; in Greece, it was sacred to Apollo and Athena and related to rebirth and eternal youth.[53] Snakes also enjoyed a position of prominence among Egyptian royalty. As the classicist Sarah Pomeroy notes, "It was surely by design that Cleopatra chose to be killed by cobra's poison, for this animal was an ancient symbol of Pharaonic power."[54] The snake, even as it links Charoba with Eve, also reaffirms her reign, her wisdom, the greatness of her posterity, and her status as an Egyptian queen. Although Charoba dies shortly after being bitten, her death does not diminish her "fame," nor does it lessen the "fear" and "respect" accorded her (275), but instead suggests her lasting reputation as a great and independent monarch. The same may be said of Charoba's resulting blindness:[55] though apparently fulfilling Gebirus's deathbed warning, it may also be considered prophetic in light of Charoba's endorsement by Abraham. The blindness lasts only a single day, functioning as a precursor to her death and what may be termed her transcendence or apotheosis, for Charoba's "name died not with her, for it remaineth, and is honoured unto this day" (211). Like Charoba's snakebite, her blindness rewrites the possibility of just punishment suggested by Gebirus in the Vattier-Davies translations.[56]

Charoba's death by snakebite also recalls Euphrasia's description of the metaphorical perils of the critical enterprise earlier in *The Progress of Romance*. I argue that, in explicitly uniting Charoba's death with Euphrasia's project, Reeve's inclusion of Charoba's story complements Euphrasia's claims by creating a parallel between Gebirus's denunciation of Charoba's success and the critical hostilities directed towards romance fiction. At the beginning of the second volume as Euphrasia prepares to move from romance to the novel, she anticipates the new difficulties associated with discussing a more recent genre of less ancient pedigree. "[N]ew dangers await us every step we set. – We may tread upon serpents that may rise and sting us; or, we may rouse a hornet's nest that may stun us with its noise, or wound us with its deadly weapons" (225). In imagining the threat of venomous serpents, Euphrasia refers not only to the living authors who might take umbrage at her critiques, but also to the critics who jealously guard the novel, opportunistically distinguishing it from romance. Like the serpent that arguably, in the Vattier-Davies translation, fulfils Gebirus's curse by punishing Charoba, the metaphorical serpents that await Reeve's trio police, with their stings, the process of canon formation. The image links hostile critics to Gebirus while Charoba emerges as a symbol of the romance-inflected novel: Reeve's adaptation and translation take Charoba's story beyond the realms of romance (of which it serves as an exemplar) and history (from which it originally comes) in favour of a hybrid romance historiography that grants Reeve the same licence as her seventeenth-century forebears. That is, like the French romancers who based their voluminous novels on legitimate history, Reeve maintains the basic facts of Charoba's fate but implies different conclusions, highlighting the prejudicial interpretive work represented by Gebirus and his modern critical counterparts.

I conclude this project with Reeve's *Progress of Romance* because it powerfully illustrates the stakes of the preceding chapters: the narrative pattern that marks Dido and Cleopatra as epic's and history's losers attempts, finally, to ensure the subordination of the genre that accommodates their defeat. In offering a revision of the Dido-Cleopatra narrative, in which Charoba doubles for the North African queens and Gebirus for the interloper Aeneas-Augustus, Reeve implicitly suggests the extent to which the *Aeneid* and Augustan historiography shape not only subsequent literature and historiographic practices but also literary history itself. In *The Progress of Romance*, reading Charoba's story back into the trio's discussion reveals that the privileging of Aeneas over Dido has consequences beyond its local context in the *Aeneid*: it leads to the canonizing of epic over romance, even men's novels over women's. In turn, Charoba's story first reverses, and finally upends altogether, the mythologizing process that threatens to exclude Barker's Jacobite readers from history, and to transform Fielding's Amelia into an unwitting sacrifice to the Noble Peer. In foregrounding Gebirus's manifest bias, it likewise undermines the easy proclamations, among Lennox's male characters, that a well-known queen of Egypt can achieve fame only as an object of sexual scandal, and further refutes the historiographic practices staged so vividly in *The Lives of Cleopatra and Octavia*. Although Reeve intends, in concluding *The Progress* with *Charoba*, to provide an example of romance's ancient lineage, her decision to translate and adapt an actual history also foregrounds the blurred lines between history, epic, and romance. There is no formal reason, *Charoba* suggests, that the same confluence of genres that enshrined Aeneas's heroism or Augustus's mastery cannot be deployed to more egalitarian ends. By ending with a history deeply inflected with Greek and Roman narratives yet derived from the "Traditions of the Arabians," Reeve takes advantage of an unfamiliar story to destabilize the Dido-Aeneas binary and therefore to frustrate its apparent inevitability. That she does so at the end of a literary-critical dialogue describing the development of Charoba's romance into the modern novel further argues for the centrality of Dido and Cleopatra to eighteenth-century fiction – not as foils for the allegedly superior genre of epic, but as subjects of heroism in their own right.

Epilogue

I'd like to end this project where it began: with the story of Inkle and Yarico that ignited, thanks to Steele's *Spectator* 11, a literary phenomenon that captivated the eighteenth century. By showcasing Yarico's story in one of his earliest issues, Mr Spectator enshrines the memory of Yarico's fate at the heart of the *Spectator* project, immediately following Addison's justification of that project, for a broad range of readers, in *Spectator* 10. In Arietta's drawing-room rebuke to the so-called Commonplace Talker so fond of stories of women's inconstancy, Steele traces the pervasiveness of the Dido myth as a model for abandoned women: he at once acknowledges the fertile ground for self-critique that narrative embodies and confronts the limits of that narrative for women like Arietta and Yarico. Although Arietta silences her companion and moves Mr Spectator to tears, Yarico arguably repeats Dido's fate, seemingly over and over again, as though no other outcome were possible. In "always" serving, as Steele hopes, as a "counterpart" to the Ephesian Matron, Yarico's narrative may make its point, but so, too, will it always enact the betrayal and abandonment of its heroine.

Yet the unsettling ending of Yarico's story, like the *Aeneid*'s discomfort with Dido's death beyond her fate, also signals a narrative rupture with the past, here embodied by the Ephesian Matron. The Commonplace Talker retails traditional stories of women's infidelity, including the Matron's infamous tale, in order to support his biases with the weight of example. The Widow, though she appears a model of chastity weeping over her husband's grave, soon becomes an exemplar of ridicule when she succumbs to the seductions of a Roman soldier. Magnifying her inconstancy, she allows the soldier to substitute her husband's body for one of the crucified corpses that has disappeared during their romantic interlude. In this way, Petronius's *Satyricon*, the *locus classicus* for the Matron's story, coarsely compares Dido to the Widow: although Dido has no choice but to abandon her vow to Sychaeus, forced by Cupid to fall in love with Aeneas, she becomes yet another example of women's infidelity. Arietta rebuffs the misogyny of the Commonplace Talker by referring to an ancient story of her own, invoking Aesop's fable of the lion and the man in order to seize the fabulist's licence to speak subversively. Deploying fable in order to foreground the falsity of her companion's assumptions, as well as the inequities that make those assumptions possible, she explains, "your Quotations put me in Mind of the Fable of the Lion and the Man."[1] "The Man walking with that noble Animal, showed him," she recounts, "in the Ostentation of human Superiority, a Sign of a Man killing a Lion. Upon which the Lion said very justly, *We are None of us Painters, else we could show a hundred Men killed by Lions, for one Lion killed by a Man.*" Arietta concludes, "You Men are Writers and can represent us Women as unbecoming as you please in your Works, while we are unable to return the Injury."[2]

In the Introduction, I argued that the story of Inkle and Yarico takes on the status of a modern fable, according to Laura Brown's definition of the term in *Fables of Modernity*. Brown writes, "a cultural fable might perform the demystifying tasks of revealing the underlying contradiction of its historical moment or uncovering the mystified social relations behind its formation, but it might also augment a particular structure or judgment, consolidate a specific contemporary prejudice, expose the problematic constituents of an accepted belief, or open an imaginative route to a new mode of knowing or being."[3] In mobilizing the familiar pattern of Dido's betrayal, Arietta's decision to remain faithful to the original narrative signals, in fact, new imaginative routes by moving Mr Spectator to tears. His affective response not only models appropriate sentiment for the reader, but suggests that other forms of engagement with the Dido myth are possible.

By relating the fable of the lion and the man in response to the Ephesian Matron, Arietta explicitly critiques the Commonplace Talker's easy deployment of an age-old story: instead of contrasting the fop's account with a "true" story of her own, she subversively relies on Aesop's fable to initiate a more fundamental critique of the means of representation, one that generates new narrative potential. That critique takes the shape of Yarico's story, itself a recasting of the longstanding monopoly of male writers' representational power, from Virgil, Ovid, and Petronius through the eighteenth century. Dido's plight comes to furnish an originary narrative, at the dawn of Augustan epic and history, that both inaugurates and prefigures the pattern of critique embodied in Arietta's rebuke.

The writers in *Novel Cleopatras* take their cue from the same inequities that motivate Arietta's challenge to the Commonplace Talker by turning to the fertile crucible of the Dido narrative. Some of these works are central to understanding the novel and key novelists in this period. Such is the case, for example, with Charlotte Lennox's *The Female Quixote* (1752), which often serves, particularly in introductory classes, as a referendum on the novel at mid-century, and Henry Fielding's *Amelia* (1751), still considered the ugly stepchild of his oeuvre despite Fielding's characterization of the novel as his favourite offspring.[4] The other novels I discuss have received growing critical recognition in recent years. This is true of Jane Barker (*Exilius*, 1715), Sarah Fielding (*The Lives of Cleopatra and Octavia*, 1757), and Clara Reeve (*The Progress of Romance*, 1785), who were important innovators of the novel and classically trained theorists of eighteenth-century literary culture. For all of these writers, returning to classical origins means undermining the categories enforced by Roman propaganda, including the *Aeneid*, and inherited by future writers: reworking the twin fates of Dido and Cleopatra allows eighteenth-century writers to upend familiar conventions and to suggest dissenting ways of thinking about epic and history.

In this way, the stakes of Dido's story – like Yarico's – extend beyond Virgil's heroine to the subject position she occupies. The Dido position makes legible the easy affinities between the categories "woman," "foreigner," and "loser," for these three categories intersect powerfully in the figure of Virgil's Carthaginian queen. They meet, too, in her real-life analogue, whose very otherness as a woman and "Egyptian" made possible, in her defeat, the actual, and especially rhetorical, birth of an empire. A fourth category – romance – attempts to ensure that epic's outcasts will never achieve the success denied them by its victors. As David Quint has argued in *Epic and Empire*, "particularly defined from the perspective of epic," romance is the losers' genre, inexorably linked "to the condition of defeat." Where "the victors experience history as a coherent, end-directed story told by their own power … the losers," he states, "experience a contingency that they are powerless to shape their own ends."[5]

While the pattern Quint identifies may hold for the *Aeneid* and the poems it inspired, the post-Virgilian fortunes of romance – from the ancient novel, to the medieval vernacular tradition, and the continental romances of the seventeenth century – engender new contexts for understanding the narratives of epic's so-called losers. As *Novel Cleopatras* demonstrates, by the advent of the eighteenth century, writers began to undermine the dichotomy between epic and romance that Quint identifies. Where the *Aeneid* imagines romance and epic as antithetical,[6] romance – particularly in the form, as I have argued, of the eighteenth-century novel – rejects the categories superficially embraced by Virgil, exploiting instead the *Aeneid*'s own instabilities in order to challenge Aeneas's heroics as well as teleological notions of history. It is perhaps unsurprising that romance – defined by, and in relation to, epic – would emerge as an inferior genre, its protagonists denied the narrative authority of epic's victors. Yet such an outcome is far from inevitable. As Clara Reeve argues in *The Progress of Romance*, even the categories of "epic" and "romance" are less rigid than they appear; for her mouthpiece Euphrasia, romance is merely an "epic in prose."[7] Although romance "from the perspective of epic" may indeed consign Dido and similar challengers to defeat, it also, more broadly conceived, makes possible Dido's escape from the narrative template created by Virgil.

In eschewing epic teleology and the subjection conventionally associated with Dido's narrative, the writers in this project give value to epic's so-called losers. Undermining familiar narratives and hierarchies, both generic and ideological, they seek to explore possibilities beyond the univocal perspective celebrated, even if uneasily, in the *Aeneid*. In revisiting the victor/loser paradigm, these writers at once encourage readers to rethink the simplistic dichotomies on which the legacy of Augustan propaganda depended, and to locate new narrative possibilities that reject the subject position advanced by traditional epic and typified in Augustan history. These authors refuse the victor/loser model altogether: the historical "losers" will not aspire to the narrative power denied them by the victors if it means reductively embodying the victor position themselves.[8] In this way, writers like Barker, Lennox, the Fieldings, and Reeve carry forward the project of *Spectator* 11: where reimagining Dido and Aeneas as Yarico and Inkle still results in Yarico's enslavement, these writers return to originary patterns in order to seek alternative outcomes for their heroines and heroes – outcomes that seek to transform, rather than to reinscribe, familiar narratives.

Throughout this project, I have used the term "romance historiography" to signal the strategy embraced by many eighteenth-century writers at a time when "romance," "novel," and "history" were still synonymous terms. Even as late as Reeve's *Progress of Romance* in 1785, the definition of romance – and even epic – remained hotly contested by Euphrasia and her contemporaries. Romance historiography depends on romance in order to reinvigorate conventional notions of history, including historiographic practices; this is nowhere clearer than its intervention in ancient – and modern – Augustan propaganda, which it refuses to accept as indisputable fact. As a novelistic strategy, romance historiography also aims to recuperate the diverse and capacious origins of the novel, from its ancient roots to its nearer continental influences, especially the seventeenth-century French heroic novel inspired by ancient history. Of course, romance militates against history even in the *Aeneid*, not only in the subordination of Dido's narrative to Aeneas's, but in the sympathy Virgil generates for Dido's plight. Although that sympathy cannot save her, it brings her to a crossroads that proliferates Didos, centralizing her resistance alongside her defeat. As a result, Dido's story marks the possibility of new narrative origins: returning to Dido means disrupting the patterns of epic and history in order to create new narrative trajectories in the English novel.

Future Neoclassicisms

This project began with a much broader interest in the contours of neoclassicism in eighteenth-century British culture. Part of its aim has been to encourage renewed investment in the neoclassical impulse as an object (and mode) of inquiry in the long eighteenth century. Central to this enterprise, I hope to have modelled some of the ways in which classical languages and literatures reinvigorate our appreciation of the generic fluidity of eighteenth-century fiction, as well as some of the ways in which early modern and eighteenth-century writers mediated antiquity – from a place of unmistakable modernity – both in England and abroad. The twin narratives of Dido and Cleopatra, though significant because of their positioning at the dawn of Western civilization, offer only one example of the literary and historical patterning that neoclassicism seeks to unsettle. In *Novel Cleopatras*, I have attempted to suggest some of the ways in which engagements with the Dido model – with the feminine, dilatory world of romance, capable of rewriting epic teleologies – model other kinds of engagements with the classical past in the British present, especially for readers and writers traditionally denied classical authority.

The common critical epithets for the decades between 1660 and 1789 – the "Augustan Age" and "neoclassical period" – emphasize the legacy, inherited from humanism, of the classical, especially Roman, past. Although these terms may sometimes suggest a uniform attitude towards antiquity, there was, importantly, no monolithic interpretation of the classical tradition in the eighteenth century, no single set of precepts that gave birth to a "neoclassical" sensibility. Far from a universal reverence for the classics, the conflict between Ancients and Moderns reveals, on both scientific and literary fronts, complex attitudes towards England's classical inheritance. Indeed, rhetorical uses of the figure of Augustus suggest that writers were often as willing to censure Augustan ideals as they were to identify themselves with the advent of a new Augustan Age.

The most prominent chroniclers of a now out-of-fashion debate between Augustans and anti-Augustans, Ancients and Moderns, remain those of the 1960s and 1970s, scholars such as James William Johnson, Joseph Levine, and Howard Weinbrot, who have spent their careers problematizing our understanding of the relationship between ancient Augustans and their modern descendants. These critics, having disputed Restoration and eighteenth-century reverence for the classics, have served as the point of departure for this project, which has sought to render a more detailed portrait of the period from roughly 1688 to 1785 and its various, sometimes competing, responses to a classical legacy that many writers both emulated and challenged. Whereas earlier scholars have argued that eighteenth-century authors exploited or criticized the ancients in order to advance the supremacy of a particularly *neo*classical model, this project has shown some of the ways in which other writers were equally interested in rethinking and expanding the values of the "new" classicism itself.

Critics such as those cited above have focused primarily on the historical and literary similarities and differences between the long eighteenth century and its Roman model. Restoration writers in particular repeatedly identified their era with (or against) Augustan Rome, the period from roughly 27 BCE to 14 CE when Octavian became Augustus and united East and West under his rule. For many Romans, it was a time of prosperity and peace, when trade and the arts flourished, and Augustus's role as creator of the *pax Augusta* led seventeenth-century writers to praise their own leaders on his model.[9] "[G]iven the facts of English history," J.W. Johnson writes,

> it was unavoidable that analogies be drawn … Despite time gaps and variant conditions, the age of Elizabeth I was akin to the Roman Republic

> after the Third Punic War: Carthage (Spain) was defeated and national power and wealth reached a new height with expanding commerce. The Cromwellian Wars were the internecine struggles between Marius and Sulla or Caesar and Pompey. Quite obviously, to the English classicist, an Augustus had to emerge to settle the world and throw open prematurely the gates to the temple of peace.[10]

So strongly felt was the kinship between England and Rome – and so disputed – that the turn of the eighteenth century saw a heated debate, in France as well as England: supporters of the Ancients ranged against admirers of the Moderns in the "Battle of the Books," fuelled especially on the English side by William Temple and William Wotton and perhaps best remembered from Swift's eponymous satire.[11] "[T]he basic condition of the quarrel," Levine writes, "was a broad insistence that the ancient Greeks and Romans had set the supreme models and standards for every sort of endeavor, most particularly for politics and the humanistic arts associated with it: rhetoric and oratory, history, poetry, moral philosophy." "[E]veryone," Levine notes, "was profoundly concerned about the authority of classical antiquity … [T]here was no subject, from art and literature to philosophy and science, from religion to politics, that was exempt from its concerns."[12]

As the Battle of the Books demonstrates, the "Augustan" epithet had its limits as an accurate descriptor of the period. Although early twentieth-century critics such as George Sherburn have tended to view appreciation for the classical tradition as normative, scholars such as Weinbrot and Levine have revised our understanding of eighteenth-century neoclassicism.[13] "There was indeed," Weinbrot acknowledges, "much deserved and continuing respect for classical literature and values … But there was also mistrust, suspicion, and outright hostility as well as emulation of the best sort."[14] At a time of political upheaval and imperial expansion, writers found the authority of the ancients appealing but also questioned their dominance; as a new age of discovery and learning dawned, many authors viewed with scepticism the so-called superiority of Greece and especially of England's nearer cultural ancestor, Rome.

In light of the sometimes contradictory attitudes expressed by the epithets "Augustan" and "neoclassical," more recent critics have offered new ways of interpreting eighteenth-century neoclassicism, highlighting the important cultural and rhetorical roles it performs. Their contributions have helped to create a more multidimensional understanding of the interaction between Ancients and Moderns, and this project aims to extend even further the implications of their work. Scholars like Philip Ayres and Richard Kroll, for example, have demonstrated that neoclassicism functioned as a method of reinforcing an imperilled hegemony; emulation of Rome legitimated aristocratic values in the wake of the Glorious Revolution, providing a way to "revise and police an entire panoply of cultural norms," for which the English used the "ancient world as a map of their present circumstances."[15] Indeed, the reality of the period was quite vexed, as Michael McKeon has argued. "[T]he affirmation of tradition and stability," he writes, "is likely to be most insistent precisely at those moments when tradition and stability are most thought to be endangered."[16]

The erosion of classical authority began as early as the 1650s, following the execution of Charles I, and gained momentum after the turmoil of the 1660s, with the Restoration and Glorious Revolution. The political trauma initiated by the execution of Charles I, and later the revolution of 1688, undermined the doctrine of the divine right of kings and, at the same time, the *Aeneid*'s epic of political destiny. For scholars like Tanya Caldwell, Dryden's translation of Virgil in 1697 marks the end of an era, offering the last prominent full-scale engagement with Virgil's poem, despite the continued importance of Virgilian epic into subsequent decades.[17] The period that produced Dryden's translation showed its ambivalence towards Virgil in other ways. A number of keys to the *Aeneid* emphasized its foreignness to many eighteenth-century readers; attempting to interpret the epic as allegory, or to historicize its elements, these keys aimed to make Virgil legible to contemporary audiences. Still other writers were openly hostile, producing a variety of parodies vulgarly satirizing Aeneas's heroism.[18] At the same time, Dryden and Pope make Virgil and Homer more accessible to a broader range of readers, especially women, who were denied access, by and large, to the learned languages and certainly to a formal classical education. While the move from translation to satire may seem to herald a decline in the fortunes of classical epic, I argue, instead, that "neoclassicism" is a dynamic phenomenon, a set of tools and strategies for reinvigorating literary culture outside of the reductive Ancients/Moderns divide.

Indeed, crucial to reconceptualizing the so-called Augustan age is a revaluation of women's participation in neoclassical culture. Although *Novel Cleopatras* did not begin as a book about predominantly female novelists, it became clear, early in my research, that female authors were especially innovative in their use of the classical past: Barker's "unfashionable romance," Lennox's *female* Quixote, Sarah Fielding's revision of classical history, and Reeve's ground-breaking literary-critical dialogue are all, in their own ways, milestones in the wake of the Ancients/Moderns debate. Yet, because of eighteenth-century hostility towards women's learning, scholars have tended to dismiss their influence as critics of, and their conflicted relationship to, (neo)classical culture. Though it is perhaps not surprising for early surveys of the period, such as Sherard Vines's *The Course of English Classicism* (1930) or J.A.K. Thomson's *Classical Background of English Literature* (1948) and *Classical Influences on English Prose* (1956), to ignore the role of women writers, it is certainly striking to find this conspicuous silence in more recent work. Levine's introduction to *Ancients and Moderns* remains typical: because classical knowledge was intended to "prepar[e] an elite group of men for public life," Levine implies that non-elite readers would have had little interest in the classics, and would have taken up arms, accordingly, for the Moderns. It was "natural," he writes, "for the few women writers in the period largely to disregard a quarrel that did not concern them directly, though they must inevitably have inclined to the modern side."[19] Yet the situation is more complex: as this project demonstrates, many women writers embraced ancient epic and history via the medium of romance, especially the seventeenth-century French heroic novel, a stance that could only be articulated from a position of modernity.

Novel Cleopatras has suggested some of the ways in which eighteenth-century writers – still attached to, yet unwilling to promote uncritically, their classical heritage – give new life to ancient epic and history even as they grant space and power to the unrepresented and effaced. In doing so, this project aims to enlarge our understanding of eighteenth-century neoclassicism as a complex set of often-contradictory responses to the past, equally capable of critique and emulation; it argues that we view neoclassicism as a more inclusive phenomenon, available both to women writers and to their male contemporaries, a phenomenon more productive than reductive, more dynamic than static. This project has demonstrated that, for many authors, "neoclassicism" served as a set of tools with which to question concepts of gender and genre, fact and fiction, ancient and modern, suggesting that the new classicism is as capable of destabilizing, as it is of reinforcing, cultural assumptions and forms.

Notes

Introduction

1 Richard Steele and Joseph Addison, *The Spectator*, ed. Donald F. Bond, 5 vols. (Oxford: Clarendon Press, 1965), 1:44. Subsequent references will be cited parenthetically. A complete version of my argument about Steele can be found in Nicole Horejsi, "'A Counterpart to the Ephesian Matron': Steele's 'Inkle and Yarico' and a Feminist Critique of the Classics," *Eighteenth-Century Studies* 39.2 (2006): 201–26.

2 Peter Ure's "The Widow of Ephesus: Some Reflections on an International Comic Theme," in *Elizabethan and Jacobean Drama: Critical Essays by Peter Ure*, ed. J.C. Maxwell (Liverpool: Liverpool University Press, 1974), 221–36, discusses some of the incarnations of the Ephesian Matron in different cultures, including eighteenth-century England. Although other versions of the story became well known as the eighteenth century progressed, Steele would have been most familiar with Petronius's anecdote, the version he cites in *Spectator* 11.

3 See Frank Felsenstein, ed., *English Trader, Indian Maid: Representing Gender, Race, and Slavery in the New World* (Baltimore: Johns Hopkins University Press, 1999): The Inkle and Yarico story has been told and retold into the twentieth century, in poetry, drama, and prose, numbering "well over sixty discrete versions and a sizable number of translations" between 1711 and 1810 alone (1–2). Among these were successful theatrical adaptations: Felsenstein notes that "between 1787 and 1800, *Inkle and Yarico* was staged a total of 164 times" (168).

4 For the epistolary tradition, see Felsenstein's compendium of Inkle and Yarico tales in *English Trader, Indian Maid*. Ovid's *Heroides* consists of a series of heroic epistles that permit heroines such as Dido to tell their own

stories. For another discussion of the similarities between the twin fortunes of Dido and Yarico, see also Peter Hulme, *Colonial Encounters: Europe and the Native Caribbean, 1492–1797* (New York: Methuen, 1986).

5 Laura Brown, *Fables of Modernity: Literature and Culture in the English Eighteenth Century* (Ithaca: Cornell University Press, 2001), 2–3. According to Brown, "the cultural fable provides a way of reading not only literary texts, but the relation between literature and history" (3). She further argues that "Women and non-Europeans provide a template, a catalyst, a reference point, a precedent, a strategy, or a conclusion for the imaginative exercises that these cultural fables undertake" (10).

6 Of the ideological work cultural fables do, Brown writes, "a cultural fable might perform the demystifying tasks of revealing the underlying contradiction of its historical moment or uncovering the mystified social relations behind its formation, but it might also augment a particular structure or judgment, consolidate a specific contemporary prejudice, expose the problematic constituents of an accepted belief, or open an imaginative route to a new mode of knowing or being" (*Fables of Modernity*, 4).

7 Though foundation myths were common in antiquity, Dido is an extremely unusual example of a foundation heroine rather than hero. For more on this phenomenon, see Nita Krevans, "Medea as Foundation-Heroine" in *Medea: Essays on Medea in Myth, Literature, Philosophy, and Art*, ed. James Clauss and Sarah Iles Johnston (Princeton: Princeton University Press, 1996), 71–82.

8 For Reeve's *The Progress of Romance*, see *Bluestocking Feminism: Writings of the Bluestocking Circle, 1738–1785*, vol. 6: *Sarah Scott and Clara Reeve*, ed. Gary Kelly (London: Pickering and Chatto, 1999), 176.

9 For more on this, see Françoise Waquet, *Latin, or, the Empire of a Sign: From the Sixteenth to the Twentieth Centuries*, trans. John Howe (New York: Verso, 2001), especially ch. 7, "Making the Man" (178–206).

10 Craig Kallendorf, *The Other Virgil: "Pessimistic" Readings of the Aeneid in Early Modern Culture* (Oxford: Oxford University Press, 2007), 3.

11 See Nancy Mace, *Henry Fielding's Novels and the Classical Tradition* (Newark: University of Delaware Press, 1996): "M.L. Clarke estimates that, according to this course of study, a student would also have read the *Aeneid* twice and Homer's *Iliad* one and a half times by the end of the sixth form. The list [of studied authors] is striking because it emphasizes Latin authors over Greek and poets over prose writers; it also shows that the average public school boy knew a few classical masterpieces well: he memorized Virgil, Horace, Homer, and Ovid, but only learned short selections from

Cicero and the authors in the anthologies" (21). For Clarke, see *Classical Education in Britain, 1500–1900* (Cambridge: Cambridge University Press, 1959).

12 Kallendorf, *The Other Virgil*, 215. See also Kallendorf, "Virgil's Post-Classical Legacy," in *A Companion to Ancient Epic*, ed. John Miles Foley (Malden, MA: Blackwell, 2009): 574–88.

13 Marilynn Desmond, *Reading Dido: Gender, Textuality, and the Medieval Aeneid* (Minneapolis: University of Minnesota Press, 1994), 7–8. Indeed, eighteenth-century writers often viewed the classics as indistinguishable from manliness. See Carolyn D. Williams, *Pope, Homer and Manliness: Some Aspects of Eighteenth-Century Classical Learning* (New York: Routledge, 1993). Though Williams's subject is Homer, her conclusions apply to the study of Latin as well.

14 Jane Stevenson, *Women Latin Poets: Language, Gender, and Authority from Antiquity to the Eighteenth Century* (Oxford: Oxford University Press, 2005), 391.

15 Ibid., 369.

16 See Linda Bree, *Sarah Fielding* (New York: Twayne Publishers, 1996), 20–2.

17 As Stevenson notes, "There is a substantial amount of evidence that seventeenth- and eighteenth-century England was well stocked with educated, more or less Latinate gentlewomen" (*Women Latin Poets*, 372).

18 Joseph Levine, *Between the Ancients and the Moderns: Baroque Culture in Restoration England* (New Haven: Yale University Press, 1999), xii. By contrast, there has been excellent work on women's participation in neoclassical culture on the American side. See, for example, Caroline Winterer, *The Mirror of Antiquity: American Women and the Classical Tradition, 1750–1900* (Ithaca: Cornell University Press, 1997).

19 On the importance of the *Aeneid* in the Western tradition, see especially Richard Waswo, *The Founding Legend of Western Civilization: From Virgil to Vietnam* (Hanover, NH: University Press of New England, 1997).

20 The first six books of the *Aeneid* rewrite, in reverse, the adventures of the *Odyssey*, while the second half follows the martial ethos of the *Iliad*. In this context, Aeneas's dalliance with Dido marks him as a potentially defeated Antony, but his ability to prioritize his heroic destiny over his own desires aligns him with the successful Octavian. Virgil mentions Cleopatra briefly in Book 8, but not by name; she is merely Antony's "*Egyptian* Wife" (6:8.912). Cleopatra thus makes her appearance as a static image on Aeneas's shield. For the *Aeneid*, see *The Works of John Dryden*, vols. 5–6: *Poems: The Works of Virgil in English, 1697*, ed. William Frost and Vinton Dearing (Berkeley: University of California Press, 1987). Volume 5 contains *Aeneid* 1–6; volume 6, *Aeneid* 7–12.

21 See *OED*, "dido," n1.

22 See the Loeb edition of Ovid in six volumes, vol. 5: *Tristia and Ex Ponto*, trans. Arthur Wheeler (Cambridge, MA: Harvard University Press, 1988), 2.535–6. As Richard Thomas writes in *Virgil and the Augustan Reception* (Cambridge: Cambridge University Press, 2001), "The reception of Dido is the richest aspect of Virgilian reception, and the one around which the Augustan battle has perhaps been fought most intensely" (154). See ch. 5, "Dido and Her Translators." For more on the reception history of the *Aeneid*, see Joseph Farrell and Michael C.J. Putnam, eds., *A Companion to Vergil's* Aeneid *and Its Tradition* (Malden, MA: Blackwell, 2010) and Kallendorf, *The Other Virgil*. On the Dido legend, with an overview of early commentators and the early modern stage tradition, see Don Cameron Allen, "Marlowe's *Dido* and the Tradition," in *Essays on Shakespeare and Elizabethan Drama in Honor of Hardin Craig*, ed. Richard Hosley (Columbia: University of Missouri Press, 1962), 55–68. On some of the political implications of Dido's story via Tate's *Dido and Aeneas* in the early eighteenth century, see Deborah Payne Fisk and Jessica Munns, "'Clamorous with War and Teeming with Empire': Purcell and Tate's *Dido and Aeneas*," *Eighteenth-Century Life* 26.2 (2002): 23–44, and Anthony Welch, "The Cultural Politics of *Dido and Aeneas*," *Cambridge Opera Journal* 21.1 (2009): 1–26. For scepticism toward the *Aeneid* more generally, see also Tanya Caldwell, *Virgil Made English: The Decline of Classical Authority* (New York: Palgrave, 2008), and Paul N. Hartle, "'Lawrels for the Conquered': Virgilian Translation and Travesty in the English Civil War and Its Aftermath," in *Reinventing the Middle Ages and the Renaissance: Constructions of the Medieval and Early Modern Periods*, ed. William F. Gentrup (Turnhout: Brepols, 1998).

23 See, respectively, Marilynn Desmond, *Reading Dido*, and Margaret Ferguson, *Dido's Daughters: Literacy, Gender, and Empire in Early Modern England and France* (Chicago: University of Chicago Press, 2003). Desmond has argued that "thematizing Dido's story (sometimes only momentarily) as the central plot of the Virgilian text constitutes a visible response to the *Aeneid* story. By displacing the epic hero Aeneas, the tradition of reading Dido disrupts the patrilineal focus of the *Aeneid* as an imperial foundation narrative" (*Reading Dido*, 2), so that the Dido episode "offers the reader an opportunity to intervene in the gendered discourses of colonialism and the canon" (ibid., 13). In many ways, Ferguson's work picks up where Desmond's ends, mapping the usefulness of the Dido figure from the fifteenth through seventeenth centuries. She focuses primarily on Christine de Pizan (an author she shares in common with Desmond, and the only

woman writer whom Desmond discusses at length), Marguerite de Navarre, Elizabeth Cary, and Aphra Behn. These women become catalysts for a larger discussion about competing modes of literacy in the early modern period (manuscript culture vs print; Latin vs the vernacular) and the gendered nature of such modes, especially in a vexed era of nation and empire building when women writers were just beginning to gain access to means of representation.

24 Cassius Dio, *Dio's Roman History*, 9 vols., trans. Ernest Cary, on the basis of the version of Herbert Baldwin Foster (Cambridge, MA: Harvard University Press, 1914–27), 5:497.

25 On the dilatory nature of romance, see especially Patricia Parker, *Inescapable Romance: Studies in the Poetics of a Mode* (Princeton: Princeton University Press, 1979). As Parker notes in the Introduction, romance (vs epic) "is characterized primarily as a form which simultaneously quests for and postpones a particular end, objective, or object" (4).

26 Scudéry in fact cites Heliodorus in the prefaces to her novels *Ibrahim* (1641) and the *The Grand Cyrus* (1649). For more on the relationship between Heliodorus and the development of the French prose romance just preceding Scudéry and La Calprenède, see Gerald N. Sandy, "Classical Forerunners of the Theory and Practice of Prose Romance in France: Studies in the Narrative Form of Minor French Romances of the Sixteenth and Seventeenth Centuries," *Antike und Abendland* 28.2 (1982): 169–91. Heliodorus was one of the most popular of the ancient Greek novelists, but he wasn't alone: the revival also included Chariton's *Chaereas and Callirhoe* (first century CE), Xenophon of Ephesus's *Ephesiaca* (second century CE), Achilles Tatius's *Leucippe and Clitophon* (late second century CE), and Longus's *Daphnis and Chloe* (late second century CE).

27 For the initial rediscovery of Heliodorus, see especially Michael Reeve, "The Re-Emergence of Ancient Novels in Western Europe, 1300–1810," in *The Cambridge Companion to the Greek and Roman Novel*, ed. Tim Whitmarsh (Cambridge: Cambridge University Press, 2008), 282–98.

28 On the novel as an ancient form, or a form with ancient roots, see Margaret Anne Doody, *The True Story of the Novel* (New Brunswick, NJ: Rutgers University Press, 1996), still the standard for this kind of study; Arthur Heiserman, *The Novel before the Novel: Essays and Discussions about the Beginnings of Prose Fiction in the West* (Chicago: University of Chicago Press, 1977); Ioan Williams, *The Idea of the Novel in Europe 1600–1800* (London: Macmillan, 1979); Gerald N. Sandy, "Ancient Prose Fiction and Minor Early English Novels," *Antike und Abendland* 25:1 (1979): 41–55; Gerald N. Sandy and Stephen Harrison, "Novels Ancient and Modern," in *The*

Cambridge Companion to the Greek and Roman Novel, ed. Whitmarsh, 299–320; Elizabeth Archibald, "Ancient Romance," in *A Companion to Romance: From Classical to Contemporary*, ed. Corinne Saunders (Malden, MA: Blackwell, 2004), 10–25; James J. Lynch, *Henry Fielding and the Heliodoran Novel: Romance, Epic, and Fielding's New Province of Writing* (Rutherford, NJ: Farleigh Dickinson University Press, 1986); Gareth Schmeling, ed., *The Novel in the Ancient World* (Leiden: E.J. Brill, 1996); James Tatum, ed., *The Search for the Ancient Novel* (Baltimore: Johns Hopkins University Press, 1994); and Thomas Hägg, *The Novel in Antiquity* (Oxford: Basil Blackwell, 1983). For an early modern perspective on Heliodorus's influence on prose fiction, see Steve Mentz, *Romance for Sale in Early Modern England: The Rise of Prose Fiction* (Burlington, VT: Ashgate, 2007).

29 For Johnson, see *Rambler* 4 in *The Rambler*, in *The Yale Edition of the Works of Samuel Johnson*, vol. 3, ed. W.J. Bate and Albrecht B. Strauss (New Haven: Yale University Press, 1969). For some recent accounts of the relationship between history and fiction in the eighteenth century, see especially Devoney Looser, *British Women Writers and the Writing of History, 1670–1820* (Baltimore: Johns Hopkins University Press, 2000); Ruth Mack, *Literary Historicity: Literature and Historical Experience in Eighteenth-Century Britain* (Stanford: Stanford University Press, 2009); Robert Mayer, *History and the Early English Novel: Matters of Fact from Bacon to Defoe* (Cambridge: Cambridge University Press, 1997); Karen O'Brien, *Women and Enlightenment in Eighteenth-Century Britain* (Cambridge: Cambridge University Press, 2009); and Mark Salber Phillips, *Society and Sentiment: Genres of Historical Writing in Britain, 1740–1820* (Princeton: Princeton University Press, 2000).

30 Seventeenth-century romancers insisted on the historicity of their novels, citing ancient sources and explaining the logic behind narrative departures. For more on this phenomenon, see chapter 3.

31 In contrast to epic, and even to other forms of romance (e.g., chivalric romance), the ancient novel (and the romances it subsequently inspired) foregrounded the adventures of both heroine and hero.

32 For more on the *Nights*, see, for example, Saree Makdisi and Felicity Nussbaum, eds., *The Arabian Nights in Historical Context: Between East and West* (Oxford: Oxford University Press, 2008); Rosalind Ballaster, *Fabulous Orients: Fictions of the East in England, 1662–1785* (Oxford: Oxford University Press, 2005); and Peter Caracciolo, *The "Arabian Nights" in English Literature: Studies in the Reception of "The Thousand and One Nights" into British Culture* (London: Macmillan Press, 1988).

33 Edward Gibbon in a letter to Lord Sheffield dated 4 October 1788. See Gibbon, *Memoirs of My Life and Writings*, ed. A.O.J. Cockshut and Stephen Constantine (Halifax: Ryburn Publications, 1994), 223.

34 Aeneas was distinguished as a hero by what the Romans called "pietas"; "pious Aeneas" is the poetic equivalent of "swift-footed Achilles" or "crafty Odysseus" in Homer. In English, "pietas" loosely translates to "piety," but the full range of its signification is much broader in Latin. "Pietas" refers not only to religious devotion but also to filial duty and service to one's country. Aeneas's *pietas* marks him as an exemplar, in part, because of the extent to which he must sacrifice his own desires for the sake of his heroic destiny.

35 Horace Walpole, *Yale Edition of Horace Walpole's Correspondence*, ed. W.S. Lewis (New Haven: Yale University Press, 1937–83), 11:20.

36 This fluidity occurred as a result of shifting constructions of womanhood and femininity in the seventeenth and eighteenth centuries. See, for example, Thomas Laqueur, *Making Sex: Body and Gender from the Greeks to Freud* (Cambridge, MA: Harvard University Press, 1990); Toni Bowers, *Politics of Motherhood: British Writing and Culture, 1680–1760* (New York: Cambridge University Press, 1996); and Susan C. Greenfield and Carol Barash, eds., *Inventing Maternity: Politics, Science, and Literature, 1650–1865* (Lexington: University Press of Kentucky, 1999). See also Laura Brown, *Ends of Empire: Women and Ideology in Early Eighteenth-Century English Literature* (Ithaca: Cornell University Press, 1993).

37 Phillips, *Society and Sentiment*, 17.

38 O'Brien, *Women and Enlightenment in Eighteenth-Century Britain*, 1.

39 Ibid., 87–8.

40 Phillips, *Society and Sentiment*, 114.

41 O'Brien, *Women and Enlightenment in Eighteenth-Century Britain*, 112.

42 Especially Angela Smallwood, *Fielding and the Woman Question: The Novels of Henry Fielding and Feminist Debate, 1700–1750* (New York: St Martin's Press, 1989), and Jill Campbell, *Natural Masques: Gender and Identity in Fielding's Plays and Novels* (Stanford: Stanford University Press, 1995).

1. "Pulcherrima Dido"

1 Barker wrote passionately of her political allegiance throughout her career, even winning the patronage of the Prince of Wales in 1700, when she dedicated to him "A Collection of Poems Referring to the times; since the Kings accession to the Crown." For an overview of this collection,

and of Barker's poetry collections more generally, see Kathryn R. King's Introduction to *The Poems of Jane Barker: The Magdalen Manuscript* (Oxford: Magdalen College, 1998), 1–23.

2 "Dido" famously means "wanderer." See Howard Jacobson, "Dido," *Mnemosyne* 58.4 (2005): 581–2.

3 For a detailed discussion of the opposition of epic and romance as the winner's and loser's genres, respectively, see David Quint, *Epic and Empire: Politics and Generic Form from Virgil to Milton* (Princeton: Princeton University Press, 1993). However, as Barker knew, this is only part of the story: epic and romance were also often indistinguishable. See Colin Burrow, *Epic Romance: Homer to Milton* (Oxford: Clarendon Press, 1993).

4 In Jane Barker, *Poetical Recreations: Consisting of Original Poems, Songs, Odes, &c. with Several New Translations. In Two Parts. Part I. Occasionally Written by Mrs. Jane Barker. Part II. By several Gentlemen of the Universities, and Others* (London: Printed for Benjamin Crayle, 1688), 1:28–9. Kathryn R. King also reproduces this poem in her edition of the Magdalen manuscript. See King, *The Poems of Jane Barker*, 49. There are slight orthographical variations between *Poetical Recreations* (excerpted and quoted here) and the Magdalen text.

5 Murray H.G. Pittock notes, "It was possibly not till the time of the Patriot Whigs in the 1730s that British Trojanness was significantly recaptured from a Jacobite context." See "The *Aeneid* in the Age of Burlington: A Jacobite Text?" in *Lord Burlington: Architecture, Art, and Life*, ed. Toby Barnard and Jane Clark (London: Hambledon Press, 1995), 238.

6 For the divine import of the Stuart position, see Paul Monod, *Jacobitism and the English People, 1688–1788* (Cambridge: Cambridge University Press, 1993), as well as Pittock, *Poetry and Jacobite Politics in Eighteenth-Century Britain and Ireland* (Cambridge: Cambridge University Press, 1994).

7 See Pittock, *Poetry and Jacobite Politics*, 42–3.

8 James Boswell and Samuel Johnson, *The Journal of a Tour to the Hebrides and A Journey to the Western Islands of Scotland*, ed. Peter Levi (New York: Penguin, 1984), 233–41.

9 Jane Barker, *Exilius: or, The Banish'd Roman*, ed. Josephine Grieder (New York: Garland, 1973), 2:141. Subsequent references will be cited parenthetically.

10 The classic accounts come from Appian's *Wars of the Romans in Iberia* and Polybius's *Rise of the Roman Empire*. For a more recent view of the Roman genocide, see Odai Johnson, "Unspeakable Histories: Terror, Spectacle, and Genocidal Memory," *Modern Language Quarterly* 70.1 (March 2009): 97–116.

11 See Serge Lancel, *Hannibal* (Malden, MA: Blackwell, 1988), 60.

12 *Aeneid*, trans. Dryden, 5:299; 298. References to Dryden's *Aeneid* come from *The Works of John Dryden*, vols. 5–6: *Poems: The Works of Virgil in English, 1697*, ed. William Frost and Vinton Dearing (Berkeley: University of California Press, 1987) and will be cited parenthetically. Volume 5 contains *Aeneid* 1–6; volume 6, *Aeneid* 7–12.

13 As Kathryn R. King summarizes, "Roughly the first third of the volume – fifty-one poems on 109 octavo pages – consists of verse by Jane Barker … Part 2 includes a scattering of poems to and about Jane Barker but consists mostly of unrelated verse by a number of men, many unidentified. Largely forgotten today – Charles Cotton and 'Sir C.S.' (Sir Charles Sedley) are the biggest names in the group – they appear to have been an uncelebrated lot even in their own time." See "Jane Barker, *Poetical Recreations*, and the Sociable Text," *English Literary History* 61.3 (1994): 552.

14 Kathryn R. King, "Barker, Jane (*bap.* 1652, *d.* 1732)," in *The Oxford Dictionary of National Biography*, ed. David Cannadine (Oxford: Oxford University Press, 2004), http://www.oxforddnb.com.huntington.idm.oclc.org/view/article/37153, accessed 20 June 2018.

15 "Virgo" has several possible meanings emphasizing female chastity. Thus the *OLD* supplies the following definitions: "1 A girl of marriageable age"; "2 A woman who is sexually intact, a virgin"; "3 A woman existing in a (permanent) state of virginity." See the *Oxford Latin Dictionary*, ed. P.G.W. Glare (Oxford: Clarendon Press, 1997), 2071.

16 Elizabeth I ("Eliza") was also popularly associated with Dido ("Elissa"). On the mythology associated with the monarchy, Murray H.G. Pittock further writes, "The Astraea myth was later to be used as a code of hope for [the Stuart] return; and after 1688 it was linked to Virgil's more famous *Aeneid*, which, in its turn[,] was the root text for the Brut myth" ("The *Aeneid* in the Age of Burlington" 232). In *Poetry and Jacobite Politics*, Pittock adds, "Indeed, so strong was the Stuart inheritance of Astraea that it could usurp the gender of its subject, leading to a feminization in portrayals of some of the family such as Charles I and Charles Edward" (15).

17 For a succinct discussion of the two Dido traditions, see Deanne Williams, "Dido, Queen of England," *English Literary History* 73.1 (2006): 31–59.

18 King writes, Barker's "self-portrayal points toward the paradoxical character of a literary innovator, a self-consciously modern novelist who continued to identify strongly with the values of the authoritarian, hierarchically ordered, and largely discredited Stuart world she had lost. This is the figure I call JANUS Barker, an author who looks back to traditional ways of thinking and feeling as much as she looks forward to

the triumph of bourgeois domesticity, a novelist whose fictions distrust the modernity they articulate." See Kathryn R. King, *Jane Barker, Exile: A Literary Career, 1675–1725* (Oxford: Oxford University Press, 2000), 9. On the particularly transgressive nature of women wanderers, see Silvia Montiglio, *Wandering in Ancient Greek Culture* (Chicago: University of Chicago Press, 2005), 17.

19 Barker regretted the apparently old-fashioned sensibilities of *Exilius* in the Preface, but her reports of romance's demise seem greatly exaggerated. The great seventeenth-century French heroic romances were still being printed in 1715, and even by 1752, Charlotte Lennox's *Female Quixote* would rely on readers' extensive knowledge of these texts in order to craft her satire.

20 See, for example, Joan DeJean, *Tender Geographies: Women and the Origins of the Novel in France* (New York: Columbia University Press, 1991).

21 Cf. Quint, *Epic and Empire*: "To the victors belongs epic, with its linear teleology; to the losers belongs romance, with its random or circular wandering. Put another way, the victors experience history as a coherent, end-directed story told by their own power; the losers experience a contingency that they are powerless to shape their own ends" (9).

22 The country retreat is also politically charged. As Pittock notes, "The monarch's authentic power resided in the country not the city … Rural renewal and retreat grew into one of the chief metaphors of Stuart political authority in the period 1630–60." He adds, "after 1688, the upheaval of exile did much to endorse the retreat and topographical poem as a Stuart-leaning subgenre" (*Poetry and Jacobite Politics*, 18–19). For the relationship between Jacobitism and the idealization of country life, and its precedent in Horace in particular, see Maren-Sofie Røstvig, *The Happy Man: Studies in the Metamorphoses of a Classical Ideal, 1600–1700* (Oxford: Basil Blackwell, 1953).

23 Monod, *Jacobitism and the English People*, 63–4.

24 Ibid., 68.

25 "By a Gentleman of St. John's College, Cambridge" (2:35–6), and signed "Exilius" at the end of the poem.

26 "By J.N. Fellow of St. John's Colledge in Cambridge" (2:29–32), and signed "Philaster" at the end of the poem.

27 See Susan Stewart, *On Longing: Narratives of the Miniature, the Gigantic, the Souvenir, the Collection* (Durham, NC: Duke University Press, 1993), 65.

28 Ibid., 60.

29 Ibid., 69.

30 Ibid., 86.

31 On the theatricality of nostalgia, see Judith Broome, *Fictive Domains: Body, Landscape, and Nostalgia, 1717–1770* (Lewisburg, PA: Bucknell University Press, 2007): "imbued with supportive illusions, [it] is a self-constituted performance that needs to be constantly repeated … the lack of any historical referent is concealed by the repetition of a performance in and by nostalgic cultural products" (17).

32 Maurizio Bettini, "Ghosts of Exile: Doubles and Nostalgia in Vergil's *parva Troia* (*Aeneid* 3.284ff)," *Classical Antiquity* 16.1 (1997), argues that the "parva Troia" is the "'double' of the destroyed city: it is an *effigies* built by the hands of its inhabitants, a consolation, in the form of a simulacrum, for the *desiderium* that afflicts them" (27).

33 Stewart, *On Longing*, 65.

34 In his discussion of the *Aeneid*, Bettini reminds us that "the act of erecting a statue to someone (a king, a minister, a dictator) explicitly signals a 'faithfulness' to that person's memory, it means that the pact is being respected – at least until the act of demolishing the image openly violates that pact, breaking the bonds of that former attachment" ("Ghosts of Exile," 28).

35 See the Loeb edition of the *Aeneid*, trans. H. Rushton Fairclough (Cambridge, MA: Harvard University Press, 1965). The original Latin reads "parvam Troiam simulataque magnis / Pergama."

36 As Bettini has noted, "Virgil's *parva Troia* is something far more uncanny than the simple imitation of a city that exists elsewhere. It is a piece of the past come alive, inhabited by people who come from the past, and above all by the ghosts of those who were lost (or seemed to have been lost?) in the past" ("Ghosts of Exile," 19).

37 Stewart, *On Longing*, 20.

38 David Quint, "Painful Memories: 'Aeneid' 3 and the Problem of the Past," *Classical Journal* 78.1 (1982): 30 and 33. For Quint, this problem is also political: "The emphasis in Virgil's fiction upon the need to forget the past and to start over again cannot be separated from the *Aeneid*'s political context, the establishment of a new Augustan order after the catastrophe of the Roman civil wars" (30–1).

39 By contrast, Quint argues that "the *Aeneid* itself is implicated in a program of Augustan propaganda which seeks to suppress and rewrite Rome's political legacy" (ibid., 31); it "elevates the therapeutic effects of forgetting into one of its major themes" (6).

40 Cf. Bettini's discussion of Virgil's little Troy: "In Virgil's parva Troia we find the two opposite extremes of possible responses to exile: nostalgic obsession with one's own identity or, alternatively, detachment, amnesia, forced assimilation" ("Ghosts of Exile," 31).

41 Stewart, *On Longing*, 86.
42 As Quint notes, the "parade of replica Troys" in the *Aeneid* are "explicitly revealed to be a place of death," so that "the fiction of Book 3 has emphasized the Trojans' need to escape their past and its memories" ("Painful Memories," 34).
43 Stewart, *On Longing*, 86.
44 Broome, *Fictive Domains*, 138.
45 This is also, of course, the project of the *Aeneid*, despite its limitations for Barker's audience. See Bettini, "Ghosts of Exile," and Quint, "Painful Memories."
46 Monod, *Jacobitism and the English People*, 287.
47 For an excellent recent discussion of Barker's similar experimentation in the *Galesia Trilogy*, see Rivka Swenson, "Representing Modernity in Jane Barker's *Galesia Trilogy*: Jacobite Allegory and the Patch-Work Aesthetic," *Studies in Eighteenth-Century Culture* 34 (2005): 55–80.

2. "What Is There of a Woman Worth Relating?"

1 For Henry Fielding's *The Life of Mr. Jonathan Wild the Great*, see *Miscellanies*, vol. 3, ed. Betrand A. Goldgar and Hugh Amory (Middleton, CT: Wesleyan University Press, 1997), 46. Subsequent references will be cited parenthetically.
2 English references to Dryden's translation of the *Aeneid* come from *The Works of John Dryden*, vols. 5–6: *Poems: The Works of Virgil in English, 1697*, ed. William Frost and Vinton Dearing (Berkeley: University of California Press, 1987). Volume 5 contains *Aeneid* 1–6; volume 6, *Aeneid* 7–12. Latin references come from the Loeb edition, ed. H. Rushton Fairclough (Cambridge, MA: Harvard University Press, 1965).
3 As Angela Smallwood writes in *Fielding and the Woman Question: The Novels of Henry Fielding and Feminist Debate, 1700–1750* (New York: St Martin's Press, 1989), "Greatness in its most destructive form, segregated from goodness and indeed inimically opposed to it, is the theme of *Jonathan Wild*. The presentation of this theme depends extensively upon the elaboration of basic contrasts between qualities associated with an aggressively masculine ethos and those associated with the feminine" (91).
4 See Fielding, *Covent-Garden Journal and A Plan of the Universal Register-Office*, ed. Bertrand A. Goldgar (Middleton, CT: Wesleyan University Press, 1988), 65. Fielding dedicates parts of numbers 7–8 to the defence of his novel.

5 In the preface to his edition of *Amelia* (Middleton, CT: Wesleyan University Press, 1983), Martin Battestin writes, "No one who scribbled for bread in [the] weeks after *Amelia* appeared could afford, it seems, to refrain from heaping a little abuse on the book and its 'doting' author" (liii). Indeed, *Amelia* was not a success for its publisher, Andrew Millar: whereas *Tom Jones* went into four editions totalling ten thousand copies mere months after its debut, only five thousand copies of *Amelia* were printed; Millar cancelled a second edition of three thousand additional volumes, and copies of the first edition were still available by 1759 (ibid., xlix–l). Despite Fielding's evident affection for the text, *Amelia* would not fare much better at the pens of modern critics. J. Paul Hunter argues that Fielding "comes close, in the rhetoric of *Amelia*, to writing the kind of novel he set out to travesty and subvert." See Hunter, *Occasional Form: Henry Fielding and the Chains of Circumstance* (Baltimore: Johns Hopkins University Press, 1975), 210. Of *Amelia*, Hunter further comments that "Moving from the world of *Tom Jones* – with its sunshine, vitality, spaciousness, and health – to that of *Amelia* is rather like entering an over-heated, small, and quarantined room, and most readers feel grudging about it, vaguely misled, even betrayed by a writer who has without warning led them to anatomize some of the more dingy and sordid concerns of the human mind" (193). Robert Alter goes further by suggesting that Fielding could not maintain authority over his own text: "One gets a disconcerting sense," he claims, "that the tone of the writing is not always fully under the writer's control, and the whole fiction threatens at times to slip down between the two literary stools on which it is precariously perched." See Alter, *Fielding and the Nature of the Novel* (Cambridge, MA: Harvard University Press, 1968), 141.

6 See Peter Sabor, "*Amelia*," in *Henry Fielding*, ed. Claude Rawson (New York: Cambridge University Press, 2007), 96.

7 Of Amelia's nose, Maurice Johnson notes that it was the "physical disfigurement … that earned the novel its greatest notoriety," so much so that "it was this flaw, more than the others, that diminished the novel's critical reputation and damaged irreparably its chances for widespread public acceptance." See Johnson, *Fielding's Art of Fiction: Eleven Essays on "Shamela," "Joseph Andrews," "Tom Jones," and "Amelia"* (Philadelphia: University of Pennsylvania Press, 1961), 121. Though the critical outcry might imply a greater catastrophe, Fielding describes the result of Amelia's accident as merely a "little Scar on her Nose" (184), and even the unflattering portrait drawn by the envious Mrs James characterizes it as nothing more than "a visible Scar on one Side" (454). As Battestin notes

in his edition (66n1), "Fielding appears to have modeled Amelia … on his beloved first wife, Charlotte Cradock."

8 Fielding, *Covent-Garden Journal*, 65–6.

9 George Sherburn, Lyall Powers, Maurice Johnson, and John Loftis have each traced some of the correspondences between the two texts, mapping the extent to which Fielding follows and deviates from Virgil. None has, however, offered a particularly compelling reason why Fielding chose the *Aeneid* for imitation and revision. Although each writer notes that eighteenth-century England, because of its Christian values, cannot support epic's pagan ideals, this explanation alone remains unsatisfactory, ignoring many of Fielding's important revisions. See Sherburn, "Fielding's *Amelia*: An Interpretation," *English Literary History* 3.1 (1936): 1–14, reprinted in *Fielding: A Collection of Critical Essays*, ed. Ronald Paulson (Englewood Cliffs, NJ: Prentice-Hall, 1962), 146–57; Lyall Powers, "The Influence of the *Aeneid* on Fielding's *Amelia*," *Modern Language Notes* 71.5 (1956): 330–6; Johnson, *Fielding's Art of Fiction*, 139–56; and Loftis, "Imitation in the Novel: Fielding's *Amelia*," *Rocky Mountain Review of Language and Literature* 31 (1977): 214–29. Subsequent critics have tended to avoid the subject. Leo Braudy argues that a too literal comparison "naturally enough does violence to both works"; he adds, "[a] more fruitful comparison of the *Aeneid* and *Amelia* might follow the lines of a distinction between the male world of war and history and the female world of emotion and domesticity." See Braudy, *Narrative Form in History and Fiction* (Princeton: Princeton University Press, 1970), 202 note n. Yet this, too, is an oversimplification, part of the very dichotomy Fielding seeks to upend: one might easily object that the true "warrior" in *Amelia* is the heroine herself; the "male world" intrudes on the "female world" in such a way as to complicate easy distinctions.

10 Indeed, critics tend to read Booth as Fielding's modern Aeneas, leading one scholar to declare, "If a concentration upon the figure of Tom impedes an appreciation of the full range of moral concern in *Tom Jones*, a preoccupation with the figure of Booth in *Amelia* is misguided to the point of irony." See Smallwood, *Fielding and the Woman Question*, 144.

11 Despite its epic structure, divided into twelve books that loosely follow the *Aeneid*, *Amelia* represents a synthesis of romance and epic reminiscent of the Heliodoran novel. See James Lynch, *Henry Fielding and the Heliodoran Novel: Romance, Epic, and Fielding's New Province of Writing* (Rutherford, NJ: Farleigh Dickinson University Press, 1986).

12 For feminist critiques of *Amelia*, see especially Smallwood, *Fielding and the Woman Question*, as well as Jill Campbell, *Natural Masques: Gender and*

Identity in Fielding's Plays and Novels (Stanford: Stanford University Press, 1995).

13 Because she begins the narrative as Mrs Bennet and ends as Mrs Atkinson, I will often refer to her hereafter as Mrs Bennet-Atkinson.

14 Objections to Fielding's privileging of Amelia over Booth may account for more of the critical hostility than most scholars have realized. As Campbell argues, "Just as the craze for 'she-tragedies' in the first decades of the century expresses an early interest in the serious possibilities of female heroism, the elements of incredulity, ridicule, and resistance in the reception of *Amelia* demonstrate a continuing readiness to see powerful female figures as necessarily either silly or threatening" (*Natural Masques*, 211). J. Paul Hunter points to one possible reason for this discomfort in his observations on the complex interplay between gender and genre: "Confronting even the possible fall of a good woman darkens the tone of *Amelia*; once Fielding decided to write mostly about a woman and not about a man, his sexual ethic virtually guaranteed a darker book than either *Joseph Andrews* or *Tom Jones*, and perhaps a wholly different mode. *Amelia*'s flirtation with romance on one side and tragedy on the other may well derive partly from the simple choice of choosing a heroine instead of a hero" (*Occasional Form*, 211). As Hunter's assessment demonstrates, there is something culturally uncomfortable about mixing "epic" and "(good) woman," a combination so destabilizing that it creates generic rifts, suggesting "a wholly different mode," a "flirtation with romance" as well as "tragedy." Calling Fielding's experiment a noncommittal vacillation between modes or "flirtation" between genres therefore dismisses the centrality of generic blending, manipulation, and collision in the text.

15 See, for example, Mark Salber Phillips, *Society and Sentiment: Genres of History Writing in Britain, 1740–1820* (Princeton: Princeton University Press, 2000).

16 See Battestin's edition of *Amelia*, 15. Subsequent references will be cited parenthetically.

17 Revealing her insights into James's behaviour, Mrs Bennet-Atkinson exclaims, "I am sure the Colonel is in Love with somebody"; then, relieved to hear that he is already married, she continues, "I think, I never saw a more luscious Picture of Love drawn than that which he was pleased to give us, as the Portraiture of Friendship. I have read, indeed, of *Pylades* and *Orestes*, *Damon* and *Pythias*, and other great Friends of old … but as for that fine, soft, tender, delicate Passion, which he was pleased to describe, I am convinced there must go a He and a She to the Composition" (336–7). See also Campbell: "Mrs. Atkinson's examples point to a specific literary

past in which the old stories of idealized male friendship might be found – that of classical drama and epic; and the emphasis on male-male relationships in those forms contrasts sharply with the premise of *Amelia* itself, and of the English novel more generally, that the most important and central narratives (whatever Booth may assume) have to do with heterosexual love" (*Natural Masques*, 223).

18 Colonel James also schemes to rid himself of his rival by arranging for Booth to command a company in the West Indies (369).

19 Fielding was deeply troubled by the unchristian equation of "honour" and "duelling." See also Battestin's comments in his edition at 135n1, 364n1, and 456n1.

20 In addition to the example of Bath's duel with Booth in order to avoid injuring the honour of his brother-in-law, James, Bath tellingly urges Booth to duel with Monsieur Bagillard after Bath has already challenged him on Booth's account.

21 On the ways in which Bath's experience of shame aligns him with Homeric heroism, see E.R. Dodds, *Greeks and the Irrational* (Berkeley: University of California Press, 1966), especially ch. 2, "From Shame Culture to Guilt Culture," 28–63.

22 This episode derives from the medieval romance *Floris and Blancheflour* (*Filocopo*, in Boccaccio's version). Similarly, the incident of the forgotten casket – in which Booth omits to bring with him a small collection of items prepared by Amelia before his departure for Gibraltar – has its source in Ariosto's *Orlando Furioso*.

23 A storm also drives Dido and Aeneas to a cave during the hunt, and they consummate their marriage. See *Aeneid* 4.166–72.

24 Ann Bermingham, "The Simple Life: Cottages and Gainsborough's Cottage Doors," in *Land, Nation and Culture, 1740–1840: Thinking the Republic of Taste*, ed. Peter de Bolla, Nigel Leask, and David Simpson (Basingstoke: Palgrave, 2005), 46. For the definition of sensibility, see Janet Todd, *Sensibility: An Introduction* (New York: Methuen, 1986), 7.

25 Bermingham, "The Simple Life," 48.

26 This is the assessment of an "anonymous enthusiast" at the Royal Academy in 1780, commenting on Gainsborough's *The Cottage Door*. Qtd. in Amal Asfour and Paul Williamson, "Gainsborough's Cottage-Door Scenes: Aesthetic Principles, Moral Values," in *Sensation and Sensibility: Viewing Gainsborough's Cottage Door*, ed. Ann Bermingham (New Haven: Yale University Press, 2005), 99–100.

27 For Eve, the narrator quotes *Paradise Lost* 8.482–4, 488–9: " – adorned / With what all Earth or Heaven could bestow / To make her amiable – "

The comparison to a nymph comes from Waller, "Of Loving at First Sight," 2.11–14: "Sweetness, Truth, and every Grace, / Which Time and Use are wont to teach, / The Eye may in a Moment reach, / And read distinctly in her Face." The final comparison, to Cupid, comes from Suckling's "The crafty Boy, that had full oft essay'd," 7–12: " – All his lovely Looks, his pleasing Fires, / All his sweet Motions, all his taking Smiles, / All that awakes, all that inflames Desires, / All that sweetly commands, all that beguiles, / He does into one Pair of Eyes convey, / And there begs Leave that he himself may stay." See *Amelia*, 230nn1–3.

28 Battestin in the Introduction to his edition of *Amelia*, xxxix.

29 On attitudes towards Gibraltar in the eighteenth century, see Stetson Conn, *Gibraltar in British Diplomacy in the Eighteenth Century* (New Haven: Yale University Press, 1942), especially ch. 11, "The Value of Gibraltar," 256–68.

30 Henry Fielding, *A Serious Address to the People of Great Britain, in Which the Certain Consequences of the Present Rebellion Are Fully Demonstrated* (London, 1745), 43.

31 Ibid., 44.

32 Qtd. in James Falkner, *Fire over the Rock: The Great Siege of Gibraltar, 1779–1783* (Barnsley, UK: Pen & Sword Military, 2009), 4.

33 Ibid., 4.

34 In his edition, Battestin notes of this scene at the beginning of Book 3, Chapter 2 (101ff): "Fielding's classical readers may have been tempted to compare this 'tender' scene with the farewell of Hector and Andromache (*Iliad*, vi. 390–502), the *locus classicus* of the parting of a soldier and his wife on the eve of battle" (101–2n1). The name of the chapter is "Containing a Scene of the tender Kind." Indeed, Andromache was evidently important to Fielding, as he mentions her on 368, 426, and 504.

35 Although I agree with Campbell that "However deep Amelia's personal authority as a living paragon of Christian virtue, her active, persuasive power over others is radically circumscribed and ultimately dependent on the authority of men" (*Natural Masques*, 239), I also read the novel as a consistent effort to undermine male authorities, starting with the magistrate and Hebbers in Book 1 and concluding with Robinson's confession of wrongdoing in Book 12. To the extent that Amelia's influence is circumscribed, the novel critiques that circumscription at every turn.

36 Campbell, *Natural Masques*, 230. See also Tiffany Potter, "The Mature Faces of Libertinism: *Amelia*," in *Honest Sins: Georgian Libertinism and the Plays and Novels of Henry Fielding* (Montreal and Kingston: McGill-Queen's University Press, 1999), 145–68.

37 Fielding is, of course, playing on the second definition, too: "A member of a bodyguard or retinue; a faithful follower; one of a group or team of attendants, servants, or assistants." See the *Oxford English Dictionary* n2.

38 See Helene P. Foley, "'Reverse Similes' and Sex Roles in the *Odyssey*," in *Women in the Ancient World: The Arethusa Papers*, ed. John Peradotto and J.P. Sullivan (Albany: State University of New York Press, 1984), 59–78.

39 Lattimore translates, "So speaking he set his child again in the arms of his beloved / wife, who took him back again to her fragrant bosom / smiling in her tears." See Homer, *The Iliad* (Chicago: University of Chicago Press, 1961).

40 In addition to his conversation with Bath (cited above), which emphasizes the tender nature of Booth's character, the narrator tells us, for example, that Booth was "a Man of a very sweet Disposition" (39), later reiterating that he is a "sweet-tempered Man" (309). These traits, which bring him closer to the "tender" and "sweet" Amelia (and Andromache), demonstrate his readiness for eventual conversion to her model.

41 Harrison, of course, quotes the original Greek, even after having "forgot," as he speciously claims, that Mrs Bennet-Atkinson "was a Scholar" (426). He proceeds to offer additional classical examples that would seem to argue for the separation of masculine and feminine activities (427).

42 E.g., *Iliad* 6.441–3: "I would feel deep shame / before the Trojans, and the Trojan women with trailing garments, / if like a coward I were to shrink aside from the fighting."

43 In *Odyssey* 11.488, Achilles says to Odysseus, "O shining Odysseus, never try to console me for dying. / I would rather follow the plow as thrall to another / man, one with no land allotted him and not much to live on, / than be king over all the perished dead." See Homer, *The Odyssey*, trans. Richmond Lattimore (New York: HarperPerennial, 1999).

44 The world of the *Iliad* is also more starkly divided than the world of the *Aeneid*, which is even more self-critical than Homer of the martial and imperialist ethos it espouses.

45 To say nothing of the mercenary society in which Amelia lives: whereas Mrs Bennet-Atkinson willingly compromises the appearance of her virtue by relating her story for Amelia's sake, Amelia's good friend Mrs James not only knows of the Noble Peer's criminal history and never tells her (246) but also later aids her husband's efforts to ensnare Amelia (494), despite her formerly close friendship with the heroine.

46 Patricia Parker, *Literary Fat Ladies: Rhetoric, Gender, Property* (New York: Methuen, 1987), 13.

47 Battestin argues in his edition that the "satire of Mrs Bennet's bookishness ... places Fielding on the negative, conservative side of a contemporary debate over the appropriateness of a learned education to the female character" (255n1). However, I contend that the problem rests not with women's "bookishness" but with classical learning more generally. To the extent that Mrs Bennet-Atkinson's learning serves as an object of critique, it is an object of critique for all similarly learned characters in the novel. Because classical training among women was so unusual, it is merely the case that her character presents, in stark relief, the inadequacies of such an education for men as well as women. Linda Bree also argues, in her recent Broadview edition of the novel (Peterborough, ON, 2010), that Fielding depicts Mrs Bennet-Atkinson in a negative light (see her Introduction, 20–2), but I would counter that the seemingly comical aspects of her treatment – much like Amelia's imperfections – are meant to humanize her character. The figures who treat Mrs Bennet-Atkinson with the least sympathy – Booth, Harrison, and the narrator – exhibit suspect judgment, as I have argued, at various points in the novel.

48 Nancy Mace, *Henry Fielding's Novels and the Classical Tradition* (Newark: University of Delaware Press, 1996), 97.

49 In the dedication to his translation of the *Aeneid* (5:299). Dryden, in fact, condemns Mercury's characterization, writing, "*Virgil* does well to put those words into the mouth of *Mercury*. *If a God had not spoken them, neither durst he have written them, nor I translated them*" (299). See also Martin Battestin's note in his edition, 409n4.

50 It is possible (though unlikely) that the passage contains grammatical errors, as Virgil left the *Aeneid* unfinished at the time of his death. See James O'Hara, "The Unfinished *Aeneid*?" in *A Companion to Virgil's "Aeneid" and Its Tradition*, ed. Joseph Farrell and Michael C.J. Putnam (Malden, MA: Blackwell, 2010), 96–106.

51 Indeed, a similar sentiment, carrying the same force, appears earlier in *Amelia*, an obvious shorthand for the dangerous mutability of female character. As the narrator, ostensibly through Booth's perspective, reflects on the intrigue with Miss Mathews, he relates, "Besides the general Knowledge of – *Furens quid Foemina posit* [what a woman can do in frenzy], he had more particular Reasons to apprehend the Rage of a Lady, who had given so strong an Instance how far she could carry her Revenge" (171). The line from *Aeneid* 5.6 reflects Aeneas's unease as he looks back at the Carthaginian coast, not yet knowing for certain that Dido has killed herself.

52 The line comes from Juno's rebuke to Venus (*Aeneid* 4.95): "… when Imperial *Juno*, from above, / Saw *Dido* fetter'd in the Chains of Love; / Hot with the Venom, which her Veins inflam'd, / And by no sense of Shame to be reclaim'd: / With soothing Words to *Venus* she begun. / High Praises, endless Honours you have won, / And mighty Trophees with your worthy Son: / Two Gods a silly Woman have undone."

53 In this way, she rewrites, as Terry Castle has argued, the first, tragic masquerade in a second, comic one that ends happily: Mrs Bennet-Atkinson apologizes for casting aspersions, through her actions, on Amelia's moral character, and Atkinson receives his commission, which, upon learning of the scheme, the Peer does not revoke (229). See Castle, "Masquerade and Allegory: Fielding's 'Amelia,'" in her *Masquerade and Civilization: The Carnivalesque in the Eighteenth Century* (Stanford: Stanford University Press, 1986).

3. "A Pattern to Ensuing Ages"

1 Charlotte Lennox, *The Lady's museum. By the author of the Female Quixote* (London: Printed for J. Newbery in St. Paul's Church-Yard, and J. Coote in Pater Noster Row, 1760–1). Subsequent references will be cited parenthetically.

2 In addition to Judith Dorn, "Reading Women Reading History: The Philosophy of Periodical Form in Charlotte Lennox's *The Lady's Museum*," *Historical Reflections/Reflexions Historiques* 18.3 (1992): 7–27, see also Devoney Looser, *British Women Writers and the Writing of History, 1670–1820* (Baltimore: Johns Hopkins University Press, 2000), for more on Lennox's relationship to British historiography.

3 The narrator describes the library as "large and well-furnished" (6). The marquis, we learn, upon taking note of Arabella's early love of reading, "permitted her therefore the Use of his Library, in which, unfortunately for her, were great Store of Romances" (7). See *The Female Quixote*, ed. Margaret Dalziel (New York: Oxford University Press, 2008). Subsequent references will be cited parenthetically. Regarding the translations, I suggest that Lennox, herself a translator, invites the audience to read this characterization with scepticism, as the Grub Street renderings are faithful to the originals.

4 In this way, the novel demonstrates the need for Arabella to distinguish between proper and improper reading through the exhortations of the Clergyman at the end of the text. See Kate Levin, "'The Cure of Arabella's mind': Charlotte Lennox and the Disciplining of the Female Reader," *Women's Writing: The Elizabethan to Victorian Period* 2.3 (1995): 271–90.

Arabella's father provides added incentive for the marriage by requiring, in his will, that Arabella forfeit one-third of the estate to Glanville should she persist in refusing the match.

5 As Joan DeJean reminds us, romances "are never solely about love, but always stress the political and social implication of affective choices." See *Tender Geographies: Women and the Origins of the Novel in France* (New York: Columbia University Press, 1991), 11. DeJean speaks of the same seventeenth-century romances that inspire Arabella.

6 I side with critics such as Doody in reading the ending ironically, even though other scholars accept a straightforward reading of the text; see, for example, Miriam Small, *Charlotte Ramsay Lennox: An Eighteenth-Century Lady of Letters* (New York: Archon Books, 1969) and W.J. Bate, *From Classic to Romantic: Premises of Taste in Eighteenth-Century England* (New York: Harper and Row, 1961). Nor do I accept the attribution of the ending to Samuel Johnson, though the Divine is certainly a Johnsonian figure. As Duncan Isles has suggested, there is no evidence to do so, especially since Lennox was more than capable of adopting Johnson's moralizing tone. See Isles's appendix to the Oxford edition (422–8). For more on Lennox's relationship to Johnson, see Norma Clarke, *Dr. Johnson's Women* (New York: Hambledon and London, 2000). See also Brian Hanley, "Henry Fielding, Samuel Johnson, Samuel Richardson, and the reception of Charlotte Lennox's *The Female Quixote* in the Popular Press," *ANQ: A Quarterly Journal of Short Articles, Notes, and Reviews*, 13.3 (2000): 27–32.

7 For more on the interrelationship between history and fiction, see especially Mark Salber Phillips, *Society and Sentiment: Genres of Historical Writing in Britain, 1740–1820* (Princeton: Princeton University Press, 2000).

8 Anne H. Stevens, "Sophia Lee's Illegitimate History," *Eighteenth-Century Novel* 3 (2002): 264.

9 Vivienne Mylne, *The Eighteenth-Century French Novel: Techniques of Illusion* (Cambridge: Cambridge University Press, 1965), 21.

10 As Karen O'Brien notes, a desire to generate newly intimate understandings of the past "underwrote a new emphasis upon the moral and cognitive benefits for the reader to be gained from entering imaginatively into the lives of less significant historical personages, or, at least, of those who acted in only supporting roles to the truly great and famous." See *Women and Enlightenment in Eighteenth-Century Britain* (Cambridge: Cambridge University Press, 2009), 211.

11 See ibid., and Phillips, *Society and Sentiment*.

12 Catherine Gallagher, *Nobody's Story: The Vanishing Acts of Women Writers in the Marketplace, 1670–1820* (Berkeley: University of California Press, 1995), 184.

13 Ibid.
14 Though Ruth Mack doesn't pursue this point, she makes a similar connection in *Literary Historicity: Literature and Historical Experience in Eighteenth-Century Britain* (Stanford: Stanford University Press, 2009): Lennox "revists Cervantes in order to comment on the romance that has always been at the root of the modern novel. In this sense, she is a very early literary historian of the novel form" (97).
15 It is worth noting that classicists do not typically make the distinction between "novel" and "romance" that has been so prejudicial to histories of the English novel, nor does the French term for the heroic romance, the *roman héroïque*.
16 Thomas DiPiero, *Dangerous Truths and Criminal Passions: The Evolution of the French Novel, 1569–1791* (Stanford: Stanford University Press, 1992), 63; 91.
17 Doody notes in her Introduction to the Oxford edition (xvii) that Lennox certainly would have known – as did Scudéry's contemporaries – that Scudéry was a woman.
18 See, for example, Livy's *History of Rome, Books I–II*, trans. B.O. Foster (Cambridge, MA: Harvard University Press, 1919), 2.13.6–11.
19 La Calprenède specifically acknowledged his debt to Homer, Virgil, and Tasso.
20 See Mark Bannister, *Privileged Mortals: The French Heroic Novel, 1630–1660* (New York: Oxford University Press, 1983), 168; 177.
21 Ibid., 166.
22 Ibid., 176.
23 Ibid., 181.
24 Madeleine de Scudéry, *The Story of Sapho*, trans. Karen Newman (Chicago: University of Chicago Press, 2003), 1.
25 Scudéry, *Madeleine de Scudéry: Selected Letters, Orations, and Rhetorical Dialogues*, ed. and trans. Jane Donawerth and Julie Strongson (Chicago: University of Chicago Press, 2004), 1.
26 DeJean, *Tender Geographies*, 91.
27 Marianne Legault, *Female Intimacies in Seventeenth-Century French Literature* (Burlington, VT: Ashgate, 2012), 122–3.
28 Ibid., 123.
29 DeJean, *Tender Geographies*, 17; 35.
30 Ibid., 28; 33.
31 Joan DeJean, "Violent Women and Violence against Women: Representing the 'Strong' Woman in Early Modern France," *Signs* 29.1 (Autumn 2003): 128.
32 Ibid., 125–6.

33 See Renée-Claude Breitenstein, "Speaking of Women and Giving Voice to Women: The Example of Madeleine and Georges De Scudéry's *Femmes Illustres ou les harangues héroïques*," in *Creating Women: Representation, Self-Representation, and Agency in the Renaissance*, ed. Manuela Scarci (Toronto: Centre for Reformation and Renaissance Studies, 2013), 54.
34 DeJean, *Tender Geographies*, 32.
35 Scudéry, *Madeleine de Scudéry: Selected Letters*, ed. Donawerth and Strongson, 14.
36 Ibid., 116.
37 For Arabella's declamations against raillery and indifference, see Scudéry, *Conversations upon several subjects.* Written in French by Mademoiselle de Scudery. And done into English by Mr. Ferrand Spence. In two tomes (London: Printed for H. Rhodes next door to the Bear Tavern near Bride-lane in Fleet-street, 1683).
38 Scudéry, *Madeleine de Scudéry: Selected Letters*, ed. Donawerth and Strongson, 114.
39 See Lennox, *The Female Quixote*, 394 (note to page 83).
40 Patricia Meyer Spacks comments that "Arabella's consistent commitment to principle and her contempt for meretricious social enticements make her potentially more threatening to a male-dominated order of things than seventeen-year-old fictional heroines usually appear." See *Desire and Truth: Functions of Plot in Eighteenth-Century English Novels* (Chicago: University of Chicago Press, 1990), 541.
41 On the Amazons, see the eponymous entry in the *OCD* (69–70).
42 Josine Blok, *The Early Amazons: Modern and Ancient Perspectives on a Persistent Myth* (New York: E.J. Brill, 1995), 432–3.
43 See Richard Barney, *Plots of Enlightenment: Education and the Novel in Eighteenth-Century England* (Stanford: Stanford University Press, 1999), 227.
44 See Patricia Meyer Spacks, who also argues that Arabella "wishes, without relinquishing her femininity – indeed, by virtue of her redefined femininity – to inhabit the public sphere." See "The Subtle Sophistry of Desire: Dr. Johnson and *The Female Quixote*," *Modern Philology: A Journal Devoted to Research in Medieval and Modern Literature* 85.4 (1988): 541.
45 This is perhaps a mild assessment. The narrator describes the gentleman as "extremely glad at having so beautiful a Creature in his Power" and "willing to have her at his own House" (100), suggesting his predatory intentions.
46 See also Jane Spencer, "Not Being a Historian: Women Telling Tales in Restoration and Eighteenth-Century England," in *Contexts of Pre-Novel Narrative: The European Tradition*, ed. Roy Eriksen (New York: Mouton

de Gruyter, 1994): "[Arabella's] romantic conception is of a virtuous Cleopatra defending herself from a ravisher. But is the gentleman's opposing view of Cleopatra as a whore any more historical?" (338).

47 In insisting on the chastity of Julia and other romance heroines maligned by history, Arabella adopts a strategy that Lennox herself would have recognized from contemporary histories. See Susan Staves, *A Literary History of Women's Writing in Britain, 1660–1789* (Cambridge: Cambridge University Press, 2006), 293–4.

48 On Arabella as an Ancient, see, for example, Looser, *British Women Writers*, and Ruth Mack, "Quixotic Ethnography: Charlotte Lennox and the Dilemma of Cultural Observation," *Novel* 38.2/3 (2005): 193–213.

49 Joan DeJean, *Fictions of Sappho, 1546–1937* (Chicago: University of Chicago Press, 1989), 112.

50 This was indeed the case. See Sarah B. Pomeroy, *Women in Hellenistic Egypt: From Alexander to Cleopatra* (New York: Schocken Books, 1984), 24.

51 DeJean, *Tender Geographies*, 88.

52 Ibid. The quotation from Father Porée is on 91.

53 Jeffrey N. Peters, *Mapping Discord: Allegorical Cartography in Early Modern French Writing* (Newark: University of Delaware Press, 2004), 99.

54 Scudéry, *Madeleine de Scudéry: Selected Letters*, ed. Donawerth and Strongson 17.

55 In Melissa Matthes, *The Rape of Lucretia and the Founding of Republics: Readings in Livy, Machiavelli, and Rousseau* (University Park: Pennsylvania State University Press, 2000), 40.

56 Ibid., 43–4.

57 Livy, *History of Rome, Books I–II*, 435–7.

58 The Latin reads, "Pace redintegrata Romani novam in femina virtutem novo genere honoris, statua equestri, donavere: in summa Sacra via fuit posita virgo insidens equo" (Livy, *History of Rome, Books I–II*, 2.13.11).

59 Scudéry, *Les femmes illustres or The heroick harangues of the illustrious women*, trans. James Innes (Edinburgh: Printed by Thomas Brown James and John Weir book sellers, 1681), 181–2. Subsequent references will be cited parenthetically.

60 Pierre Le Moyne, *The Gallery of Heroick Women*, trans. the Marquesse of Winchester (London: Printed by R. Norton for Henry Seile, over against S. Dunstans Church in Fleetstreet, 1652). Subsequent references will be cited parenthetically.

61 One might even call the raped woman a requisite condition for writing (ancient) history: this is certainly true of many of the major episodes in Roman history, and even Herodotus, the "first historian," begins his *Histories* with a litany of rapes, both mortal and divine.

62 Carol Dougherty, "Sowing the Seeds of Violence: Rape, Women, and the Land," in *Parchments of Gender: Deciphering the Bodies of Antiquity*, ed. Maria Wyke (Oxford: Clarendon Press, 1998), 272.

63 Ibid., 279.

64 See Carol Berkin, *Revolutionary Mothers: Women and the Struggle for America's Independence* (New York: Alfred A. Knopf, 2005), 39–41.

65 It is significant, along these lines, that the heroic romance offers the safest of all possible fictions, for heroines rarely fall victim to rape despite other persecutions. In a sense, the worst has certainly happened to Arabella. It is no coincidence that the Divine's conversion leaves her with a strong sense of shame and humiliation; Margaret Anne Doody argues that the scene "represents a brainwashing session as sexual taming" (Introduction to the Oxford edition, xxxi). This would explain why the Countess cannot convince Arabella of her error: she lacks the power to force such a conversion.

66 Pericles says, in full, "Perhaps I should say a word or two on the duties of women to those among you who are now widowed. I can say all I have to say in a short word of advice. Your great glory is not to be inferior to what God has made you, and the greatest glory of a woman is to be least talked about by men, whether they are praising you or criticizing you." See Thucydides' *The History of the Peloponnesian War: Revised Edition*, trans. Rex Warner, ed. M.I. Finley (New York: Penguin, 1972), 2:46.

4. Performing Augustan History in Sarah Fielding's *Lives of Cleopatra and Octavia*

1 Sarah Fielding, *The Lives of Cleopatra and Octavia*, ed. Christopher D. Johnson (Lewisburg, PA: Bucknell University Press, 1994), 54. Subsequent references will be cited parenthetically. Johnson's is the only modern annotated version of the text, following the facsimile reproduction edited by R. Brimley Johnson in 1928.

2 See the modern facsimile edition, Arnaud Berquin, *The Looking-Glass for the Mind or Intellectual Mirror* (New York: S.R. Publishers, 1969). Berquin's compilation of stories was serially published in French in 1782–3, and, by 1840, the English version had reached its twentieth edition (Preface, viii–ix). Subsequent references will be cited parenthetically.

3 References to the *Aeneid* come from the Dryden translation and will be cited parenthetically. See *The Works of John Dryden*, vols. 5–6: *Poems: The Works of Virgil in English, 1697*, ed. William Frost and Vinton Dearing (Berkeley: University of California Press, 1987). Volume 5 contains *Aeneid* 1–6; volume 6, *Aeneid* 7–12.

4 For the Latin text of the *Aeneid*, see the Loeb edition, trans. H. Rushton Fairclough, 2 vols. (Cambridge, MA: Harvard University Press, 1965).

5 Cassius Dio, *Dio's Roman History*, 9 vols., trans. Ernest Cary, on the basis of the version of Herbert Baldwin Foster (Cambridge, MA: Harvard University Press, 1914–27), 6:43.

6 Ibid.

7 See Michael Grant, *Cleopatra* (New York: Barnes and Noble, 1992). Grant writes that Cleopatra was "the ideal national foe, the oriental woman who had ensnared the Roman leader in her evil luxury, the harlot who had seized Roman territories, until even Rome itself was not safe from her degenerate alien hordes" (201).

8 See Fielding's Preface to *The History of the Countess of Dellwyn* (London: Printed for A. Millar, 1759), xiii–xiv.

9 Patricia Meyer Spacks, *Imagining a Self: Autobiography and Novel in Eighteenth-Century England* (Cambridge, MA: Harvard University Press, 1976), 18. See also Felicity Nussbaum, *Autobiographical Subject: Gender and Ideology in Eighteenth-Century England* (Baltimore: Johns Hopkins University Press, 1989): "In short, I am arguing in the pages that follow that the 'self' of autobiography is an effect of ideology and a mediation of its conflicts, and that a politics of writing and reading is implicit within it" (xxi). Nussbaum notes that "Autobiographical writing parallels history writing in its claims to represent what *is*" (16).

10 Although her primary source was Charles Fraser's *Life of Antony*, which appeared in Dryden's edition of Plutarch's *Lives*, Christopher D. Johnson, in his excellent edition of Fielding's text, traces her reading to Velleius Paterculus (30 CE), Pliny the Elder (77 CE), Josephus (74–9 CE), Seneca the Elder (first century CE), Suetonius (121 CE), Appian (145–65 CE), Florus (second century CE), Athenaeus of Naucratis (end of second century CE), and Cassius Dio (third century CE). In addition to her reliance on ancient sources, Fielding evidently turned to several popular historical texts to colour her portraits, including François Catrou and Pierre Julien Rouille's *Historie romaine, depuis la foundation de Rome* (1725–37); Laurence Echard's *Roman History from the Building of the City, to the Present Settlement of the Empire* (1695); John Lockman's *New Roman History, by Question and Answer* (1737); and especially Charles Rollin and Jean Baptiste Crevier's *Roman History to the Battle of Actium* (1739–50). Perhaps because Cleopatra, from her own reign through her subsequent historical reception, was so distinguished by spectacle and theatricality, Fielding also drew, in addition to historical accounts, on Shakespeare's *Antony and Cleopatra* (1623), Thomas May's *Cleopatra* (1639), John Fletcher and Philip

Massinger's *The False One* (1647), Dryden's *All for Love* (1678), and Colley Cibber's *Cæsar in Ægypt* (1725).

11 Betty Schellenberg, *The Professionalization of Women Writers in Eighteenth-Century Britain* (Cambridge: Cambridge University Press, 2005), 98–9.

12 Of Sarah's relationship with Henry, Hester Thrale remarked that "as soon [as] he perceived She once read Virgil, farewell to Fondness, the Author's jealousy was become stronger than the Brother's Affection, and he saw her further progress in literature not without pleasure only – but with Pain." See Thrale, *Thraliana, the Diary of Mrs. Hester Lynch Thrale, 1776–1809*, ed. Katherine C. Balderston, 2 vols. (Oxford: Clarendon Press, 1951), 1:79. For a different view, see Martin Battestin, *Henry Fielding: A Life* (New York: Routledge, 1989), 381.

13 Linda Bree, *Sarah Fielding* (New York: Twayne Publishers, 1996), 20.

14 On this project she received help from James Harris, a scholar of Greek and Latin, who was also a close friend of her brother's. As Clive Probyn notes, the translation was "well received," and "[o]ne section was often reprinted [and] remained in print until well into the twentieth century." See "Fielding, Sarah (1710–1768)," in *The Oxford Dictionary of National Biography*, ed. H.C.G. Matthew and Brian Harrison (Oxford: Oxford University Press, 2004).

15 Christopher D. Johnson, Introduction to his edition of *The Lives of Cleopatra and Octavia*, 18. Johnson reprints the full list of subscribers, 42–53.

16 Bree, *Sarah Fielding*, 10. This critical silence largely continues to prevail, despite the availability of Johnson's valuable edition. Discussions of *The Lives* generally serve to bolster arguments about Fielding's other texts.

17 See Susan Carlile's Introduction to *Masters of the Marketplace: British Women Novelists of the 1750s*, ed. Susan Carlile (Bethlehem: Lehigh University Press, 2011), 17. Carlile later adds, "Clearly, these pioneering women had arrived at a crucial intersection in literary history, one in which their interest in fostering a public persona merged with a more amenable marketplace. Thus these novelists were able to subvert standard plots; highlight both a woman's plight as well as her potential; engage with, expand on, and define accepted ways of action; and ultimately expand the possibilities of this new genre" (22).

18 Donna Landry, "Picturing Benevolence against the Commercial Cry, 1750–98: Or, Sarah Fielding and the Secret Causes of Romanticism," in *The History of British Women's Writing, 1750–1830*, vol. 5, ed. Jacqueline M. Labbe (Basingstoke: Palgrave Macmillan, 2010), 153.

19 On Fielding's reputation as an English novelist, see Peter Sabor, Introduction, in Sarah Fielding, *The Adventures of David Simple and The*

Adventures of David Simple, Volume the Last (Lexington: University Press of Kentucky, 1998), xxiii; xxiv. On Fielding's popularity relative to Henry Fielding and Laurence Sterne, see James Raven, *British Fiction 1750–1770: A Chronological Check-List of Prose Fiction Printed in Britain and Ireland* (Newark: University of Delaware Press, 1987).

20 On Fielding's reputation, see Schellenberg, *The Professionalization of Women Writers in Eighteenth-Century Britain*, 11. On Sarah Fielding as an author-function, see 99: "Lady Mary Wortley Montagu's tendency to make false attributions of works to Sarah Fielding is a typical effect of Fielding's having achieved an author function, an effect complained of as well by such contemporaries as Alexander Pope and her brother Henry."

21 For Christopher D. Johnson, see "Novel Forms and Borrowed Texts: Genre and the Interpretive Challenge in Sarah Fielding," in *Experiments in Genre in Eighteenth-Century Literature*, ed. Sandro Jung (Lebanon, NH: University Press of New England, 2011), 181. See also Downs-Miers, "Springing the Trap: Subtexts and Subversions," in *Fetter'd or Free?: British Women Novelists, 1670–1815*, ed. Mary Anne Schofield and Cecilia Macheski (Athens: Ohio University Press, 1986) and Carolyn Woodward, "Sarah Fielding's Self-Destructing Utopia: *The Adventures of David Simple*," in *Living by the Pen: Early British Women Novelists*, ed. Dale Spender (New York: Teachers College Press, 1992).

22 Kate Rumbold, "Shakespeare's 'Propriety' and the Mid-Eighteenth-Century Novel: Sarah Fielding's *The History of the Countess of Dellwyn*," in *Reading 1759: Literary Culture in Mid-Eighteenth-Century Britain and France*, ed. Shaun Regan (Lewisburg, PA: Bucknell University Press, 2013), 190.

23 Landry, "Picturing Benevolence," 153.

24 Ibid., 154; 160.

25 Daniel Gross, *The Secret History of Emotion: From Aristotle's Rhetoric to Modern Brain Science* (Chicago: University of Chicago Press, 2006), 143.

26 Nussbaum, *Autobiographical Subject*, 125.

27 Grant, *Cleopatra*, 241.

28 The following titles are representative: Christopher Pelling, *Plutarch and History: Eighteen Studies* (Swansea: Classical Press of Wales, 2011); Tim Duff, *Plutarch's Lives: Exploring Virtue and Vice* (Oxford: Clarendon Press, 1999); and Philip Stadter, ed., *Plutarch and the Historical Tradition* (New York: Routledge, 1992).

29 Duff, *Plutarch's Lives*, 48.

30 Ibid., 250.

31 Ibid., 54–5; 56.

32 Ibid., 56.

33 Ibid., 243.
34 Christopher D. Johnson, "Novel Forms," 190.
35 Pelling, *Plutarch and History*, 238.
36 For an excellent overview that properly historicizes Pope's argument according to seventeenth- and eighteenth-century debates about the passions, see Bertrand Goldgar, "Pope's Theory of the Passions: The Background of Epistle II of the *Essay on Man*," *Philological Quarterly* 41.4 (1962): 739.
37 Samuel Johnson, "Life of Pope," in *Samuel Johnson: Selected Poetry and Prose*, ed. Frank Brady and W.K. Wimsatt (Berkeley: University of California Press, 1978), 520–1.
38 See Henry Fielding, *Amelia*, ed. Linda Bree (Peterborough, ON: Broadview, 2010), 57.
39 References to Plutarch are from *The Lives of the Noble Grecians and Romans*, trans. John Dryden et al., rev. Arthur Hugh Clough (New York: Modern Library, 1932) and will be cited parenthetically.
40 On the relationship between women and animals such as monkeys in the eighteenth century, see Laura Brown, *Homeless Dogs and Melancholy Apes: Humans and Other Animals in the Modern Literary Imagination* (Ithaca: Cornell University Press, 2010).
41 For Josephus, *Jewish Antiquities* and the *Wars of the Jews*, see the Loeb edition, trans. H. St J. Thackeray and Ralph Marcus, 9 vols. (Cambridge, MA: Harvard University Press, 1966). Subsequent references will be cited parenthetically as *JA* and *WJ*. On Josephus, see Grant: "he is savagely biased against the queen" (*Cleopatra*, 240).
42 See Appian's *Civil War*, trans. John Carter (London: Penguin, 1996), 5.2.8–9.
43 See John Lockman, *A New Roman History, by Question and Answer, in a Method much more Comprehensive than any of the Kind extant. Extracted from Ancient Authors, and the Most celebrated among the Modern, and Interspersed with such Customs as serve to illustrate History. With a Complete Index. Designed principally for Schools* (Dublin: Printed by John Exshaw, 1778), 316; hereafter cited parenthetically as *NRH*. According to the *English Short Title Catalogue*, there were at least eleven editions between 1737 and 1791.
44 See, for example, Cassius Dio's *Roman History*, 50:33. Lucy Hughes-Hallett notes how "the character that Octavius imagined for Cleopatra is shaped and endorsed by racist expectations" as well as "by sexual prejudice … Taken together … they add up to a perfect image of otherness, of all the vices and weaknesses that a good Roman soldier-male must shun." See *Cleopatra: Histories, Dreams and Distortions* (New York: HarperPerennial, 1991), 49.

45 Christopher D. Johnson suggests Fielding's specific debt to Rollin and Crevier's *The Roman History from the Foundation of Rome to the Battle of Actium: That is, To the End of the Commonwealth. Translated from the French* (London: Printed for J. and P. Knapton, 1754). Crevier revised and completed volumes 8 and 9, and wrote 10–16 following Rollin's death. But it seems likely that, owing to its popularity and her interest in classical scholarship, Fielding would also have known Rollin's far more popular *Ancient History of the Egyptians, Carthaginians, Assyrians, Babylonians, Medes and Persians, Macedonians, and Grecians. Translated from the French in ten volumes* (London: Printed for J. Rivington and sons; G.G.J. and J. Robinson; B. Law; T. Carnan; T. Verner, etc., 1778). Both histories saw multiple editions: the *ESTC* lists at least three editions of the *Roman History* between 1739 and 1768, and nine of the *Ancient History* between 1738 and 1800. Rollin and Crevier's *Roman History from the Foundation of Rome to the Battle of Actium* will be cited parenthetically as *RH*.

46 James Sambrook, "Lockman, John (1698–1771)," in *The Oxford Dictionary of National Biography*, ed. Lawrence Goldman (Oxford: Oxford University Press, 2004) http://www.oxforddnb.com/view/article/16912 (accessed 20 June 2018).

47 See Grant, *Cleopatra*, 241–2.

48 Denis Diderot, "The Paradox of Acting," in *Actors on Acting*, ed. Toby Cole and Helen Krich Chinoy (New York: Crown, 1949), 163–6.

49 Nancy Armstrong, *Desire and Domestic Fiction: A Political History of the Novel* (Oxford: Oxford University Press, 1987).

50 R. Brimley Johnson, Introduction, in Sarah Fielding, *The Lives of Cleopatra and Octavia*, ed. R. Brimley Johnson (London: Scholartis Press, 1928), xxv.

51 See Tanya Caldwell's Introduction in *The Broadview Anthology of Restoration and Early Eighteenth-Century Drama*, ed. J. Douglas Canfield (Peterborough, ON: Broadview, 2001), 218. References to Dryden's *All for Love* come from *The Works of John Dryden*, vol. 13: *Plays: All for Love, Oedipus, Troilus and Cressida*, ed. Maximillian E. Novak and George R. Guffey (Berkeley: University of California Press, 1984) and will be cited parenthetically.

52 Aelius Donatus was a fourth-century Latin grammarian, whose *Life of Virgil* was based on Suetonius's treatment of Virgil in *De viris illustribus* (from a section now lost).

53 Duff, *Plutarch's Lives*, 250.

54 I am not suggesting that Fielding was necessarily familiar with *Les Femmes illustres*, but rather that the contrast is instructive.

55 Dryden, *Aureng-Zebe*, in *The Works of John Dryden*, vol. 12, ed. Vinton Dearing (Los Angeles: University of California Press, 1994), 156.

56 Ibid.
57 Ibid.
58 Richard Steele and Joseph Addison, *The Spectator*, ed. Donald F. Bond, 5 vols. (Oxford: Clarendon Press, 1965), 4:269–72. As Bond notes of the anecdote, "The incident referred to is the famous legend of the *Weibertreue*, and is supposed to have taken place when Conrad III besieged the town of Weinsburg (Hensburg) in the year 1140. Guelphus, or Welf, was the brother of Henry the Proud, Conrad's powerful rival in Bavaria and Saxony, who had just died in the preceding year. The story has been often told" (4:269n2).
59 Grant, *Cleopatra*, 152.
60 Ibid., 134.
61 Cf. Rollin-Crevier: "she cried, and bewailed her fortune, being sincerely affected at finding herself one of the causes of civil war" (*RH*, 16:24).

5. Whose "Wild and Extravagant Stories"?

1 On the relationship between Landor and Orientalism, see especially Mohammed Sharafuddin, *Islam and Romantic Orientalism: Literary Encounters with the Orient* (New York: Tauris, 1994).
2 See Landor, *The Poetical Works of Walter Savage Landor*, 2 vols., ed. Stephen Wheeler (Oxford: Clarendon Press, 1937), 1:474.
3 In the 1798 Preface to *Gebir*, reproduced in ibid., 1:473.
4 Gary Kelly writes, for example, that *The Progress* "was the most comprehensive type of work by a woman in English until the Victorian Age." See Kelly's Introductory Note to his edition of *The Progress of Romance* in *Sarah Scott and Clara Reeve*, vol. 6 of *Bluestocking Feminism: Writings of the Bluestocking Circle, 1738–1785* (London: Pickering and Chatto, 1999), 167. Further references to both *The Progress of Romance* and *Charoba* will be cited parenthetically from this edition. Dale Spender identifies Reeve as the "first 'woman of letters' I can find who concerns herself with an assessment of fiction." See Spender, *Mothers of the Novel: 100 Good Women Writers before Jane Austen* (New York: Pandora Press, 1986), 177. Brian Corman enlarges this perspective, concluding, "There is, in other words, virtually no historical criticism of the novel before Clara Reeve." See Corman, "Clara Reeve's *The Progress of Romance* and the Canon of the Novel in 1785," in *New Windows on a Woman's World: Essays for Jocelyn Harris*, ed. Colin Gibson and Lisa Marr (Dunedin, NZ: University of Otago Department of English, 2005), 127. Though criticism – as Landor's remark suggests – was not considered an appropriate occupation for

women, Reeve's *Progress of Romance* marked the start of a new era: women writers were "begin[ning] to appear as reviewers" by the 1780s. See Susan Staves, *A Literary History of Women's Writing in Britain, 1660–1789* (Cambridge: Cambridge University Press, 2006), 437.

5 As Betty Schellenberg further notes, "The temporary space within which Reeve holds these competing notions of literary value in play is that of the dialogue, soon to be displaced by a more monologic and unitary narrative of literary history within which there is simply room for fewer writers." See *The Professionalization of Women Writers in Eighteenth-Century Britain* (Cambridge: Cambridge University Press, 2005), 177.

6 See Gary Kelly, "Clara Reeve, Provincial Bluestocking: From the Old Whigs to the Modern Liberal State," in *Reconsidering the Bluestockings*, ed. Nicole Pohl and Betty A. Schellenberg (San Marino, CA: Huntington Library, 2003), 105–25, where Kelly details Reeve's education.

7 Quoted in ibid., 117.

8 Kelly, Introductory Note to Reeve, *The Progress of Romance*, lxii. Corman disagrees with Kelly's assessment of Reeve's politics: "She is far too concerned with the ill effects of Circulating Libraries to have much time for a fiction promoting Republican politics" ("Clara Reeve's *The Progress of Romance*," 138).

9 On Charoba's relationship to classical texts, see also Robert Mack's brief Introduction in his edition of *Oriental Tales* (New York: Oxford University Press, 1992), xxxiv–xl.

10 Of course, "epic" and "romance" are not mutually exclusive, but the addition of romance to epic tends to create uncomfortable, even unresolvable, tensions in the text.

11 The *Arabian Nights' Entertainments* was first translated into English from Antoine Galland's French edition between 1704 and 1717.

12 See also Srinivas Aravamudan, "In the Wake of the Novel: The Oriental Tale as National Allegory," *Novel: A Forum on Fiction* 33.1 (1999): 16.

13 As Susan Staves notes, contrasting Reeve with James Beattie, one of the literary critics with whom Reeve was in dialogue: "She criticizes James Beattie's discussion of romance in *Dissertations Moral and Critical* for inattention to significant works and she treats women writers Beattie and other contemporaries ignored, including Behn, Manly, Haywood, Griffith, and Brooke (a particular favorite)" (*A Literary History of Women's Writing in Britain*, 383).

14 As Corman notes, "Reeve makes clear that she knows the earlier novel criticism well; the text of *The Progress of Romance* is filled with quotations

and citations from virtually every authority" ("Clara Reeve's *The Progress of Romance*," 132).

15 As Barbara Fuchs writes in *Romance* (New York: Routledge, 2004), romance is hard to define precisely because "different conceptions of the term emerge dynamically, and in opposition to other types of literary production" (2). Hence, as the novel became a popular form in eighteenth-century England, the French novels of the previous century became mere romances, and critics dismissed as "romance" many fictions they perceived to fall short of the new novelistic standards, whatever those happened to be.

16 Jonathan Kramnick, *Making the English Canon: Print-Capitalism and the Cultural Past, 1700–1770* (Cambridge: Cambridge University Press, 1999), 4.

17 Ibid.

18 Ibid., 107; 204.

19 Ibid., 133.

20 It is worth noting that this view of Shakespeare was also contested even in the eighteenth century: Charlotte Lennox's *Shakespeare Illustrated* (1753) traced the plays to their romance origins, emphasizing his indebtedness to a larger tradition.

21 See William St Clair, *The Reading Nation in the Romantic Period* (Cambridge: Cambridge University Press, 2004), 122.

22 Ibid.

23 Ibid.

24 Ibid., 137.

25 April London, *Literary History Writing, 1770–1820* (New York: Palgrave, 2010), 111.

26 Ibid., 111–12.

27 For more on Milton's ambiguous status in the eighteenth century, see Adeline Johns-Putra, *The History of the Epic* (New York: Palgrave, 2006), 87–90.

28 See the *OLD*, ed. P.G.W. Glare (Oxford: Clarendon Press, 1997), 1971.

29 Further blurring distinctions, the division into twelve volumes is also associated with romance, as the Earl of Chesterfield suggested in 1774: "A Novel is a kind of abbreviation of a Romance; for a Romance generally consists of twelve volumes, all filled with insipid love nonsense, and most incredible adventures" (cited in Fuchs, *Romance*, 109).

30 For more on the relationship between Scheherazade and Dinarzade, see Rosalind Ballaster, "Playing the Second String: The Role of Dinarzade in Eighteenth-Century English Fiction," in *The Arabian Nights in Historical*

Context: Between East and West, ed. Saree Makdisi and Felicity Nussbaum (Oxford: Oxford University Press, 2008), and *Fabulous Orients: Fictions of the East in England, 1662–1785* (Oxford: Oxford University Press, 2005).

31 For a more recent critical perspective on this phenomenon, see Margaret Anne Doody, *The True Story of the Novel* (New Brunswick, NJ: Rutgers University Press, 1996).

32 Reeve emphasizes these false oppositions more explicitly in the dialogue preceding *Charoba*. Martha Pike Conant has argued that the oriental tale is a reaction against classicism. See *The Oriental Tale in England in the Eighteenth Century* (New York: Columbia University Press, 1908). Outdated as it is, this is one of the few critical works that engages in any depth with the English vogue for the oriental tale in this period.

33 On the oriental tale, see, for example, Mack's Introduction to *Oriental Tales*; Peter Caracciolo's Introduction to *The "Arabian Nights" in English Literature: Studies in the Reception of "The Thousand and One Nights" into British Culture* (London: Macmillan Press, 1988); and Ballaster, *Fabulous Orients*. On the romance genre, see especially Ballaster, *Seductive Forms: Women's Amatory Fiction from 1648–1740* (Oxford: Clarendon Press, 1992); Fuchs, *Romance*; Patricia Parker, *Inescapable Romance: Studies in the Poetics of a Mode* (Princeton: Princeton University Press, 1979); and, in the spirit of Reeve, Doody's *True Story of the Novel*.

34 Critics have often enlisted Reeve on the side of the novel, believing that "progress" marks an evolution *from* something *to* something superior, but Reeve desires to establish a romance genealogy precisely in order to prevent such teleological arguments.

35 As Mohammed Sharafuddin further notes in his discussion of Landor, "According to the Koran, the Adites were tyrannical, corrupt and vainglorious; thus their punishment (the decline and destruction of their city and nation) was correspondingly severe" (*Islam and Romantic Orientalism*, 11).

36 Reeve's Charoba differs from its source material in this respect. See John Davies' *The Egyptian history, treating of the pyramids, the inundation of the Nile, and other prodigies of Egypt, according to the opinions and traditions of the Arabians. Written originally in the Arabian tongue by Murtadi the son of Gaphiphus. Rendered into French by Monsieur Vattier, Arabick professor to the King of France. And thence faithfully done into English by J. Davies of Kidwelly* (London: Printed by R[obert]. B[attersby]. for Thomas Basset, at the George, near Cliffords-Inn in Fleet-street, 1672), 109–10. For Vattier's French edition, see *L'Egypte de Mvrtadi, fils dv Gaphiphe;*

ov il est traite des pyramides, du de bordement du Nil, & des autres merueilles de cette Prouince, selon les opinions & traditions des Arabes (Paris: T. Ioly, 1666).

37 There is no mention of Hagar's origins in the Christian Bible, and Abraham's wealth upon leaving Egypt remains unexplained.

38 See also Gary Kelly's note on Reeve's preface to *Charoba*: "This passage does not correspond to that in the English translation by J. Davies; it may be Reeve's own, but it differs from Vattier's French in certain respects, too, most notably in substituting a reference to Ovid's *Metamorphoses* for a reference to the fourth book of Virgil's *Georgics* in both Vattier and Davies" (311n2).

39 See *Amores* 1.1 in Ovid, *Heroides and Amores*, trans. Grant Showerman, Loeb edition (Cambridge, MA: Harvard University Press, 1977).

40 In the opening lines of the prologue, Ovid begins, "My mind is bent to tell of bodies changed into new forms." See *Metamorphoses*, 2 vols., trans. Frank Justice Miller (Cambridge, MA: Harvard University Press, 1916–26), 1:3.

41 See Leo Curran, "Rape and Rape Victims in the *Metamorphoses*," in *Women in the Ancient World: The Arethusa Papers*, ed. John Peradotto and J.P. Sullivan (Albany: State University of New York Press, 1984), 263–86. For a more generous interpretation of sexual violence in Ovid, see Lynn Enterline, *The Rhetoric of the Body from Ovid to Shakespeare* (Cambridge: Cambridge University Press, 2000).

42 See Helene P. Foley, "Tragic Wives: Medea's Divided Self," in Foley, *Female Acts in Greek Tragedy* (Princeton: Princeton University Press, 2001), 243–71.

43 Indeed, Hercules in Sophocles' *Trachiniae* issues a dying lament very similar to Gebirus's, listing his many accomplishments before inveighing against Deianeira. As Page duBois notes, "Hercules lists soldiers, giants, beasts, Greeks and barbarians, and ends with *gunê*, woman, in an emphatic position in the line which stresses heavily the fact, most repellent to the hero, that his final, victorious opponent substitutes for all other opponents." See *Centaurs and Amazons: Women and the Pre-History of the Great Chain of Being* (Ann Arbor: University of Michigan Press, 1991), 104.

44 "Deianeira" literally means "destroying her spouse." See the eponymous entry in Henry Liddell and Robert Scott, *A Greek-English Lexicon* (Oxford: Clarendon Press, 1996).

45 On the rough and impious character of Achilles, see, for example, the entry in the *OCD*, 6–7.

46 See Homer, *The Iliad*, trans. Richmond Lattimore (Chicago: University of Chicago Press, 1961).

47 Reeve brings out this parallel to the *Iliad* by rearranging Gebirus's speech: whereas the Vattier-Davies versions include Gebirus's dying words at the moment of the snakebite, Reeve presents them earlier.

48 Davies, *The Egyptian history, treating of the pyramids*, 134–5; Vattier, *L'Egypte de Mvrtadi*, 156.

49 See Lucy Hughes-Hallet, *Cleopatra: Histories, Dreams, and Distortions* (New York: HarperPerennial, 1991), 26; Sarah B. Pomeroy, *Women in Hellenistic Egypt: From Alexander to Cleopatra* (New York: Schocken Books, 1984).

50 Cassius Dio, *Dio's Roman History*, 9 vols., trans. Ernest Cary, on the basis of the version of Herbert Baldwin Foster (Cambridge, MA: Harvard University Press, 1914–27), 6:497.

51 Arsinoe, daughter of Ptolemy and Berenice I, achieved divine status in her lifetime, the first "Ptolemaic ruler to enter the Egyptian temples as 'temple-sharing goddess' ... Her career was marked by ambition and political deftness, her death memorialized by Callimachus ... and the festival of the Arsinoeia." See the *OCD*, ed. Simon Hornblower and Antony Spawforth (Oxford: Oxford University Press, 2003), 177. Berenice II, whose dedication of her lock inspired Pope's mock-epic, was also deified. Hypatia was an Alexandrian scholar learned in philosophy, mathematics, and astronomy, who wrote several commentaries (now, for the most part, lost) on ancient authors. Zenobia, originally queen of Palmyra, took advantage of Roman political instability in the late third century CE in order to take over Egypt and parts of Asia Minor, before finally being subdued by Aurelian.

52 "The Egyptians made King in her stead her Cousin-german Dalic; or rather (as others affirm) they made Queen her Cousin Dalica: for she had continued a Virgin, and was never married" (Davies, *The Egyptian history, treating of the pyramids*, 136; Vattier, *L'Egypte de Mvrtadi*, 158).

53 Gertrude Jobes, *Dictionary of Mythology: Folklore and Symbols* (New York: Scarecrow Press, 1961–2), 1469. See also Annis Pratt's *Dancing with Goddesses: Archetypes, Poetry, and Empowerment* (Bloomington: Indiana University Press, 1994).

54 Pomeroy, *Women in Hellenistic Egypt*, 26.

55 For more on the symbolism of blindness at the end of the eighteenth, and beginning of the nineteenth, centuries, see Edward Larrissy, *The Blind and Blindness in Literature of the Romantic Period* (Edinburgh: Edinburgh University Press, 2007).

56 Despite Charoba's divinely sanctioned defence of her kingdom, the source texts suggest a cause-and-effect relationship between her defeat of Gebirus and her own demise: Gebirus warns her not to triumph in his death because a similar moment awaits her; the narrator immediately relates

how Charoba "lived [not] above a year after him" when she treads on a poisoned serpent. Reeve, however, alters the order of events: although Gebirus issues the same warning, Reeve rearranges some of the narrative elements in order to distance Charoba's death from Gebirus's dying words, which also emphasizes the chance nature of her encounter with the serpent: "Now it happened about three years after the death of Gebirus … It so happened that the Queen trod upon a serpent" (274–5).

Epilogue

1 Richard Steele and Joseph Addison, *The Spectator*, ed. Donald F. Bond, 5 vols. (Oxford: Clarendon Press, 1965), 1:48.
2 Ibid. 1:48–9.
3 Laura Brown, *Fables of Modernity: Literature and Culture in the English Eighteenth Century* (Ithaca: Cornell University Press, 2001), 4.
4 See Henry Fielding, the *Covent-Garden Journal and A Plan of the Universal Register-Office*, ed. Bertrand A. Goldgar (Middleton, CT: Wesleyan University Press, 1988), 65–6. Fielding dedicates parts of numbers 7–8 to the defence of his novel.
5 David Quint, *Epic and Empire: Politics and Generic Form from Virgil to Milton* (Princeton: Princeton University Press, 1993), 9.
6 Not only in the opposition of Dido's story to Aeneas's, but in the very structure of the narrative: Books 1–6 recount Aeneas's Odyssean adventures while the second epic invocation at the beginning of Book 7 signals a turn to the Iliadic model that will cement his success as a forebear of Augustus. That is, Aeneas must cast off and leave behind the romance wanderings of Odysseus in order to embrace his epic destiny. More generally, the opposition between epic and romance also has roots in the origins of "romance" as a term: originally, "romance" described works written in the vernacular as opposed to Latin (see *OED* n1).
7 Clara Reeve, *Progress of Romance*, 173. See *The Progress of Romance*, in *Sarah Scott and Clara Reeve*, vol. 6 of *Bluestocking Feminism: Writings of the Bluestocking Circle, 1738–1785*, ed. Gary Kelly (London: Pickering and Chatto, 1999), 173. Euphrasia is not, of course, wrong: see Richard Martin, "Epic as Genre," in *A Companion to Ancient Epic*, ed. John Miles Foley (Malden, MA: Blackwell, 2009), 9–19. See also Colin Burrow, *Epic Romance: Homer to Milton* (Oxford: Clarendon Press, 1993): "The creation of [the] antithesis [between epic and romance] goes back a long way, and is intricately entangled in the reception history of epic. It derives ultimately from a determination to see the two Homeric poems as rootedly distinct

from each other: the *Iliad* shows fighting, and heroic goings-on, so it is epic; the *Odyssey* relates wanderings, magical adventures abroad, and a final comic reunion in the return of the hero to his wife and home, so it is a romance" (2). As Barbara Fuchs writes, "romance" is a shifting signifier: "different conceptions of the term emerge dynamically, and in opposition to other types of literary production." See *Romance* (New York: Routledge, 1994), 2.

8 Cf. Quint, who argues that "the losers' epics would all – not so secretly – like to be epics of history's winners" (*Epic and Empire*, 209). See also Margaret Ferguson, who notes, "Dido's case shows that some alternative versions of an imperial story, even those that quite aggressively challenge an influential writer's claims to truth, may work to extend the empire's ideological dominion over its subjects – including those who live in later regimes that adapt aspects of that empire's regulatory vision." See *Dido's Daughters: Literacy, Gender, and Empire in Early Modern England and France* (Chicago: University of Chicago Press, 2003), 19.

9 Around 1654, for example, Edmund Waller favourably compares Cromwell with Augustus in *A Panegyric to my Lord Protector*; Dryden later, in 1660, praises Charles in this same way in *Astraea Redux*.

10 James William Johnson, *The Formation of English Neo-Classical Thought* (Princeton: Princeton University Press, 1967), 19.

11 See especially Joseph Levine, *The Battle of the Books: History and Literature in the Augustan Age* (Ithaca: Cornell University Press, 1991) and *Between the Ancients and the Moderns: Baroque Culture in Restoration England* (New Haven: Yale University Press, 1999), as well as *Doctor Woodward's Shield: History, Science, and Satire in Augustan England* (Berkeley: University of California Press, 1977) and *Humanism and History: Origins of Modern English Historiography* (Ithaca: Cornell University Press, 1987).

12 Levine, *Between the Ancients and the Moderns*, ix; viii.

13 See Howard Weinbrot, *Augustus Caesar in "Augustan" England: The Decline of a Classical Norm* (Princeton: Princeton University Press, 1978) and *Britannia's Issue: The Rise of British Literature from Dryden to Ossian* (New York: Cambridge University Press, 1993).

14 Weinbrot, *Britannia's Issue*, 74. For Weinbrot, this "outright hostility" manifests itself through modes like the burlesque and mock-heroic, whereas my book focuses on more ambivalent and generically productive responses toward the clash between past and present.

15 Richard Kroll, *The Material Word: Literate Culture in the Restoration and Early Eighteenth Century* (Baltimore: Johns Hopkins University Press, 1991), 3; 8. For Philip Ayres, see *Classical Culture and the Idea of Rome in*

Eighteenth-Century England (Cambridge: Cambridge University Press, 1997).

16 Michael McKeon, "Cultural Crisis and Dialectical Method: Destabilizing Augustan Literature," in *The Profession of Eighteenth-Century Literature*, ed. Leo Damrosch (Madison: University of Wisconsin Press, 1992), 46.

17 For Tanya Caldwell, see *Virgil Made English: The Decline of Classical Authority* (New York: Palgrave, 2008) and *Time to Begin Anew: Dryden's "Georgics" and "Aeneis"* (Lewisburg, PA: Bucknell University Press, 2000). On Virgilian parodies, see Caldwell, and Paul N. Hartle, "'Lawrels for the Conquered': Virgilian Translation and Travesty in the English Civil War and Its Aftermath," in *Reinventing the Middle Ages and the Renaissance: Constructions of the Medieval and Early Modern Periods*, ed. William F. Gentrup (Turnhout: Brepols, 1998), 127–46.

18 For an excellent overview of this process, see Caldwell, *Virgil Made English*.

19 Levine, *Ancients and Moderns*, xii.

Bibliography

Allen, Don Cameron. "Marlowe's *Dido* and the Tradition." In *Essays on Shakespeare and Elizabethan Drama in Honor of Hardin Craig*, ed. Richard Hosley, 55–68. Columbia: University of Missouri Press, 1962.

Alter, Robert. *Fielding and the Nature of the Novel*. Cambridge, MA: Harvard University Press, 1968.

Appian. *Civil War*. Trans. John Carter. London: Penguin, 1996.

Aravamudan, Srinivas. "In the Wake of the Novel: The Oriental Tale as National Allegory." *Novel: A Forum on Fiction* 33.1 (1999): 5–31. https://doi.org/10.2307/1346025.

Archibald, Elizabeth. "Ancient Romance." In *A Companion to Romance: From Classical to Contemporary*, ed. Corinne Saunders, 10–25. Malden, MA: Blackwell, 2004. https://doi.org/10.1002/9780470999172.ch2.

Armstrong, Nancy. *Desire and Domestic Fiction: A Political History of the Novel*. Oxford: Oxford University Press, 1987.

Asfour, Amal, and Paul Williamson. "Gainsborough's Cottage-Door Scenes: Aesthetic Principles, Moral Values." In *Sensation and Sensibility: Viewing Gainsborough's Cottage Door*, ed. Ann Bermingham, 97–119. New Haven: Yale University Press, 2005.

Ayres, Philip. *Classical Culture and the Idea of Rome in Eighteenth-Century England*. Cambridge: Cambridge University Press, 1997.

Ballaster, Rosalind. *Fabulous Orients: Fictions of the East in England, 1662–1785*. Oxford: Oxford University Press, 2005.

– "Playing the Second String: The Role of Dinarzade in Eighteenth-Century English Fiction." In *The Arabian Nights in Historical Context: Between East and West*, ed. Saree Makdisi and Felicity Nussbaum, 83–102. Oxford: Oxford University Press, 2008.

– *Seductive Forms: Women's Amatory Fiction from 1648–1740*. Oxford: Clarendon Press, 1992.

Bannister, Mark. *Privileged Mortals: The French Heroic Novel, 1630–1660*. New York: Oxford University Press, 1983.

Barker, Jane. *Exilius: or, The Banish'd Roman*. Ed. Josephine Grieder. New York: Garland, 1973.

– *The Galesia Trilogy and Selected Manuscript Poems of Jane Baker*. Ed. Carol Shiner Wilson. New York: Oxford University Press, 1997.

– *The Poems of Jane Barker: The Magdalen Manuscript*. Ed. Kathryn R. King. Oxford: Magdalen College, 1998.

– *Poetical Recreations: Consisting of Original Poems, Songs, Odes, &c. with Several New Translations. In Two Parts. Part I. Occasionally Written by Mrs. Jane Barker. Part II. By several Gentlemen of the Universities, and Others*. London: Printed for Benjamin Crayle, 1688.

Barney, Richard. *Plots of Enlightenment: Education and the Novel in Eighteenth-Century England*. Stanford: Stanford University Press, 1999.

Bate, Walter Jackson. *From Classic to Romantic: Premises of Taste in Eighteenth-Century England*. New York: Harper and Row, 1961.

Battestin, Martin. *Henry Fielding: A Life*. New York: Routledge, 1989.

– *Henry Fielding Companion*. Westport, CT: Greenwood Press, 2000.

– Introduction. In Henry Fielding, *Amelia*, ed. Martin Battestin, xv–lxxx. Middleton, CT: Wesleyan University Press, 1983.

Battestin, Martin C., and Clive T. Probyn. General Introduction. In *The Correspondence of Henry and Sarah Fielding*, ed. Martin C. Battestin and Clive T. Probyn, xv–xliii. Oxford: Clarendon Press, 1993.

Berkin, Carol. *Revolutionary Mothers: Women and the Struggle for America's Independence*. New York: Alfred A. Knopf, 2005.

Bermingham, Ann. "The Simple Life: Cottages and Gainsborough's Cottage Doors." In *Land, Nation and Culture, 1740–1840: Thinking the Republic of Taste*, ed. Peter de Bolla, Nigel Leask, and David Simpson, 37–62. Basingstoke: Palgrave, 2005. https://doi.org/10.1057/9780230502048_3.

Berquin, Arnaud. *The Looking-Glass for the Mind or Intellectual Mirror*. New York: S.R. Publishers, 1969.

Bettini, Maurizio. "Ghosts of Exile: Doubles and Nostalgia in Vergil's *parva Troia* (*Aeneid* 3.284ff)." *Classical Antiquity* 16.1 (1997): 8–33. https://doi.org/10.2307/25011052.

Blok, Josine. *The Early Amazons: Modern and Ancient Perspectives on a Persistent Myth*. New York: E.J. Brill, 1995.

Boswell, James, and Samuel Johnson. *The Journal of a Tour to the Hebrides and A Journey to the Western Islands of Scotland*. Ed. Peter Levi. New York: Penguin, 1984.

Bowers, Toni. *Politics of Motherhood: British Writing and Culture, 1680–1760.* New York: Cambridge University Press, 1996.
Bowra, C.M. *From Virgil to Milton*. London: Macmillan & Co., 1948.
Boyle, A.J., ed. *Roman Epic*. New York: Routledge, 1993. https://doi.org/10.4324/9780203439463.
Braudy, Leo. *Narrative Form in History and Fiction*. Princeton: Princeton University Press, 1970.
Bree, Linda. Introduction. In Henry Fielding, *Amelia*, ed. Linda Bree, 9–30 New York: Broadview, 2010. https://doi.org/10.1017/CBO9780511782534.002.
– *Sarah Fielding*. New York: Twayne Publishers, 1996.
Breitenstein, Renée-Claude. "Speaking of Women and Giving Voice to Women: The Example of Madeleine and Georges De Scudéry's *Femmes illustres ou les Harangues héroïques*." In *Creating Women: Representation, Self-Representation, and Agency in the Renaissance*, ed. Manuela Scarci, 45–56. Toronto: Centre for Reformation and Renaissance Studies, 2013.
Broome, Judith. *Fictive Domains: Body, Landscape, and Nostalgia, 1717–1770.* Lewisburg, PA: Bucknell University Press, 2007.
Brown, Laura. *Ends of Empire: Women and Ideology in Early Eighteenth-Century English Literature*. Ithaca: Cornell University Press, 1993.
– *Fables of Modernity: Literature and Culture in the English Eighteenth Century.* Ithaca: Cornell University Press, 2001.
– *Homeless Dogs and Melancholy Apes: Humans and Other Animals in the Modern Literary Imagination*. Ithaca: Cornell University Press, 2010.
Burden, Michael, ed. *A Woman Scorn'd: Responses to the Dido Myth*. London: Faber and Faber, 1998.
Burrow, Colin. *Epic Romance: Homer to Milton*. Oxford: Clarendon Press, 1993. https://doi.org/10.1093/acprof:oso/9780198117940.001.0001.
Buxton, John. *The Grecian Taste: Literature in the Age of Neo-Classicism, 1740–1820*. New York: Harper and Row, 1978. https://doi.org/10.1007/978-1-349-03867-1.
Caldwell, Tanya. Introduction to *All for Love*. In *The Broadview Anthology of Restoration and Early Eighteenth-Century Drama*, ed. J. Douglas Canfield, 218. Peterborough, ON: Broadview, 2001.
– *Time to Begin Anew: Dryden's Georgics and Aeneis*. Lewisburg, PA: Bucknell University Press, 2000.
– *Virgil Made English: The Decline of Classical Authority*. New York: Palgrave, 2008.
Campbell, Jill. *Natural Masques: Gender and Identity in Fielding's Plays and Novels*. Stanford: Stanford University Press, 1995.

Camps, W.A. *An Introduction to Virgil's Aeneid*. London: Oxford University Press, 1969.

Canfield, J. Douglas, and J. Paul Hunter, eds. *Rhetorics of Order/Ordering Rhetorics in English Neoclassical Literature*. Newark: University of Delaware Press, 1989.

Caracciolo, Peter, ed. *The "Arabian Nights" in English Literature: Studies in the Reception of "The Thousand and One Nights" into British Culture*. London: Macmillan Press, 1988. https://doi.org/10.1007/978-1-349-19620-3.

Carlile, Susan. *Charlotte Lennox: An Independent Mind*. Toronto: University of Toronto Press, 2018.

– Introduction. In *Masters of the Marketplace: British Women Novelists of the 1750s*, ed. Susan Carlile, 11–27. Bethlehem: Lehigh University Press, 2011.

Cassius Dio. *Dio's Roman History*. 9 vols. Trans. Ernest Cary, on the basis of the version of Herbert Baldwin Foster. Cambridge, MA: Harvard University Press, 1914–27.

Castle, Terry. "Masquerade and Allegory: Fielding's 'Amelia." In Castle, *Masquerade and Civilization: The Carnivalesque in Eighteenth-Century English Culture and Fiction*, 177–252. Stanford: Stanford University Press, 1986.

Chauveau, Michel. *Cleopatra: Beyond the Myth*. Trans. David Lorton. Ithaca: Cornell University Press, 2002.

Cibber, Colley. *Cæsar in Ægypt*. In *The Dramatic Works of Colley Cibber, Esq. In Five Volumes. Volume the Fifth. Containing Cæsar in Ægypt. Flora; or, Hob in the Well. School Boy. Xerxes. Venus and Adonis. Papal Tyranny. Damon and Phillida.* London: Printed for J. Rivington and Sons, et al., 1777.

Clarke, M.L. *Classical Education in Britain, 1500–1900*. Cambridge: Cambridge University Press, 1959.

Clarke, Norma. *Dr. Johnson's Women*. New York: Hambledon and London, 2000.

– *The Rise and Fall of the Woman of Letters*. London: Pimlico, 2004.

Clayton, Barbara. *A Penelopean Poetics: Reweaving the Feminine in Homer's Odyssey*. Lanham, MD: Lexington Books, 2004.

Clery, E.J. *The Feminization Debate in Eighteenth-Century England: Literature, Commerce, and Luxury*. New York: Palgrave, 2004. https://doi.org/10.1057/9780230509047.

Conant, Martha Pike. *The Oriental Tale in England in the Eighteenth Century*. New York: Columbia University Press, 1908.

Conn, Stetson. *Gibraltar in British Diplomacy in the Eighteenth Century*. New Haven: Yale University Press, 1942.

Corman, Brian. "Clara Reeve's *The Progress of Romance* and the Canon of the Novel in 1785." In *New Windows on a Woman's World: Essays for Jocelyn*

Harris, ed. Colin Gibson and Lisa Marr, 126–40. Dunedin, NZ: University of Otago Department of English, 2005.

Curran, Leo. "Rape and Rape Victims in the *Metamorphoses*." In *Women in the Ancient World: The Arethusa Papers*, ed. John Peradotto and J.P. Sullivan, 263–86. Albany: State University of New York Press, 1984.

Davies, John. *The Egyptian history, treating of the pyramids, the inundation of the Nile, and other prodigies of Egypt, according to the opinions and traditions of the Arabians.* Written originally in the Arabian tongue by Murtadi the son of Gaphiphus. Rendered into French by Monsieur Vattier, Arabick professor to the King of France. And thence faithfully done into English by J. Davies of Kidwelly. London: Printed by R[obert]. B[attersby]. for Thomas Basset, at the George, near Cliffords-Inn in Fleet-street, 1672.

DeJean, Joan. *Fictions of Sappho, 1546–1937.* Chicago: University of Chicago Press, 1989.

– *Tender Geographies: Women and the Origins of the Novel in France.* New York: Columbia University Press, 1991.

– "Violent Women and Violence against Women: Representing the 'Strong' Woman in Early Modern France." *Signs (Chicago, Ill.)* 29.1 (Autumn 2003): 117–47. https://doi.org/10.1086/375709.

Desmond, Marilynn. *Reading Dido: Gender, Textuality, and the Medieval Aeneid.* Minneapolis: University of Minnesota Press, 1994.

Diderot, Denis. "The Paradox of Acting." In *Actors on Acting: The Theories, Techniques, and Practices of the Great Actors of All Time as Told in Their Own Words*, ed. Toby Cole and Helen Krich Chinoy, 160–9. New York: Crown, 1949.

DiPiero, Thomas. *Dangerous Truths and Criminal Passions: The Evolution of the French Novel, 1569–1791.* Stanford: Stanford University Press, 1992.

Dodds, E.R. *Greeks and the Irrational.* Berkeley: University of California Press, 1966.

Doody, Margaret Anne. Introduction. In Charlotte Lennox, *The Female Quixote or The Adventures of Arabella*, ed. Margaret Dalziel, xi –xxxii. New York: Oxford University Press, 2008.

– *The True Story of the Novel.* New Brunswick, NJ: Rutgers University Press, 1996.

Dorn, Judith. "Reading Women Reading History: The Philosophy of Periodical Form in Charlotte Lennox's *The Lady's Museum*." *Historical Reflections/Reflexions Historiques* 18.3 (1992): 7–27.

Dougherty, Carol. *The Poetics of Colonization: From City to Text in Archaic Greece.* Oxford: Oxford University Press, 1993.

– "Sowing the Seeds of Violence: Rape, Women, and the Land." In *Parchments of Gender: Deciphering the Bodies of Antiquity*, ed. Maria Wyke, 267 –84. Oxford: Clarendon Press, 1998.

Downes, Jeremy M. *Recursive Desire: Rereading Epic Tradition*. Tuscaloosa: University of Alabama Press, 1997.

Downs-Miers, Deborah. "Springing the Trap: Subtexts and Subversions." In *Fetter'd or Free: British Women Novelists, 1670–1815*, ed. Mary Ann Schofield and Cecilia Macheski, 308–23. Athens: Ohio University Press, 1986.

Dryden, John. *All for Love*. In vol. 13 of *The Works of John Dryden*. Ed. Vinton Dearing. Los Angeles: University of California Press, 1984.

– *Aureng-Zebe*. In vol. 12 of *The Works of John Dryden*. Ed. Vinton Dearing. Los Angeles: University of California Press, 1994.

Dryden, John, et al., trans. Plutarch. *Lives of the Noble Grecians and Romans*. Rev. Arthur Hugh Clough. New York: Modern Library, 1932.

Dryden, John, trans. Virgil. *Aeneid*. In vols. 5–6 of *The Works of John Dryden: The Works of Virgil in English, 1697*. Ed. William Frost and Vinton Dearing. Berkeley: University of California Press, 1987.

duBois, Page. *Centaurs and Amazons: Women and the Pre-History of the Great Chain of Being*. Ann Arbor: University of Michigan Press, 1991. https://doi.org/10.3998/mpub.8096.

Duff, Tim. *Plutarch's Lives: Exploring Virtue and Vice*. Oxford: Clarendon Press, 1999.

Echard, Laurence. *The Roman History from the Building of the City to the Perfect Settlement of the Empire by Augustus Caesar. Containing the Space of 727 Years. Design's as well for the Understanding of the Roman Authors, as the Roman Affairs*. London: Printed for H. Bonwicke, J. Tonson, W. Freeman, T. Goodwin, et al., 1702.

Enterline, Lynn. *The Rhetoric of the Body from Ovid to Shakespeare*. Cambridge: Cambridge University Press, 2000.

Erskine-Hill, Howard. *The Augustan Idea in English Literature*. London: Edward Arnold, 1983.

Falkner, James. *Fire over the Rock: The Great Siege of Gibraltar, 1779–1783*. Barnsley, UK: Pen & Sword Military, 2009.

Farrell, Joseph, and Michael C.J. Putnam, eds. *A Companion to Vergil's Aeneid and Its Tradition*. Malden, MA: Blackwell, 2010. https://doi.org/10.1002/9781444318050.

Felsenstein, Frank, ed. *English Trader, Indian Maid: Representing Gender, Race, and Slavery in the New World*. Baltimore: Johns Hopkins University Press, 1999.

Ferguson, Margaret. *Dido's Daughters: Literacy, Gender, and Empire in Early Modern England and France*. Chicago: University of Chicago Press, 2003. https://doi.org/10.7208/chicago/9780226243184.001.0001.

Fielding, Henry. *Amelia*. Ed. Martin Battestin. Middleton, CT: Wesleyan University Press, 1983.

– *Amelia*. Ed. Linda Bree. Peterborough, ON: Broadview, 2010.

– *Covent-Garden Journal and A Plan of the Universal Register-Office*. Ed. Bertrand A. Goldgar. Middleton, CT: Wesleyan University Press, 1988.

– *The Life of Mr Jonathan Wild the Great*. Ed. Bertrand A. Goldgar and Hugh Amory. Middleton, CT: Wesleyan University Press, 1997.

– *A Serious Address to the People of Great Britain, in Which the Certain Consequences of the Present Rebellion Are Fully Demonstrated*. London, 1745.

– *The Works of Henry Fielding*. Philadelphia: John D. Morris and Company, 1902.

Fielding, Sarah. *The Adventures of David Simple and The Adventures of David Simple, Volume the Last*. Lexington: University Press of Kentucky, 1998.

– *The History of the Countess of Dellwyn*. London: Printed for A. Millar, 1759.

– *The Lives of Cleopatra and Octavia*. Ed. Christopher D. Johnson. Lewisburg, PA: Bucknell University Press, 1994.

– *The Lives of Cleopatra and Octavia*. Ed. R. Brimley Johnson. London: Scholartis Press, 1928.

Fisk, Deborah Payne, and Jessica Munns. "'Clamorous with War and Teeming with Empire': Purcell and Tate's *Dido and Aeneas*." *Eighteenth Century Life* 26.2 (2002): 23–44. https://doi.org/10.1215/00982601-26-2-23.

Fletcher, John, and Philip Massinger. *The False One*. In vol. 8 of *The Dramatic Works in the Beaumont and Fletcher Canon*, ed. Fredson Bowers. Cambridge: Cambridge University Press, 1992.

Foley, Helene P. "'Reverse Similes' and Sex Roles in the *Odyssey*." In *Women in the Ancient World: The Arethusa Papers*, ed. John Peradotto and J.P. Sullivan, 59–78. Albany: State University of New York Press, 1984.

– "Tragic Wives: Medea's Divided Self." In Foley, *Female Acts in Greek Tragedy*, 243–71. Princeton: Princeton University Press, 2001.

Foley, John Miles, ed. *A Companion to Ancient Epic*. Malden, MA: Blackwell, 2009.

Fowler, R. "'On Not Knowing Greek': The Classics and the Woman of Letters." *Classical Journal* 78.4 (1983): 337–49.

Fuchs, Barbara. *Romance*. New York: Routledge, 2004.

Fussell, Paul. *Rhetorical World of Augustan Humanism: Ethics and Imagery from Swift to Burke*. Oxford: Clarendon Press, 1965.

Gallagher, Catherine. *Nobody's Story: The Vanishing Acts of Women Writers in the Marketplace, 1670–1820*. Berkeley: University of California Press, 1995. https://doi.org/10.1093/acprof:oso/9780198182436.001.0001.

Galland, Antoine. *Arabian Nights' Entertainments*. Ed. Robert Mack. Oxford: Oxford University Press, 2006.

Gibbon, Edward. *Memoirs of My Life and Writings*. Ed. A.O.J. Cockshut and Stephen Constantine. Halifax: Ryburn Publications, 1994.

Goldgar, Bertrand. "Pope's Theory of the Passions: The Background of Epistle II of the *Essay on Man*." *Philological Quarterly*. 41.4 (1962): 730–43.

Grant, Michael. *Cleopatra*. New York: Barnes and Noble Books, 1992.

Greenfield, Susan C., and Carol Barash. *Inventing Maternity: Politics, Science, and Literature, 1650–1865*. Lexington: University Press of Kentucky, 1999.

Gross, Daniel. *The Secret History of Emotion: From Aristotle's Rhetoric to Modern Brain Science*. Chicago: University of Chicago Press, 2006. https://doi.org/10.7208/chicago/9780226309934.001.0001.

Gruen, Eric. *Rethinking the Other in Antiquity*. Princeton: Princeton University Press, 2010. https://doi.org/10.1515/9781400836550.

Guest, Harriet. *Small Change: Women, Learning, and Patriotism, 1750–1810*. Chicago: University of Chicago Press, 2000.

Hägg, Thomas. *The Novel in Antiquity*. Oxford: Basil Blackwell, 1983.

Hamer, Mary. *Signs of Cleopatra: History, Politics, Representation*. London, New York: Routledge, 1993.

Hanley, Brian. "Henry Fielding, Samuel Johnson, Samuel Richardson, and the Reception of Charlotte Lennox's *The Female Quixote* in the Popular Press." *ANQ: A Quarterly Journal of Short Articles, Notes, and Reviews* 13.3 (2000): 27–32.

Hardwick, Lorna, and Christopher Stray, eds. *A Companion to Classical Receptions*. Malden, MA: Blackwell, 2008.

Hartle, Paul N. "'Lawrels for the Conquered': Virgilian Translation and Travesty in the English Civil War and Its Aftermath." In *Reinventing the Middle Ages and the Renaissance: Constructions of the Medieval and Early Modern Periods*, ed. William F. Gentrup, 127–46. Turnhout: Brepols, 1998.

Heiserman, Arthur. *The Novel before the Novel: Essays and Discussions about the Beginnings of Prose Fiction in the West*. Chicago: University of Chicago Press, 1977.

Hill, Herbert. *La Calprenède's Romances and the Restoration Drama*. Reno: University of Nevada, 1910–11.

Homer. *The Iliad*. Trans. Richmond Lattimore. Chicago: University of Chicago Press, 1961.

Homer. *The Odyssey.* Trans. Richmond Lattimore. New York: HarperPerennial, 1999.

Horejsi, Nicole. "'A Counterpart to the Ephesian Matron': Steele's 'Inkle and Yarico' and a Feminist Critique of the Classics." *Eighteenth-Century Studies* 39.2 (2006): 201–26. https://doi.org/10.1353/ecs.2005.0061.

Hughes-Hallett, Lucy. *Cleopatra: Histories, Dreams, and Distortions.* New York: HarperPerennial, 1991.

Hulme, Peter. *Colonial Encounters: Europe and the Native Caribbean, 1492–1797.* New York: Methuen, 1986.

Hunter, J. Paul. *Occasional Form: Henry Fielding and the Chains of Circumstance.* Baltimore: Johns Hopkins University Press, 1975.

Hunter, Richard, ed. *Studies in Heliodorus.* Cambridge: Cambridge Philological Society, 1998.

Huzar, Eleanor. *Mark Antony, a Biography.* Minneapolis: University of Minnesota Press, 1978.

Jacobson, Howard. "Dido." *Mnemosyne* 58.4 (2005): 581–2.

Jobes, Gertrude. *Dictionary of Mythology: Folklore and Symbols.* New York: Scarecrow Press, 1961–2.

Johnson, Christopher D. Introduction. In Sarah Fielding, *The Lives of Cleopatra and Octavia,* ed. Christopher D. Johnson, 15–37 Lewisburg, PA: Bucknell University Press, 1994. https://doi.org/10.3138/9781442623118-002.

– "Novel Forms and Borrowed Texts: Genre and the Interpretive Challenge in Sarah Fielding." In *Experiments in Genre in Eighteenth-Century Literature,* ed. Sandro Jung, 179–201. Lebanon, NH: University Press of New England, 2011.

Johnson, James William. *The Formation of English Neo-Classical Thought.* Princeton: Princeton University Press, 1967. https://doi.org/10.1515/9781400877485.

Johnson, Maurice. *Fielding's Art of Fiction: Eleven Essays on "Shamela," "Joseph Andrews," "Tom Jones," and "Amelia."* Philadelphia: University of Pennsylvania Press, 1961. https://doi.org/10.9783/9781512817195.

Johnson, Odai. "Unspeakable Histories: Terror, Spectacle, and Genocidal Memory." *Modern Language Quarterly* 70.1 (March 2009): 97–116. https://doi.org/10.1215/00267929-2008-031.

Johnson, R. Brimley. Introduction. In Sarah Fielding, *The Lives of Cleopatra and Octavia,* ed. R. Brimley Johnson, xv –xxvii. London: Scholartis Press, 1928.

Johnson, Samuel. "Life of Pope." In *Samuel Johnson: Selected Poetry and Prose,* ed. Frank Brady and W.K. Wimsatt, 473–559. Berkeley: University of California Press, 1978.

– *The Yale Edition of the Works of Samuel Johnson*. Ed. W.J. Bate and Albrecht B. Strauss. New Haven: Yale University Press, 1969.

Johnson, W.R. *Darkness Visible: A Study of Vergil's Aeneid*. Berkeley: University of California Press, 1976. https://doi.org/10.7208/chicago/9780226252377.001.0001.

Johns-Putra, Adeline. *The History of the Epic*. New York: Palgrave, 2006. https://doi.org/10.1057/9780230595729_4.

Jones, Prudence. *Cleopatra: A Sourcebook*. Norman: University of Oklahoma Press, 2006.

Josephus. *Jewish Antiquities and the Wars of the Jews*. Trans. H. St. J. Thackeray and Ralph Marcus. Loeb edition. Cambridge, MA: Harvard University Press, 1966.

Kallendorf, Craig. *The Other Virgil: "Pessimistic" Readings of the Aeneid in Early Modern Culture*. Oxford: Oxford University Press, 2007. https://doi.org/10.1093/acprof:oso/9780199212361.001.0001.

– "Virgil's Post-Classical Legacy." In *A Companion to Ancient Epic*, ed. John Miles Foley, 574–88. Malden, MA: Blackwell, 2009.

Karydas, Helen Pournara. *Eurykleia and Her Successors: Female Figures of Authority in Greek Poetics*. New York: Rowman and Littlefield, 1998.

Keith, A.M. *Engendering Rome: Women in Latin Epic*. Cambridge: Cambridge University Press, 2000. https://doi.org/10.1017/CBO9780511605925.

Kelly, Gary. "Clara Reeve, Provincial Bluestocking: From the Old Whigs to the Modern Liberal State." In *Reconsidering the Bluestockings*, ed. Nicole Pohl and Betty A. Schellenberg, 105–25. San Marino: Huntington Library, 2003.

– "Reeve: Introductory Note." In Clara Reeve, *The Progress of Romance, Through Times, Countries, and Manners; With Remarks on the Good and Bad Effects of it, on them Respectively; In a Course of Evening Conversations*, ed. Gary Kelly. In vol. 6 of *Bluestocking Feminism: Writings of the Bluestocking Circle, 1738–1785*, ed. Gary Kelly, xxiii–lxii. London: Pickering and Chatto, 1999.

King, Kathryn R. "Barker, Jane (*bap.* 1652, *d.* 1732)." In *The Oxford Dictionary of National Biography*, ed. David Cannadine. Oxford: Oxford University Press, 2004. http://www.oxforddnb.com.huntington.idm.oclc.org/view/article/37153, accessed 20 June 2018.

– Introduction. In *The Poems of Jane Barker: The Magdalen Manuscript*, ed. King, 1–23 Oxford: Magdalen College, 1998.

– *Jane Barker, Exile: A Literary Career, 1675–1725*. Oxford: Oxford University Press, 2000.

– "Jane Barker, *Poetical Recreations*, and the Sociable Text." *English Literary History* 61.3 (1994): 551–70. https://doi.org/10.1353/elh.1994.0025.

– "Of Needles and Pens and Women's Work." *Tulsa Studies in Women's Literature* 14.1 (Spring 1995): 77–93. https://doi.org/10.2307/464249.

Kleiner, Diana. *Cleopatra and Rome*. Cambridge, MA: Belknap Press of Harvard University Press, 2005. https://doi.org/10.4159/9780674039667.

Kolodny, Annette. *The Land before Her: Fantasy and Experience of the American Frontiers, 1630–1860*. Chapel Hill: University of North Carolina Press, 1984.

Konstan, David, and Kurt A. Raaflaub, eds. *Epic and History*. Malden, MA: Blackwell, 2010.

Kramer, David Bruce. *The Imperial Dryden: The Poetics of Appropriation in Seventeenth-Century England*. Athens: University of Georgia Press, 1994.

Kramnick, Jonathan. *Making the English Canon: Print-Capitalism and the Cultural Past, 1700–1770*. Cambridge: Cambridge University Press, 1999. https://doi.org/10.1017/CBO9780511483653.

Krevans, Nita. "Medea as Foundation-Heroine." In *Medea: Essays on Medea in Myth, Literature, Philosophy, and Art*, ed. James J. Clauss and Sarah Iles Johnston, 71–82. Princeton: Princeton University Press, 1997.

Kroll, Richard. *The Material Word: Literate Culture in the Restoration and Early Eighteenth Century*. Baltimore: Johns Hopkins University Press, 1991.

La Calprenède, Gaultier de Costes, Seigneur de. *Cassandra: The Fam'd Romance*. London: Printed for A. Mosley, 1667.

– *Hymen's Praeludia or Love's Master-Piece. Being that so much admired Romance, entituled Cleopatra*. London: Printed for A. Mosley and John Crooke, 1668.

– *Pharamond: or, the History of France. A Fam'd Romance*. London: Printed for T. Bassett, T. Dring, and W. Cademan, etc., 1677.

Lancel, Serge. *Hannibal*. Malden, MA: Blackwell, 1988.

Landor, Walter Savage. *The Poetical Works of Walter Savage Landor*. 2 vols. Ed. Stephen Wheeler. Oxford: Clarendon Press, 1937.

Landry, Donna. "Picturing Benevolence against the Commercial Cry, 1750–98: Or, Sarah Fielding and the Secret Causes of Romanticism." *The History of British Women's Writing, 1750–1830*, vol. 5. Ed. Jacqueline M. Labbe, 150–71. Basingstoke: Palgrave Macmillan, 2010. https://doi.org/10.1057/9780230297012_8.

Langbauer, Laurie. *Women and Romance: The Consolations of Gender in the English Novel*. Ithaca: Cornell University Press, 1990.

Laqueur, Thomas. *Making Sex: Body and Gender from the Greeks to Freud*. Cambridge, MA: Harvard University Press, 1990.

Larrissy, Edward. *The Blind and Blindness in Literature of the Romantic Period*. Edinburgh: Edinburgh University Press, 2007. https://doi.org/10.3366/edinburgh/9780748632817.001.0001.

Legault, Marianne. *Female Intimacies in Seventeenth-Century French Literature*. Burlington, VT: Ashgate, 2012.

Le Moyne, Pierre. *The Gallery of Heroick Women*. Trans. the Marquesse of Winchester. London: Printed by R. Norton for Henry Seile, over against S. Dunstans Church in Fleetstreet, 1652.

Lennox, Charlotte. *The Female Quixote, or The Adventures of Arabella*. Ed. Margaret Dalziel. New York: Oxford University Press, 2008.

– *The Lady's Museum*. London: Printed for J. Newbery in St. Paul's Church-Yard, and J. Coote in Pater Noster Row, 1760–1.

Levin, Kate. "'The Cure of Arabella's mind': Charlotte Lennox and the Disciplining of the Female Reader." *Women's Writing: The Elizabethan to Victorian Period* 2.3 (1995): 271–90. https://doi.org/10.1080/0969908950020305.

Levine, Joseph. *The Battle of the Books: History and Literature in the Augustan Age*. Ithaca: Cornell University Press, 1991.

– *Between the Ancients and the Moderns: Baroque Culture in Restoration England*. New Haven: Yale University Press, 1999.

– *Doctor Woodward's Shield: History, Science, and Satire in Augustan England*. Berkeley: University of California Press, 1977.

– *Humanism and History: Origins of Modern English Historiography*. Ithaca: Cornell University Press, 1987.

Liddell, Henry, and Robert Scott. *A Greek-English Lexicon*. Oxford: Clarendon Press, 1996.

Lipking, Lawrence. *Abandoned Women and the Poetic Tradition*. Chicago: University of Chicago Press, 1988.

Livy. *History of Rome, Books I–II*. Trans. B.O. Foster. Loeb edition. Cambridge, MA: Harvard University Press, 1919.

Lockman, John. *A New Roman History, by Question and Answer, in a Method much more Comprehensive than any of the Kind extant. Extracted from Ancient Authors, and the Most celebrated among the Modern, and Interspersed with such Customs as serve to illustrate History. With a Complete Index. Designed principally for Schools*. 4th ed. Dublin: Printed by John Exshaw, 1778.

Loftis, John. "Imitation in the Novel: Fielding's *Amelia*." *Rocky Mountain Review of Language and Literature* 31 (1977): 214–29.

London, April. *Literary History Writing, 1770–1820*. Basingstoke: Palgrave, 2010. https://doi.org/10.1057/9780230283336.

Looser, Devoney. *British Women Writers and the Writing of History, 1670–1820*. Baltimore: Johns Hopkins University Press, 2000.

Lynch, James J. *Henry Fielding and the Heliodoran Novel: Romance, Epic, and Fielding's New Province of Writing*. Rutherford, NJ: Farleigh Dickinson University Press, 1986.

MacCarthy, B.G. *Women Writers: Their Contribution to the English Novel, 1621–1744*. Cork: Cork University Press, 1944.

MacDougall, Hugh. *Racial Myth in English History: Trojans, Teutons, and Anglo-Saxons*. Montreal: Harvest House, 1982.

Mace, Nancy. *Henry Fielding's Novels and the Classical Tradition*. Newark: University of Delaware Press, 1996.

Mack, Robert. Introduction. In *Oriental Tales*, ed. Robert Mack, vii–xlix. New York: Oxford University Press, 1992. https://doi.org/10.1016/0009-2541(92)90001-L.

Mack, Ruth. *Literary Historicity: Literature and Historical Experience in Eighteenth-Century Britain*. Stanford: Stanford University Press, 2009.

– "Quixotic Ethnography: Charlotte Lennox and the Dilemma of Cultural Observation." *Novel* 38.2/3 (2005): 193–213.

Makdisi, Saree, and Felicity Nussbaum, eds. *The Arabian Nights in Historical Context: Between East and West*. Oxford: Oxford University Press, 2008. https://doi.org/10.1093/acprof:oso/9780199554157.001.0001.

Martin, Richard. "Epic as Genre." In *A Companion to Ancient Epic*, ed. John Miles Foley, 9–19. Malden, MA: Blackwell, 2009.

Martindale, Charles, and Richard F. Thomas, eds. *Classics and the Uses of Reception*. Malden, MA: Blackwell, 2006. https://doi.org/10.1002/9780470774007.

Matthes, Melissa. *The Rape of Lucretia and the Founding of Republics: Readings in Livy, Machiavelli, and Rousseau*. University Park: Pennsylvania State University Press, 2000.

May, Thomas. *The Tragœdy of Cleopatra, Queene of Ægypt*. Ed. Denzell S. Smith. New York: Garland, 1979.

Mayer, Robert. *History and the Early English Novel: Matters of Fact from Bacon to Defoe*. Cambridge: Cambridge University Press, 1997. https://doi.org/10.1017/CBO9780511582066.

McBurney, William H. "Edmund Curll, Mrs. Jane Barker, and the English Novel." *Philological Quarterly* 37.4 (1958): 385–99.

McKeon, Michael. "Cultural Crisis and Dialectical Method: Destabilizing Augustan Literature." In *The Profession of Eighteenth-Century Literature*, ed. Leo Damrosch, 42–61. Madison: University of Wisconsin Press, 1992.

– *Origins of the English Novel, 1600–1740*. Baltimore: Johns Hopkins University Press, 1987.

Mentz, Steve. *Romance for Sale in Early Modern England: The Rise of Prose Fiction*. Burlington, VT: Ashgate, 2007.

Monod, Paul. *Jacobitism and the English People, 1688–1788*. Cambridge: Cambridge University Press, 1993.

Montiglio, Silvia. *Wandering in Ancient Greek Culture*. Chicago: University of Chicago Press, 2005.

Mylne, Vivienne. *The Eighteenth-Century French Novel: Techniques of Illusion*. Cambridge: Cambridge University Press, 1965.

Nussbaum, Felicity. *Autobiographical Subject: Gender and Ideology in Eighteenth-Century England*. Baltimore: Johns Hopkins University Press, 1989.

– *Torrid Zones: Maternity, Sexuality, and Empire in Eighteenth-Century English Narratives*. Baltimore: Johns Hopkins University Press, 1995.

– "Women Novelists 1740s–1780s." In *The Cambridge History of English Literature, 1660–1780*, ed. John Richetti, 745–67. Cambridge: Cambridge University Press, 2005.

O'Brien, Karen. *Women and Enlightenment in Eighteenth-Century Britain*. Cambridge: Cambridge University Press, 2009. https://doi.org/10.1017/CBO9780511576317.

O'Hara, James. "The Unfinished *Aeneid*?" In *A Companion to Virgil's "Aeneid" and Its Tradition*, ed. Joseph Farrell and Michael C.J. Putnam, 96–106. Malden, MA: Blackwell, 2010. https://doi.org/10.1002/9781444318050.ch7.

OCD. Hornblower, Simon, and Antony Spawforth, eds. *Oxford Classical Dictionary*. Oxford: Oxford University Press, 2003.

OLD. Glare, P.G.W., ed. *Oxford Latin Dictionary*. Oxford: Clarendon Press, 1997.

Ovid. *Heroides and Amores*. Trans. Grant Showerman. Loeb edition. Cambridge, MA: Harvard University Press, 1977.

– *Metamorphoses*. 2 vols. Trans. Frank Justice Miller. Loeb edition. Cambridge, MA: Harvard University Press, 1916–26.

– *Tristia and Ex Ponto*. Trans. Arthur Wheeler. Loeb edition. Cambridge, MA: Harvard University Press, 1988

Parker, Patricia. *Inescapable Romance: Studies in the Poetics of a Mode*. Princeton: Princeton University Press, 1979.

– *Literary Fat Ladies: Rhetoric, Gender, Property*. New York: Methuen, 1987.

Paulson, Ronald, ed. *Fielding: A Collection of Critical Essays*. Englewood Cliffs, NJ: Prentice-Hall, 1962.

Pearson, Jacqueline. *Women's Reading in Britain, 1750–1835: A Dangerous Recreation*. Cambridge: Cambridge University Press, 1999. https://doi.org/10.1017/CBO9780511582899.

Pelling, C.B.R. Introduction. In *Plutarch's Life of Antony*, ed. C.B.R. Pelling, 1–47 Cambridge: Cambridge University Press, 1988.

– *Plutarch and History: Eighteen Studies*. Swansea: Classical Press of Wales, 2011.

Perry, B.E. *The Ancient Romances: A Literary-Historical Account of Their Origins*. Berkeley: University of California Press, 1967.

Peters, Jeffrey N. *Mapping Discord: Allegorical Cartography in Early Modern French Writing*. Newark: University of Delaware Press, 2004.

Petronius. *Satyricon*. Trans. Michael Heseltine. Cambridge, MA: Harvard University Press, 1961.

Phillips, Mark Salber. *Society and Sentiment: Genres of Historical Writing in Britain, 1740–1820*. Princeton: Princeton University Press, 2000. https://doi.org/10.1515/9781400823628.

Pittock, Murray H.G. "The *Aeneid* in the Age of Burlington: A Jacobite Text?" In *Lord Burlington: Architecture, Art and Life*, ed. Toby Barnard and Jane Clark, 231–50 London: Hambledon Press, 1995.

– *Poetry and Jacobite Politics in Eighteenth-Century Britain and Ireland*. Cambridge: Cambridge University Press, 1994.

Plutarch. *Lives of the Noble Grecians and Romans*. Trans. John Dryden et al. Rev. Arthur Hugh Clough. New York: Modern Library, 1932.

Pomeroy, Sarah B. *Women in Hellenistic Egypt: From Alexander to Cleopatra*. New York: Schocken Books, 1984.

Potter, Tiffany. *Honest Sins: Georgian Libertinism and the Plays and Novels of Henry Fielding*. Montreal and Kingston: McGill-Queen's University Press, 1999.

Powers, Lyall. "The Influence of the *Aeneid* on Fielding's *Amelia*." *Modern Language Notes* 71.5 (1956): 330–6. https://doi.org/10.2307/3043446.

Pratt, Annis. *Dancing with Goddesses: Archetypes, Poetry, and Empowerment*. Bloomington: Indiana University Press, 1994.

Probyn, Clive. "Fielding, Sarah (1710–1768)." In *The Oxford Dictionary of National Biography*, ed. H.C.G. Matthew and Brian Harrison. Oxford: Oxford University Press, 2004. http://www.oxforddnb.com/view/article/9405, accessed 20 June 2018.

Quint, David. *Epic and Empire: Politics and Generic Form from Virgil to Milton*. Princeton: Princeton University Press, 1993.

– "Painful Memories: 'Aeneid' 3 and the Problem of the Past." *Classical Journal* 78.1 (1982): 30–8.

Raven, James. *British Fiction 1750–1770: A Chronological Check-List of Prose Fiction Printed in Britain and Ireland*. Newark: University of Delaware Press, 1987.

Rawson, Claude. *Henry Fielding and the Augustan Ideal under Stress: "Nature's Dance of Death" and Other Studies*. London, Boston: Routledge and Kegan Paul, 1972.

Reardon, Bryan P., ed. *Collection of Ancient Greek Novels*. Berkeley: University of California Press, 2008.

– *The Form of Greek Romance*. Princeton: Princeton University Press, 1991.

Reeve, Clara. *The Progress of Romance, Through Times, Countries, and Manners; With Remarks on the Good and Bad Effects of it, on them Respectively; In a Course of Evening Conversations*. Ed. Gary Kelly. In vol. 6 of *Bluestocking Feminism:*

Writings of the Bluestocking Circle, 1738–1785, ed. Gary Kelly. London: Pickering and Chatto, 1999.

Reeve, Michael. "The Re-Emergence of Ancient Novels in Western Europe, 1300–1810." In *The Cambridge Companion to the Greek and Roman Novel*, ed. Tim Whitmarsh, 282–98. Cambridge: Cambridge University Press, 2008. https://doi.org/10.1017/CCOL9780521865906.017.

Richetti, John. *English Novel in History, 1700–1780*. New York: Routledge, 1999. https://doi.org/10.4324/9780203393079.

– Introduction. In *The Cambridge Companion to the Eighteenth-Century Novel*, ed. John Richetti, 1–8 Cambridge: Cambridge University Press, 1996.

– *Popular Fiction before Richardson: Narrative Patterns, 1700–1739*. Oxford: Clarendon Press, 1992.

Roller, Duane. *Cleopatra: A Biography*. Oxford: Oxford University Press, 2010.

Rollin, Charles. *Ancient History of the Egyptians, Carthaginians, Assyrians, Babylonians, Medes and Persians, Macedonians, and Grecians. Translated from the French in ten volumes*. London: Printed for J. Rivington and sons; G.G.J. and J. Robinson; B. Law; T. Carnan; T. Verner, etc., 1778.

Rollin, Charles, and Jean Baptiste Louis Crevier. *The Roman History from the Foundation of Rome to the Battle of Actium: That is, To the End of the Commonwealth. Translated from the French*. London: Printed for J. and P. Knapton, 1754.

Røstvig, Maren-Sofie. *The Happy Man: Studies in the Metamorphoses of a Classical Ideal, 1600–1700*. Oxford: Basil Blackwell, 1953.

Rudd, Niall. *The Classical Tradition in Operation*. Toronto: University of Toronto Press, 1994. https://doi.org/10.3138/9781442673007.

Rumbold, Kate. "Shakespeare's 'Propriety' and the Mid-Eighteenth-Century Novel: Sarah Fielding's *The History of the Countess of Dellwyn*." In *Reading 1759: Literary Culture in Mid Eighteenth-Century Britain and France*, ed. Shaun Regan, 187–205. Lewisburg, PA: Bucknell University Press, 2013.

Runge, Laura. *Gender and Language in British Literary Criticism, 1660–1790*. Cambridge: Cambridge University Press, 1997. https://doi.org/10.1017/CBO9780511553530.

Sabor, Peter. "Amelia." In *Henry Fielding*, ed. Claude Rawson, 94–108. New York: Cambridge University Press, 2007. https://doi.org/10.1017/CCOL0521854512.008.

– Introduction. In Sarah Fielding, *The Adventures of David Simple and The Adventures of David Simple, Volume the Last*, ed. Peter Sabor, xi–xxxvi. Lexington: University Press of Kentucky, 1998.

Sachs, Jonathan. *Romantic Antiquity: Rome in the British Imagination, 1789–1832*. Oxford: Oxford University Press, 2010.

Said, Edward. *Orientalism*. New York: Pantheon Books, 1978.

Sambrook, James. "Lockman, John (1698–1771)." In *The Oxford Dictionary of National Biography*, ed. Lawrence Goldman. Oxford: Oxford University Press, 2004. https://doi-org.huntington.idm.oclc.org/10.1093/ref:odnb/16912, accessed 20 June 2018.

Sandy, Gerald N. "Ancient Prose Fiction and Minor Early English Novels." *Antike und Abendland* 25.1 (1979): 41–55.

– "Classical Forerunners of the Theory and Practice of Prose Romance in France: Studies in the Narrative Form of Minor French Romances of the Sixteenth and Seventeenth Centuries." *Antike und Abendland* 28.2 (1982): 169–91.

Sandy, Gerald N., and Stephen Harrison. "Novels Ancient and Modern." In *The Cambridge Companion to the Greek and Roman Novel*, ed. Tim Whitmarsh, 299–320. Cambridge: Cambridge University Press, 2008.

Saunders, Corinne, ed. *A Companion to Romance: From Classical to Contemporary*. Malden, MA: Blackwell, 2004.

Schellenberg, Betty A. "The Bluestockings and the Genealogy of the Modern Novel." *University of Toronto Quarterly* 79.4 (Fall 2010): 1023–34. https://doi.org/10.3138/utq.79.4.1023.

– *The Professionalization of Women Writers in Eighteenth-Century Britain*. Cambridge: Cambridge University Press, 2005.

Schiff, Stacy. *Cleopatra: A Life*. New York: Little, Brown and Company, 2010.

Schmeling, Gareth, ed. *The Novel in the Ancient World*. Leiden: E.J. Brill, 1996. https://doi.org/10.1163/9789004217638.

Scudéry, Madeleine de. *Artamenes; or, the Grand Cyrus. That Excellent Romance*. London: Printed for J. Darby, R. Roberts, etc., 1690–1.

– *Clelia, an Excellent New Romance*. London: Printed by H. Herringman, D. Newman, etc., 1678.

– *Clélie. Histoire romaine*. 5 vols. Ed. Chantal Morlet-Chantalat. Paris: Honoré Champion, 2001.

– *Conversations upon several subjects*. Written in French by Mademoiselle de Scudery. And done into English by Mr. Ferrand Spence. In two tomes. London: Printed for H. Rhodes next door to the Bear Tavern near Bride-lane in Fleet-street, 1683.

– *Les femmes illustres or The heroick harangues of the illustrious women*. Trans. James Innes. Edinburgh: Printed by Thomas Brown James and John Weir book sellers, 1681.

– *Madeleine de Scudéry: Selected Letters, Orations, and Rhetorical Dialogues*. Ed. and trans. Jane Donawerth and Julie Strongson. Chicago: University of Chicago Press, 2004.

– *The Story of Sapho*. Trans. Karen Newman. Chicago: University of Chicago Press, 2003.

Séjourné, Philippe. *The Mystery of Charlotte Lennox, First Novelist of Colonial America*. Paris: Editions Ophrys, 1967.

Shankman, Steven. *Pope's Iliad: Homer in the Age of Passion*. Princeton: Princeton University Press, 1983.

Sharafuddin, Mohammed. *Islam and Romantic Orientalism: Literary Encounters with the Orient*. New York: Tauris, 1994.

Sherburn, George. "Fielding's *Amelia*: An Interpretation." *English Literary History* 3.1 (1936): 1–14. https://doi.org/10.2307/2871654.

Small, Miriam. *Charlotte Ramsay Lennox: An Eighteenth-Century Lady of Letters*. New York: Archon Books, 1969.

Smallwood, Angela. *Fielding and the Woman Question: The Novels of Henry Fielding and Feminist Debate, 1700–1750*. New York: St Martin's Press, 1989.

Spacks, Patricia Meyer. *Desire and Truth: Functions of Plot in Eighteenth-Century English Novels*. Chicago: University of Chicago Press, 1990.

– *Imagining a Self: Autobiography and Novel in Eighteenth-Century England*. Cambridge, MA: Harvard University Press, 1976. https://doi.org/10.4159/harvard.9780674435780.

– "The Subtle Sophistry of Desire: Dr. Johnson and *The Female Quixote*." *Modern Philology: A Journal Devoted to Research in Medieval and Modern Literature* 85.4 (1988): 532–42. https://doi.org/10.1086/391661.

Spencer, Jane. "Not Being a Historian: Women Telling Tales in Restoration and Eighteenth-Century England." In *Contexts of Pre-Novel Narrative: The European Tradition*, ed. Roy Eriksen, 319–40. New York: Mouton de Gruyter, 1994.

Spender, Dale. *Mothers of the Novel: 100 Good Women Writers before Jane Austen*. New York: Pandora Press, 1986.

St Clair, William. *The Reading Nation in the Romantic Period*. Cambridge: Cambridge University Press, 2004.

Stadter, Philip, ed. *Plutarch and the Historical Tradition*. New York: Routledge, 1992. https://doi.org/10.4324/9780203312926.

Starke, Sue. *The Heroines of English Pastoral Romance*. Woodbridge: D.S. Brewer, 2007.

Staves, Susan. *A Literary History of Women's Writing in Britain, 1660–1789*. Cambridge: Cambridge University Press, 2006. https://doi.org/10.1017/CBO9780511484513.

Steele, Richard, and Joseph Addison. *The Spectator*. Ed. Donald F. Bond. 5 vols. Oxford: Clarendon Press, 1965.

– *The Tatler*. Ed. Donald F. Bond. Oxford: Clarendon Press, 1987.

Stevens, Anne H. "Sophia Lee's Illegitimate History." *Eighteenth-Century Novel* 3 (2002): 263–91.

Stevenson, Jane. *Women Latin Poets: Language, Gender, and Authority from Antiquity to the Eighteenth Century*. Oxford: Oxford University Press, 2005. https://doi.org/10.1093/acprof:oso/9780198185024.001.0001.

Stewart, Susan. *On Longing: Narratives of the Miniature, the Gigantic, the Souvenir, the Collection*. Durham, NC: Duke University Press, 1993.

Stray, Christopher. *Classics Transformed: Schools, Universities, and Society in England*. Oxford: Clarendon Press, 1998.

Suzuki, Mihoko. *Metamorphoses of Helen: Authority, Difference, and the Epic*. Ithaca: Cornell University Press, 1989.

Sweet, Rosemary. *Antiquaries: The Discovery of the Past in Eighteenth-Century Britain*. New York: Hambledon and London, 2004.

Swenson, Rivka. "Representing Modernity in Jane Barker's *Galesia Trilogy*: Jacobite Allegory and the Patch-Work Aesthetic." *Studies in Eighteenth-Century Culture* 34.1 (2005): 55–80. https://doi.org/10.1353/sec.2010.0022.

Tatum, James, ed. *The Search for the Ancient Novel*. Baltimore: Johns Hopkins University Press, 1994.

Thomas, Richard. *Virgil and the Augustan Reception*. Cambridge: Cambridge University Press, 2001. https://doi.org/10.1017/CBO9780511482403.

Thomson, J.A.K. *Classical Background of English Literature*. London: Allen and Unwin, 1948.

– *Classical Influences on English Poetry*. London: Allen and Unwin, 1951.

– *Classical Influences on English Prose*. London: Allen and Unwin, 1956.

Thrale, Hester. *Thraliana, the Diary of Mrs. Hester Lynch Thrale, 1776–1809*. 2 vols. Ed. Katherine C. Balderston. Oxford: Clarendon Press, 1951.

Thucydides. *The History of the Peloponnesian War: Revised Edition*. Trans. Rex Warner and ed. M.I. Finley. New York: Penguin, 1972.

Tillyard, E.M.W. *The Epic Strain in the English Novel*. London: Chatto and Windus, 1958.

Todd, Janet. *Sensibility: An Introduction*. New York: Methuen, 1986.

Turner, Cheryl. *Living by the Pen: Women Writers in the Eighteenth Century*. New York: Routledge, 1992. https://doi.org/10.4324/9780203296905.

Ure, Peter. "The Widow of Ephesus: Some Reflections on an International Comic Theme." In *Elizabethan and Jacobean Drama: Critical Essays by Peter Ure*, ed. J.C. Maxwell, 221–36. Liverpool: Liverpool University Press, 1974.

Vattier, Pierre. *L'Egypte de Mvrtadi, fils dv Gaphiphe; ov il est traitedes pyramides, du debordement du Nil, & des autres merueilles de cette Prouince, selon les opinions & traditions des Arabes*. Paris: T. Ioly, 1666.

Velleius Paterculus. *Compendium of Roman History*. Trans. Frederick W. Shipley. Cambridge, MA: Harvard University Press, 1992.

Vines, Sherard. *The Course of English Classicism from the Tudor to the Victorian Age*. London: L. and V. Woolf, 1930.

Virgil. *Aeneid*. Trans. John Dryden. In vols. 5–6 of *The Works of John Dryden: The Works of Virgil in English, 1697*. Ed. William Frost and Vinton Dearing. Berkeley: University of California Press, 1987.

– *Aeneid*. Trans. H. Rushton Fairclough. 2 vols. Loeb edition. Cambridge, MA: Harvard University Press, 1965.

– *Aeneid*. Trans. Robert Fitzgerald. New York: Vintage Classics, 1986.

Walpole, Horace. *Yale Edition of Horace Walpole's Correspondence*. Ed. W.S. Lewis. New Haven: Yale University Press, 1937–83.

Waquet, Françoise. *Latin, or, the Empire of a Sign: From the Sixteenth to the Twentieth Centuries*. Trans. John Howe. New York: Verso, 2001.

Waswo, Richard. *The Founding Legend of Western Civilization: From Virgil to Vietnam*. Hanover, NH: University Press of New England, 1997.

Waters, Mary. *British Women Writers and the Profession of Literary Criticism, 1789–1832*. Basingstoke: Palgrave, 2004. https://doi.org/10.1057/9780230514515.

Waters, Mary, ed. *British Women Writers of the Romantic Period: An Anthology of Their Literary Criticism*. New York: Basingstoke, 2009.

Watkins, John. *Specter of Dido: Spenser and Virgilian Epic*. New Haven: Yale University Press, 1995.

Weinbrot, Howard. *Augustus Caesar in "Augustan" England: The Decline of a Classical Norm*. Princeton: Princeton University Press, 1978.

– *Britannia's Issue: The Rise of British Literature from Dryden to Ossian*. New York: Cambridge University Press, 1993.

Welch, Anthony. "The Cultural Politics of *Dido and Aeneas*." *Cambridge Opera Journal* 21.1 (2009): 1–26. https://doi.org/10.1017/S0954586709990012.

Williams, Carolyn D. *Pope, Homer, and Manliness: Some Aspects of Eighteenth-Century Classical Learning*. New York: Routledge, 1993.

Williams, Deanne. "Dido, Queen of England." *English Literary History* 73.1 (2006): 31–59. https://doi.org/10.1353/elh.2006.0010.

Williams, Ioan. *The Idea of the Novel in Europe 1600–1800*. London: Macmillan, 1979. https://doi.org/10.1007/978-1-349-04081-0.

Winterer, Caroline. *The Mirror of Antiquity: American Women and the Classical Tradition, 1750–1900*. Ithaca: Cornell University Press, 1997.

Woodward, Carolyn. "Sarah Fielding's Self-Destructing Utopia: *The Adventures of David Simple*." In *Living by the Pen: Early British Women Novelists*, ed. Dale Spender, 65–81. New York: Teachers College Press, 1992.

Young, Robert. *White Mythologies: Writing History and the West*. New York: Routledge, 2004.

Zimmerman, Everett. *The Boundaries of Fiction: History and the Eighteenth-Century British Novel*. Ithaca: Cornell University Press, 1996.

Index

Aeneas, 4–5, 6, 11, 13, 16, 18, 21, 22, 25, 27, 35, 42, 43, 45, 50, 51, 52, 54, 55, 57, 59, 80, 81, 83, 95, 129, 132, 162, 163, 179, 184, 192, 193, 194, 197, 198, 200, 202, 203, 206, 210n20, 215n34, 222n10, 224n23, 245n6
Achilles, 63, 65, 75, 76, 77, 99, 109, 124, 184, 190, 191, 243n45
Actium, Battle of, 7, 12, 15, 142, 144, 146, 151, 156
Addison, Joseph, 3, 38, 163, 199, 239n58
Aesop, 200
Alexander the Great, 54, 55, 56, 57, 58, 195
Alter, Robert, 221n5
Amazons, 38, 79, 101, 102, 106, 109, 114
Ancients, 95, 111, 112, 204, 205, 207
Andromache, 58, 67, 70, 71, 72, 73, 75, 76, 77, 226n40
Anne of Austria, 34, 101
Antony, Mark, 7, 12, 13, 15, 52, 80, 110, 126–8, 129, 130, 134, 136, 137, 139, 140, 141, 142, 143, 144, 146, 147, 148, 150, 151, 152, 153, 156, 157, 158, 159, 160, 161, 163, 164, 210n20
Apollodorus, 109
Arabian Nights' Entertainments, 16, 170, 175, 179–80, 183, 240n11
Armstrong, Nancy, 150
Augustine, 13
Augustus, 12, 13, 16, 20, 21, 42, 52, 94, 95, 110, 126–7, 129, 130, 133, 141, 142, 143, 146, 147, 148, 152, 153, 154, 157, 161, 162, 163, 164, 165, 184, 192, 194, 197, 204, 210n20
autobiography, 20, 134, 135, 141, 234n9
Ayres, Philip, 206

Bannister, Mark, 99, 100
Barbados, 3, 5
Barbauld, Anna Letitia, 90, *91*, 167
Barclay, John, 12, 169
Barker, Jane, 6, 8, 12, 14, 18–19, 25, 27, 31–2, 46–7, 48, 52–3, 55, 94, 95, 184, 202, 215n1, 217n18; *Amours of Bosvil and Galesia*, 32; as alternative Dido, 33; Catholicism, 32; circle of Cambridge friends, 31, 46–7, 52; education in Latin and medicine, 31; *Entertaining Novels of Mrs Jane Barker*, 32; *Exilius*, 8, 15, 18–19, 20, 21, 27–8, 30–1, 33–4, 35–6, 40, 44–5,

46, 47, 48, 51–2, 53, 57, 84, 94, 183, 206–7; *Galesia Trilogy*, 32, 37, 47, 53, 220n47; *Lining of the Patch-Work Screen*, 32; *Love Intrigues*, 32; and manuscript culture, 31; *Patch-Work Screen for the Ladies*, 32; *Poetical Recreations*, 25, 26–7, 29, 31–3, 37, 46, 47, 48
Battestin, Martin, 68, 72, 221n5, 221n7, 224n19, 225n34, 227n47
Beckford, William, 183
Berkin, Carol, 123
Berquin, Arnaud, 126–9, 164–5, 233n2
biography, 9, 17, 54, 59, 95, 125, 126, 130, 131, 132, 133, 136, 137–8, 140, 141, 146, 164
Blok, Josine, 109
Boileau, Nicolas, 101, 112
Bond, Donald F., 239n58
Boswell, James, 27
Braudy, Leo, 222n9
Bree, Linda, 227n47
Broome, Judith, 52
Brown, Laura, 5, 200, 210nn5–6
Burrow, Colin, 245n7
Byron, Lord, 166

Caesar, Julius, 15, 19, 42, 43, 54, 55, 57, 58, 110, 130, 157
Caldwell, Tanya, 206
Campbell, Jill, 74, 222n12, 223n14, 223n17, 225n35
canon, literary, 21, 27, 92, 169, 170, 172, 173, 174, 175, 177, 178, 191, 195, 196, 197
Carlile, Susan, 134, 235n17
Carter, Elizabeth, 12, 90, *91*
Carthage, 13, 19, 28, 29–30, 31, 33, 34, 35, 38, 39, 40, 42, 47, 52, 84
Cassius Dio, 13–14, 130, 144, 194
Castle, Terry, 228n53
Cato, Marcus, 29
Cervantes, Don Miguel de, 90, 94; *Don Quixote*, 20, 91, 94
Charles I, 206
Charles II, 246n9
Chaucer, Geoffrey, 13
Clelia, 94, 98, 113–23
Cleopatra (Cleopatra VII), 6, 7–8, 9–10, 12–14, 15, 16, 17, 18, 19, 20, 21, 52, 69, 73, 74, 80, 85, 93, 94, 95, 96, 98, 109, 110, 112, 113, 123, 124, 125, 126–8, 129, 130, 131, 132, 134, 136, 138, 139–54, 155, 156, 158, 160, 161, 162, 164, 165, 166, 167, 181, 184, 188, 191, 193, 194, 195, 196, 197, 201, 203, 210n20, 232n46
Cleopatra VIII, 19, 38, 94, 110
Collier, Arthur, 12, 133
Collier, Jane, 133, 135
Corman, Brian, 239n4, 240n14
Crayle, Benjamin, 31
Crevier, Jean Baptiste Louis, 144, 145, 147

Davies, John, 167, 184, 192
Deianeira, 184, 187, 188, 189, 190, 191, 243nn43–4
DeJean, Joan, 34, 102, 114, 229n5
Desmond, Marilynn, 13, 212n23
Diderot, Denis, 149–50
Dido, 4–5, 6–8, 9–10, 13, 14, 16, 17, 18, 19, 20, 21, 22, 25, 26, 27, 28, 29–30, 31, 32, 33, 35, 36, 37, 38, 43, 44, 45, 46, 48, 50, 52, 53, 54, 55, 57, 59, 67, 69, 70, 71, 73, 74, 76, 77, 78, 79, 80, 81, 82, 83, 84, 85, 94, 95, 96, 123, 129, 130, 132, 148, 162, 166, 167, 184, 188, 193, 194, 197, 198,

199, 200–1, 202, 203, 210n4, 210n7, 216n2, 224n23, 245n6
DiPiero, Thomas, 97
Donatus, Aelius, 154
Donawerth, Jane, 116
Doody, Margaret Anne, 230n17, 233n65
Dougherty, Carol, 123
Downs-Miers, Deborah, 135
Dryden, John, 26; *Aeneis*, 30, 80, 154, 206, 227n49; *All for Love*, 150–1, 160; *Astraea Redux*, 246n9; *Aureng-Zebe*, 160; translation of Plutarch, 137
duelling, 60, 61, 62, 71, 224nn19–20
Duff, Tim, 137, 138, 155–6

education, 7, 8, 10–12, 21, 128–9, 168, 169, 175–6, 211n17
Elizabeth I, 32, 90, 217n16
Ephesian Matron, 3–5, 7, 55, 83, 199–200, 209n2
epic, 4, 5, 6, 7, 8, 9, 10, 13, 14, 15, 16, 17, 18, 19, 20, 21, 22, 25, 26, 27, 28, 29, 30, 32, 37, 43, 47, 52, 53, 55, 56, 57, 58, 59, 60, 61, 62, 63, 64, 67, 70, 71, 74, 76, 77, 78, 79–80, 81, 83, 84, 95, 96, 99, 109, 111, 129, 130, 131, 132, 154, 166, 167, 168, 169, 170, 171, 172, 174, 175, 176, 177, 179, 180, 183, 184, 185, 186, 187, 188, 189, 190, 191, 193, 194, 195, 197, 198, 201, 202, 203, 206, 207, 212n23, 213n25, 214n31, 216n3, 218n21, 222n9, 222n11, 223n14, 240n10, 245n6, 245n7, 246n8

fable, 5
Felsenstein, Frank, 209nn3–4
femme forte, 38, 101, 102, 121. *See also* Amazons
Ferguson, Margaret, 13, 212n23, 246n8
Fielding, Henry, 6, 8, 56–7, 90, 92, 94, 95, 133, 134, 140, 182, 202, 235n12; *Amelia*, 8, 9, 19, 53, 56, 57, 59, 63, 64, 68, 69, 70, 81, 94, 140, 197, 201, 221n5, 221n7, 222nn9–12, 223n14, 223n17, 224n22, 226n40, 226n45, 227n51; *Covent-Garden Journal*, 56–7, 80; *Jonathan Wild*, 54–6, 57, 58, 220n3; *Joseph Andrews*, 19, 56; *Serious Address to the People of Great Britain*, 68–9; *Shamela*, 56; *Tom Jones*, 19, 56, 68, 79, 182, 221n5
Fielding, Sarah, 6, 8, 95, 132–6, 182, 202, 235n12, 236n20; *Adventures of David Simple*, 135, 136; background reading for *The Lives*, 234n10; *Cry* 135; *Governess*, 135; *History of the Countess of Dellwyn*, 125, 131, 135; *History of Ophelia*, 135; *Lives of Cleopatra and Octavia*, 9, 12, 20–1, 94, 124, 125–6, 130–1, 133, 134, 135, 137, 138, 139, 140, 141, 145, 169, 182, 197, 201, 207; *Xenophon's Memoirs of Socrates*, 12, 133
Finch, Anne, 12
Fronde (French civil war), 34, 38, 101, 102, 106
Fuchs, Barbara, 241n15, 246n7

Gainsborough, William, 65, *66*, 224n26
Gallagher, Catherine, 93
Galland, Antoine, 16, 183
Geoffrey of Monmouth, 11, 25–6
Gibbon, Edward, 16
Gibraltar, 64, 67, 68, 69, 70, 225n29
Glorious Revolution, 18, 25, 26, 31, 206

Goldgar, Bertrand, 140
Grant, Michael, 136, 164, 234n7
Greek, 12, 58, 77, 133, 226n41
Griffith, Elizabeth, 90, *91*
Gross, Daniel, 136

Hannibal, 18–19, 29, 30, 33, 34, 35, 39, 40, *41*, 44, 47, 52
Harris, James, 235n14
Haywood, Eliza, 134, 181, 183
Hector, 65, 71, 72, 75, 76, 77, 99, 190, 191
Helen of Troy, 58, 67, 70, 71, 72, 73, 77
Heliodorus, 14, 15, 96, 213n26
Hercules, 67, 68, 69, 70, 179, 184, 187, 189, 243n43
Herodotus, 15, 33, 92, 96, 111, 112, 121, 232n61
historiography, romance, 15, 17, 20, 21, 26, 33, 35, 67, 93, 132, 145, 202, 203
history, 6, 7, 8, 9, 13, 15, 16, 17, 18, 19, 20, 21, 22, 26, 27, 30, 31, 33, 34, 35, 37, 38, 42, 43, 47, 49, 50, 51–2, 53, 55, 59, 65, 67, 74, 84, 85, 89, 90, 91, 92, 93, 94, 95, 96, 97, 102, 106, 107, 109, 110, 111, 112, 113, 114, 116, 119, 123, 124, 125, 126, 127–8, 129, 131, 132, 133, 134, 136, 139, 141, 144, 145, 146, 148, 149, 151, 152, 153, 157, 161, 164, 165, 169, 170, 171, 174, 181, 182, 183, 184, 185, 186, 187, 188, 189, 191, 193, 194, 195, 197, 201, 202, 203, 205, 207, 210n5, 214n29, 218n21, 229n7, 232n47, 232n61, 234n9, 234n10, 246n8
history, literary, 8, 9, 13, 95
Homer, 10, 16, 53, 58, 59, 61, 62, 63, 75, 77, 96, 132, 168, 170, 174, 175, 177, 179, 188, 206; *Iliad*, 11, 56, 58, 71, 75, 76, 109, 190, 191, 226n44, 244n47; *Odyssey*, 75, 76, 175, 187, 189, 226n44
Horejsi, Nicole, 209n1
Hughes-Hallett, Lucy, 237n44
Hulme, Peter, 210n4
Hume, David, 92, 136
Hunter, J. Paul, 221n5, 223n14

"Inkle and Yarico" (*Spectator* 11), 3–5, 16, 21, 55, 83, 124, 199, 200, 202, 209n3

Jacobites, 14, 18, 19, 25, 26, 28, 35, 43, 44, 46, 47, 48, 50, 51, 52, 53, 197
James I, 26
James II, 14, 18, 25, 26, 27, 43, 45, 46
Johnson, Christopher D., 135, 144, 234n10, 238n45
Johnson, James William, 204
Johnson, Maurice, 221n7, 222n9
Johnson, R. Brimley, 150
Johnson, Samuel, 15, 27, 90, 140, 141, 173, 183
Josephus, 142–3
Julia (daughter of Augustus), 94, 109, 110, 111, 112, 113, 232n46, 246n9
Juvenal, 77, 176

Kallendorf, Craig, 11
Kauffman, Angelica, 90, *91*, 154, *155*
Kelly, Gary, 169, 239n4, 240n8, 243n38
King, Kathryn, 32
Kroll, Richard, 206

La Calprenède, Gauthier de Costes, Seigneur de, 14, 15, 20, 33, 92, 94, 96, 99, 100, 230n19; *Cassandre* (*Cassandra*), 14, 99, 100, 109; *Cléopâtre* (*Cleopatra*), 14, 38, 99

Landor, Walter Savage, 166–8
Landry, Donna, 134, 135, 136
Latin, 10, 11, 12, 58, 129, 245n6
Legault, Marianne, 101
Le Moyne, Pierre, 102, *103*, *104*, 116, *117*, *118*, 119, 121, 122
Lennox, Charlotte, 6, 8, 9, 15, 84–5, 89–90, *91*, 132, 169, 202; *Female Quixote*, 14, 19–20, 21, 84–5, 90, 91–2, 95, 96, 112, 113, 126, 156, 165, 183, 197, 201, 207, 228nn3–4; history of Elizabeth I, 90; in *The Nine Living Muses of Great Britain*, 90, *91*; *Lady's Museum*, 89–90; *Life of Harriot Stuart*, 90; *Memoirs of the Countess of Berci*, 90; *Memoirs of the Duke of Sully*, 90; *Memoirs for the History of Madame de Maintenon*, 90; *Shakespear Illustrated*, 90, 241n20
Levine, Joseph, 12, 204, 205, 207
Ligon, Richard, 3, 5
Linley, Elizabeth, 90, *91*
Livy, 15, 33, 96, 98, 111, 113, 116, 120, 122, 123
Lockman, John, 144, 145–6, 147
Loftis, John, 222n9
London, April, 174
Louis XIV, 34, 38, 101
Lucretia, 94, 98, *118*, 119, 120, 122, 123

Macaulay, Catharine, 90, *91*
Mace, Nancy, 79, 210n11
Mack, Ruth, 230n14
Matthes, Melissa, 119
McKeon, Michael, 206
Medea, 73, 184, 187, 188, 189, 190, 191, 210n7
Moderns, 95, 96, 111, 112, 204, 205, 207
Monod, Paul, 46
More, Hannah, 12, 90, *91*
Montagu, Elizabeth, 90, *91*
Montagu, Lady Mary Wortley, 173, 236n20

Newman, Karen, 100
North, Thomas, 136
novel, ancient, 3, 14, 20, 96, 201, 213n28, 222n11, 230n15; heroic (*see* romance, heroic); eighteenth-century, 5, 6, 8, 9, 14, 20, 21–2, 84, 90, 92, 96, 134, 168, 170, 179, 180, 181, 182, 183, 196, 198, 202, 203, 241n15, 242n34
Nussbaum, Felicity, 234n9

O'Brien, Karen, 17, 18, 229n10
Octavia, 20, 21, 124, 125, 130–1, 132, 133, 134, 136, 138, 139, 142, 145, 152, 154–65
Octavian. *See* Augustus
Odysseus, 16, 132
Orientalism, Romantic, 166; oriental tale, 16, 20, 21, 166, 168, 169, 178, 179, 183, 184, 185, 186, 188, 192, 242n32
Ovid, 36; *Amores*, 187; *Heroides*, 5, 26, 27, 32, 106, 200, 209n4; *Metamorphoses*, 187, 188, 189; *Tristia*, 13

Parisatis, 94, 109
Parker, Patricia, 78–9, 213n25
Parthenissa, 110
pax Romana, 12, 15
Pelling, Christopher, 137, 138
Penelope, 184, 187, 188, 189, 191
Penthesilea, 124
Pericles, 124, 233n66
Peters, Jeffrey, 114
Petronius, 3–5, 200, 209n2
Phillips, Mark Salber, 17, 18

Pittock, Murray H.G., 218n22
Plutarch, 111, 112, 133, 134, 136, 137, 138, 141, 142, 144, 145, 146, 149, 150, 151, 155, 157, 158, 161, 163
Pomeroy, Sarah, 196
Pompey, 19, 35, 42, 43, 146, 157
Pope, Alexander, 16, 63, 140, 175, 181, 206, 237n36
Powers, Lyall, 222n9
Probyn, Clive, 235n14
propaganda, Augustan, 7, 9, 15, 17, 20, 74, 95, 126, 129, 142, 151, 153, 166, 167, 182, 194, 197, 201, 202, 203
Punic War, First, 28, 29, 33, 40
Punic War, Second, 28, 29, 30, 33, 35, 40
Punic War, Third, 29
Purcell, Henry, 13
Pygmalion, 157, 158

Querelle des femmes (woman question), 101–2
Quint, David, 201, 202, 246n8

Reeve, Clara, 6, 8, 9, 12, 95, 166, 168–9, 202, 239n4, 240n5, 240n8, 240n13, 242n34; *Argenis*, 12, 169; *Castle Connor*, 167; *Destination*, 167; education, 169; *Edwin, King of Northumberland*, 167; *Exiles*, 167; *History of Charoba*, 14, 21–2, 166, 167, 183–98, 244n47, 244n56; *Memoirs of Sir Roger de Clarendon*, 167; *Old English Baron*, 9, 167; *Original Poems on Several Occasions*, 167; *Plans of Education*, 167; *Progress of Romance*, 8, 10, 15, 166, 167–8, 169, 170–83, 191, 197, 201, 202, 203, 207, 240nn4–5, 240n14; *School for Widows*, 167; *Two Mentors*, 167
Revolution, American, 123, 169
Revolution, French, 169, 173
Reynolds, Sir Joshua, 65, 90
Riccobini, Marie Jeanne, 134
Richardson, Samuel, 8, 56, 90, 92, 134, 150, 182
Robertson, William, 90, 92
Rollin, Charles, 144, 145, 147, 149, 150, 238n45
romance, 5, 6, 7, 8, 9, 10, 13, 14–15, 16, 17, 18, 19, 20, 21, 22, 26, 27, 30–1, 32, 33, 34, 35, 38, 42, 44, 45, 46, 47, 52, 53, 57, 58, 59, 61, 63, 67, 74, 76, 77, 78, 83, 84, 85, 90, 91–2, 93, 94, 95, 96, 97, 98, 99, 100, 102, 106, 107, 108, 109, 110–11, 112, 113, 114, 123, 124, 126, 129, 131, 132, 134, 145, 146, 151, 162, 165, 166, 167, 168, 169, 170, 171, 172, 173, 174, 175, 176, 177, 178, 179, 180, 181, 182, 183, 184, 186, 187, 188, 189, 190, 191, 192, 194, 195, 196, 197, 198, 201–2, 203, 207, 213n25, 213n26, 214n30, 214n31, 216n3, 218n19, 218n21, 222n11, 223n14, 224n22, 228n3, 229n5, 230n15, 232n47, 233n65, 240n10, 241n15, 241n20, 241n29, 242n34, 245n6, 245n7
romance, heroic, 14, 15, 20, 33, 34, 38, 84–5, 90, 91–2, 96, 97, 99–100, 101, 107, 108, 110, 111, 124, 197, 202, 203, 214n30, 218n19, 230n15, 233n65, 241n15
Roman Empire, 11, 12, 26, 35, 94, 128, 152, 162, 165
Rome, 19, 28, 31, 33, 34, 35, 38, 39, 40, 42, 47, 52, 84; Augustan, 4, 10, 42, 129, 130, 204; Early Republican, 29; Middle Republican, 28; Republican, 94

ruling passion, 140, 141, 150, 156, 158, 159, 237n36
Rumbold, Kate, 135

St Clair, William, 173
salon culture, 93, 99, 101, 106, 111
Samuel, Richard, 90, *91*
Sappho, 94, 98
Schellenberg, Betty, 8, 133, 135, 236n20, 240n5
Scipio Africanus, 18, 28, 29, 30, 31, 33, 34, 35, 39, 40, 42, 44, 45, 46, 47, 48, 50, 52, 53
Scudéry, Madeleine de, 14, 15, 20, 33, 90, 92, 94, 96, 97, 99, 100, 102, *105*, 106, 107, 110, 112, 113, 116, 119, 122, 123, 213n26; *Artamène, ou le Grand Cyrus*, 14, 92, 99, 100, 106, 107, 213n26; *Carte de Tendre*, 101, 113, *114*, 116; *Clélie, histoire romaine* (*Clelia*), 14, 99, 100, 101; *Conversations morales*, 100; *Conversations sur divers sujets*, 106; *Femmes illustres*, 100, 102, *105*, 106, 116, 120, 121, 156; *Ibrahim*, 213n26; *Nouvelles conversations de morale*, 100; *Nouvelles conversations sur divers sujets*, 106; salon of, 101; *Story of Sapho*, 100
sensibility, 64, 65
Seward, Anna, 12
Sewell, George, 32
Shakespeare, William, 150, 172–3, 241n20
Sharafuddin, Mohammed, 242n35
Shelley, Percy, 166
Sherburn, George, 205, 222n9
Sheridan, Frances, 183
Sindbad, 16
slavery, 4
Smallwood, Angela, 220n3, 222n12
Southey, Robert, 166
Spacks, Patricia Meyer, 132, 231n40, 231n44
Spanish Succession, War of, 68
Spectator, the, 126. *See also* Addison, Joseph; "Inkle and Yarico"; Steele, Richard
Spencer, Jane, 231n46
Spender, Dale, 239n4
Stadter, Philip, 137
Stanyan, Temple, 91, 107
Statira, 94, 95, 109
Staves, Susan, 240n4, 240n13
Steele, Richard, 3, 4, 8, 19, 199. *See also* "Inkle and Yarico"
Sterne, Laurence, 134, 182
Stevenson, Jane, 12
Stewart, Susan, 49, 51
Strongson, Julie, 116
Stuart monarchy, 25, 27, 32, 35, 44, 45, 46, 50, 52, 53, 68
Swift, Jonathan, 205

Tate, Nahum, 13
Temple, William, 205
Thalestris, 109, 110, 113
Thomson, J.A.K., 207
Thrale, Hester, 12, 235n12
Thucydides, 92, 112, 124
Trojan War, 50, 51, 58, 67, 109

Vattier, Pierre, 167, 184, 192
Verginia, 119, 120, 122, 123
Vines, Sherard, 207
Virgil, 6, 7, 10, 35, 36, 58, 59, 61, 62, 63, 132, 174, 175, 177, 188, 193, 200, 203, 206; *Aeneid*, 4, 5, 6, 7, 8, 9, 10–11, 13, 14, 18, 20, 25, 27, 28, 29, 30, 32, 33, 36, 37, 44, 47, 50, 51, 52, 53, 54, 55, 57, 58, 59, 67, 71, 77, 78, 79, 80, 81, 82, 83,

84, 95, 129, 154, 162, 163, 166, 167, 179, 193, 194, 197, 199, 201, 202, 206, 219n32, 219n34, 219n36, 219nn38–40, 220n42, 220n45, 221n9, 222n11, 226n44, 227n49, 227n51, 245n6

Walpole, Horace, 9, 16, 167
Weinbrot, Howard, 204, 205, 246n14
Widow of Ephesus. *See* Ephesian Matron
William III, 27, 53
Woodward, Carolyn, 135
Wotton, William, 205

Xenophon, 12, 133
Xerxes, 29, 63

www.ingramcontent.com/pod-product-compliance
Lightning Source LLC
LaVergne TN
LVHW090153080826
844660LV00013B/793/J

* 9 7 8 1 4 4 2 6 4 7 1 4 5 *